D0598135

TypePad®

FOR

DUMMIES®

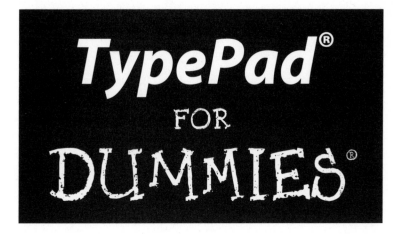

by Melanie Nelson and Shannon Lowe

RETIRÉ DE LA COLLECTION UNIVERSELLE
Bibliothèque et Archives nationales du Québec

WILEY

Wiley Publishing, Inc.

TypePad® For Dummies®

Published by
Wiley Publishing, Inc.
111 River Street
Hoboken, NJ 07030-5774

www.wiley.com

Copyright © 2010 by Wiley Publishing, Inc., Indianapolis, Indiana

Published by Wiley Publishing, Inc., Indianapolis, Indiana

Published simultaneously in Canada

No part of this publication may be reproduced, stored in a retrieval system or transmitted in any form or by any means, electronic, mechanical, photocopying, recording, scanning or otherwise, except as permitted under Sections 107 or 108 of the 1976 United States Copyright Act, without either the prior written permission of the Publisher, or authorization through payment of the appropriate per-copy fee to the Copyright Clearance Center, 222 Rosewood Drive, Danvers, MA 01923, (978) 750-8400, fax (978) 646-8600. Requests to the Publisher for permission should be addressed to the Permissions Department, John Wiley & Sons, Inc., 111 River Street, Hoboken, NJ 07030, (201) 748-6011, fax (201) 748-6008, or online at http://www.wiley.com/go/permissions.

Trademarks: Wiley, the Wiley Publishing logo, For Dummies, the Dummies Man logo, A Reference for the Rest of Us!, The Dummies Way, Dummies Daily, The Fun and Easy Way, Dummies.com, Making Everything Easier, and related trade dress are trademarks or registered trademarks of John Wiley & Sons, Inc. and/or its affiliates in the United States and other countries, and may not be used without written permission. TypePad is a registered trademark of Six Apart, Ltd. All other trademarks are the property of their respective owners. Wiley Publishing, Inc. is not associated with any product or vendor mentioned in this book.

LIMIT OF LIABILITY/DISCLAIMER OF WARRANTY: THE PUBLISHER AND THE AUTHOR MAKE NO REPRESENTATIONS OR WARRANTIES WITH RESPECT TO THE ACCURACY OR COMPLETENESS OF THE CONTENTS OF THIS WORK AND SPECIFICALLY DISCLAIM ALL WARRANTIES, INCLUDING WITHOUT LIMITATION WARRANTIES OF FITNESS FOR A PARTICULAR PURPOSE. NO WARRANTY MAY BE CREATED OR EXTENDED BY SALES OR PROMOTIONAL MATERIALS. THE ADVICE AND STRATEGIES CONTAINED HEREIN MAY NOT BE SUITABLE FOR EVERY SITUATION. THIS WORK IS SOLD WITH THE UNDERSTANDING THAT THE PUBLISHER IS NOT ENGAGED IN RENDERING LEGAL, ACCOUNTING, OR OTHER PROFESSIONAL SERVICES. IF PROFESSIONAL ASSISTANCE IS REQUIRED, THE SERVICES OF A COMPETENT PROFESSIONAL PERSON SHOULD BE SOUGHT. NEITHER THE PUBLISHER NOR THE AUTHOR SHALL BE LIABLE FOR DAMAGES ARISING HEREFROM. THE FACT THAT AN ORGANIZATION OR WEBSITE IS REFERRED TO IN THIS WORK AS A CITATION AND/OR A POTENTIAL SOURCE OF FURTHER INFORMATION DOES NOT MEAN THAT THE AUTHOR OR THE PUBLISHER ENDORSES THE INFORMATION THE ORGANIZATION OR WEBSITE MAY PROVIDE OR RECOMMENDATIONS IT MAY MAKE. FURTHER, READERS SHOULD BE AWARE THAT INTERNET WEBSITES LISTED IN THIS WORK MAY HAVE CHANGED OR DISAPPEARED BETWEEN WHEN THIS WORK WAS WRITTEN AND WHEN IT IS READ.

For general information on our other products and services, please contact our Customer Care Department within the U.S. at 877-762-2974, outside the U.S. at 317-572-3993, or fax 317-572-4002.

For technical support, please visit www.wiley.com/techsupport.

Wiley also publishes its books in a variety of electronic formats. Some content that appears in print may not be available in electronic books.

Library of Congress Control Number: 2010920258

ISBN: 978-0-470-55094-6

Manufactured in the United States of America

10 9 8 7 6 5 4 3 2 1

WILEY

About the Authors

Melanie Nelson: Melanie has been blogging since 1998 and working with social media since 1995. In that time she has worked with every major blogging platform, including TypePad. She currently owns and writes Blogging Basics 101 (www.bloggingbasics101.com), where she provides tips, instructions, and advice for bloggers. She has spoken at both the Blissdom and BlogHer blog conferences as well as local professional development events. Melanie is also a social media consultant, a Contributing Editor at BlogHer.com, and a technical writer and editor. She has a master's degree in technical writing. Melanie lives in Oklahoma with her husband and two children.

Shannon Lowe: Shannon has been a TypePad blogger since 2006, writing the award-winning parenting blog Rocks In My Dryer (www.rocksinmydryer.net). She is a freelance writer whose work has appeared in books and magazines such as *Good Housekeeping, Parenting, Chicken Soup for the New Mom's Soul,* and *The Social Cause Diet.* She has been a guest speaker at several blogging conferences, including BlogHer, Blissdom, and SheSpeaks. In February 2008, she and a team of U.S. bloggers traveled to Uganda with Compassion International to live-blog their child advocacy work. She lives in Oklahoma with her husband and four children.

Dedication

To Bill and Mac, for everything.

Authors' Acknowledgments

This book was a team effort, in every sense. We heartily thank our hard-working and patient project editor, Susan Pink — we learned so much from you! Many thanks to Amy Fandrei and Jodi Jensen of Wiley Publishing, who helped us in countless ways. Still more thanks to the rest of the Wiley team. Thank you, too, to Andy Wibbels of Six Apart for serving as our technical editor.

We give our deep thanks to the readers of our blogs, Blogging Basics 101 and Rocks In My Dryer. You guys are the reasons we get to do what we do and we're endlessly thankful you've taken the time to offer us your support and encouragement over the years.

Melanie: I would like to thank my husband, Bill, and our awesome, funny children. Without your patience and support my blogging endeavors, let alone writing a book, wouldn't be possible. Our life is the life I always wanted.

I also want to thank Jann Nelson, Donna Monthei, and John and Robin Monthei for always being available to help with anything that came up; Robert M. Brown, PhD for being a constant voice in my head telling me to write well; and Kathy Cordeiro for so many things I couldn't possibly list them all. I appreciate all of you.

Shannon: I'd like to thank my parents, Don and Cathy Dunn, and my grandmother, Bonnie Young, for all the practical help and support through this hectic book-writing process. To the other family members and friends who offered healthy doses of sanity and encouragement — thank you. I couldn't have done it without you!

A very special thanks to my four fantastic kids for being such good sports. I'm proud of this book, but I'm a million times prouder to be your mom.

Most of all, thank you to Mac for being Mac, which is always just exactly what I need.

Publisher's Acknowledgments

We're proud of this book; please send us your comments at http://dummies.custhelp.com. For other comments, please contact our Customer Care Department within the U.S. at 877-762-2974, outside the U.S. at 317-572-3993, or fax 317-572-4002.

Some of the people who helped bring this book to market include the following:

Acquisitions and Editorial

Project Editor: Susan Pink

Acquisitions Editor: Amy Fandrei

Copy Editor: Susan Pink

Technical Editor: Andy Wibbels

Editorial Manager: Jodi Jensen

Editorial Assistant: Amanda Graham

Sr. Editorial Assistant: Cherie Case

Cartoons: Rich Tennant
(www.the5thwave.com)

Composition Services

Project Coordinator: Patrick Redmond

Layout and Graphics: Carl Byers, Christine Williams

Proofreaders: Lindsay Littrell, Kathy Simpson

Indexer: Potomac Indexing, LLC

Publishing and Editorial for Technology Dummies

> **Richard Swadley,** Vice President and Executive Group Publisher

> **Andy Cummings,** Vice President and Publisher

> **Mary Bednarek,** Executive Acquisitions Director

> **Mary C. Corder,** Editorial Director

Publishing for Consumer Dummies

> **Diane Graves Steele,** Vice President and Publisher

Composition Services

> **Debbie Stailey,** Director of Composition Services

Contents at a Glance

Table of Contents

Introduction

The blogosphere is a busy place. It's hard to nail down a firm number, but the best estimates indicate that there are more than 200 million blogs bumping around globally in cyberspace. It can be daunting for a beginning blogger (or even an intermediate one) to comfortably find a spot of his or her own in such a crowd. Where can you learn all the technical jargon you need to know? How do you host a blog? How do you manage a community? What do you do about privacy concerns? Is it really even possible to make money in the blogosphere?

Fortunately, TypePad exists as a very large and streamlined toolbox to help bloggers of all levels of experience and interest manage their home on the Web. It is widely regarded in the blogging world as a simple, affordable, and easy-to-manage platform, used by millions of bloggers around the world. TypePad is frequently updated with new features — including a complete overhaul in 2009 — in an effort to offer users the best of the blogosphere.

We have our own TypePad history — professional *and* personal. Melanie is a technical writer who has blogged professionally for years on numerous blogging platforms, including TypePad, giving her a solid basis for comparison. Shannon is a personal blogger who has been hammering out posts from the TypePad Dashboard since 2006. Just like you, we started out as beginners. We studied the TypePad help section and submitted help tickets. We discovered some shortcuts and found out other things the hard way. We asked the same questions you're asking now, and we're eager to show you what our own TypePad experience has taught us.

About This Book

Because you've picked up this book, chances are you fall into one of two categories: You want to start your first blog, and you've heard that TypePad is a user-friendly way to find your place in the blogosphere; or you already have a TypePad blog, and you want to better understand some of the significant changes Six Apart made in 2009 when it released the newest version of TypePad. Or we may be completely off-base and you just picked up this book because it's a pretty yellow color. Whatever the reason, we're glad you're reading it.

We've written this book with the beginning to intermediate TypePad user in mind and have included information on the most recent features available to users as of late 2009.

Even beginners can expect to find TypePad a hassle-free tool for building a polished, professional blog. Just as TypePad is known for its user-friendliness, we've written this book to be user-friendly as well. You won't find an abundance of technical talk, because we know that many TypePad users choose TypePad specifically to avoid technical headaches. We tell you the terms, techniques, and processes you need to know to navigate this software like a pro, even if you do not bring a lot of technical experience to the table. Whether you're blogging as a hobbyist or as a professional, we fully expect this book to give you what you need to build a stellar TypePad blog.

Conventions Used in This Book

Conventions are large and scary gatherings of unknown people with name tags, but don't worry — we don't have any of those in this book. The conventions we're talking about in this book are simply formatting rules we'll follow to make it easier to navigate the information we've shared. Here are the ones we'll use.

When we place a word in italics, we're telling you that it's an important word you need to know, and we define it immediately. Let's try it out:

> Your userpic can be a picture of yourself or your brand. A *brand* is simply a concept or visual image your readers associate with you.

When you see a word written in bold, we're referring to specific text that you need to enter in the designated field on your screen. Here's an example:

> If you're looking for a post you wrote about the world's best hash brown casserole, typing **hash brown** in the search bar will pull up every post you've written that contains those words.

When we change the font to `look like this`, we're indicating that this is a Web address (URL), an e-mail address, or a piece of code. Here's one last example:

> Choose your blog URL. The *URL* is your blog's address online (for example, `http://www.typepadfordummies.typepad.com`).

What You're Not to Read

You certainly don't have to read this book from cover to cover. We expect that you'll likely jump around between chapters, searching for answers to your particular questions. We've written this book with that in mind — you'll notice that we frequently point you toward another chapter where the topic is discussed in further detail.

If you already have a decent amount of TypePad experience, you'll probably skip some parts of this book altogether. The earliest chapters, especially, are geared toward true beginners. If that isn't you, skip ahead until you find the information you need. Likewise, if you're just starting out as a blogger, some of the later chapters about custom CSS (Cascading Style Sheets) and advanced templates may seem overwhelming. Don't sweat it. Get comfortable with the easier parts of the process and then look at the later chapters in a few weeks or months. They won't feel so overwhelming then.

So scan ahead, reread, underline, make notes, draw daisies in the margins — do whatever you have to do to make this book helpful. That's why we wrote it.

Foolish Assumptions

Assumptions can be dangerous, but we had to make a few as we wrote this book. We've assumed the following:

✔ You either own a computer or have access to one, and you are familiar with its most basic functions.

✔ You know how to access the Internet, and you know how to maneuver around Web sites by pointing and clicking. (If not, you might want to check out *The Everyday Internet All-in-One Desk Reference For Dummies,* by Peter Weverka.)

✔ You have an e-mail address and know how to use it.

✔ You have a general sense of what a blog is and probably have already read at least a few of them. (If not, you'd benefit from *Blogging For Dummies,* 2nd Edition, by Susannah Gardner and Shane Birley.)

✔ You may not know much about TypePad (at least, not yet — we'll fix that soon enough), but you do understand that TypePad has something to do with blogging, and you want to find out more.

How This Book Is Organized

This book is organized into five parts. Our goal is to introduce you to everything you'll need to best use TypePad as your blogging platform. We start by explaining the basic premise of blogging, move on to setting up your TypePad account and blog, and then show you how to take your blog to the next level (with customized designs, for example).

Part I: The Basics of Blogging

If you're new to blogging, Part I is where you want to start. We explain the dynamics of blogging so you can understand why people blog and why community is such an important part of blogging. We also discuss how you can develop your own blogging identity and build a community around your particular niche. Then we introduce you to some of the basic technology that powers blogs (such as RSS feeds and search engine optimization). By the end of Chapter 1, you'll know the difference between hosted and self-hosted blogging platforms and which is right for your blog's purposes.

In Chapter 2, we introduce you to Six Apart (TypePad's parent company). We explain the costs of TypePad and help you decide which pricing level to choose based on whether you're blogging for business, pleasure, or both.

Part II: Getting Started with TypePad

Part II helps you establish your account with basic settings and billing information. Then we describe a TypePad Profile and why it's important, and we walk you through setting up your own Profile. We show you what the Dashboard is and discuss each of the options and features it offers. Next, we get to what you've been waiting for: setting up your first blog. We walk you through choosing your basic blog settings (for example, handling your RSS feeds and sharing your content), checking your stats (to see who's visiting your blog), and managing your posts after you've written them. We not only give you instructions to compose a blog post (including how to insert images into the post, format the text, and set keywords for your post) but also address how TypePad can help you manage your blogging community as your blog readership grows.

Part III: Adding Useful Elements to Your TypePad Blog

In Part III, you find the real nuts and bolts. You begin to customize your TypePad blog to reflect what suits you — and your readers — best. We tell you about dozens of tools available to TypePad bloggers who want to maximize their online space. We show you how to use TypeLists (TypePad's way of sharing content in your blog's sidebars) and widgets (bits of code that offer additional functionality for your blog, such as a search bar) to help you organize your content and make your blog more user-friendly. We also explain how to integrate podcasting and video into your blog.

We figure if you're blogging, you probably have other social media accounts as well (maybe Twitter or Facebook?), and you'll want to connect those Profiles with your blog. We have you covered. If you don't have other social

Chapter 1

Understanding Blogging and TypePad

*B*efore we move ahead with some technical TypePad how-tos, let's start at the beginning. If you're not an experienced blogger, this chapter provides a simple framework for you, explaining the basic social dynamics and technology of blogging. The definitions and concepts we introduce in this chapter are used throughout the book, so a solid understanding of them is helpful. If you've already been blogging for some time, feel free to skip ahead to the next chapter.

In this chapter, we help you understand the social dynamics of a blog — how it works and why people even do it in the first place. We discuss the idea of community — a key difference between writing for a blog versus writing for a book or magazine — and we offer considerations for managing this community. We also explain some of the fundamental technological elements of a blog (including RSS feeds and search engine optimization) and how you can harness these elements to create a successful blog. All these points work toward producing a polished, attractive, user-friendly blog that invites participation from readers.

Dynamics of Blogging

Even if you don't have a blog yourself, you probably at least read a few of them. You may already have a sense of the general ebb and flow of a blogger's relationship with his or her readers. But reading a blog and writing a blog are two very different creatures — if you're just starting out, you'd be wise to have a solid understanding of the blogging dynamic before you jump in with both feet. This section gives those of you in the planning stages a few things to consider.

What is a blog?

The word *blog* is short for *weblog*. It's an online journal written by one or more authors. Some are updated multiple times a day; others are updated rarely, perhaps once a month. Most of the time, the author's most recent post is the first thing you see when you visit his or her blog, and as you scroll down, you'll be able to read the posts in reverse sequence, from the most recent to the oldest.

Unlike writing for a book or magazine, writing a blog offers the author immediate access to readers. There is no waiting around for editorial approval. A blogger can write a post and click Publish, and his or her words are instantly transmitted to the Web. Blogs have quickly joined the ranks of mainstream media as a cutting-edge and (sometimes!) accurate source of information for readers on a wide range of subjects.

Fundamental to the blogging experience is the presence of reader feedback in the form of a comments section for each post. The *comments section* is the place where readers can instantly agree, disagree, encourage, or ask questions of the author. Any comment you leave will, most likely, be visible to other readers of the blog. Many bloggers will tell you that some of the best, most robust discussion happens not in their own posts, but in the comments section. (You will occasionally encounter a blog that does not have a comments section, but this is rare.)

Why do people blog?

In the grand scheme of things, blogging is a relatively new form of human interaction. Engaging with readers through a computer screen can be enjoyable, but it can generate its fair share of headaches. Considering the millions of blogs that currently exist, countless people clearly think blogging is worth the effort. But why? Most of the answers to that question fall under two main categories: blogging for fun and blogging for business.

Blogging for fun

It's the reason most of us first ventured into the blogosphere — to have an online spot of our own that documents something important to us. Some people blog as a way to keep long-distance family members updated on the kids. Others enjoy using their blog as a journal for a specific process, such as a house remodeling or a weight-loss journey. Others document a hobby, such as knitting or woodworking, by sharing their achievements and offering tutorials. Plenty of others write a blog with no specific aim in mind — they keep a blog as a life journal, with no thematic thread running through it. You certainly don't need an official reason to start a blog.

You may often hear tips about how to develop your blog and gain a large readership; in reality, a large readership and a vocal comments section are not even remotely necessary to enjoy the process of blogging. You may start a blog and, quite unexpectedly, develop a following. Conversely, you may happily churn out posts for the benefit of only a handful of readers. Either option is acceptable, and you will find that your blogging satisfaction is highest when you focus on the quality of your own content, not on the number of people who may or may not be reading. Some of the finest blogs around are those written purely as a hobby, and the authors' clear passion for their topic makes the blogs so appealing to readers.

Most bloggers will tell you that a benefit of blogging (perhaps an unexpected one) is honing your writing and communication skills. As with most activities, we get better with practice, and preparing posts for a readership of any size can help us sharpen our writing abilities. Many people stumbled into blogging to document a particular process, only to realize that they enjoyed the act of crafting a good sentence. Think of it as your payoff for staying awake in freshman composition!

How to find related blogs

Wondering whether there's already a blog on your topic of interest? Visit `blogsearch.google.com` a search engine specifically for searching other blogs (as opposed to other Web sites). Or visit `blogs.com`, a site owned by TypePad's parent company, Six Apart. This site regularly links to blogs offering quality content on a range of subjects. Sites like these give you an opportunity to find out how (or whether) your particular topic is being addressed in the blogging community. Is left-handed cake decorating your thing? You'll probably find that there's a blog on the subject. Even if someone already has your particular topic or idea covered, don't hesitate to jump in and start, especially if you think you can offer a fresh perspective or an interesting twist.

Blogging for business

A growing number of bloggers are earning income on their blogs, primarily through selling ad space, a subject we tackle more fully in Chapter 12. Especially in your early blogging days, keep your expectations realistic when it comes to earning income — only a small minority of bloggers are able to earn enough income to fully support themselves through blogging. But it's not a bad way to supplement your main income, even if only modestly.

Business blogging isn't just for individuals; companies large and small are setting up interactive spots in the blogosphere where they can engage with customers. Even if these blogs don't generate income themselves, they are a valuable (and very inexpensive) marketing tool for talking about new products, offering technical support, or explaining your creative process. If you're a book author or musician, you may find the blogosphere is an efficient way to support your primary artistic purpose by connecting with the people who buy your books or music. In this interactive age, consumers increasingly expect to be able to engage online. Chapter 2 offers you some information about TypePad's services geared toward business bloggers.

Specifically, small business owners with limited marketing budgets may find blogging to be invaluable in showcasing their product or service. Use a blog to host a giveaway of your product or offer photographs of new products coming out soon. Allow customers to give you feedback, and you might find your next big idea in your own comments section.

Building a blogging community

Blogging is, at its core, an instant form of dialogue between blogger and reader. People connect online by agreeing, disagreeing, laughing, commiserating, learning, or questioning, among other things. This dialogue creates connection, which in turn leads to a word you'll hear often in the blogosphere: community. Whether you're blogging as an individual or as part of a bigger team or corporate entity, establishing a community is key to increasing readership. To encourage that community, you'll need to consider a few things before you start blogging, such as how you will engage with your readers, handle negative comments, and project your intended image.

Understanding online community

Community, as described in the context of blogging, is simply the idea that people connect with one another online. Community refers to the way that people congregate in cyberspace, bound together by common interests or causes. People engage with one another online through comments, e-mails, social media (see Chapter 10), and other means, forming a sense of togetherness. A common element (usually) of the most widely read blogs is a strong sense of community — a feeling that the blog in question is a reliable place to gather, receive information, share ideas, and possibly even generate friendships.

It's important to note that in defining what blogging community is, we should also take note of what it isn't. Most wise and experienced bloggers will tell you that the online connection can be a strong one, but it should never take the place of real-life relationships. Avoid the temptation of engaging so heartily in your online community that you neglect the real one. Finding balance as a blogger is key, and you can do this by seeking out blogging tools that help you engage in the online community without letting it govern your life. In Chapter 7, we discuss TypePad's commenting features, explaining how you can use those tools to streamline your blog interactions in a practical way.

Engaging effectively in the online community

You may be blogging just for fun, with no intention of developing a readership. As we say earlier in this chapter, this is a perfectly valid reason to write a blog, and you shouldn't feel any sense of obligation to draw readers to your blog if that's not why you're blogging. But if your aim is to turn your TypePad blog into a place where people want to gather, be deliberate in how you engage in the blogosphere. Some bloggers pay consultants big bucks to help generate a sense of community on their blog. The truth is that there is no magic formula for this — just hard work, good manners, and common sense. Here are a few things you can try:

- ✔ **Offer your readers something useful.** Building a successful blog ultimately involves offering good content with a clear purpose — for example, to inform, entertain, or encourage. Write for your own enjoyment, but (if you want to develop a readership) do it with your readers in mind — what is valuable to them? Chapter 6 offers more advice about writing good posts.

- ✔ **Participate generously in the blogging community.** Especially as you're starting out, you can encourage dialogue at your own blog by participating in the dialogue elsewhere. Leave thoughtful comments at other blogs, and when you find something worth reading, link to it from your own blog. This builds goodwill with other bloggers and has a way of coming back to you.

- ✔ **Elicit feedback.** If it's feedback you're after, write in a way that invites it! Ask a question of your readers, or bring up a topic that you're sure people want to discuss.

- ✔ **Write often.** People are more likely to gather at a blog that is updated at least a few times per week. Don't have the time or inclination to post this often? Depending on the TypePad level you choose, you can write posts ahead of time and then schedule them to publish in the future (see Chapter 6). This helpful feature allows you to write multiple posts when the mood strikes you and publish them at your desired pace.

- ✔ **Be user-friendly.** Offer a design that is easy on your readers' eyes (see Chapter 11) and use categories to make your blog searchable and streamlined (see Chapter 6).

Setting standards

The give-and-take dynamic of an online community is generally a good thing for bloggers; most of us find the dialogue intriguing and stimulating. Many blogs with large readerships have grown, at least in part, because they've engaged effectively with readers and other bloggers. They've offered their readers something that is useful or entertaining or both. They've asked their readers for feedback, offering them a chance to interact with one another.

It's not a bad idea for bloggers to set some commonsense ground rules at their blog, defining how they'll manage things and how they expect their readers to interact. Many bloggers will go so far as to set up a separate page in which they spell out their guidelines for community interaction and etiquette. (See Chapter 6 for instructions on how TypePad allows you to set up a page and to find out how a page is different from a regular blog post.) Especially if you plan to blog about hot-button issues that can breed controversy, setting guidelines might be a sanity saver for you. Some suggestions for these guidelines include

- ✔ Explaining whether or not you delete comments and if so, on what grounds (such as offensive language or name-calling, spam, or off-topic comments).

- ✔ Letting readers know that they can always expect a response to your private e-mails or that they can never expect one, or (perhaps more realistically) something in between.

- ✔ Spelling out your own guidelines on whether you accept payments for posts or free products in exchange for a review (see Chapter 12). Transparency in this department, particularly, is an important element of developing trust in your readers.

The blogosphere is a wide-open space, which means there is limitless potential for interaction from a wide variety of people. Don't fear the occasional *troll,* which is blogspeak for a commenter who hangs around your comment section purposely to stir up trouble. It happens to nearly every blogger at some point, even those who are blogging about noncontroversial topics. It is generally prudent to ignore trollish behavior; giving attention to it often makes it worse. (The exception, of course, is if the behavior reaches a level that is threatening. In this case, you should always contact the proper authorities.) Don't let yourself become discouraged by the occasional negativity; dust yourself off and think of what you enjoy about blogging. For every story about negative comments, there are a dozen stories about positive, helpful interactions that may even lead to real-life friendships.

Considering privacy issues

Privacy is understandably a big deal to many bloggers. You may be starting a blog with the intention of growing a large readership and even building a business — if this is the case, you may be happy to have as many eyes as possible browsing through your blog. But particularly for people who blog as hobbyists or to chronicle more personal items such as daily family life, it can be disconcerting to know that complete strangers may read the words you write. TypePad offers several privacy options, including password protection, comment blocking, and search-engine blocking (we tell you how to apply these options in Chapters 4, 7, and 5, respectively). Even with these options in place, it's still a good idea for bloggers to apply common sense and restraint when dealing with the issue of privacy. Use the TypePad tools that best suit your needs, but use your head as well. Here are a few things to consider:

- ✔ **Think of others.** You might not be an especially private person, but perhaps your spouse, boss, or mother-in-law is. It's a common courtesy to consider others' privacy preferences before you write something about them.

- ✔ **It's a small world.** Ask any blogger you know, and they will probably be able to tell you a story about the time a real-life acquaintance unexpectedly ran across the blog. If you write a post about how much you hate your neighbor's dog, be aware that your neighbor might find the post. You'd be surprised how often this type of thing happens in the blog world, so remember what you already learned the hard way in eighth grade: If you won't say something to someone's face, don't say it behind his or her back.

- ✔ **Remember that you can't take it back.** Even if you delete something you've written, it may continue to be referenced by search engines indefinitely. There's not much you can do to change that, other than changing your publicity options. Your mom's advice to "think before you speak" applies to blogging too.

- ✔ **Start slowly.** Especially if you're a new blogger and you're not sure where your comfort level lies along the privacy spectrum, err on the side of revealing too little instead of too much. Perhaps you'll want to withhold information such as real names and geographical locations until you've spent a little more time in the blogging community. You could use a pseudonym for yourself or your family, or you might not want to include photographs of your children, for example. After you've blogged for a while, you will likely develop a better sense of what privacy levels make you most comfortable. At that point, you can always begin to fill in more private details for your readers, should you so choose.

Finding an online identity

Your *online identity* is the face you present to the online world. It consists of, among other things, the name of your blog, your domain name, the name you use as a user id, your writing tone (on your own blog and in the comments you leave elsewhere), and the content of your posts. As a blogger, the words you write convey something about yourself, so be intentional about communicating authentically.

Using your own voice

It might initially sound appealing to invent an online persona for yourself, and certainly some bloggers have done this with varying degrees of success. Ultimately, though, you will likely find the greatest personal satisfaction from conducting your online interactions the way you would conduct your real-life ones. In other words, be yourself. As you write your posts (see Chapter 6), avoid the temptation to imitate another blogger. Instead, develop your own writing style or refine the one you already have. If you fall in love with blogging and use your blog as an online "home" for many years, you'll be glad that you use the voice you're most comfortable with — your own.

Choosing a name for your blog

It's one of the first decisions you have to make about your blog, and it's a big one: what should you name your blog? In Chapter 3, we tell you how to set up your TypePad account, and you'll be asked right away to name your TypePad URL (your blog's online address, such as `http:// typepadfordummies. typepad.com`). We strongly suggest naming your URL the same name as your blog, as a way to keep one cohesive online identity. If your URL is `http:// typepadfordummies.typepad.com`, you can see why your readers might be confused if they visit your blog and see "A Million and One Uses for Orange Juice" splashed across the top of your header design. (See Chapter 3 for a further explanation of the difference between a URL and a header.)

Remember that the name of your blog will help a reader form an initial opinion about the purpose and tone of your content. When you browse at a bookstore, aren't you more likely to pick up a book with a catchy and descriptive title? It's the same for blogs — if your blog title makes an impression, a new reader is likely to stick around and read more. Keep the following advice in mind as you develop your blog's name:

- ✔ **Check domain availability.** Many bloggers like to have their own domain name (such as `typepadfordummies.com`). It's a good idea to check the availability of your blog name as a domain name (and buy it right away) even if you're not quite ready to use it. See Appendix A for an explanation of domain names and how to map one to your TypePad blog.

- ✔ **Be descriptive.** Ideally, your title is an accurate reflection of your content. If you write snarky political commentary in your posts, reflect that tone in your title. If your blog is general in nature (such as a journal), you'll probably want to choose a more general name.

- ✔ **Avoid commonplace wording.** Terms such as *reflections, musings,* and *thoughts* aren't catchy and are overused. If you want your blog to be memorable, steer away from bland wording in your title.

- ✔ **Use a thesaurus.** Think of the words and concepts you hope to communicate to a potential reader. Write the words down and then use a thesaurus to list even more variations. Play around with them until something seems right.

✔ **Keep it short.** A long URL is hard to type, and a long blog title is hard to remember. Corporations choose short slogans because they stick in our heads, so apply the same logic to your blog name. Anything more than four or five words is probably too long.

✔ **Brainstorm.** Don't just think of words that describe your blog. Especially if your blog is a personal journal, think of any creative word or phrase from your past that might translate into a good title. The name of the street where you grew up? A compelling phrase from your favorite poem? A goofy nickname your spouse calls you? Interesting blog titles can lurk in unexpected places. See Chapter 17 for some examples of TypePad bloggers who have made great title selections.

Understanding Blogging Technologies

When you decide to start a blog, you'll need to choose a blogging platform. A *blogging platform* is simply the software you use for blogging. It's the site you sign in to when you're ready to write, edit, or manage your blog. Several platforms are available (TypePad, Blogger, and WordPress, for example), and they all offer a wide range of technical options. We offer a few comparisons of those platforms in Chapter 2. This section explains the basic blogging technologies present in most blogging platforms, including Rich Text and basic HTML editing choices, RSS feeds, and search engine optimization options. We also explain the difference between hosted and self-hosted platforms.

Rich Text

All major blogging platforms offer two ways to compose a blog post: HTML mode or Rich Text mode. HTML (short for Hypertext Markup Language) is the basic programming language (or code) that allows your browser to "read" your blog post and display it correctly. If you're familiar with HTML, you can make changes or tweaks as necessary to manipulate how your text and images appear. Don't worry if you don't know a thing about HTML; you can still blog. You'll just want to use the Rich Text editor instead of the HTML editor.

Rich Text is sometimes referred to as *WYSIWYG* (pronounced wiz-ee-wig) — it's the acronym for What You See Is What You Get. In other words, when you type your post in the Rich Text (WYSIWYG) editor, you'll see a preview of how the text and images of your post will look when published. The Rich Text editor is similar to what you're used to working with in Microsoft Word or Apple's Pages. The Rich Text editor has buttons to click to format text (such as bold, italic, and underline), to insert images and other multimedia files easily, and to change the alignment of your text. Chapter 6 explains these buttons more thoroughly.

Figures 1-1 and 1-2 show the difference between TypePad's Rich Text editor and HTML editor.

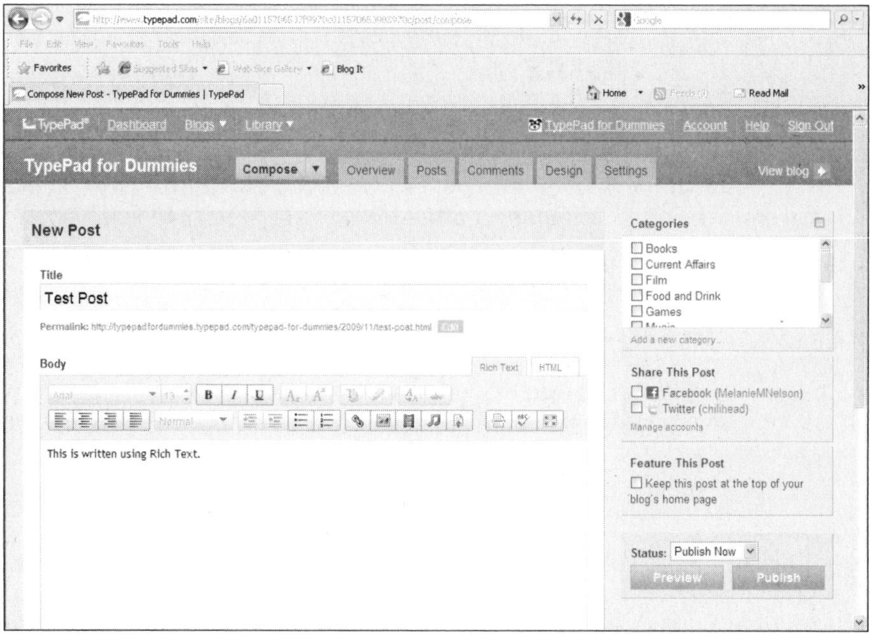

Figure 1-1:
Use the Rich Text editor for writing your blog posts.

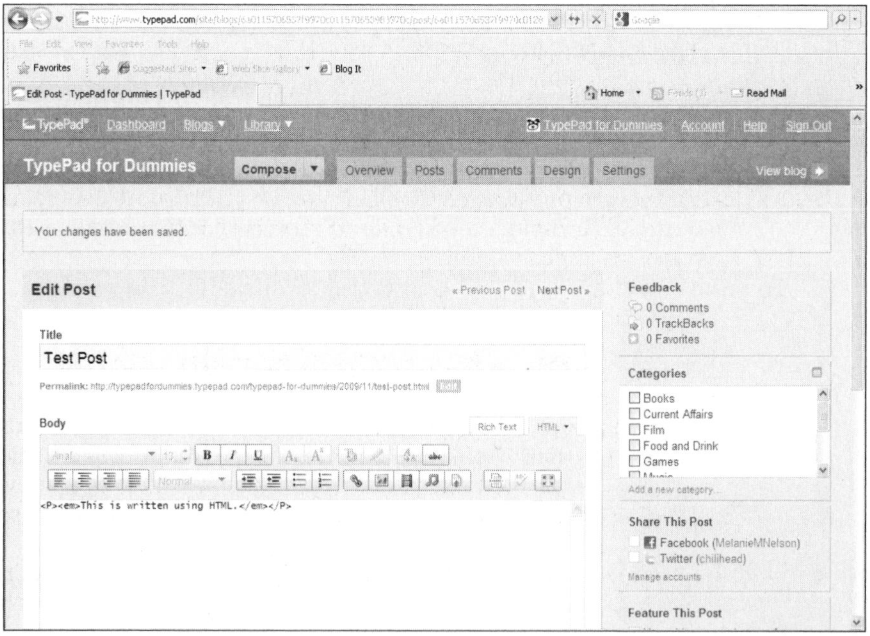

Figure 1-2:
Use the HTML editor if you need to tweak your HTML code.

Depending on the blogging platform you choose, your WYSIWYG mode may be called Rich Text (TypePad), Compose (Blogger), or Visual (WordPress). They all mean WYSIWYG.

RSS feeds

If you read a blog regularly and want to know when it's updated, you could visit that blog several times a day to see whether the author has posted anything new, or you could subscribe to the RSS feed and let it do the work for you. *RSS* stands for *Really Simple Syndication* and is the standard way for your readers to be alerted when you update your blog. The RSS feed sends new content to a feed reader as that content is available.

A *feed reader* (also known as an *aggregator*) is a site that allows you to sign up for an account and add the RSS feeds of blogs and Web sites you're interested in. The feed reader provides the updates for all the feeds you're subscribed to in one place. Two of the most widely used feed readers are Google Reader (www.google.com/reader) and NewsGator (www.NewsGator.com).

Using a feed reader yourself is easy. All you have to do is establish an account with a feed reader, subscribe to the RSS feed you want to monitor, and then check your feed reader when you have the time.

An RSS feed for your blog is automatically generated when you sign up with any of the major blogging platforms (TypePad, WordPress, or Blogger). There are several formats for RSS feeds: Atom, RSS 2.0, and RSS 1.0. Atom and RSS are basically the same types of blog feeds; it should not matter which feed you choose to offer or subscribe to. However, if you are podcasting and want to offer a feed for that service, you will want to offer RSS 2.0 to your readers because it offers the necessary parameters for that function.

Another way for readers to subscribe to your RSS feed is through e-mail. Many people prefer to receive new alerts in their e-mail inbox instead of through a third-party feed reader. You can offer this option with FeedBurner (which we discuss in Chapter 5).

Search engine optimization (SEO)

If you want people to find your blog when they do a search on a particular topic, you'll want to think about how to use SEO (search engine optimization) on your blog. *Search engine optimization* is simply using keywords effectively in your posts and titles so search engines can catalog your blog and include it in search results.

Before we explain how to use SEO on your blog, though, let us first explain how search engines work. Search engines send out virtual search teams of code called *robots* (also known as *bots* or *spiders)* that visit blogs and Web sites to look for words people use when they search for information. As these spiders crawl around each Web site or blog, they gather data relevant to what people are searching for and rank that data. (How they rank the data is based on algorithms and constantly changing formulas and is dependent on the search engine.) When spiders crawl your blog looking for relevance, they are looking specifically at semantic data (what you're writing about and which words you use) as well as contextual data (who is linking to you and what words they're using when they link to you). The more relevant your blog is to a specific topic or search term, the higher your blog appears on the results page for that topic or search term.

SEO is such a large topic that hundreds of books, blogs, and Web sites are devoted to teaching you how to use it effectively. We want to give you a few pointers to get you started, but this list is in no way exhaustive. Here are few suggestions on how to use keywords to help your blog's SEO rankings:

- **Use relevant keywords in your main post title.** Titles have more weight with search engines than paragraph text (though that's important, too). Including a keyword or two in your post title will help your SEO ranking. The title of your post will also be the permalink of your article. A *permalink* is the address of an individual blog post. Each post you write has its own address (permalink). Search engines consider your post titles and permalinks as they rank your site for relevance to a topic. Here are two examples of titles:

  Not so great: Back from Vacation!

  SEO friendly: New Orleans French Quarter: Cafe Du Monde, St. Louis Cathedral, and Bourbon Street!

  Not only is the second title more helpful to your readers by telling them what your post is about, but it's also more likely to be picked up by search engines because it uses terms people search for regularly (that is, if they're looking for information about New Orleans).

- **Use keywords associated with your topic and niche within your post.** One way to ensure that you're using relevant keywords throughout your blog is to think about how you would find the information if you were searching for it. What words would you type into a search engine to find information on your topic? Use those words in your titles and articles.

- **Choose your link words carefully.** Try to be as descriptive as possible when making words into a link. For example, if you'd like your readers to read your blog policies, instead of writing "My blog policies are <u>here</u>" (where the word "<u>here</u>" is a link to your policies) or "<u>Click here</u> for my blog policies" (where the phrase "<u>Click here</u>" is the link to your policies), write something like "Before you leave a comment, read my <u>blog policy for commenters</u>" (where "<u>blog policy for commenters</u>" is the link to your policy). Not only are the longer links more descriptive, but also, they're more search-engine-friendly. Spiders and bots are looking for interpretive word strings — phrases such as *click here* are everywhere on the Web and are hardly useful in setting your content apart from the crowd. Make your content stand out by using descriptive words and phrases as links.

✔ **Assign relevant keywords and categories to your post before you publish.** Chapter 6 shows you how to create categories that fit your topic and how to attach tags (or keywords) to your posts to make them more SEO-friendly.

Search engine optimization is important if you'd like to expand your readership or make your content readily available to others, but it shouldn't take over your blog. Your readers will be turned off if all your content reads like a commercial or search results page. Write content that appeals to your readers (interests them, helps them, or answers a question for them) and creates community. Incorporate SEO as you go, but not at the expense of alienating your readers. As your blog content grows, so will your SEO because it's information people want to know. The bottom line: Create content for people, but keep it friendly for the machines.

Hosted versus self-hosted blogging platforms

When you are comparing blog platforms to see which one is right for you, one of the things you'll need to consider is whether the platform is hosted or self-hosted. A *hosted blogging platform* is one that allows the blog to reside on the host's server. TypePad is an example of a hosted blogging platform. TypePad allows you to keep your blog on its server and use its software to blog — you don't have to download anything to your computer. All updates to the server or software are handled by TypePad instead of you. Hosted blogging platforms such as TypePad are very popular because they offer an easy way to get started with a blog without having to know anything about HTML, CSS, or Perl (a few of the types of programming code that build your blog behind the scenes and allow your browser to read your blog design properly) — using a hosted blogging platform is pretty much a point-and-click affair.

Although hosted blogging platforms are popular and easy to use, they have some issues you should consider before you commit:

✔ Blogs on hosted platforms can appear to be less professional because they have `.typepad.com` (or `.blogspot.com` for Blogger blogs) at the end of the URL (for example, `http://typepadfordummies.typepad.com`). However, you can skirt this issue by buying your own domain name and mapping it to your account (see Chapter 3 and Appendix A for further information and instructions). What that means is that you can buy your own domain name (for example, `www.typepadfordummies.com`) and map it to your TypePad account so when someone visits your blog, they see `http://www.typepadfordummies.com` in the address bar instead of `http://www.typepadfordummies.typepad.com`.

✔ Hosted blogging platforms give you less control over HTML and CSS, and you won't see any Perl. Although you can tweak your HTML in your Rich Text editor, that applies only to individual posts. If you're fluent with CSS and HTML and are used to making changes to your blog by changing the code by hand, you'll be disappointed. You're not allowed to access the full code of your blog directly. There are work-arounds (see Chapter 14, where we discuss how to use Advanced Templates with TypePad), but you'll still be limited. If you don't know the first thing about HTML and are fine not messing with your code (and, in fact, prefer not to), this issue won't be a problem for you.

A *self-hosted blogging platform* is one that allows you to use its blogging software but asks you to house your blog on your own server. Because you likely aren't set up with your own server, you will need to pay a third-party Web host to host your blog (you can learn more about choosing a server provider at WebHosting Talk: `webhostingtalk.com`). Movable Type (sister to TypePad) and WordPress.org are self-hosted blogging platforms. The thing that makes self-hosted platforms attractive to bloggers is that they allow you to have full control over your HTML, CSS, Perl, and PHP. Code junkies love to have access to their code. The biggest con to using a self-hosted blogging platform is the learning curve. A self-hosted platform requires you to contact a server provider and rent space, install the software on the server (usually a one-click install with CPanel, which most server providers offer), and transfer files from your computer to the server (this is called File Transfer Protocol, or FTP). Although updates to the server will most likely be handled by your server provider, software updates will be handled by you (again, usually a simple one-click procedure, but one you're responsible for).

If you're new to the blogging world and aren't sure if you'll be staying or just want to get your feet wet before you commit to so much responsibility, we suggest going with a hosted blogging platform such as TypePad. The hosted platforms will help you slowly familiarize yourself with blogging and the mechanics behind it without overwhelming you. If you decide you want to manage your own code down the line, you can migrate your blog to a self-hosted platform such as Movable Type or WordPress.org.

Considering some of the basic concepts and terminologies we've given you in this chapter will help you navigate more smoothly throughout the blogosphere (whichever platform you ultimately choose). A successful blogger is one who is well-informed about blogging trends and solidly connected in the blogging community. Along with what we've told you here, keep a keen eye out for changing technologies and engage honestly and fairly in the blogging community around you. Most important, don't let yourself get mired down in what you *don't* know — the best way to learn is to jump in and start!

Chapter 2

The Benefits of TypePad

Whether you're blogging for personal pleasure or to help your business establish a solid online presence (or you're somewhere in between), this chapter gives you an overview of where TypePad came from and what it does well. We explain the pros and cons of using TypePad and discuss which pricing options and features are right for your blog.

Discovering the History of TypePad

If you've read much about TypePad, you may have heard of Six Apart, the company that produces TypePad. In 2001, husband-and-wife team Mena and Ben Trott were looking for a better way to manage Mena's personal blog, Dollarshort (www.dollarshort.org). In 2001, they developed and released Movable Type, a blogging platform geared toward people with a decent amount of technical know-how. The release of Movable Type was so well-received that Mena and Ben formed their own company, Six Apart, to support Movable Type (interestingly, Six Apart's name comes from the six-day span between Ben and Mena's birthdates).

About the same time that Movable Type was taking off, the rest of the world had been bitten by the blogging bug. Less experienced bloggers were eager for software similar to Movable Type, but they wanted one that didn't require advanced technical knowledge. With the addition of some new employees and some venture capital, Six Apart launched TypePad in October 2003. TypePad offered a simple, fee-based service to people who just wanted to blog without the hassles of coding and hosting issues.

Now, many years later, TypePad continues to thrive as a leading platform for bloggers of all sizes and niches. TypePad is home to millions of blogs around the world. It has a strong presence internationally and has continued to roll out new features to keep users on the cutting edge of blogging technologies. In late 2009, TypePad released a new version of its platform, bringing about the most significant changes since the product was first released in 2003.

Blogging for Personal or Business Use with TypePad

Getting started with TypePad is fast and easy. Before we start, though, let's look at how TypePad stacks up against some of the other blogging platforms. Several platforms are available, and they offer a range of technical options and price points:

✔ Google Blogger is free and takes care of hosting your blog, but it has limited design options unless you possess Web design experience (or can hire someone who does). Additionally, many users opt to install third-party commenting software for additional functionality.

✔ WordPress.com is also free and hosts your site for you, but it doesn't allow you to be part of ad networks — an important consideration if you're hoping to earn a little money from your blog. WordPress.*org* (which is different from WordPress.*com*) requires that you have a significant degree of comfort with managing code (if you don't, you may want to hire someone who does). In addition, you are responsible for managing and paying for your own site hosting. WordPress.org allows you to have ads on your blog.

✔ Movable Type is also free. But as with WordPress.org, you must be comfortable with managing code (or hire somebody to do it for you). And again as with WordPress.org, you are responsible for managing and paying for your own site hosting. Movable Type does allow you to have ads on your blog.

✔ TypePad also has several account options, both free and paid. The free option, called Micro, is not as customizable as Blogger, though it does offer some significant advantages. In particular, Micro allows you to integrate your content with your social media accounts. The paid TypePad account options are Pro Plus, Pro Unlimited, and Business Class and are priced comparably to what you would spend if you were paying for a server host. All TypePad account levels offer access to TypePad's well-known customer support, a significant advantage over Google Blogger. You might say that TypePad is the happy medium of blogging platforms — the polish and flexibility of WordPress.org or Movable Type with the simplicity of Blogger.

If you want more information about what the other blogging platforms offer, check out *Google Blogger For Dummies,* by Susan Gunelius, or *WordPress For Dummies,* 2nd Edition, by Lisa Sabin-Wilson.

We understand that all products have pros and cons. We've laid those out for you here. We include a few direct comparisons to some of the other well-known blogging platforms available on the Web.

Pros

- ✔ **It's simple.** For many users, this is one of TypePad's biggest benefits. With TypePad, you can be a professional blogger with a polished and sophisticated-looking blog, and you never have to deal with coding or hosting.

- ✔ **Reliable tech support is readily available.** If issues do arise, TypePad is known for quick, round-the-clock customer service, and its help section is written without a lot of overwhelming techspeak.

- ✔ **It's affordable.** As of this writing, TypePad's monthly pricing ranges from free to $14.95 a month (Business Class rates are significantly higher, but more on that in a minute). Frequent coupon codes are available, as are discounts if you pay for a year at a time. That's a pretty inexpensive hobby. And for those who use their TypePad blog as a revenue-generating business, those are nominal business costs (and possibly tax-deductible; ask your tax professional for details on this). This monthly charge is comparable to the amount you'd spend paying for hosting with a WordPress.org or Movable Type blog.

- ✔ **TypePad has an impressive track record regarding security.** TypePad's sign-in information is transmitted via encrypted SSL login. *SSL* stands for *Secure Sockets Layer* and is the standard way to encrypt information as it passes between a Web server and a browser. Millions of Web sites use SSL to protect customer transactions. TypePad manages security issues for users, eliminating the need to install additional plug-ins or upgrade current ones as security technology advances. (With WordPress.org, users are responsible for this themselves.)

- ✔ **The design templates are attractive and visually pleasing.** TypePad offers dozens of design themes and several page layouts, ranging from very simple to more complex. Your design can be changed with a few clicks, which may be a big benefit if you like to change the look of your blog often.

- ✔ **Custom designs don't have to be complicated, either.** Maybe you don't want a standard design template, but you don't want to pay a designer for an elaborate, allover blog design. TypePad makes it easy to install a simple personalized design by using a custom header. In Chapter 11, we tell you how to install a custom header, giving you a personalized look on a budget. In Chapter 14, we explain some of the more sophisticated, coding-related customization tools available to TypePad users with a Pro Unlimited account and above.

✔ **Frequent updates are provided automatically.** Six Apart frequently rolls out new and improved features for TypePad users. You don't have to download anything or install any additional plug-ins (as you might have to do in WordPress). TypePad does it for you! When you have a TypePad account, you can have updates on new features e-mailed right to your inbox, so you'll never miss a thing.

✔ **TypeLists are simple tools for organizing sidebars.** TypeLists are a feature much loved by most TypePad users. They're streamlined ways to categorize and organize your sidebar information (links, reading lists, images, and so on). TypeLists are easy to add, edit, delete and move around, and they make managing your sidebar very simple. We tell you how to use them in Chapter 8.

✔ **You can manage multiple blogs with one account.** Although you may begin writing a single blog, eventually you may want to start an additional one, or a member of your family may want a separate blog under your account. Instead of creating an entirely new TypePad account, you can simply add another blog to your existing one. The Pro Plus package allows you to have up to three blogs on one account, whereas the Pro Unlimited and Business Class packages allow unlimited blogs on a single account, and each can have its own domain.

Cons

✔ **If you want customization, it isn't free.** TypePad's Micro option won't cost you a thing, but you have access to only one design theme. The only elements of this theme you can personalize are your banner photo and color scheme. If you're firmly set on using a free platform that gives you full design customization, Google Blogger may suit you better. If you're not sure yet, our best advice is to start with a free TypePad Micro blog and see whether the features suit you. If you decide you want to stake a more permanent, customized claim in the blogosphere, you can upgrade to a paid TypePad account later.

✔ **You have limited access to your code.** If you're using the Micro or Pro Plus option, you'll never see a single dot of code. It depends on your outlook as to whether you define this as a pro or a con (see the first item in the "Pros" list). If you're the technical sort who loves to mess around in code, or if you're starting your blog specifically because you want to learn coding, TypePad's simplicity might be a turnoff. Bloggers who choose WordPress.org, for example, have to jump in to meatier technical issues from the first day, which might be your cup of tea. If you have a TypePad Pro Unlimited or Business Class account, you do have *some* access to your code, either through custom CSS or Advanced Templates (both of which are covered in Chapter 14).

✔ **It's not as customizable as WordPress.org** (see *WordPress For Dummies,* 2nd Edition, by Lisa Sabin-Wilson). WordPress.org has a bajillion templates available for your blog. (Okay, that's an exaggeration, but you'd be hard-pressed to count them all.) Most of those templates are customizable to some degree. You need to be familiar with the coding necessary to make significant changes (PHP, CSS, and HTML), but because you have access to all that code in your WordPress.org template, you (or your hired designer or developer) can easily find problems and make changes as necessary. TypePad has dozens of templates available, but depending on which type of account you have, you may or may not be able to customize your template. If you have the Pro Plus package or above, it's fairly easy to add a custom header to your blog. Completely customizing your template and styles requires using the Advanced Templates option (which is available only in the Pro or Business Class packages and is discussed in Chapter 14). A customizing option that's less complicated than Advanced Templates is custom CSS, also addressed in Chapter 14.

✔ **TypePad is not open source software.** *Open source software* allows users to be the driving force of people who constantly create new plugins, features, and templates for the vast open community. The advantage is that everyone is working together to better the software. TypePad offers several forums for community discussion, but any development released to the community is controlled by Six Apart.

✔ **TypePad is not ideal as a Content Management System.** A Content Management System (or CMS) is a way to manage more technologically complicated streams of content, such as rotating displays and aggregated content. If you've seen blog designs that look more like a magazine than a typical blog (for example, rotating images with article excerpts or a list of additional article with links), you're seeing a site that uses a CMS to populate certain areas of the design with specific new content. TypePad isn't set up to do that. Content management systems aren't for everyone — most typical bloggers don't need one. If you do, though, you may want to consider Movable Type (also owned by Six Apart and a sister to TypePad; it's a self-hosted blogging platform) or installing WordPress.org on your own hosted service.

Choosing the Right TypePad Blogging Package

TypePad offers its users four blogging packages, with widely varied features and pricing. Whether you think of blogging as a lone endeavor with the individual pounding out posts from a solitary kitchen table or as a necessary business tool with posts from multiple authors, TypePad has a package that addresses your needs. Depending on your specific blogging needs, you can choose which pricing package offers you the features you want. Table 2-1 is a quick reference of pricing and features (a more thorough listing is at `typepad.com/pricing`). We explain these features further in the rest of this section.

Table 2-1		Overview of TypePad Pricing Options and Features
Package	*Price*	*Features*
Micro	Free	Includes basic blogging necessities such as allowing you to post images and video.
		Offers only one design option (the Chroma theme). The only customizable design elements are the banner photo and the color scheme.
		Forbids the use of your own domain name (for example, `www.yourblogname.com`).
		Enables you to host only one blog on this account.
		Built-in integration with your social media accounts.
		Provides 3GB of storage.
Pro Plus	$8.95/ month	Includes everything in the Micro plan.
		Allows hosting of up to three blogs on your account.
		Allows you to use your own domain name.
		Enables you to use a customer header in your design.
		Provides unlimited storage (although no more than 150MB can be uploaded in any one month).
Pro Unlimited	$14.95/ month	Includes everything in the Micro and Pro Plus plans.
		Allows unlimited blogs on your account.
		Allows unlimited authors on your account.
		Gives you total control over your design; you can customize as you see fit (see Chapter 14 for instructions on how to use custom CSS and Advanced Templates to tweak your theme).
		Provides unlimited storage (although no more than 1000MB can be uploaded in any one month).

Package	Price	Features
Business Class	$89.95/ month	Includes everything in the Micro, Pro Plus, and Pro Unlimited plans.
		Allows multiple administrators (as opposed to just multiple authors).
		Assigns you an account manager to oversee the deployment of the blog.
		Provides yearly invoicing.
		Provides unlimited storage (although no more than 2000MB can be uploaded in any one month).

The Micro package offers 3GB of storage, which refers to how much space TypePad gives you to store your files (such as photos or audio) on its server. The three paid packages all offer you an unlimited amount of storage, but the rate at which you can upload files differs. For example, Pro Plus offers you 150MB per month of uploads. This means that in the month of, say, January, you could upload 150MB worth of photos, audios, PDF documents, and so on. After you upload 150MB, you would not be able to upload anything else until February 1, at which point you could again upload 150MB. The files you uploaded in January would still be there, perfectly safe under the "unlimited storage" feature.

As you choose which package is right for you, consider how often you upload files, and at what size. Images, video files, and audio files can be quite large. A photo blogger or podcaster who uploads multiple large files a week may need a higher monthly upload number. A blogger who writes only text (and posts the occasional photo) would not need a very high monthly upload amount.

Each of TypePad's packages also offers

- ✔ Access to TypePad's customer support and design portfolio (except Micro, which offers you only the Chroma design theme)
- ✔ The option to post photos, video, and audio
- ✔ Password protection and comment blocking
- ✔ Full integration with social media accounts (for example, Facebook and Twitter)
- ✔ Mobile-posting options
- ✔ RSS feeds

It's at this point that the different levels begin to part ways, so let's break down a few considerations for each one (please note that all pricing and feature options are current as of November 2009).

Micro

The Micro option is the newest addition to the TypePad family, added in November 2009. As mentioned, it's free, offering a bare-bones approach to TypePad blogging. You have access to the most basic blogging functions (posting text, photos, video, and so on), and you can interact fully with your readers in your comments section. You're limited to 3GB of storage, which is probably enough for most bloggers posting text only. If you plan to include a significant number of photos in your blog, or if you have a very long stash of archived posts, you might run out of space quickly.

Also, the Micro package has no design customization (except for your banner image and color scheme), and you have access only to the Chroma theme (pictured in Figure 2-1).

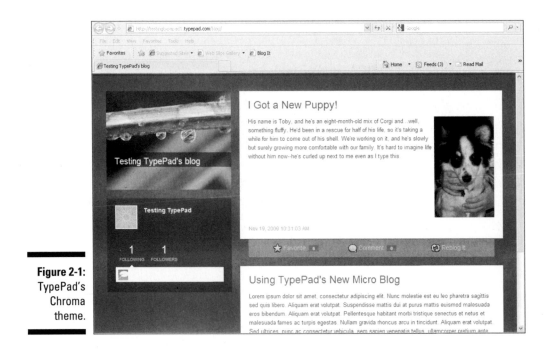

Figure 2-1:
TypePad's
Chroma
theme.

The functionalities of the Micro package are good ones — certainly more than adequate for a hobbyist blogger who wants to learn the ins and outs of blogging, or share posts with friends and family. With a Micro account, you can

- ✔ Use the Blog It widget (see Chapter 15)
- ✔ Post via e-mail
- ✔ Integrate your content with your various social media accounts
- ✔ Have a fully functioning comments section
- ✔ Search TypePad's Knowledge Base (the help files)
- ✔ Follow the Profiles of other TypePad users to develop a sense of community

In the interest of keeping you fully informed, though, you should be aware that some features aren't available to Micro users. With a Micro account, you *cannot*

- ✔ Schedule a post to publish in the future
- ✔ Customize your design (except a color scheme and banner)
- ✔ Have multiple authors
- ✔ Use trackbacks
- ✔ Create pages (Chapter 6 explains how pages differ from blog posts)
- ✔ Create or use TypeLists or widgets (therefore, you can't include additional information or ad networks on your sidebars)
- ✔ Create a help ticket for your specific blogging issue

If you enjoy TypePad Micro but decide that more functionalities are attractive, you are perfectly positioned to upgrade to a paid TypePad account with just one click.

If you are a Micro user, you will still find much relevant information in this book. However, many of the features we explain in later chapters may not be available to you — when this happens, just skip ahead to a section that covers a feature you *do* have!

Pro Plus

Pro Plus is a middle-of-the road package that offers significantly more features than the Micro package, and they're features that are generally important to bloggers (especially those who plan to build a readership and possibly earn some revenue). For example, the Plus package allows you to engage in *domain mapping,* which means you can use your own personal URL (that is, `www.mypersonalurl.com`) to point back to your TypePad blog. We show you how to do this in Appendix A. The Pro Plus package also allows you to create two additional blogs under the same account and at least a measure of design flexibility (in particular, allowing you to insert a custom-designed header, as described in Chapter 11). The Pro Plus package (as well as the Pro Unlimited and Business Class packages) allow you to schedule posts into the future — more on this in Chapter 6.

Your storage in Pro Plus is unlimited, but as we explain earlier, you can upload files at a rate of only 150MB per month. When they're in, though, you can store them in perpetuity.

Pro Unlimited

The next level is Pro Unlimited, which brings in still more features. It provides a significant jump in the amount of monthly uploads allowed — a whopping 1000MB. For users who want a truly custom design (as opposed to just a custom header), Pro Unlimited gives you (or your blog designer) access to CSS. (We define and discuss CSS in Chapter 14.) The Pro Unlimited package offers unlimited additional blogs, which may make it a good option for a family who wants to host several blogs from the same account. This level lets you give an unlimited number of additional authors access to your Dashboard, which is often an important feature for small-business blogs.

Business Class

Savvy companies are jumping on board with blogging, providing their customers highly interactive venues for learning about new products, leaving feedback, and engaging socially with other customers. It has become the norm, not the exception, for companies to have some kind of presence in the blogosphere. TypePad offers Business Class as a service aimed at midsize-to-large companies. Unlike a corporate Web site, which may not be geared toward two-way communication, a corporate blog allows your business to jump feet first into the dialogue taking place online.

You'll notice a significant price jump between the first three pricing levels and the Business Class package. This fourth level is designed for corporate users who need a blogging platform with some very specific features. Most notably, Business Class allows for additional administrators. This is different from having an additional author; unlike an author, an administrator has full authorization to make fundamental, account-level decisions. This feature may be important to a large corporation that needs more than one employee to help maintain a large-scale blogging effort. Additionally, being a Business Class member of TypePad gives you access to higher-level services (for an additional fee), such as implementing custom designs, coaching on how to knit together an entire social media presence, and access to priority support.

If you have a small or even midsize business, you will likely find that the Pro Unlimited level is sufficient for your company blog, especially if you're primarily using it for issuing updates on new products or general company news. The Pro level offers plenty of powerful features to produce a highly polished blog without requiring the business owner to incur the additional cost of Business Class.

The rest of this book focuses on bloggers using the Micro, Pro Plus, and Pro Unlimited pricing levels. If you're a Business Class blogger, your Dashboard will have many similarities with those of these other levels, and you will certainly find plenty of helpful tips for managing your Business Class blog. But we do not address some of the more advanced options available to Business Class bloggers, such as multiple administrators and yearly invoicing — instead, you should contact the TypePad priority support team specifically assigned to you when you set up your Business Class blog.

Discovering TypePad's Technical Support Services

Ask TypePad bloggers what they love most about this platform, and odds are that you will hear a mention of the excellent technical support. It's one of the things TypePad is most known for throughout the blogosphere — quick and easy-to-understand help from a team of real-live people at TypePad's help desk. You won't find this same level of service with Blogger (which offers limited help files and virtually no personal assistance) or WordPress (which has a more open and vocal community, but its documentation tends to be laced with technical jargon and can be difficult to understand if you're a beginner).

In Chapter 4, we explain how you can access TypePad's Knowledge Base, or help section, from your Dashboard. We show you how to easily search for Knowledge Base articles that will answer your questions. If you can't find the answer, we show you how to submit a help ticket. When you open a ticket, someone from the TypePad support community will get back to you (usually within 24 hours) with an answer. The best part? The answer is usually exactly what you were looking for, and if instructions are necessary and included, they're incredibly easy to follow.

The Knowledge Base isn't the only place to brush up on your TypePad skills. Six Apart provides ongoing support for users, educating them about how to implement the best TypePad has to offer and informing them of changes just around the bend. In Chapter 16, we point you toward several of these resources in detail, including the Everything TypePad blog (TypePad's official blog, full of company news), TypePad User Forums (a place to talk through your questions with other TypePad users), and Live Events (online and in-person seminars you can access to help you polish your TypePad knowledge). See Chapter 16 for even more resources available to TypePad users.

Whether you're a blogging newbie or have years of online experience under your belt, rest assured that TypePad users don't have to do it alone. With an impressive amount of technical support behind you and opportunities to find out more being presented all the time, you're sure to find the support you need from TypePad. This support, along with the other features offered to TypePad users, gives bloggers everything they need to produce a top-notch blog.

Part II
Getting Started with TypePad

The 5th Wave   By Rich Tennant

"I know it's a short About Me page, but I thought 'King of the Jungle' sort of said it all."

In this part . . .

This part of the book gets you up and running with your TypePad account and shows you the basic lay of the land of your Dashboard. You also get moving on some of the most fundamental activities for a blogger: creating a blog, writing a post, and interacting with your readers.

Chapter 3

Creating Your TypePad Account and Profile

*B*efore you can begin using TypePad, you need to sign up for an account. It's a simple process, requiring an e-mail address and a password (for Micro, the free option), plus a credit card (if you're opting for a Pro Plus or Pro Unlimited account). TypePad does the rest for you. You don't need to find a server (TypePad will host your blog on its server) or install software (because TypePad is hosting your blog in their data center, the software is already there and ready to go). You just create an account, sign in, and get started!

Although the process isn't complex, you do have to jump through a few hoops before you start blogging on TypePad. In this chapter, we tell you what you need to think about before and during the getting-started process. We give you some advice on specifying your blog's title as well as its URL, offer a quick look at the TypePad Dashboard, and tell you what it takes to create a TypePad Profile and why you need one. After we have you set up with your account, we discuss a few issues you need to consider before you start blogging — for example, how much personal information you want to share and whether you want to connect your TypePad Profile with your other social media accounts (such as Facebook or Twitter).

Signing Up for a TypePad Account

For an explanation of the different TypePad account options, both free and paid, see Chapter 2.

Ready to get started with your TypePad account? Before you do, spend a little time thinking about the face you want to present to the blogging world. It's a good idea to decide on your blog's name and the URL you want (they should match) before you start typing stuff on the sign-up page.

Also, think about the e-mail address you want to associate with TypePad. TypePad uses the address you provide when you create an account to send you updates on TypePad features and communicate with you about support tickets you might submit. Also, if you set up your account to have your comments e-mailed to you (see Chapter 7), this is the e-mail address where the comments will be sent.

TypePad offers a free blogging option (Micro) or a free trial period before you commit to a paid option (see Chapter 2 for a complete overview of TypePad's blogging tiers). Before you commit to anything, we suggest that you consider how much you're willing to pay. TypePad accepts Visa, MasterCard, American Express, and Discover cards but doesn't accept PayPal or personal checks as payment. Of course, if you choose TypePad Micro, you won't need a credit card because it's free.

Finally, you need to consider whether or not you want your blog to be found via search engines. If you're hoping people will find and read your blog, and you want to develop a community around your topic, you'll want search engines to include your blog in their results. If you are writing a private, password-protected blog, search engines will not index your blog. TypePad gives you this option when you sign up. Don't worry if you change your mind later; you can change your settings using the Dashboard.

After you have your blogging ducks in a row, you just need to set up a TypePad account. We'll explain how to do that, whether you choose the free Micro account or a paid Pro account.

TypePad Micro

Creating a TypePad Micro account is easy. In just a few short clicks, you'll be ready to blog! To get started, follow these steps:

1. **Type** www.TypePad.com **in your browser's address box and press Enter.**

   The TypePad home page appears. Look for the title Create Your Free Micro Blog in Seconds.

2. **Type your e-mail address and password in the text boxes provided.**

3. **Click the Create Blog Now button.**

   A new page with your TypePad Micro blog appears. Figure 3-1 shows what this page looks like.

4. **Click the image you want to use for your banner.**

If you'd like to use your own image instead of one TypePad offers, you can do that by clicking the Browse button and uploading an image from your hard drive. Keep in mind that your blog's color scheme is pulled from the colors in the image you choose for your banner; the more colorful the image, the more colorful your blog's color scheme options.

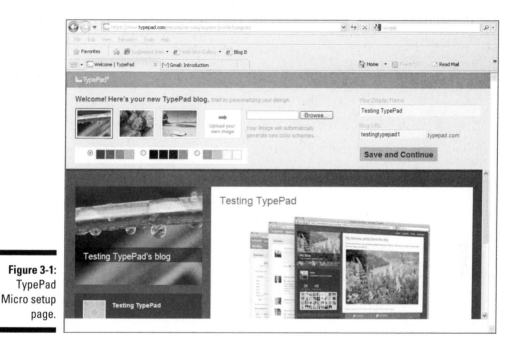

Figure 3-1:
TypePad
Micro setup
page.

5. **Click to select the button next to the color scheme you want to use for your blog.**

   The bottom half of the screen shows you how your blog will look with those colors.

6. **Click in the Your Display Name text box and type the display name you want to use with your blog.**

   Your display name is the name that appears as the author of your blog posts and any comments you leave at other TypePad blogs.

7. **Click in the Blog URL text box and type the URL you want to use for your blog.**

   A little later in this chapter, we advise you on how to choose the best URL for your blog.

8. **Click the Save and Continue button.**

   Your blog's Dashboard, as shown in Figure 3-2, appears. From here, you can start blogging immediately or choose to familiarize yourself with your Dashboard (see Chapter 4) or blog settings (Chapter 5).

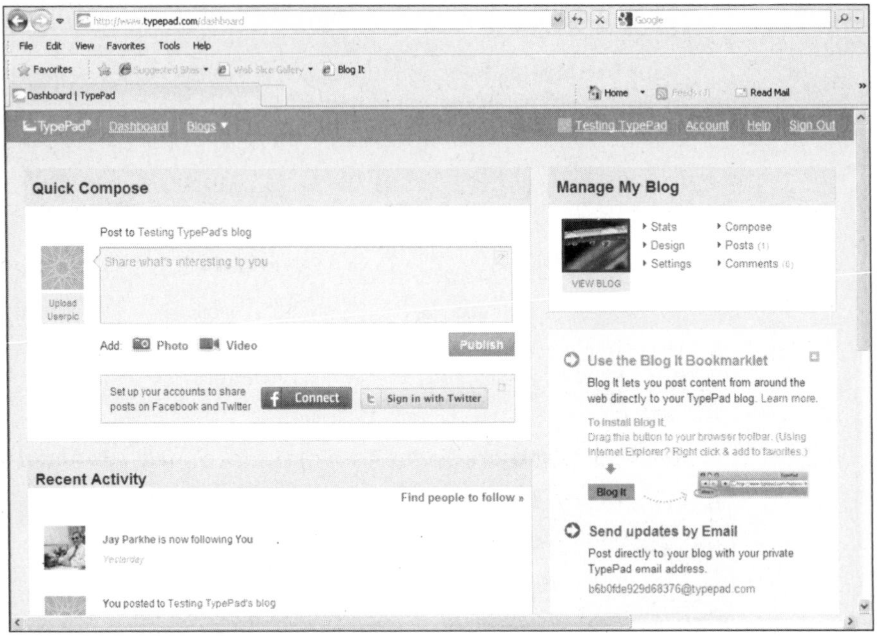

Figure 3-2:
TypePad
Micro
Dashboard.

Customizing your Micro color scheme

If you're a TypePad Micro user and aren't happy with the color scheme pulled from your banner image, we have a little trick that may help. You'll need two images saved to your hard drive: one with very vibrant colors that you want to use as your color scheme and the image you want to use as your banner. When you have those two images ready, follow these instructions:

1. **Go to your blog's Design tab.**

2. **Click the Banner link.**

   The Banner page appears.

3. **Click the Browse button to find and upload the vibrant image.**

   Several color scheme options are pulled from the picture's colors and appear as choices.

4. **Click to select the button next to the color scheme you want to use.**

5. **Click Save Changes.**

6. **Click the Browse button to find and upload the image you want to use as your banner.**

   Several color schemes are offered, based on the new image. You also see Existing Color Scheme as a choice.

7. **Click to select Existing Color Scheme.**

8. **Click the Preview button to see how your changes look.**

9. **Click Save Changes to save your new image and color scheme.**

TypePad Pro

TypePad offers three paid options for your blogging account: Pro Plus, Pro Unlimited, and Business Class (each option is discussed at length in Chapter 2). Because Business Class is a fairly customized option, you should contact TypePad directly to set up this option. To create a TypePad Pro (either Plus or Unlimited) account, follow these instructions:

1. **Type** www.TypePad.com **in your browser's address box and press Enter.**

   The TypePad home page appears.

2. **Find the Blog Like a Pro box. Click the TypePad Pro: Try It For Free button.**

   A new page appears, listing each of the three paid account options.

3. **Click to select the button for the type of account that's right for you (Pro Plus or Pro Unlimited).**

4. **Click the Continue button.**

   On the resulting page, shown in Figure 3-3, you see several blanks that you must fill in before you can create your account.

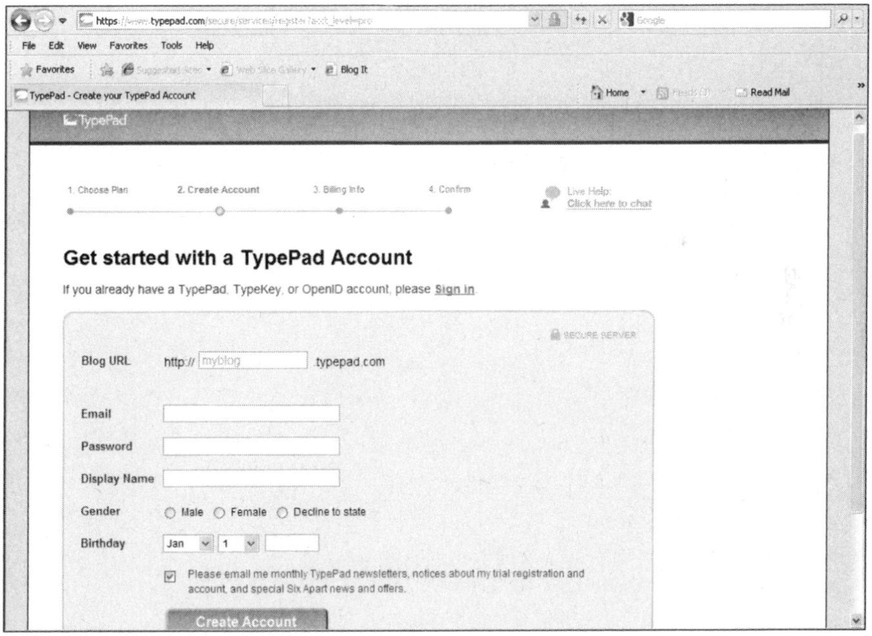

Figure 3-3: Get Started with a TypePad account on this page.

5. Fill in the blanks on the Get Started with a TypePad Account form.

You need to provide the following information:

- **Your blog *URL*,** which is your blog's address online (for example, `http://typepadfordummies.typepad.com`). It is advisable, though not required, that your URL be the same as the title you want to appear in your blog's header. The *title* is the name of your blog, and the *header* is where that title appears at the top of your blog. The title also appears in the *title bar,* which is at the top of your blog's browser page (see Figure 3-4). Refer to Chapter 1 for advice on choosing a name for your blog

  If your aim is to use a blog to establish a solid online identity, readers may find it confusing if the title of your blog is different from the URL. For consistency, the URL, blog title, blog header, and title bar should match. In other words, if your blog is *TypePad for Dummies,* your blog items will look like the URL, title, and header in Figure 3-4.

- **Your e-mail address,** which TypePad uses to send you feature updates, blog comments, and responses to help tickets. You can click the links to TypePad's Terms of Service and Privacy Policy under the Create Account button at the bottom of the page to see additional information about how your e-mail address will be used. You can change your e-mail address at any time.

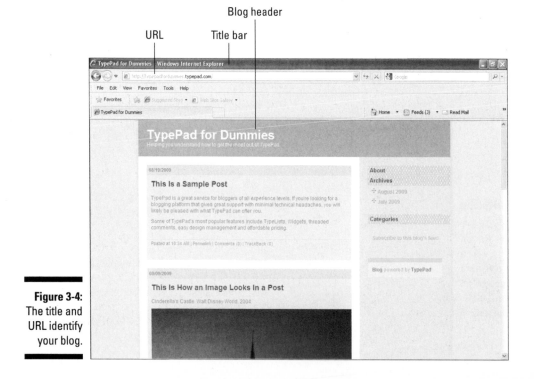

Figure 3-4:
The title and
URL identify
your blog.

• **A password,** which secures the access to your account. As always, when creating any sort of online account, choose a password that cannot be easily guessed, especially if you plan to share personal information on your blog. For example, if you plan to write about your dog Walter in your TypePad blog, you might not want to use Walter as your TypePad password!

Be very careful when setting your password. The TypePad setup process asks you to type your password only once (instead of twice to verify that it's typed correctly). If you accidentally make a typo, you could have trouble later.

• **A display name,** which is the name associated with you on your blog. The display name also appears in your RSS feeds (as the author) and when you comment at other blogs. Your display name can be your real name or a pseudonym.

• **Your gender,** which you mark by selecting an option.

• **Your birthday,** which helps TypePad determine that you are at least 13 years old, as required by law. TypePad does not share your birthday publicly.

6. **Select the check box if you'd like to receive monthly TypePad newsletters.**

Although many people may be hesitant to sign up for e-mail newsletters of any sort, signing up for the monthly TypePad newsletter will keep you updated on new features, events, and offers from Six Apart (TypePad's parent company). These e-mails frequently offer helpful information about changes to TypePad or useful suggestions on how to use your account more efficiently.

7. **Click the Create Account button.**

A new page appears, asking for your billing information.

8. **Select your payment options, enter billing information, and click the Continue button.**

You need to make the following decisions and provide the following information:

• **Monthly billing or annual billing:** You can prepay your TypePad account for one year and receive two months free, or you can be billed monthly.

• **A discount code (if you have one):** If you do a Google search using the phrase *TypePad coupon code,* you can generally find several offers. TypePad is offering *TypePad For Dummies* readers a 10 percent discount when you sign up for a TypePad Pro Plus or TyepPad Pro Unlimited account. The discount is good for your first year of service. When you sign up, just enter **DUMMIES** as your discount code.

- **The type of credit card you'll be paying with:** You can use Visa, MasterCard, American Express, or Discover. You cannot use PayPal or a personal check.

- **Your credit card information:** You need your full card number, the credit card's expiration date, and the security code (the three-digit number on the back of your card).

- **Your billing information:** Your billing information is your name, address, city and state, postal code, and country of residence. Note that you won't be billed until your two-week trial is over.

9. **Click the Continue button.**

   The Confirm Your Information page appears.

10. **Review the information you've entered so far.**

    You can edit your blog URL, e-mail address, or billing information.

11. **Click the Confirm and Start Your Blog button.**

    A new page appears that looks like the one in Figure 3-5.

12. **Type a title for your blog in the box on the left.**

13. **Click the check box next to Publicize This Blog on Search Engines and My TypePad Profile if you would like your blog to be visible to search engines.**

    Unless you're writing a private password-protected blog, you'll probably want search engines to index your blog so readers can find you.

Figure 3-5: Choose what to do first.

14. **Choose what to do first:**

- Write your first post (see Chapter 6).

- Design your blog (see Chapter 11).

- Skip these options and head directly to your TypePad Dashboard (see the next section and Chapter 4).

After you confirm your new TypePad account, you'll receive a confirmation e-mail at the e-mail address you provided. This e-mail includes instructions on how to get started with your blog by writing a post, adding a picture, or changing your blog's design.

Signing In to Your TypePad Account

Now that you have a TypePad account, you'll need to sign in to access that account. After you sign in, you can visit the Dashboard or your account page, or search the Help section if you have questions. You can also edit your blog (or blogs) and connect your Profile to your other social media accounts (such as Facebook, LinkedIn, or Twitter).

If you're ready to customize your TypePad information, type **www.TypePad. com/dashboard** in your browser's address bar and press Enter. The TypePad Sign In screen appears, as shown in Figure 3-6.

You can sign in to your TypePad account in two ways:

✔ **Enter your e-mail address and password.** Click inside the text boxes and enter the necessary information. Then click the Sign In button.

If you are using your own computer and are the only one with access to it, you might want to consider selecting the Remember Me option if you're using your e-mail and password to sign in to your TypePad account. That way, you won't have to sign in each time you want to edit your blog. If you're using a common computer at a library or other public place, you should not select the Remember Me option.

✔ **Use an existing social media account (for example, Facebook, Twitter, or Google).** Click the pull-down menu and choose the social media account you want to use as your sign-in. A button for that social media network appears; click it. A new page appears, asking you to confirm that you want to allow TypePad to access that account information. Complete the ID and password information as necessary and confirm that it's okay for TypePad to access that account information.

After you've signed in to your TypePad account, the Dashboard appears (see Figure 3-7).

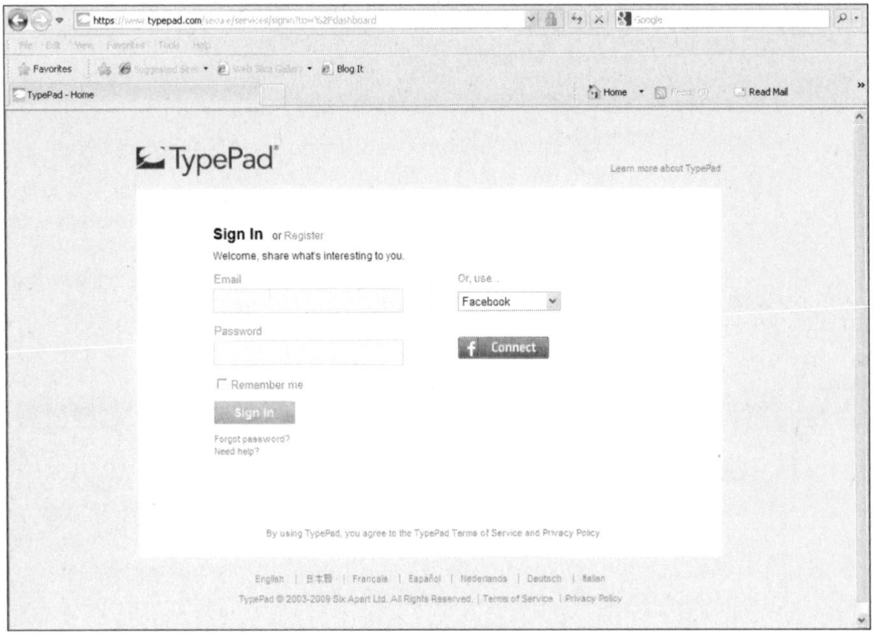

Figure 3-6:
Sign in
to your
TypePad
account.

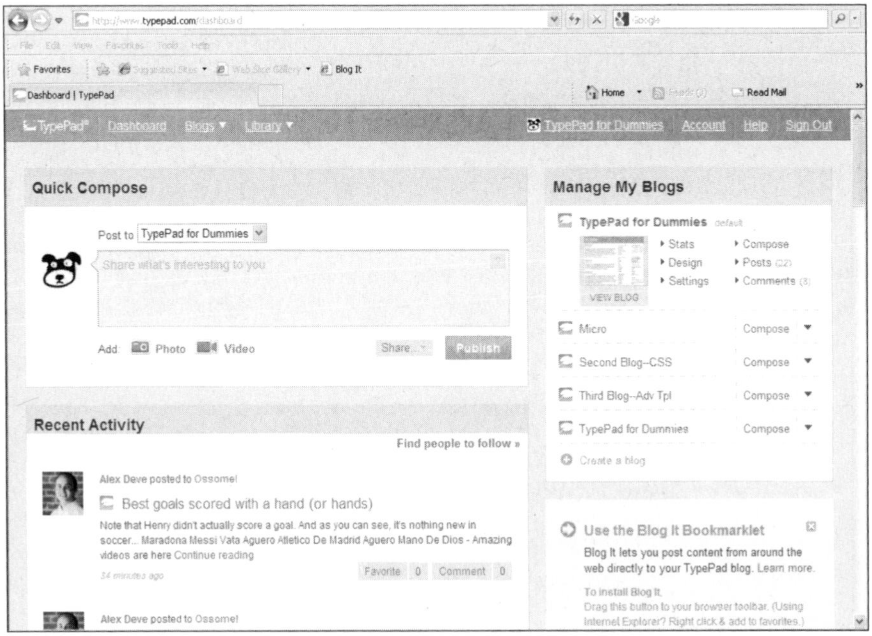

Figure 3-7:
The
Dashboard
is your start-
ing point.

Your Dashboard is your starting point every time you sign in, so you'll want to be familiar with all its features. Think of the TypePad Dashboard the same way you'd think of a car's dashboard: It's where all the basic controls for operation are gathered. From the Dashboard, you can access every part of your TypePad account (including your TypePad Library, your account information, and your blogs). We cover how to use the Dashboard at length in Chapter 4, so in the next section, we move on to creating your TypePad Profile.

Creating Your TypePad Profile

Before you start creating your blog (see Chapter 5), you'll want to set up your Profile. A TypePad Profile is similar to an About page (and, in fact, TypePad uses some of the information you include in your Profile to populate your About page — which we discuss in Chapter 4). Your Profile includes information such as your display name, bio, interests, and userpic. Your Profile also lists social media accounts you may have, any blogs you write that are housed at TypePad, and your homepage URL.

Think of your TypePad Profile as a hub that shows others where you can be found online. It integrates all your online presences into one central location. When you leave a comment at any blog that uses the TypePad commenting system (see Chapter 7), readers can click your comment and be taken directly to your TypePad Profile. You may even want to link directly to your Profile from your own sidebar, in place of a more traditional About page, an option we discuss in Chapter 4.

You should be aware that your Profile page is public and shows your commenting activity on TypePad blogs.

To create and edit your TypePad Profile, you need to go from your Dashboard to your Profile page:

1. **Click your display name.**

    You can find your display name in the green account-level bar at the top of the Dashboard.

2. **Click the Edit Your Profile button.**

    Your Profile page appears (see Figure 3-8).

3. **Fill in the information you want to share in your Profile.**

    The rest of this chapter explains the options you have when choosing what information to share in your Profile.

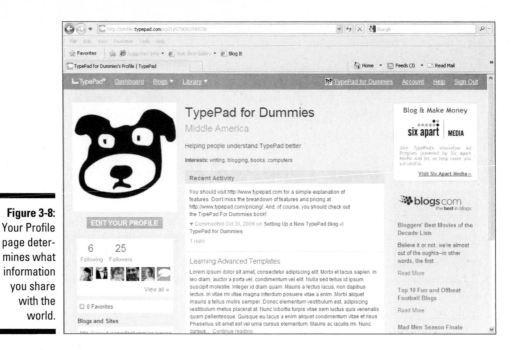

Figure 3-8:
Your Profile
page deter-
mines what
information
you share
with the
world.

Sharing your personal information

You may want to share the following information in your TypePad Profile:

- ✔ **Display name**: This is the name that appears as the author of your blog posts, when you leave comments at other blogs, and when you respond to comments at your own blog. To edit your display name, click the Edit Display Name link, change the display name to your desired name or nickname, and save your changes.

- ✔ **Profile URL**: This is the address of your public Profile and is the URL you can link to if you'd like to share your Profile on your blog. Although the initial part of the URL (`http://profile.typepad.com/`) is static, you can choose the end of the URL (after the final /) — for example, `http://profile.typepad.com/typepadfordummies`.

  When choosing your Profile URL, use a word or phrase that is relevant to your blog and memorable. For example, you may choose to use your display name.

- ✔ **Location:** This information is optional. It's worth considering how much information you want to share with the world at large. Do you want people to know exactly where you live (Jefferson, IA) or would you rather give them a general idea (Iowa or Midwest)? If you are not comfortable sharing any location information, leave this box blank.

The information you choose to share is public and can be seen by anyone who views your Profile.

✔ **One-line bio:** Your one-line bio can be the tagline for your site. A *tagline* is a short sentence or slogan that tells readers a bit more about your blog. If your tagline is something especially catchy, you might want to consider including it on your banner design, too (see Chapter 11). Your one-line bio can also be a short sentence that encapsulates you and your blog content (such as "I like pie and I blog about it."). Although there is no character limit to your one-line bio, it's best to keep it to about 150 characters (including spaces). You can expand on your idea in the Interests section.

✔ **Interests:** Below your one-line bio is a place to fill in your interests. You can simply list your interests, separating them with commas, or you can explain your interests in a paragraph format. Reading about your interests is one more way for readers and community members to find out more about you quickly, so consider listing items that really explain who you are.

Be specific when entering your interests: "Watching *Firefly* reruns" says more about you than simply "Watching television."

Uploading your userpic

Including a *userpic,* short for *user picture* (also referred to by some as an *avatar),* of yourself in your Profile helps readers connect with you. Your user-pic can be a picture of yourself or your *brand,* which is simply a concept or visual image your readers will associate with you. Your userpic will appear next to your comments on other TypePad blogs.

You may want to use a picture of your brand instead of a picture of yourself. For example, if you write a financial advice blog, and your logo is a bright-green dollar sign, an image of that dollar sign might have more effect than a photo of you. On the other hand, readers like to feel a connection to the people who write the blogs they visit. Including a picture of yourself helps readers feel as though you've introduced yourself to them personally.

To add or change your userpic, click the Browse button under Choose an Image File. Find the image you want to use among the files on your hard drive, and click OK or Open. Then scroll to the bottom of the Profile page and click Save Changes to see your new userpic in action.

Connecting your Profile to the rest of the Web

The bottom half of your Profile (under Around the Web) offers you the opportunity to show readers where else you can be found online. You have the following options:

- ✔ **Your Accounts Elsewhere:** You can choose to include direct links to other online accounts you have, such as Twitter and Facebook. To add a link to one or more of these accounts, simply click Add an Account; you'll be taken to the Other Accounts page of your Account Dashboard. We explain how to add links to other social media accounts in Chapter 4.

- ✔ **Your Homepage URL:** This is the URL that will be linked to your name any time you comment on a TypePad blog. You can type any URL here — it can be the URL for your blog or the URL for another Web site or blog that isn't part of TypePad.

- ✔ **Your Blogs:** If you have more than one blog hosted at your TypePad account, you can choose which ones will be listed in your Profile. Any blog you choose to have displayed on your Profile page will also show updates. In other words, each time a new article is posted at a listed blog, anyone who looks at your Profile page will see the update.

- ✔ **Show the Recent Activity Module:** If you select this option, your most recent comments on other TypePad blogs (see Chapter 7) will be visible to your followers.

- ✔ **Show the Blogs.com Module:** Blogs.com is a Six Apart–owned Web site that offers, in the company's words, "the best of blogs." If you choose to show recent posts from Blogs.com on your Profile page, those posts will show up as links on the sidebar of your Profile page. You can ensure that these links are relevant to your blog's niche or community by selecting a category from the drop-down menu under Show the Blogs. com Module.

Congratulations! You've established your TypePad account, logged in, and set up your Profile. Now you can change your personal information as necessary, access your blog (see Chapter 5 if you haven't already set yours up), and get connected with the TypePad community.

Chapter 4

Touring the TypePad Dashboard

· ·

· ·

*Y*our TypePad Dashboard is the hub of all your TypePad activity — it's the first thing you see when you sign in to your TypePad account. Your Dashboard is the starting place for all the links you need to access your blogs, change your Profile information, manage your library of stored files, search the Knowledge Base (TypePad's help files), access your account information, and keep tabs on your TypePad community. Navigating your Dashboard comfortably is critical to managing your blog well, and this chapter provides a brief overview of what you can expect to find. Think of this chapter as your Dashboard geography lesson — we show you a left-to-right, top-to-bottom explanation of each button, link, and section. In other chapters, we help you apply many of these functions in further detail.

Depending on which TypePad account you have, some of the items discussed in this chapter and others may not be part of your account. For example, TypePad Micro doesn't have access to TypeLists or File Manager.

Understanding the Navigation Bars

To access the Dashboard, you simply need to sign in to your TypePad account (instructions on how to do that are in Chapter 3). Throughout this chapter, it will be helpful to refer to Figure 4-1 because it shows the basic layout of the Dashboard.

Account-level bar

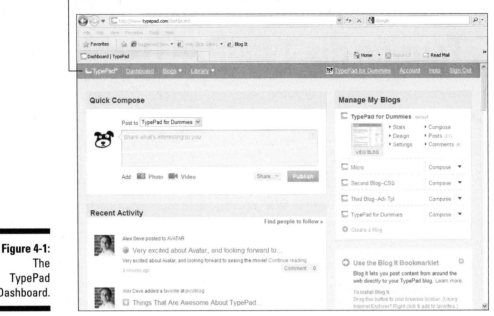

Figure 4-1:
The
TypePad
Dashboard.

The key to moving around the Dashboard is understanding the two primary *horizontal navigation bars* — the bars that run all the way across the top of the Dashboard. If you've just now logged into your account, you're probably seeing only one bar — it's a green one, and it contains links such as TypePad, Dashboard, and Blogs. This is the *account-level bar*. You use it to access core account information relevant to your entire account, not just your individual blog — an important distinction to draw, because many people manage multiple blogs from one account. When we explain how to establish and manage individual blogs (in Chapter 5), you'll also see a blue bar right below the account-level bar. The blue bar is the *blog-level bar*. This bar provides links to blog-specific information, such as your posts, settings, and comments.

Right now, we want to discuss the account-level bar and make you familiar with its options. Table 4-1 explains the purpose of each link in the account-level bar (moving from left to right).

Table 4-1	Account-Level Navigation Bar Links
Click This Link	*To Do This*
TypePad	View the TypePad Dashboard.
Dashboard	View the TypePad Dashboard.
Blogs	See a pull-down menu of the blogs you've set up with this TypePad account as well as an Add a Blog link, which allows you to create a new blog on the same account or connect blogs on other blogging platforms to your TypePad account. You can choose which of your blogs (if you have several) you want to work on from this menu. When you click a blog name, you're taken to a page that gives you an overview of that blog's statistics and links to other tasks (posting, comment moderation, design, and settings).
Library	See a pull-down menu that allows you to access your photo albums, TypeLists, and files. If you have a TypePad Micro account, you do not have this option.
[Your Username]	See your TypePad Profile page as it appears to your readers. The exception is that you also see the Edit Your Profile button — your readers don't see that. We explain how to create and edit your Profile in Chapter 3.
Account	See and update your TypePad account information — if you have one of the TypePad Pro accounts. From your account information page you can edit your personal information, notifications, billing information, and About Me page information. You can also add or delete additional social media and affiliate accounts (such as Amazon.com, Facebook, Twitter, or FriendFeed), change your password, or map a domain name to your blog (see Appendix A). We explain how you can edit account information later in this chapter.
	If you have TypePad Micro, you can update your personal information and notifications settings, and add or delete social media accounts.
Help	Find answers to your TypePad questions and access TypePad's support team.
Sign Out	Sign out of your account.

With the overview in Table 4-1 in mind, let's begin exploring.

Locating Your TypePad Library

Your TypePad library is the repository for your files and TypeLists (see Chapter 8 for an explanation of TypeLists). When you click the Library link on the account-level bar, you see a pull-down menu with these choices: Photo Albums, TypeLists, and File Manager. Each choice offers you a way to manage a variety of files.

Knowing where your files are and how they're organized helps you manage your blog as it grows. You'll be able to find the information you're looking for quickly and easily if you take the time to set up an intuitive folder system for the files you share with your readers. You may want to re-create the system you use on your home computer because you're most likely already in a groove there and are familiar with where things are.

Finding photo albums

After clicking the Library link in the green account-level bar, choose Photo Albums from the drop-down menu. This takes you to a screen listing any photo albums you have created in your TypePad account. If you haven't created any albums yet but would like to, just click Add a Photo Album in the top-right corner (more detailed instructions on photo albums are in Chapter 9). Photo albums are a particularly handy tool under the following circumstances:

 ✔ You're a photo blogger whose blog is geared largely to your photographic content, and you need a streamlined way to organize all the images.

 ✔ You're documenting a specific event (such as a vacation or a home remodel) that generates a large number of photos, and you want those photos grouped in one place. In Chapter 11, we explain how you can set up your sidebars so that you link directly to one (or all) of these photo albums.

The Photo Albums tool in TypePad is such a large and powerful feature that we devote much of Chapter 9 to it (other multimedia tools are addressed there as well). In that chapter, we walk you through the specifics of setting up your photo albums, and we tell you how you can maximize your use of this tool. For now, simply be aware that the green account-level bar is where you access your photo albums; We dive into the subject more deeply in the later chapter.

 If you're a blogger who posts primarily text, posting photos only occasionally, you may find that photo albums are not an especially integral part of your TypePad use. When you write a post, you can easily insert an image or a photo with a few quick clicks (see Chapter 6) without ever accessing your photo albums.

Navigating TypeLists

TypeLists are TypePad's way of organizing any sidebar information you include on your blog. Sidebar information can include everything from your contact information to links to your favorite or most popular posts to advertisements. To access your TypePad TypeLists, create a new TypeList, or edit an existing TypeList, click the Library link in the account-level bar and choose TypeLists from the pull-down menu.

TypePad offers four kinds of TypeLists:

- ✔ **Links TypeList:** Post basic links in the sidebar, such as a text link to your Twitter account.

- ✔ **Notes TypeList:** Post customized HTML or complex code in the sidebar. You can use this kind of TypeList to place images or buttons in the sidebar.

- ✔ **Books TypeList:** Share and rate book lists in the sidebar. You can link the list to Amazon.

- ✔ **Albums TypeList:** Share music lists in the sidebar. Similar to the Books TypeList, the Albums TypeList enables you to rate and comment on the music you've listed.

TypeLists are an important part of your blog's design because they control the contents of the sidebars. We discuss them at length, with specific instructions on how to set up individual TypeLists, in Chapter 8.

Managing stored files

A blog is often much more than just the text you see on the screen. Bloggers can share with readers a wide variety of files and media that they want readers to see (or be able to download), such as photos, spreadsheets, PDF files, music, and video. To upload or access your various blog files, you use File Manager. On the Account-level bar, click the Library link and choose File Manager from the pull-down menu.

Any time you upload a file (such as a photo), it's stored in File Manager. You don't *have* to create a filing system to organize File Manager — many TypePad bloggers just upload files and dig around for them as needed — but if you take the time to set up a clear filing system, you can avoid some serious headaches down the road. You can reference parts of your blog easily if you know where you store the files.

Your main blog hosts its files and subfolders in the main Home directory. By default, each blog you set up on your TypePad account in addition to your first blog has its own folder in the Home directory. See Figure 4-2 for an example of how File Manager might look with three blogs on the same account.

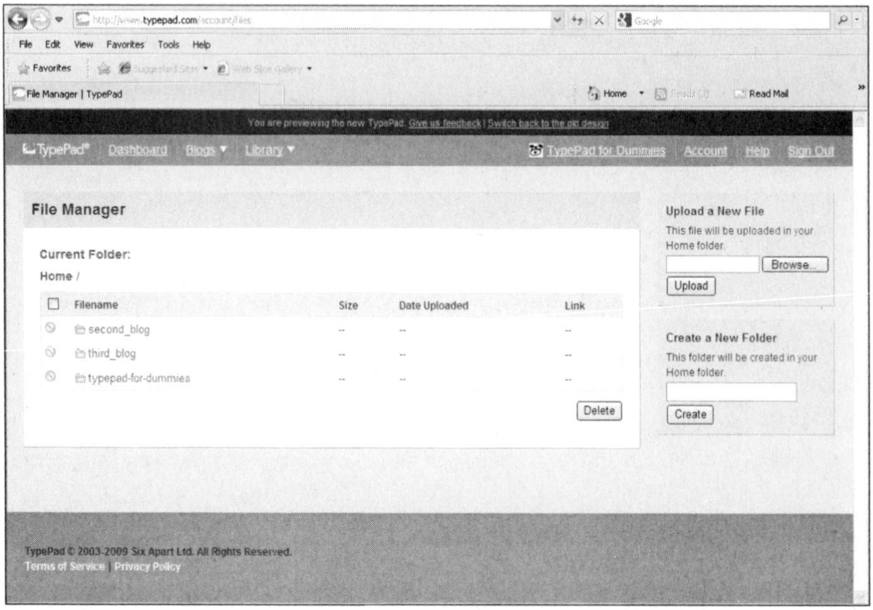

Figure 4-2:
File
Manager
set up with
multiple
blogs on
a single
account.

While in File Manager, you'll be able to create new folders and subfolders and create a file structure that makes sense to you. It may work best for you to mirror the file structure you've set up on your computer. For instance, if you keep all your PDF documents in a folder named PDF on your computer and plan to share PDF documents on your blog, it's logical to make a folder named PDF in your TypePad File Manager and store the blog's PDFs there. You may also want to consider setting up folders specifically for podcasts or video files, as shown in Figure 4-3.

To create a new folder in the Home directory:

1. **Click in the text box under Create a New Folder.**

   Create a New Folder is in the right sidebar.

2. **Type the name of the new folder.**

3. **Click the Create button.**

To create a new folder within an existing folder (in other words, to create a subfolder):

1. **Click the folder you'd like to open.**

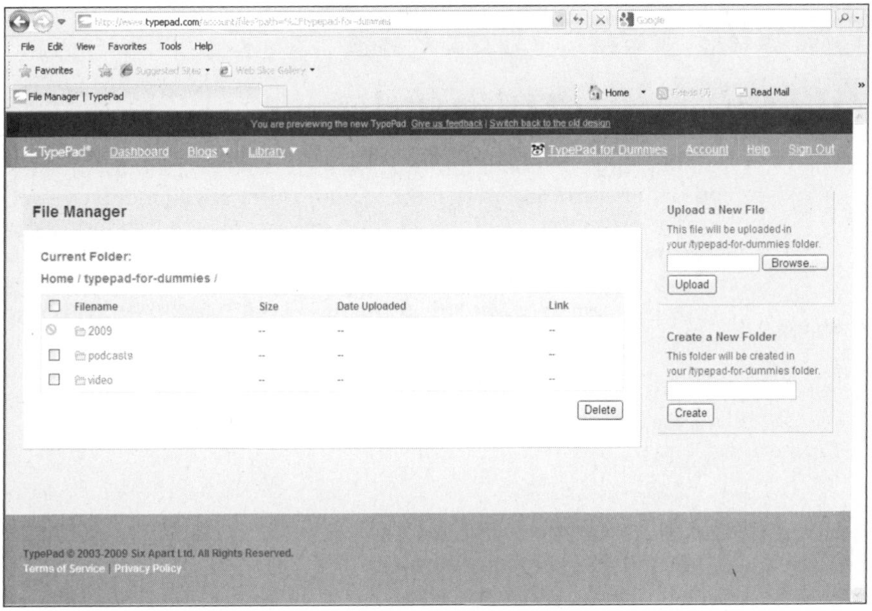

Figure 4-3:
An example
file structure
for storing
media and
other files.

2. **Click in the text box under Create a New Folder, which is in the right sidebar.**

3. **Type the name of the new folder.**

4. **Click the Create button.**

When you upload files to TypePad, the process is similar to what you're used to when uploading or downloading files to your own computer and its filing system:

1. **Click the folder where you would like to store the new file.**

2. **Click inside the text box under Upload a New File (it's the top box in the right sidebar).**

    You see your own computer's file manager.

3. **Choose the file you want to upload.**

4. **Click Upload.**

Right-click the name of the file you just uploaded and choose Copy Link Location to save the file location to your clipboard.

Editing Your TypePad Account Information

Your TypePad account information includes everything from your personal and billing information to links to your other social media accounts and password information. Only the account owner can see the information on the Account page — any guest or junior authors of your blogs can't see this information. You can change or edit any of your account information as needed by clicking the Account link at the top of the Dashboard. You'll see a page that looks like Figure 4-4.

You'll notice a list of options in the left sidebar. Each of these tabs opens a new form for you to edit. In this section, we walk you through each one, from the top down.

Summary tab

The Summary tab is exactly what you think it is: It lists a summary of the account information you shared when you initiated your TypePad account. You can change or edit the following information:

- ✔ First name
- ✔ Last name
- ✔ Display name
- ✔ E-mail address (and whether you'd like to share that e-mail address)

  You use your e-mail address to sign in to your TypePad account. If you change your e-mail address here, you'll need to remember to use the new one the next time you want to sign in to TypePad.

  Sharing your e-mail address is a good idea because it allows other bloggers to contact you when you leave a comment at their blog. This is particularly handy when you're part of a great discussion.

- ✔ Domain

  If you change your TypePad domain (for example, changing from `type padfordummies.typepad.com` to `dummies.typepad.com`), you can't change it back later. The name you stop using will be available to other TypePad users for use on their own blog(s). We suggest that you buy and map a domain to your blog (see Appendix A), rather than changing your TypePad domain here.

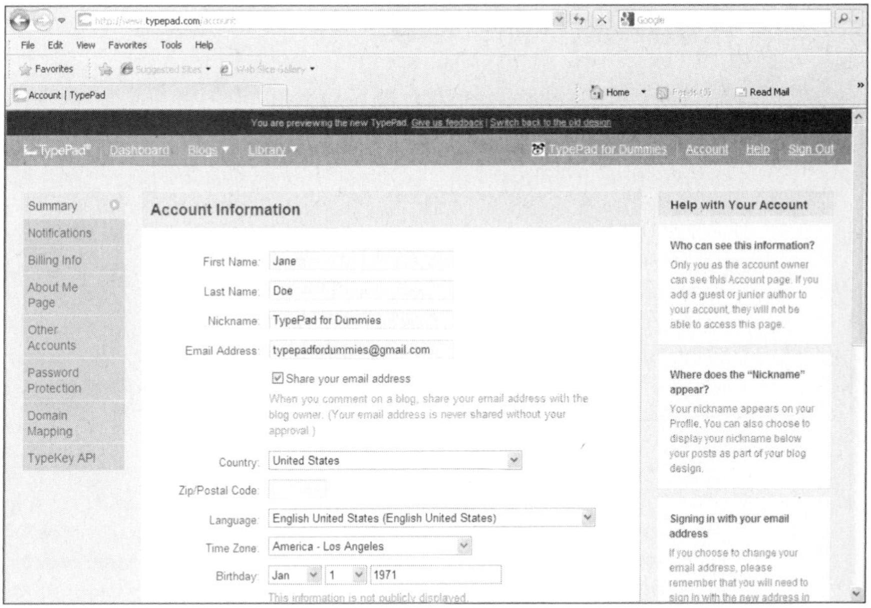

Figure 4-4:
TypePad
Account
page.

 ✔ Country

 ✔ Zip/Postal Code

 ✔ Language

 ✔ Time Zone

 ✔ Birthday (This is simply to verify that you are 13 or older; the United States Children's Online Privacy Protection Act asserts that no company can obtain information from a child under 13 without express consent from the parents.)

 ✔ Gender

If you make any changes on this Summary page, be sure to click the Save Changes button, or you'll lose the changes you made.

If you want to change your password, scroll to the bottom of the Summary page to find the box titled Password Changes and then follow these instructions:

1. **Type your current password in the Current Password box.**

2. **Type your new password in the New Password box.**

3. **Retype your new password in the Confirm Password box.**

4. **Click the Change Password button to save your changes.**

Notifications tab

The Notifications tab is where you can set up how and when you are notified via e-mail about new comments, Six Apart newsletters and offers, and how those e-mails appear (that is, plain text or with HTML formatting). The Notifications tab has three sections: News, Activity, and Email Format. We describe each next.

News: Click to select this box if you'd like to receive newsletters from Six Apart and notices about your account. We strongly recommend that you select this box. Six Apart offers users new features and themes often, and being on its mailing list means you will understand the new features available to you. The notices are not sent very often, but when they are, the information is usually important.

Activity: If you're interested in knowing when someone responds to one of your comments on a blog (explained further in Chapter 7) or starts following your updates to your blog and other social media sites, you can be notified via e-mail. You can also choose to be notified via if someone selects your blog as a favorite. Click to select the box beside each option you're interested in using.

If you think you'll be distracted by watching your inbox for comments all day long, consider setting up a separate e-mail account just for your TypePad blog. You can use that e-mail address for all things blog-related and keep your blogging correspondence separate from your private, "real-world" correspondence.

Email Format: You can receive your e-mail notifications in either HTML format or plain text. HTML format usually includes images and design elements. Plain text is just what it sounds like: words and links with no spiffy design. Your e-mail client can probably handle either format, so it's really a personal preference. Click to select the radio button beside the type of e-mail you'd like to receive.

Billing Info tab

The Billing Info tab shows an overview of the billing information you provided when you set up your TypePad account and gives you a summary of your billing history (all the monthly charges you've incurred thus far and any changes you've made to your billing information, such as changing your credit card).

Billing Summary: This section shows you which billing options you chose when you set up your TypePad account:

> ✔ Current Plan lists which package you're currently using (Chapter 2 explains the blogging packages TypePad offers and helps you decide which one is right for you). You have the option of upgrading or downgrading your current package or canceling your account.

✔ Billing Cycle tells you when you can expect to be billed (monthly or yearly). You chose your billing cycle when you established your TypePad account, but you have the option of changing it here, if you like. Your only choices for billing cycles are monthly or yearly (you get two free months of service if you choose yearly).

✔ Payment Method lists the last four digits of the credit card you have on file with the TypePad billing department (you shared this information when you set up your account). You have the option of updating your credit card. If you click the Update link, you can apply a discount code, update your credit card information, or change your credit card completely. You can also edit your billing address if necessary.

If you do a Web search for *TypePad discount code,* you'll usually find a few to choose among. Refer to Chapter 3 for a special discount code for readers of this book.

✔ Billing Rate is your monthly TypePad rate, which depends on which blogging package you chose when you signed up for your TypePad account.

✔ Next Billing tells you when you can expect your next bill.

✔ Member Since tells you when you established your TypePad account.

Transaction History: This section shows you a complete list of all your TypePad billing transactions. This list includes billing dates, payments made, and any changes you may have made to your billing information (such as changing your credit card information or your billing address).

About Me Page tab

Every blogger needs an About Me page — it's the place your readers can quickly find out more about you. New readers often look for a link to an About Me page (and click it!) the first time they stop by your blog. Your blog should include an obvious, easy-to-find link to your About Me page. (We tell you how to set up that link when we discuss blog design in Chapter 11.) You have four distinct options for setting up this important page on TypePad: your account's default About Me page, your own HTML page, your TypePad Profile, and your own personally constructed About Me page written in your WYSIWYG editor. Let's discuss all four of them, and you can decide which one fits you best.

TypePad's default About Me page

Because we're working our way through your Account Summary, you'll notice an About Me Page tab on the vertical bar on the left side of the screen. Click that tab, and you see a list of information TypePad can pull from your account to populate the default About Me page. If you choose this option, simply click the items you want TypePad to pull into the page. Also notice that the URL to the default page is listed toward the top of the screen; click that, if you want to see how it looks.

The default About Me template allows you to share specific information from your Account, Profile, and TypeLists with your audience. To choose the information and allow it to appear on your About Me page, simply click to select the box next to the item you want to include.

Account: The information listed under Account is pulled directly from the data you shared in your Account Summary and Other Accounts tabs, with the exception of the photo option (which is pulled from your Profile). You can choose to include

✔ Name

✔ Display name

✔ Photo (the photo you shared as your userpic when you set up your Profile in Chapter 3)

✔ Email (if you share your e-mail address, it's automatically encrypted to keep it safe from spammers)

✔ Other accounts (any accounts listed in the Other Accounts tab is listed if you choose to include this option)

✔ Publish FOAF file (*FOAF* is an acronym for *Friend of a Friend;* the FOAF project creates machine-readable pages that contain information about people and the things they create online)

✔ Edit Account Settings (links to the Account Summary tab, where you can edit your name, display name, and so on)

Profile: The information options listed under Profile are pulled directly from the data you shared when you set up your Profile in Chapter 3:

✔ Web address (your blog's URL)

✔ Country

✔ Interests

✔ One-line bio

✔ Amazon Wish List (you need to log in to your Amazon account and find your Wish List ID and, if you're an Amazon Associate, your Amazon Associate ID); your Amazon Wish List is an option only if you've shared this information via your Profile (see Chapter 3)

✔ Edit your Profile (links directly to your Profile so you can edit any information you've shared there)

TypeLists: You may want to include specific TypeLists in your About Me sidebar. The TypeLists option for your About Me page lists all the TypeLists you've set up for your blog (see Chapter 8 for instructions on setting up TypeLists); if you haven't set up any TypeLists yet, you won't see the option to include them on your About Me page. To include a specific TypeList in your About Me page, simply click to select the box next to the TypeList you want to include.

Biography: If you'd like to include a short biography or information that isn't covered with the previous data choices, you can type that information in the text box labeled Biography. When you're happy with your information, click to check the box next to Biography so your information will show up on your About Me page.

Choose a Style: You can choose to style your About Me page so that it reflects the theme (design) of your blog. Use the pull-down menu to choose which style you'd like to apply. If you're using one of TypePad's basic design themes, it's a good idea to apply the same theme to your About Me page for consistency. To do this, click the pull-down menu and choose your own username.

If you are not using a basic TypePad theme (perhaps you use a custom header design like the kind we discuss in Chapter 11), you can still match your About Me page to your custom design. The instructions in the previous paragraph won't work, though; you'll need to set up a specific design for your About Me page to match your custom design. We cover this issue when we address all design-related questions in Chapter 11.

When you've chosen the information you'd like to share, written your biographical information, and think you have your About Me page finished, click the Preview or Save and Publish button. If you click the Preview button, a new window opens with a preview of your About Me page. If you're not happy with the information, change what you need to by selecting new information options or deselecting current information options. Rewrite your bio if necessary or change your userpic if you want to. Click the Preview button again and see how it looks. When you're satisfied with the outcome, click the Save and Publish button.

Figure 4-5 shows you a sample of an About Me page constructed using the default template.

Your own HTML page

Below the Default Template section, you can see the Write Your Own HTML Page option. If you are comfortable with HTML and have an idea of how you'd like your About Me page to appear, you can type the code in the HTML box. You can check your progress by clicking the Preview button. When you're satisfied with how the page looks and have finished tweaking the code, click the Save and Publish button to save the page and have it automatically published to your blog. This option requires a good bit of coding knowledge, which the average blogger may not have. We advise that you tackle this option only if you have experience with HTML.

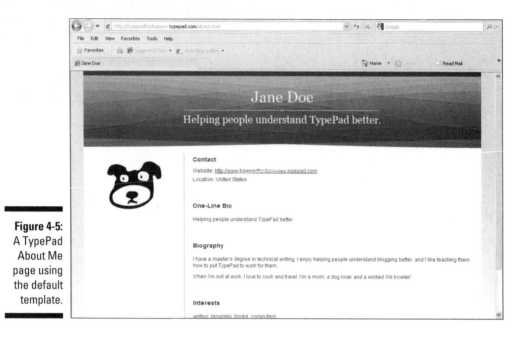

Figure 4-5:
A TypePad
About Me
page using
the default
template.

Your TypePad Profile

In Chapter 3, we explain that a TypePad Profile is essentially a hub site that you can use to show readers all the places you can be found online. Your Profile is central to your participation in the TypePad community. Because it contains so much information about you, it could serve as a decent About Me page (you can insert a direct link to your Profile into the Content portion of the Design tab — Chapter 11 details how). Figure 4-6 shows you a completed TypePad Profile. (Can't remember how to access or edit yours? See the instructions in Chapter 3.)

One of the drawbacks of using the Profile as your About Me page is that you don't have your e-mail listed on your Profile. Including a way to contact you is a crucial part of your About Me page. To get around this issue, you could easily create a TypeList (see Chapter 8) with a link to your e-mail address and include it in your blog's main sidebar.

A personally constructed About Me page

All TypePad users (except those with Micro accounts) can create pages in addition to posts. (A *page* is basically a freestanding, undated post you can create in your Rich Text editor; we explain this further in Chapter 6.) Creating a page is as simple as writing a post. When readers click a link to one of your pages, they're still at your blog, seeing your header and sidebar, just as if they were reading a post — this makes for much better design continuity. You can write an About Me page this way with great results (see Chapter 6 for instructions on publishing posts and pages). See Figure 4-7. Generally, a more narrative About Me page is preferable to a simple bulleted list of hobbies.

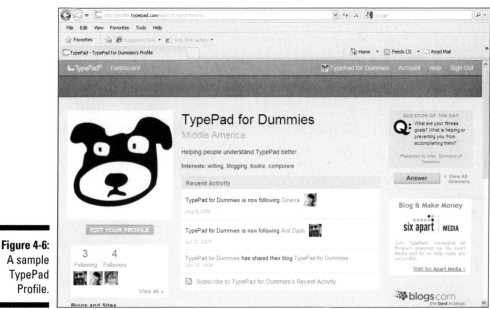

Figure 4-6:
A sample
TypePad
Profile.

Your About Me page may form a reader's first impression of you, so include succinct details that communicate who you are.

Apply your own sense of style to your About Me page (if your blog is, for example, inspirational, reflect that same tone in your About Me page). Here are some items you might want to include if you construct this page yourself:

✔ Your name (or the name you go by in the blogosphere)

✔ Where you live

✔ A general explanation of what your blog is about

✔ Your e-mail address

✔ Links to other social networking accounts, such as Twitter, Facebook, and LinkedIn

✔ Hobbies

✔ Your favorite movies, music, and sports team

Whatever option you choose, remember that sharing information online is sharing information with the world. Before you publicize certain aspects of yourself in an About Me page (or anywhere else on a blog), consider whether you really want people to know where you live or the names of your family members. If you haven't already read the "Considering privacy issues" section in Chapter 1, this is a good time to do so.

Figure 4-7:
An About
Me page
made with
the page
option.

Other Accounts tab

Your Other Accounts tab is where you list the other social media sites you belong to and link them to your blog. *Social media* includes all the ways you interact with friends and colleagues online (blogs, Twitter, Facebook, FriendFeed, Digg, LinkedIn, and so on).

You may want your readers to be able to find you on Facebook or follow you on Twitter. It's a fairly simple process to integrate this information into your TypePad account. After you've established your additional social media links, TypePad can integrate them into your TypePad Profile or your default About Me page. (If you manually create your own About page, as we recommended in the previous section, note that the accounts you link here do not automatically appear in your manually created page. You'll need to link them yourself in your Rich Text editor when you create or edit the actual page.)

To add new social media account information to your TypePad account, follow these instructions:

1. Click the pull-down menu.

You'll see a list of many social media sites, some of which you won't use. That's okay. There are so many social media sites, you can't use them all effectively. It's best to choose just a few and concentrate on using them well. TypePad offers a fairly comprehensive list of social media options because so many people use different ones.

What to include in your About Me page

Your About Me page is one of the most important pages you'll include in your blog. Think of it as your online business card of sorts. When people are new to your blog, one of the first things they will do is click your About Me link to see if the blog is a fit with their interests. Your About Me page is a way to engage with your readers and let them know a little more about you. Your About Me page is a highlight of you. It's a page devoted to what sets you apart from everyone else.

If you're at all interested in working with advertisers or marketers, your About Me page is crucial in helping you establish those relationships. Advertisers and marketers have hundreds of blogs to review to determine if they are a fit with their product or campaign. When they decide a blog is a fit, the advertiser or marketer contacts the blogger and extends an offer. If you'd like to help this relationship along, you can do a few things — and they all start with your About Me page:

✔ **Make your contact information clearly visible.** If a marketer or advertiser (or even a loyal reader) wants to contact you privately, they'll need a way to do so. If your e-mail is buried or not even listed, visitors quickly tire of trying to find it and move to the next blog. If you're worried about a text link to your e-mail being harvested by spammers, create a small image (or button) with your e-mail address and insert it into your About Me page that way.

✔ **Give a brief overview of what your blog is about.** You can give a bit of your background, why you chose to write about this particular blogging niche, your blogging goals, and so on. This is the perfect opportunity for you to explain why you're different from other bloggers in your area. When you're writing about yourself, it can be hard to decide how much information is too much. Because your blog can probably speak for itself to some degree, try to keep your About Me page short but entertaining. Short and interesting trumps long and overdone every time.

✔ **Establish your credibility.** Your About Me page is the perfect place to let readers know why you're the go-to source for your topic. If you have pertinent background experience, have won awards, or have professional designations or degrees that apply directly to your niche, mention them here.

✔ **Explain what types of advertising or marketing relationships you're interested in.** This might include giveaways for your readers, product reviews, or sharing press releases for causes you're passionate about (then tell them which causes those are). If marketers can readily see that you are a good fit for their product, they're more likely to contact you. You may also want to share a link to your disclosure policy. (Chapter 12 advises you further about how to disclose relationships and why it's important.) These details can also be packaged into what's called a media kit (see Chapter 12).

2. **Choose the social media link you want to start with, such as Facebook.**

3. **Click the Add button.**

   A pop-up window appears with sign-in information for that Web site (such as a Facebook sign-in). You must share your sign-in information so TypePad can access that account and bring the information to your blog.

 4. Continue to add accounts as you see fit.

 5. Click the Save button when you're finished.

TypePad has a strong relationship with Amazon and allows you to easily share your Amazon Wish List or your Amazon Associates ID. (You can find out more about the Amazon Associates program by visiting affiliate-program.amazon.com. It's basically a program that allows you to receive a commission from goods sold when someone clicks to their site from yours.) You need to log in to your Amazon account to determine your account information before you can share it with TypePad. After you have your Amazon account info, you can choose which Amazon vendor you want to work with (for example, Amazon.com, Amazon.co.uk, or Amazon.fr), type your Associates ID (if applicable), and type your Wish List ID (if you'd like to share it). Click the Save button, and you're all set.

Password Protection tab

Not everyone finds it appealing to have complete strangers popping in to read their blog. You may decide you want to exert a little more control over which eyes see your posts. You can easily password-protect one, some, or all blogs under your TypePad account, and you can send the sign-in details to only the people you choose.

Click the Password Protection tab. Note the simple question at the top of this page: Do you want to password-protect your entire site? You can click to select the button next to the option that best suits your needs:

✔ **No, Share My Site With Everyone:** This option makes all your blogs public. They can be found by search engines and anyone online.

✔ **Yes, Password-Protect My Entire Site:** This options makes all blogs associated with this TypePad account password-protected. If you choose this option, you're prompted to choose a username and password.

 This username and password should be different from your TypePad username and password! Remember to send this new username and password to the readers you want to invite. They'll need to use it every time they visit your blog. Click Save Changes at the bottom of the page to apply the password to all the blogs on your account.

✔ **Password-Protect Some Blogs and Not Others:** This option allows you to apply password protection to some blogs and leave other blogs open to the public. To password-protect a blog, click the Settings link next to the blog's title. You'll be taken to that blog's Settings page. Click to select the Password option, and set a username and password. Then click the Save Changes button on that page.

If you make any changes to your privacy settings on the Password Protection page, be sure to click the Save Changes button at the bottom of the page so the changes will take effect.

Password protection is your most powerful privacy tool, but it's not the only one. As we mention in Chapter 1, occasionally your blog might be visited by someone intent on stirring up trouble in your comments section. If this happens to you, don't sweat it — this happens to nearly every blogger at some point. TypePad allows you to block unwanted commenters from ever leaving comments again — all you need is the person's IP address, which you'll be able to see the first time he or she leaves a comment. We show you how to do this in Chapter 7, where we deal with all comment-related issues.

Note that although TypePad allows you to block certain IP addresses from leaving a comment, it does not currently offer a way for you to block that IP address from *viewing* your blog. The only way to keep certain viewers from seeing your site is to implement password protection.

Domain Mapping tab

Domain mapping simply means that you're using your own domain name (yourblog.com) instead of your hosted domain name (yourblog.typepad.com). When you map your domain to your blog, you're telling the browser to recognize the .com (or .net, .org, and so on) as your URL. TypePad has thorough instructions for domain mapping with several domain hosts, including Yahoo! and GoDaddy — we also tackle domain mapping in Appendix A.

When you're ready to use your own domain for your blog, you'll come to the Domain Mapping tab and start the process. If you're a new blogger, this may not mean much to you right now. If that's the case, we encourage you to become comfortable with blogging first and consider this option in a few months. When you're ready to find out more, flip to Appendix A, where we explain how to find out if your domain name is available, how to purchase the domain name, and how to map it to your blog.

TypeKey API tab

You may see an API Key tab at the bottom of the tab list on the Account page. API Key is the software that allows you to turn on the comment features in Movable Type (if you have a Movable Type account). If you see this tab but don't have a Movable Type account, you can just ignore it; you don't need it. If you don't see this tab, that's okay too.

Getting Help

Now that you've seen all the items you can edit in the Account link, let's head back up to the green account-level bar and address the next link: Help. This is an important one, of course — it's the link you should click any time TypePad issues have you stumped. As we mention in Chapter 2, TypePad prides itself on its technical support, offering a thorough help section written without a lot of complicated jargon. It also gives you quick access to a real live person, by using the help ticket system. We describe both approaches in this section.

Using the Knowledge Base

After you click the Help link, you see a help screen that looks like the one in Figure 4-8.

If you have a TypePad Micro account, your Help screen will look a bit different: You are limited to searching the Knowledge Base, and you can't open a help ticket.

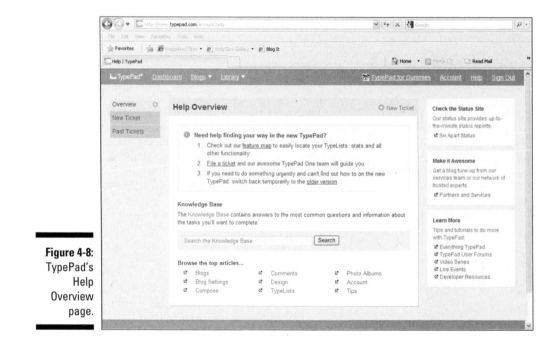

Figure 4-8:
TypePad's
Help
Overview
page.

When you're facing a technical question, your best place to start is about halfway down the page, in the section called Knowledge Base. *Knowledge Base* is simply another word for a large collection of instructional articles users can access for assistance with questions. Many times, the particular question you're facing has already been addressed here. To find an answer in the Knowledge Base, click inside the search bar under Knowledge Base. Type the word or phrase that best describes the issue. Click the Search button, and a list of relevant Knowledge Base articles appears. Take a few minutes to browse through these search results and see if they offer the information you need.

The Knowledge Base is updated so frequently that you might want to keep a close eye on new articles being issued by subscribing to Knowledge Base updates. You can do this by visiting `help.sixapart.com/tp/us` and clicking the Feed Subscribe to Updates link in the right sidebar.

If you can't find an answer to your question in the Knowledge Base, you may require more personal assistance. In this case, opening a help ticket is the next step.

Submitting a help ticket

For direct access to someone on TypePad's support staff, revisit the Help Overview page (refer to Figure 4-8). In the blue list of links on the left side of the page, click New Ticket. (TypePad Micro users don't have this option.)

The next screen asks you what area of TypePad you need help with. Choose the best answer from the drop-down menu. Next, in the subject line, describe the problem succinctly. Be specific in the subject line: "Readers can't see my comments" is more descriptive than "Comment problem."

In the last field, describe your problem at length. Be thorough and specific — the support staff can best help you when you give them as much information as possible. Because the support team will try to replicate the problem to solve it, we suggest that you explain what you were doing when the problem occurred and also mention any error messages you saw. When you have finished describing the issue, click Create Ticket at the bottom of the screen.

After submitting the ticket, simply wait until the support staff responds — nearly always within 24 hours, and usually much less. You'll be notified by e-mail with their response. You can either read their answer directly in your e-mail or use the Active Ticket section in your blog's Help Overview page — just click the subject line of the ticket in question to see the answer. This will open a new page, with TypePad's response listed.

If the support staff has answered your question fully (and we hope they have), click the Mark This Ticket as Resolved box at the bottom of the page (this serves as a helpful reminder to both you and them that no further correspondence is required) and then click Submit Response.

If you're still uncertain even after their response, however, don't hesitate to write back for additional clarification. TypePad prides itself on customer service, so take full advantage of this tool as often as you need to!

 TypePad conveniently keeps a record of all your old help tickets, making it easy for you to revisit questions. From the Help Overview page, simply click View All Past Tickets in the list of links on the left sidebar, and you're taken to a full listing of every help ticket you've ever submitted, complete with TypePad's responses.

Using Quick Compose

Near the top of the Dashboard (refer to Figure 4-1) is a Quick Compose section. You can enter text, photos, or videos here and then click Publish — the new post will publish instantly to whichever blog you've set up as your account's default blog. If you click the Share button, you can even share the content with whichever social media accounts you've linked with your blog.

Use this tool if it appeals to you, but keep in mind that (as of this writing) the Quick Compose section has no space for including a title for your post. Many bloggers consider this a glaring omission. Instead of using the Quick Compose section, we recommend that you write your posts using the Compose editor, which we discuss fully in Chapter 6.

Locating Your List of Blogs

Earlier in the chapter, we mention that a complete listing of your current TypePad blogs appears in the drop-down menu when you click Blogs in the green account-level bar. That's not the only place you'll find them listed, though. On the Dashboard, look at the right sidebar (refer to Figure 4-1). You see the name of your main blog, with links to its settings tabs. Below that is a list of the other blogs (if you have any) associated with this TypePad account. TypePad lists your blogs in both places (the Blogs pull-down menu and the right sidebar of the Dashboard), but clicking a blog's title in either spot ultimately lands you at the same place: the overview for that particular blog. Work from whichever list feels the most natural to you. If you're a beginner who hasn't yet created a TypePad blog, you won't see anything listed in that box at this point. Don't worry — we show you how to set up your first blog in the next chapter.

If you *do* already have a TypePad blog, notice that this sidebar offers you some handy shortcuts that can take you directly to where you want to go. Below the title of your main blog, you see links to the tabs available in your blog-level bar: Stats, Design, Settings, Compose, Posts, and Comments. The blogs listed below the main one have a link to the Compose tab. Clicking that link takes you to the page where you write a new post for that particular blog. Clicking the down arrow next to Compose displays a pull-down menu, offering shortcuts to various locations in that particular blog's Dashboard. We cover each of those items thoroughly in Chapter 5; for now, know that this handy sidebar is a good starting point for managing every blog in your account.

Answering the Question of the Day

The Question of the Day (also known as the QotD) feature is tucked at the bottom of the Dashboard's right sidebar. This option is just for fun, but you won't want to miss it — it's a simple way to engage in the TypePad community, and it offers you some clever posting topics. TypePad freely accepts submissions for QotD; simply e-mail a creatively compelling question (95 characters or less) to `qotd@typepad.com`. Each day, TypePad lists a new question in this box, and you'll find that the questions range from the ridiculous to the thought-provoking. Notice, too, that the author of each day's question appears in the QotD box, garnering that blogger some good attention in the TypePad community.

To participate in the Question of the Day, click the yellow Answer button below the day's question. This takes you directly to a new post, and the question is automatically inserted into the top of your new post. Write your answer, click Save (more on post publishing options in the next chapter), and your answer will post on your own blog. Conveniently, your QotD answer is also linked to all the other answers to that day's question, and the answers are all listed at `blogs.com`, Six Apart's hub site for featuring interesting content around the blogosphere. (To see that particular day's answers, click View Answers in the QotD box.) This is not only a simple way to jump feet-first into the TypePad community, but also a handy cure for writer's block.

As you can see, there's much to know and understand about the TypePad Dashboard. If you're a beginning blogger (or if you're an old TypePad pro who is still getting comfortable with the big redesign of late 2009), give yourself some time to learn the ropes. Spend some time poking around on the Dashboard, and refer to this chapter as needed to help find your way around. In no time at all, you'll be navigating with ease!

Chapter 5

Creating Your First Blog

. . . .

In This Chapter

▶ Determining your blog's settings

▶ Understanding your design choices

▶ Finding out who's visiting you and why

▶ Managing what you've already written

▶ Setting up your comment structure

. . . .

*B*efore you start writing posts, you need to set up your blog and make it as user-friendly (to you *and* your readers) as possible. Understanding and establishing your blog's basic settings on the front end saves you many headaches on the back end! In Chapter 4, we show you how to navigate your TypePad Dashboard using the green account-level bar. When you click the name of the blog you want to work on (from the Blogs link in your green account-level bar or the Dashboard's right sidebar), you see a blue blog-level navigation bar. In this chapter, we focus on the blue blog-level bar to get your blog set up and ready to share with the world.

Just as Chapter 4 gives you a road map of your green account-level bar, this chapter gives you a road map of your blue blog-level bar, explaining the purpose and function of every link and button. Some of these blog-level elements, we explain in full detail; still others contain enough features to require further explanation later in the book. But by the end of this chapter, you'll have a working knowledge of the blog-level bar, and you'll be ready to jump into writing posts in Chapter 6.

While you're still in the blog setup stage, use the steps in this chapter to set your blog's publicity options, configure your post and page options, set up your comment preferences, and ensure that your RSS feed is readily available to your readers. After you do that, we introduce you to the design options (though we cover them in more detail in Chapter 11) and show you how to check your stats (you want to know who's reading you, right?). We also tell you how to invite additional authors to contribute to your blog and how to import or export your blog if necessary. Those are a lot of decisions to make, but this chapter gives the basics you need to plan wisely.

Depending on which TypePad account you have, some of the items discussed in this chapter and others may not be part of your account.

Choosing Your Basic Blog Settings

Taking the time to choose your blog settings saves you hassle later: You'll know that search engines are finding your posts, your RSS feed is working and available, and your readers are able to comment. To establish your settings, you'll need to be signed in and looking at the blog-level bar:

1. **Type** www.typepad.com/dashboard **in the browser's address bar and press Enter.**

2. **Sign in if necessary.**

3. **Click your blog's name in the Dashboard's right sidebar.**

   A page that looks similar to Figure 5-1 appears.

4. **Click the tab that says Settings. It's the very last tab.**

   You see a page that looks similar to Figure 5-2.

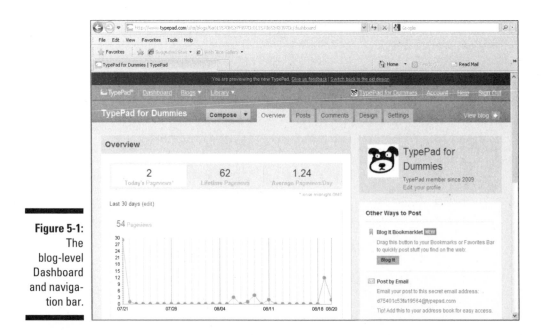

Figure 5-1:
The blog-level Dashboard and navigation bar.

Figure 5-2:
The Settings
tab.

You already established some of the necessary information for your blog's settings when you created your TypePad account and built your profile. That information is already filled in on the Settings tab. On the left side of the Settings page is a list of links to settings options. Those links are

- Basics
- SEO
- Sharing
- Stats
- Feeds
- Posts & Pages
- Categories
- Comments
- Authors
- Post by Email
- Import/Export

Let's work our way down that list of links, discussing each one in detail. After you've had your TypePad blog up and running a while, you may decide you want to edit some of these settings. Don't worry — you can come back and make changes any time.

Basics tab

The fields in the Basics tab are already populated with information you shared with TypePad when you set up your account.

SEO tab

The SEO tab deals with search engine optimization (SEO) — setting up your blog so search engines (such as Google and Yahoo!) can find and index your content. After the search engines do that, they rank your content based on its relevance to a topic. The more relevance your blog has to a topic, the higher your rank and, subsequently, the higher your blog appears on the search results page. If you want your blog to rank well, pay special attention to your blog's SEO settings. If you'd like to find out a little more about how search engines work, read Chapter 1.

Publicity: If you're interested in allowing anyone and everyone to find your blog using a search engine, click to select the Yes, Publicize This Blog option. If you allow your blog to be public, TypePad sends your newly updated blog out to search engines and blog indexes. If you don't select this option, TypePad and search engines assume you'd like to keep your blog private and won't help you promote your content publicly (though the content is still available to readers).

Keep in mind that if you don't choose to publicize your blog, you won't be able to sync your blog with your Facebook, Twitter, or other social media accounts — a feature we discuss in Chapter 10.

Google Sitemap: If you want Google to find and index your blog, you need to have a Google Sitemap. A *Google Sitemap* helps TypePad alert Google each time you create new content. When Google receives notification that you've updated your blog, it sends out search spiders to come and crawl through your blog. That's not as creepy as it sounds; it simply means Google (and Yahoo!, Ask, Bing, and other search engines) is gathering the relevant information it needs to answer search queries. TypePad generates a Google Sitemap for you if you click to select this option.

Title Format: This title is not referring to your blog's name. Rather, it's referring to the text that appears at the top of your blog page in your browser's title bar. Figure 5-3 shows the location of the title bar. Most bloggers choose to have the name of the post and the name of the blog included in the title bar. TypePad allows you to choose how those two names are displayed. Use the pull-down menu to select the option you like best.

Putting the post title first, followed by the blog name, makes for stronger SEO.

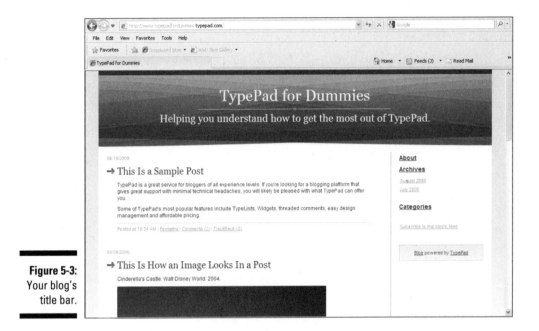

Figure 5-3:
Your blog's
title bar.

Meta Keywords: *Meta keywords* are keywords that don't appear on your blog but are coded into your blog's template (in the `<head>` tag of your template; don't worry, TypePad takes care of it for you). The meta keywords are invisible to everyone but search engines (unless someone opens your coded template; then they're visible). In the past, search engines used meta keywords to help categorize a blog and determine if it was relevant to a particular search. Now, though, most search engines don't use meta keywords in their algorithms, and using meta keywords in your own blog isn't necessary. Google and Microsoft Live Search ignore them completely. However, if you choose to use this function, use keywords that are relevant to your blog and what you're writing about. It's not wise to include words that are irrelevant to your blog's purpose just to try to garner more search engine hits for your content (you won't). The search engines are wise to this and penalize your blog by giving you lower rankings or blacklisting you completely.

Meta Description: Whereas meta keywords are basically irrelevant to your blog's SEO, your meta description is not. Your meta description is located in the `<head>` tag of your template (TypePad takes care of the coding so you don't have to) and is used by search engines to describe your blog when it's listed on a search results page. However, not all search engines use your meta description. Instead, they pull a description of your blog from the copy of the blog post listed in the search results. If you choose to write a meta description for your blog, make it a concise description of your blog's intent. Here are two examples:

Not so great: Camaro Crusade

Better: The story of how I'm restoring a 1967 Camaro to its former muscle-car glory so I can drive it along Route 66

The latter example is more descriptive and includes keywords people are likely to search for (such as *1967 Camaro, Route 66, restoring 1967 Camaro,* and *1967 muscle car*). If a search engine uses your meta description at all, the second example will have more weight in determining your search ranking.

Sharing tab

Chapter 4 explains how to link other social media accounts to your TypePad Profile. Now we explain how to link your other social media accounts with your *blog.* Social media is so prevalent these days, everyone seems to have accounts with Facebook, Twitter, FriendFeed, LinkedIn, and so on. Sometimes it makes sense to share information among accounts. You may have different audiences with different accounts (for example, you might have personal friends on Facebook and business peers on Twitter), and those audiences may be different still from your RSS subscribers. By linking your blog to these different accounts, you may be reaching several audiences without much effort on your part. Be careful, though: You don't want to inundate your friends with multiple links to the same thing. If your audiences overlap significantly (for example, you're mostly friends with the same people at Twitter and Facebook), it may not be necessary to post your link in both places.

Share Your Posts with Friends on Other Social Networks: If you've set up social media accounts and linked them with TypePad already (as we show you how to do in Chapter 4), just click to select the accounts you'd like to link with your blog. As you update your blog, TypePad automatically sends a link to your latest post to those social media accounts. If you want to configure more social media accounts for sharing, just click the Configure More Accounts link, which takes you to the Other Accounts section of your Account page. Here, you can add more accounts (Chapter 4 tells you how to do that if you're not sure).

Share This Blog on Your TypePad Profile: When you click to select this option, you're agreeing that TypePad can share your blog throughout its site. Most notably, your blog is included in the Recent Activity list on your Profile. If you have multiple blogs on your TypePad account, you can choose which ones are listed on your Profile.

Let Your Readers Share Their Comments: If a reader is signed in to his TypePad account when he comments on your blog post, his comments and a link to your blog appear on his TypePad Profile.

Stats tab

When you click the Stats tab, the Stats page appears and asks for your Google Analytics UA Number. If you're using Google Analytics, your UA number is your User Account number. See Appendix B for a full explanation of third-party statistics tracking software and how to integrate those options with your TypePad blog.

Feeds tab

Moving down the menu, you see the Feeds tab next. Chapter 1 explains what an RSS feed is and the benefits of offering one to your blog's readers. All blogging platforms offer a default RSS feed. Following are your default TypePad RSS feeds (replace the necessary information with your own):

- Atom: `http://blogname.typepad.com/folder_name/atom.xml`
- RSS 1.0: `http://blogname.typepad.com/folder_name/index.rdf`
- RSS 2.0: `http://blogname.typepad.com/folder_name/rss.xml`

These days, most people expect to see an RSS button to subscribe to your feed. The official symbol of an RSS feed is the button to the right of Subscribe in the top-right corner of Figure 5-4. That figure shows how the symbol might look in a blog's actual sidebar. Usually, but not always, the button is orange. By default, TypePad has a small orange RSS button or a text link or both in your blog sidebar that says Subscribe to This Blog's Feed. If you'd like to customize that default RSS link (such as a larger RSS button), flip to Chapters 8 and 11, where we show you how to include customized images and links on the sidebar via a TypeList.

You can find variations of this button by doing a Web search for *RSS button.*

Published Feeds: This is where you can decide whether you want to offer your readers the ability to subscribe to posts only, comments only, or both. At a minimum, you should click to select Blog Posts so your readers can include your RSS feed in their feed reader. It's a good idea to offer readers the option of subscribing to comments on individual posts or pages as well. Sometimes a reader will leave a comment and may want to stay informed about how the discussion is progressing. By subscribing to the comments, readers are alerted via their feed readers when a new comment is posted to that same article.

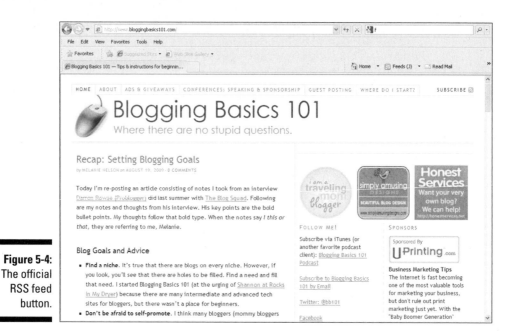

Figure 5-4:
The official
RSS feed
button.

Feed Content: You have the option of publishing full or partial feeds. This means that when a feed reader shows your new content, it either shows the entire article within the reader or only a teaser of the article (which forces the reader to click over to your blog if he'd like to read the rest of the article). There are pros and cons to each option. If you have advertisements on your blog or are hoping for more traffic to your blog, you might prefer a partial feed because it provides only a teaser of the article and asks the reader to click over for more. However, many readers prefer to read all their articles within their feed readers without clicking to individual blogs. More than a few readers have unsubscribed to blogs that offer only partial feeds. Their argument is that if your content is compelling, they will click over to your blog to leave a comment or join in the discussion. In general, readers have little time for clicking around and prefer to read full articles within their feed readers.

Connect to FeedBurner: This is optional. TypePad automatically supplies an RSS feed for each blog you establish. You can use one of TypePad's feeds, or you can use FeedBurner — a widely used, Google-owned tool for helping bloggers *burn* (or issue) an RSS feed. After you burn a feed through FeedBurner, you have access to numerous helpful features such as statistics and e-mail alerts (see more on this in Appendix B).

You can use FeedBurner by visiting `www.feedburner.com`, setting up an account, and following the helpful wizard to burn a feed for your blog (for example, `http://feeds.feedburner.com/TypePadForDummies` instead of the default feed that TypePad supplies). Once you've burned the feed, connect it to your TypePad blog by clicking the Connect to FeedBurner button on the Feeds page in your blog's Dashboard. For an alternative to FeedBurner, visit www.feedblitz.com.

Posts tab

The options in the Posts tab are the ones that make your blogging go smoothly. Your decisions here determine how your readers navigate your blog and how your posts are presented and saved. Don't worry; everything here is editable if you change your mind. Play around with your options to figure out what works best for you and your readers.

Default Publishing Status: When you write your blog posts, you have the option of publishing the post immediately, saving it as a draft, or setting a future date and time to publish the post (see Chapter 6). If you know that you usually write a post and publish it immediately, click to select the Publish Now option; if you know that you usually write a post and save it for later, click to select the Draft option.

It's a smart safeguard to set your default publishing status to draft, because it keeps you from inadvertently posting something that wasn't quite ready for public consumption.

Posts to Display: Your choices here determine how many posts appear on your blog at a given time. You have the option of choosing to display a specific number of posts or days on your blog's home page (the page your readers see when they first visit your blog). Most people choose to show posts. When someone visits your blog, they expect to see several posts listed on your page. The number you choose to display affects how long your page is. In general, visitors don't like to scroll and scroll and scroll. If you write short to medium-size posts, you might want to include up to ten posts on your main page. If your posts are fairly long, though, consider cutting that number to five or fewer.

Your archive pages list blog posts that you've already published. You can choose to list more posts on the archive pages because they are not the main page of your blog and won't be cluttering up your blog's home page. It's fine to display ten posts on an archive page.

Navigation Links: When a reader is reading an individual blog post (not just those on your blog's home page), TypePad provides navigation at the bottom of the post so the reader can move to the previous or next post easily. TypePad's default navigation link words are Previous and Next. If you'd like to customize a navigation link word, click inside the text box, select and delete the word you want to change, and type the new word(s).

Post Date Format: Including a date on your posts helps your readers determine the content's freshness. Depending on your niche, it may be important to know when you published the original content. For example, if you're writing about technology, and someone visits your blog looking for information about whether or not to use meta keywords, they'll need to know how old the post is. If you're writing about your family, dating posts is also helpful if you ever decide to make your blog into a book or print entries in chronological order. Use the pull-down menu to choose how the date displays for each blog post.

Post Time Format: Each blog post you publish has a timestamp. Use the pull-down menu to choose either standard or military (24-hour-format) time.

Front Page: Your blog's front page (or *home page,* as some call it) can either display your most recent posts (usually in reverse chronological order) or show a page (we explain the difference between posts and pages in Chapter 6). If you choose to have a page as your home page, it will most likely be static (unless you plan on updating it at regular intervals). If your front page displays your most recent posts, it will be more dynamic.

Readers tend to prefer the dynamic format and expect a list of blog posts when they visit your blog; for this reason, we strongly recommend that you choose to display your most recent posts. At any rate, remember that many times readers find you through links from other sites or a search, in which case they might never even see your front page!

Order of Posts: Most bloggers list their blog posts in reverse chronological order (in other words, the newest post is at the top). Readers are accustomed to reading blogs this way and appreciate it because the newest content is always on top and they don't have to search for it. You do have the option of listing your posts in chronological order, though, and that may work for your blog. Click to select Newest First or Oldest First, depending on your preference, but again, keep in mind that choosing Oldest First will likely confuse the average blog reader.

Limit Recent Posts: Recent Posts is a sidebar module you can add to your blog design (we discuss blog design in Chapter 11). This module lists, obviously, your most recently written posts. However, you have a bit of control over what's listed here. You can choose to include only posts within a specific category (we talk about those in a minute) or every post that comes through. Use the pull-down menu to choose whether you'd like to include all posts in your Recent Posts module, only a specific category, or multiple categories. If you choose Multiple Categories, a window with a list of your categories pops up. Press the Control key (PC) or the Command key (Mac) while you click to make multiple category selections.

Post Display Language: The default language for your blog is English United States. You can change the display language of your blog by simply clicking inside the text box and choosing the relevant language from the menu. Note that this option changes the supporting elements of the post (such as month names and archive headers), not the language of the posts.

Auto-Generated Excerpt Length: When you write a blog post, you can also write a short excerpt, or description, of the post (see Chapter 6 to find out how). Search engines use this excerpt to determine whether your post is relevant to a query; feed readers use the excerpt to send a short teaser of the post via RSS (if you chose partial feeds in the Feeds tab earlier). If you do not write a customized excerpt for each post, TypePad generates one for you by using the first 100 words of the post. Click inside the text box and change the number of words if you're not happy with 100.

Categories tab

Like most other blogging platforms, TypePad allows you to group, or organize, posts into one or more categories. Chapter 6 explains how to label a post with one or more categories, but here in the Settings tab is where you manage those categories. Using categories and including links to them is a helpful navigational feature for your readers, who can use them to see what else you might have said on a particular topic. If you choose to use this feature (and we strongly recommend that you do), each time you write a post, you'll assign that post to one more of your categories. For example, if you write a post about a trip to Dallas in which you saw the Dallas Cowboys play, you might categorize that post under both Sports and Travel.

TypePad automatically offers several categories, which are listed in the Categories tab. Look through these and see if they're sufficient for you; if they're not, you can easily add more of your own. To change an existing category, simply click Edit to the right of the current category. Type the new category you'd like to have appear in its place. If you want to delete a current category altogether, just click the Delete button on the same line.

If you need more categories than the ones listed (and you probably will), type the name of the new category in the text box entitled Add a New Category, and then click Add. The category appears alphabetically in the list. TypePad allows you to create an unlimited number of categories. And you don't have to make a decision right now about every category you expect to need in your blogging career; you can revisit this same tab to add and rename categories as you go.

When it comes to naming categories, you can be as straightforward or as creative as you want. Some bloggers rely so heavily on categories as a good navigational tool that they keep categories as concise as possible (for example, Recipes, Home Improvement, Recycling, Travel). Still other bloggers see categories as a chance to inject some cleverness and name them in ways that aren't as direct (for example, I Am Addicted to Libraries, Sometimes I

Do Stupid Stuff, I Think My Computer Hates Me). Either option is fine, but be aware that the latter option may not be quite as obvious to your readers.

The categories you create in the Settings tab appear in your Rich Text editor when you sit down to blog. In Chapter 6, we explain the specifics of writing and publishing posts, and we show you how to apply one or more categories to what you write.

Comments tab

The Comments tab is a tiny one with a big purpose: the presentation and management of your comments. As you probably know, comments are the lifeblood of the blogger/reader relationship. Understanding how to set up and manage comments effectively helps your blogging experience run more smoothly. This topic is such a big one, we devote an entire chapter (Chapter 7) to it. For now, because you're in the setup stage, keep TypePad's default comment settings. We revisit this important tab thoroughly in Chapter 7.

Authors tab

As you continue to work your way through the Settings tab, you'll see that the next link is called Authors, and this is where you can invite additional authors to guest-post on your blog.

It's important to note that you see the Authors link only if you have the Pro Unlimited or Business Class level of TypePad.

Many bloggers enjoy inviting other people to write guest posts on their blog. It's a great way to introduce your readers to a new and interesting blogger, and it's a convenient feature if you're traveling or otherwise away from your blog for an extended period of time but don't want to stop offering your readers good content.

If you're interested in having a guest blogger post only once, it would probably be more convenient and reasonable for her to e-mail you her post. You can then cut and paste it into your Compose editor (see Chapter 6), and your guest blogger doesn't have to mess with signing in to your TypePad account. If you want the other blogger to post with some degree of frequency, however, you can give the person limited access to your account as a guest or junior author.

When you click the Authors tab, you see your own name listed as the blog's *owner*. This means you are the only one authorized to make fundamental, account-level changes to your blog. (Business Class members are actually able to invite additional owners, but most TypePad users are limited to inviting guest authors or junior authors only.) You will notice you can choose to invite a guest author or a junior author. A *guest author* has the most freedom of the two: he or she can save and write posts and can publish his or her own posts without waiting for your approval. That's a significant amount of freedom, so issue a guest-author invitation only to someone whose blogging standards you trust. A *junior author,* on the other hand, cannot publish posts without your approval, giving you, the owner, final say as to what does and doesn't appear on your blog. The junior author saves a post as a draft, and you, the owner, have to approve it for publication.

Neither guest authors nor junior authors have access to other parts of your Dashboard beyond creating posts. They won't be able to see your statistics or edit your design, for example. They are authorized to do only their appointed tasks and nothing else. You, as the owner, can revoke their access at any time.

To set up additional authors, or to edit the status of existing ones, follow these steps:

 1. **Click the Authors tab in the bar on the left side of the Settings tab.**

    To invite a new author, look for the section titled Invite Additional Authors (see Figure 5-5).

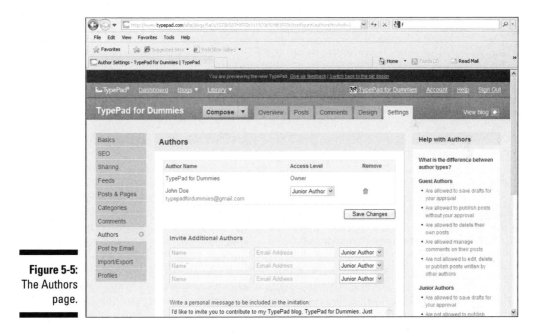

Figure 5-5:
The Authors page.

2. **Enter the name and e-mail address of the person you want to invite, and use the drop-down menu to choose whether you want to invite the person as a guest or a junior author.**

3. **(Optional) Use the text box below the name and e-mail address to send a personalized message with the invitation.**

   You can also leave the default message.

4. **Click the Send Invitation(s) button.**

Your invitee receives an e-mail with a link to accept or decline your invitation. If she doesn't have a TypePad account, she can easily set one up for free (the e-mail tells her how). If she is already a TypePad user, she'll be able to sign in with her current sign-in information. In her own TypePad Dashboard, your blog would then appear in the list of blogs to which she can post.

After she accepts the invitation, you see your new author's name listed under your own at the top of the page (refer to Figure 5-5). Revisit this page if you need to delete an author from your blog (note that this deletes just the author's posting permission, not the author's post). Also, you can use the pull-down menu next to the author's name to upgrade a junior author to a guest author or to downgrade a guest author to a junior author.

Post by Email tab

Ideas for blog posts can come into your head any time, anywhere. Unfortunately, sometimes you want to write and publish a post, but you're nowhere near your own computer. TypePad gives you the flexibility of e-mailing your post from any computer or your phone (that is, if your phone has e-mailing capability). For more about mobile posting tools (including the TypePad iPhone application), see Chapter 15.

Posting Email Address: Posting to your blog via e-mail is a quick way to update your blog while you're on the go. TypePad assigns you a random (and boy, do we mean random!) e-mail address. You can check to see yours by clicking the Post by Email tab. The TypePad crew suggests that you e-mail your super-secret special e-mail address to yourself so you'll have it in your phone address book or contacts and won't have to memorize it. We think that's a darn good idea, because the e-mail address likely contains about 15 random numbers and letters.

Reset Address: Just as it's smart to reset your passwords every once in a while, it's smart to reset your TypePad posting e-mail address. Another good time to reset the address? If you think your e-mail address book has been compromised. To reset your TypePad posting e-mail address, simply click the reset button, and you're finished. You'll get a new address automagically.

Notifications: If you want to verify that your e-mail post is successfully published on your blog, TypePad can notify you when that happens. Just click to select Notify Me Via Email When My Email Post Has Been Successfully Published.

Import/Export tab

Importing content from an existing blog is a fairly easy process with TypePad. Exporting your content for backup purposes or to another platform can be tricky, but it's not so bad (depending on where you're moving your content.). Chapter 13 covers the ins and outs of importing and exporting your TypePad content, but this section offers a quick overview of what you can expect when you click the Import/Export tab in your blog's Settings.

Import: If you're importing content from another blog platform, click to select the platform it's coming from. Depending on the platform you choose, you'll see different choices. Table 5-1 is an overview of what to expect when importing from a specific platform.

Table 5-1	Importing Blog Content from a Different Platform
If You Are Importing From	*You Need This Source Information*
TypePad, Movable Type, or other MTIF file	Choose to either upload a file from your computer or import a file from a Web address
WordPress.com	Type the blog's URL, your username, and your password
WordPress WXR file	Choose to either upload a file from your computer or import a file from a Web address

Export: When you export your blog content, TypePad will generate a simple text file that contains all of your blog's information (posts, links, comments, and so on). To start the process, just click the Export button.

Managing Your Design

Knowing how to access and edit your blog design is important. The way your blog appears on the screen matters to your readers — people tend to click away from blogs that aren't easy on the eyes. The Design tab in the blog-level bar is your starting point for managing your current design or applying a new one.

When you click the Design tab, you see several options for managing your design. You can choose a *theme* (another word for TypePad's basic designs), select a *layout* (the "bone structure" of a blog, determining where sidebars and the main content column will go), organize content (click and drag to rearrange elements on your blog), and add Custom CSS (see Chapter 14).

The good news is that TypePad makes blog design pretty painless; the interface is intuitive and highly visual. Even then, though, the topic of blog design is involved enough that we give it a chapter of its own (see Chapter 11). We revisit this Design tab there and explain how you can easily get the look you want.

Checking Your Stats in the Overview

One of the perks of writing a blog (as opposed to writing a book or a magazine) is that you have almost immediate access to details about how many readers you have and how they found you. These details are referred to as *statistics* (often shortened to *stats*). It's undeniably satisfying to see that people are stopping by to see the things you post — writers, after all, want to have readers! On the other hand, with the real-time measuring stick of blog statistics, it can be easy to get hung up on the numbers. Let's take a minute to find out where to find your blog statistics, but let's keep in mind from the start that they are not the ultimate definition of your blogging success.

From the blog-level bar, click the Overview tab. This takes you to a page that looks similar to the one pictured in Figure 5-6.

Immediately, you'll see a graph of your pageviews. Every time a reader clicks to a new page on your blog, that's a *pageview*. If they click around to several different spots on your page (for example, through your categories or archives), these clicks each count as a separate pageview. Above your statistics graph is a light blue bar giving you a quick snapshot of where your blog statistics stand right now. From left to right, you see Today's Pageviews (the number of clicks you've received since midnight GMT today), Lifetime Pageviews (the number of pageviews you've received since you started your TypePad blog), and Average Pageviews (obviously, a daily average of how many pageviews you receive).

Use your statistics graph as a handy visual tool. The default setting for the graph shows you your pageview activity for the last 30 days. If you want to change that, click the small Edit link just above the graph, and you see a drop-down menu with options to view your pageviews in 120-, 90-, 30- or 7-day increments. Click the one that serves you best.

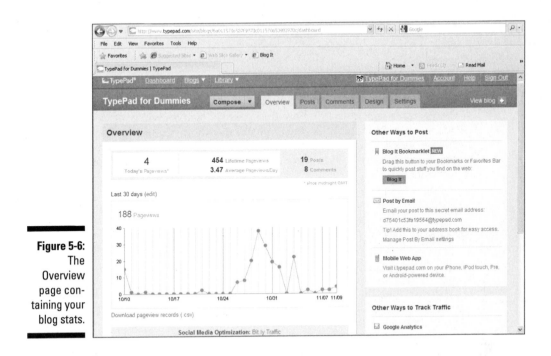

Figure 5-6:
The
Overview
page con-
taining your
blog stats.

If you want to know your pageview history beyond 120 days, you have an option that sends you much further back. Below the graph is a small link that reads Download Pageview Records (`.csv`). Click that link and save the resulting .csv file (which lists your entire pageview history from the day you started your TypePad blog to the current day) to your computer. A *csv* (or comma-separated value) file saves data in a table format and can be opened in Microsoft Excel (Windows), Numbers (Mac), or a text editor.

Below the statistics graph is a small link to Bit.ly traffic. We define Bit.ly and tell you how to use it in Chapter 10.

If you scroll down, below your graph you'll see a list titled Recent Referrers. This tells you where people are clicking *from* when they click to your blog. The left column tells you what time the pageview occurred. The center column shows you which page of your blog the visitor entered (remember, visitors won't always enter through your front page). For example, if another blogger links to one of your older posts, when a visitor clicks over, he or she will land at the post to which the other blogger linked. The third and final column of this list is especially important: It shows which outside sites (including their URLs) are sending visitors to your blog. Clicking those URLs takes you directly to the page that referred you. If the referring URL looks like a search engine (for example, `www.google.com/search`), clicking the link usually takes you to the search engine page that shows which search terms the reader used when he or she found the link to your blog.

Finding Existing Posts

In the blog-level bar, the Posts tab may be the one you use most often. The Posts tab hosts a list of all the posts and pages you've created (even those saved as drafts or those set to publish in the future). If you haven't deleted the post or page, it's listed here in reverse chronological order. From this list, you can find a post or page and edit it, change its setting (for example, change its status from draft to published or delete it), or find out at a glance whether it has open comments or is accepting trackbacks. (Wondering what a trackback is? See Chapter 7.)

You can filter the listed posts by using the drop-down menu at the top of the Posts or Pages page (as shown in Figure 5-7). Filtering your posts or pages based on category, author, or status (published, future, or draft) helps you quickly and easily find the post you're looking for. Or, if you'd rather, you can click inside the Search box, type a few keywords, and click the Search button.

When you find the post or page you're looking for in the list of returned posts, you can tell at a glance whether the post is accepting comments and trackbacks or the publish status (published or draft). Click the title of the post or page to edit the contents, change whether the file accepts comments, or change whether the file accepts trackbacks. Or, if you just want to change the status or delete the post completely, click the pull-down menu to the right of the title.

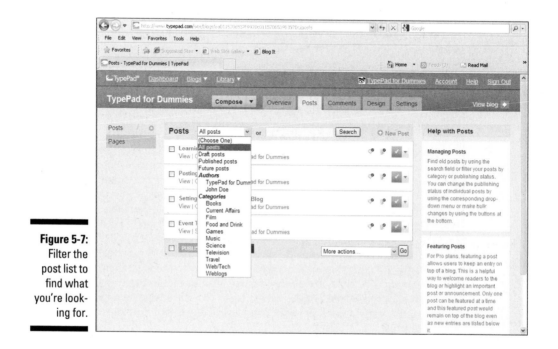

Figure 5-7:
Filter the post list to find what you're looking for.

You can perform bulk actions by clicking to select multiple posts or pages and then scrolling to the bottom of the Posts page and clicking the Publish, Draft, or Delete button. For example, you can unpublish several posts at a time by converting them to draft mode in a bulk action. You can also choose other bulk actions from the pull-down menu (as shown in Figure 5-8).

You can do all the following to a single post or page or to multiple posts or pages:

- ✔ Add categories
- ✔ Replace categories
- ✔ Open comments
- ✔ Close comments
- ✔ Accept trackbacks
- ✔ Do not accept trackbacks

Bulk actions can be especially helpful if you need to perform the same task on multiple files. For instance, if you need to close the comments on five different posts, just select those posts, scroll down to the More Actions pull-down menu (below the list of posts), and choose Close Comments from the menu. All finished!

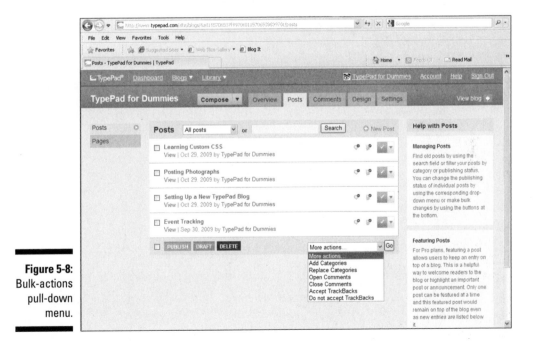

Figure 5-8:
Bulk-actions
pull-down
menu.

Managing Existing Comments

Continuing to work your way through the tabs on the blog-level bar, you see a Comments tab. Click that tab to see a current list of existing comments (if you're just now setting up your blog, you won't have any. That's okay! After we show you how to write a post in Chapter 6, you'll be able to receive comments).

Be aware that this tab is one place to find a list of your existing comments, but once again (are you detecting a theme?), we wait to address the meaty issue of comment management and this tab in Chapter 7.

Creating More Than One Blog in Your TypePad Account

After you're comfortable with setting up your first blog, you can host additional blogs in your TypePad account (unless you are a Micro user). Why would you want to host more than one blog? Well, other family members may want their own blogs, or you may want to set up a separate blog for a new niche. If you have a paid TypePad account, you can set up more than one blog on your account. The Pro Plus account allows you to have up to three blogs; the Pro Unlimited account allows you to have unlimited blogs on your account.

To set up an additional blog on your TypePad account, sign in and go to the Dashboard. In the right sidebar under Manage My Blogs, click the Create a Blog link. The Add a Blog page appears. You have the choice of creating a new TypePad blog or, if you have a blog at another platform, connecting that blog to your TypePad account.

To create a new TypePad blog, follow these steps:

1. **Click to select Create a New TypePad Blog.**

2. **Configure your new TypePad blog as follows:**

   a. **Name the blog.**

   b. **Assign a folder for the blog to reside in.**

   c. **Choose whether you'd like the blog to be publicized.**

      This option refers to whether you want the blog to be visible to search engines and listed on your Profile page.

After you choose your blog name and folder name, you shouldn't change them (if you change your blog name, it's confusing for your readers; if you change your folder name, your links won't work anymore). Your publicity settings, however, can be changed at any time.

If you have a TypePad Pro Plus or Pro Unlimited account, you can assign a mapped domain to this blog or any other new blog at any time. See Appendix A for instructions.

3. Click the Create Blog button.

That's a lot of decision-making for one chapter! You've discovered how to read your statistics, create a new blog (should you want to), manage your comments, invite other authors, and perform a host of other important tasks in the blog-level bar. You understand a little more about the alphabet soup of RSS feeds and SEO. Thinking through all your blog settings at the same time may seem tedious, but it ultimately serves you well. When you sit down to write your first post, you'll know that you're publishing it to a blog that's set up to your best standards.

Chapter 6

Writing and Editing Your Blog Posts

*I*t's the reason you started a blog in the first place, most likely: You have a story to tell, either in words or pictures, and you'd like a place to tell it. You've signed up for a TypePad account, and you're beginning to grasp the functionalities of the Dashboard. You have your first blog set up just the way you want it. Those are all important preliminary steps, but guess what? Now it's time for the fun part: writing a post.

In this chapter, we show you not only how to write a new post in the Compose editor, including how you can tweak the font with different colors and sizes, but also how to categorize and edit existing posts. We also walk you through the simple steps of inserting images into your posts.

Composing Your First Blog Post

At the heart of the TypePad Dashboard is the Compose editor. The Compose editor is where you write and edit new posts (and edit older posts).

Finding the Compose editor couldn't be simpler. On the Dashboard, look at your list of blogs (or blog, if you have only one) on the right side of the screen. Determine which blog you want to post to, and look to the right of its name for the Compose link (see Figure 6-1).

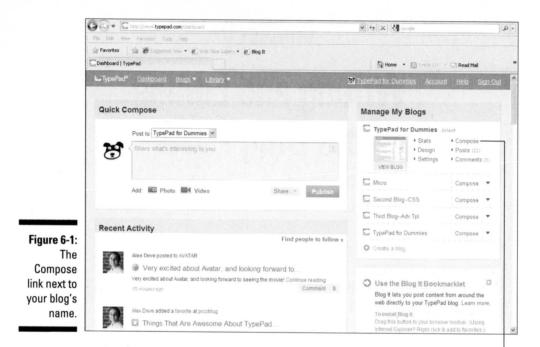

Figure 6-1:
The
Compose
link next to
your blog's
name.

Compose link

Clicking the Compose link takes you directly to the Compose editor, as shown in Figure 6-2. We will be referring to this figure often in this chapter.

As we mention in Chapter 4, you can also compose posts in the Quick Compose section on the front page of the Dashboard. The Quick Compose option may be appealing to some bloggers, but it doesn't offer you full functionality — it doesn't have a field to enter a title, for example, nor can you make many edits to your text (such as alignment and color). For the most features and flexibility, we recommend that you write your posts in the Compose editor.

The cursor is automatically inserted into the Title field. Naming your post is the most obvious place to start, of course, although you don't have to enter anything in this field if you don't want a title. If you're writing a post with the hopes of being noticed by search engines (and, thus, new readers), remember the SEO (search engine optimization) tips we share with you in Chapter 5.

Your title isn't just a place to put SEO principles in place. If you're more interested in the artistic side of blogging versus the SEO side of blogging, you can use your post title as a place to be creative and grab a reader's attention. Use a title that makes a reader want to jump into reading the post you've written. "A Bad Day at the Office" doesn't have as much zing as "My Ridiculously Horrible Encounter with a Fax Machine."

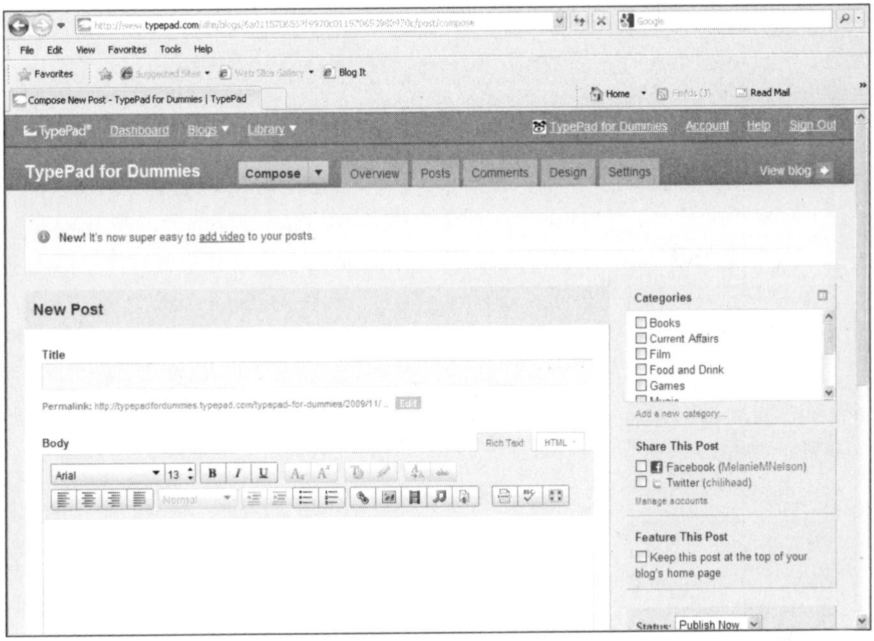

Figure 6-2:
The
TypePad
Compose
editor.

Below the Title bar is a small line of text that shows your permalink for this particular post (see an example in Figure 6-3).

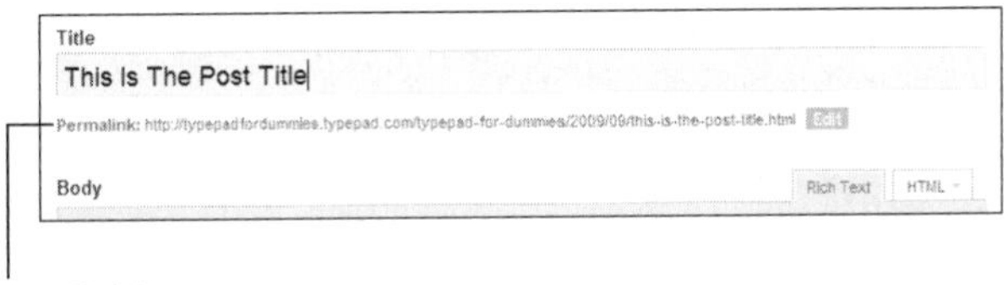

Figure 6-3:
The per-
malink
bar in the
Compose
editor.

Permalink bar

A permalink is the URL for a specific post (for example, `http://typepad fordummies.typepad.com/post_title.html`) as opposed to the main URL for the front page of your blog (for example, `http://typepadfor dummies.typepad.com`). If you (or any other bloggers) want to link to a particular post (whether on your blog or another's), the permalink is what you use to point readers to that post. TypePad automatically sets your permalink to reflect the post title (or, if you don't use a title, the first sentence of your post). If you don't like the default permalink, you can change it by clicking the blue Edit button.

Tackling writer's block

When you start your blog, you will likely find that you have many things you'd like to share with your readers. In fact, you may have so many things to write about that you find you're writing several posts in one sitting! Our advice is to harness that energy and write away. But instead of publishing those posts immediately, think about them, edit them, and then set them to post at a future date. Why? Because there will come a day when you won't have a thing to write about, and you'll appreciate having those posts in your queue ready to go.

When you're stumped for a post topic, poke around in your memory. You probably have a great story to tell about how your third-grade teacher inspired your love of history, or how your first business failed miserably, or how your gramps taught you to ride a horse.

And look around at your everyday life for ideas. Are you struggling with some health insurance difficulties? Compile a list of resources around the Web, and share them with your readers. Do you like the way the afternoon sun hits your kitchen? Find a poetic way to describe it. Your blog can be fertile ground for refining your writing skill — a built-in critique group, if you will.

Try to resist the urge to write a post about the fact that you don't have anything to write about. Some people pull off a post like with great hilarity, but most don't. Dig around for a worthwhile topic, or say nothing at all.

Which brings us to an important point: A blogging break can work wonders. The immediacy of the blogosphere can feel frantic at times, and that may throw water on your creative fires. It's true that writing with regularity helps build an audience and helps you hone your skills, but a well-timed season of rest may be just what you need. Take off a few days, a week, or even a month or more, and you may find that you come back invigorated to write like never before.

When writer's block does hit, here are a few blogs to visit that help you find your groove again:

- **ProBlogger** (`problogger.net`): Darren Rowse is one of the biggest names in blogging, and he's earned that title. He produces usable content every day (whether by him or a guest author). We suggest checking out his 31 Days to Building a Better Blog course, which gives you not only writing assignments, but also ideas to take your blog to the next level (garnering more traffic, implementing advertising, and becoming a more vocal part of your blogging community). This course is available as a workbook, but you can also find the lessons on his site if you do a search for the course name.

- **Confident Writing** (`confidentwriting.com`): With a tagline like "Power up your words and find your writing voice," how you can you go wrong? Joanna Young is a go-to gal for inspired writing. She can help you tighten things up, flesh things out, and generally improve your writing. She offers new writing tips and ideas several times a week and frequently offers a writing series on her blog that encourage your participation. These series will definitely give you writing fodder and food for thought.

- **Question Of the Day:** In Chapter 4, we show you the TypePad Question of the Day box in the Dashboard. Not only does this offer an excellent new writing prompt each day, but it's also an easy way to jump feet first into the TypePad community.

✔ **NaBloPoMo** (`www.nablopomo.com`): NaBloPoMo, which stands for National Blog Posting Month, is a monthly challenge that encourages participants to post a new article on their blog daily. Each month has a theme, but blogging to the theme is optional. The important thing is developing the habit of writing consistently so writer's block has a harder time setting in. NaBloPoMo offers groups, forums, and even prizes to help you get involved. If you need to bounce ideas off others, don't be shy — head to the forums or join one of the groups.

You can change a permalink at any time, though it's not advisable to do so after the post is published. Why? If you change the permalink after an article is published, any incoming links to the previous permalink are broken.

Moving further down the screen, you'll see a large white space titled Body, and this is where you write your post. Click inside this text box and start writing. Vast, empty white space can be overwhelming to any writer, regardless of your experience, but don't be afraid to jump in anyway. See the "Tackling writer's block" sidebar in this chapter for some encouragement.

TypePad is set up so that you are automatically posting in Rich Text (this is the same thing as the WYSIWYG editor we describe in Chapter 1). As long as you're writing in Rich Text, your text appears in your published post just as it appears here, in the Compose editor (think of it as a word processor). This is by far the clearest, simplest way to write a post, but if HTML is your thing, you can write your post using the HTML editor instead. To do this, just click the HTML tab in the top-right corner of the Body section, as shown in Figure 6-4.

If you're a blogging newbie who would like to begin to learn the nuts and bolts of HTML coding, try this: Click the HTML tab in your completed posts, and notice how the post is marked with HTML. You'll soon find intuitive codes and start to see how they work. For example, <p> is the HTML code that starts a new paragraph, and </p> is the code that ends a paragraph. As you probably know, computers don't just know how to do things; you have to tell them. That's what HTML does: It tells the browser how to read and display the posts you write.

You can find HTML tutorials online. It's worth knowing even a little HTML so you can have more control over how your posts are displayed or so you can troubleshoot any small issues that may arise (like why your image isn't centered). The HTML editor is a great place to start learning the basics.

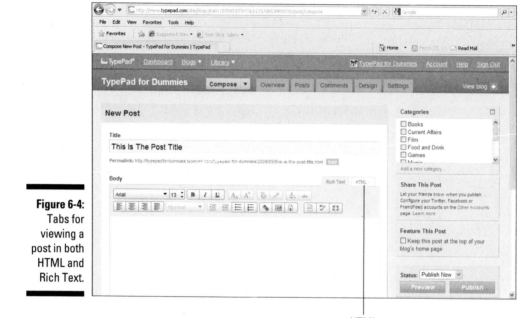

Figure 6-4:
Tabs for
viewing a
post in both
HTML and
Rich Text.

HTML

Formatting Your Text

As you write your blog posts, there are times when you want to make a word or phrase stand out. TypePad's editor makes this very easy to do by allowing you to simply highlight a word or phrase and click a toolbar button to change the font, weight, or color of the highlighted word(s).

In the Rich Text tab, you'll see a variety of buttons; Table 6-1 explains the function of each one. Feel free to write a test post and start playing around with how those buttons work. Highlight a word and change its font or color; make it bold or underlined. You can also format your paragraphs so that they are bulleted lists, indented as blockquotes, or aligned to the right instead of the left.

Table 6-1	Compose Editor Buttons
Use This Button	*To*
Arial ▼	Choose what font you'd like to use for your posts
13 ▲▼	Choose the size of the font you use for a particular word, phrase, or even paragraph
B *I* U	Make a word, phrase, or paragraph bold, italic, or underlined

Use This Button	To
A_x A^x	Use subscript and superscript
	Change the color of a word, phrase, or paragraph
	Highlight a word, phrase, or paragraph
	Remove formatting from a selection
	Strikethrough a word or phrase
	Choose the alignment of your paragraphs (left, center, right, or justified)
Normal	Assign normal formatting or header formatting to text
	Indent text as a blockquote or unindent text
	Make your text into a bulleted or numbered list
	Insert a link into your text
	Insert an image into your post
	Insert a link to a file into your post (for example, a PDF of your restaurant's menu)
	Insert a video (or a link to the video) into your post
	Insert an audio file into your post
	Insert a split entry into your post (a _split entry_ is when you publish an excerpt of a post to your blog's front page and have a "Read more" link that takes the reader to the expanded post)
	Spell-check your post before you publish it
	Expand the TypePad editor to take up the full screen

How to write a great blog post

Consultants make big bucks helping bloggers implement strategies for SEO and community management. Those are both important parts of growing a blog, but ultimately, a good blog comes down to one thing: *good content*. All the gimmicks in the world won't help a blog gain footing if the writing is tired or uninteresting, the grammar is poor, or there's no clear purpose.

You may have started a blog purely for your own enjoyment, with no intention of growing a readership. That is a perfectly valid reason to blog. But if your aim is to produce blog content that draws in *new* readers, consider the following as you sit down to write your post:

✔ **Good form matters.** Grammar, punctuation, and spelling aren't meant to be stuffy (your impressions from sixth grade notwithstanding). Instead, these tools are markers to make it easier for our eyes and brain to navigate our language. Especially when publishing on a computer screen (which is harder on the eyes than ink-and-paper format), using good grammar, punctuation, and spelling makes it that much easier for your readers to understand you. A blogger who consistently refuses to use capitalization, for example, or one who makes repeated, glaring spelling errors may push away readers who don't want to have to work so hard to interpret posts. Don't worry about being perfect (we all make mistakes), but try to edit yourself and apply some reasonable style standards.

✔ **Have a clear beginning, middle, and end.** Some bloggers can successfully write rambling lists about what they did today and still manage to be entertaining. That's hard to pull off, though. Most of us benefit from sticking to a more structured, essay-style format in blog posts, using a clear beginning, middle, and end. In other words, tell a story. For example, instead of a bulleted list that describes every single errand you ran last Saturday afternoon, write about the funny conversation you had with the 89-year-old woman at the computer store.

✔ **Be concise.** There's an old rule of thumb among writing teachers that you shouldn't use ten words when five will suffice. This is especially true in blogging; a computer screen full of long, wordy posts may make a reader's eyes glaze over. People generally visit blogs expecting shorter, bite-size stories and information, so write with that in mind. Be particularly sure, as a courtesy to your readers' eyes, that you use brief paragraphs, with a double-spaced line between them.

✔ **Use good wording.** The best way to encourage your own brevity is to choose words that pack a punch. Tighten your posts by striking as many *be* verbs as you can, replacing them with more descriptive verbs ("I was cold" isn't as interesting as "I shivered in the December air"). Keep a thesaurus at your computer desk. You may surprise yourself: By holding yourself to high standards in your word choices, you may discover a love for writing you didn't know you had!

✔ **It's not about you.** Well, technically, it *is* about you, especially if you're writing a personal blog. But it's about your readers too, and the best way to gain more of them is to write with them in mind. Depending on the type of blog you write, your purpose may vary from the bloggers around you, but you can still be mindful of offering something to your readers. You can entertain, encourage, challenge, instruct, and much more. Are you writing about the minutia of your daily life? Make it funny. Are you ranting about the state of the U.S. tax code? Give your readers information, or call them to action. Be a blogger who readers can count on to provide something of value — however small — each time they visit you.

✔ **Engage your readers in the conversation.** Remember that blogging (unlike, for example, book writing) is an immediate, real-time dialogue. At least occasionally, consider bringing your readers directly into your posts by asking for their opinion. For example, if you write a post about your best principles for leading an organization effectively, consider ending with a question: "What leadership principles have best worked for you?" This concrete invitation for dialogue draws your readers in and lets them know that their opinion matters. You may find that some of the best content on your blog occasionally appears in the comments section!

Inserting Extras into Your Blog Posts

As you write your blog posts, you'll no doubt discover that links, images, and sometimes files (for example, PDFs) will enhance your message or be useful to your readers. Inserting links, images, and files into your posts couldn't be easier with TypePad's editor, and we explain how to do it. We also provide instructions for inserting files using File Manager. The latter takes a little more effort, but we think it's worthwhile in the long run.

Inserting links using the Compose editor toolbar

Linking to other bloggers and sites is an important part of participating in the online community. Any time you want to share a link to a post (whether one of your own or from another site), a file, another blog, or somehow move your reader to another place (for example, to Amazon.com so they can see a product you're discussing), you need to use a link. TypePad makes inserting links into your post a breeze:

1. **Use the cursor to highlight the word(s) you want to use as your link.**

   See our advice on choosing link words in Chapter 1.

2. **Click the Link button on the Compose toolbar.**

   The Link button looks like a piece of chain link.

3. **Type the URL of your link in the Link URL text box.**

   As a shortcut, open the page you're linking to in another browser window or tab. Then you can copy (Ctrl+C for the PC; Command+C for the Mac) the URL from that window's browser and paste it (Ctrl+V for the PC; Command+V for the Mac) into the Link URL text box.

4. **Click to select Open in a new window.**

When you insert a link into your post, you have the option of opening that link in a new browser window or tab when a reader clicks it. We like to choose this option because, although it opens a new browser tab for the link, it keeps the current browser tab open to your site.

5. **(Optional) Type a brief description of your link, if you like.**

If you choose to include a link description, it does not appear in your article text. Instead, the description appears when a reader's cursor hovers over the link.

6. **Click OK.**

Linking generously to great posts by other bloggers is not only acceptable, but also encouraged. It builds goodwill with your blogging peers and benefits your readers by pointing them toward excellent content you've found elsewhere. It is extremely important to remember, however, that you should never cut and paste an entire post from another blogger on your blog. It is rude and illegal — it's a violation of copyright law. You can paste, at the very most, a few sentences of their post on your blog, but you must always be sure you make it clear that the words are someone else's, not your own. Any time you quote from someone else's post, link directly back to their blog, or (even better) directly to that particular post. For more on the topic of online copyright issues, visit Plagiarism Today (www.plagiarismtoday.com).

Inserting images using the Compose editor toolbar

Images add interest and depth to a post, underscoring your ideas with a visual punch. Also, remember that online reading is harder on the eyes than print reading. Using images to break up the text of your post offers readers' eyes a brief moment of rest.

To insert an image into a post, follow these instructions:

1. **Click inside the Body text box.**

If you've already written your post and know where you want to place your image, click to put the cursor where you want the image to appear.

2. **Click the Insert Image button.**

(The button is on the Compose toolbar and looks like a picture.) An Insert Image pop-up box appears.

3. **Get your image using one of these methods:**

   - Click the Browse button to search through your files for the image you'd like to use in your post.

   - Insert the image's URL, if you're using one from the Web.

   If you plan to insert a thumbnail gallery of multiple images, go ahead and choose all of them now.

4. **Click the Edit link in the Default box (listed under your images) to choose the image size and alignment.**

   The pop-up window expands to give you these options:

   - Choose whether to display one image or a thumbnail gallery of several images.

   - Use the drop-down arrow to choose how large the image is displayed within your post (image size).

   - Choose whether the post's text wraps around the image.

   - Choose whether the image links to the original (possibly larger) version when a reader clicks the image.

   - If you want, save these settings as your default image settings, by checking the appropriate box.

     The next time you insert an image, you can just click to select Default, and TypePad automatically applies those settings.

5. **Click the Insert Image button.**

   You see your image(s) in your post.

It's mighty tempting to find a picture or image online and use it in your post. Unfortunately, unless that image is royalty-free (and it will be tagged as such at a reputable site), it's a violation of copyright law for you to download it and use it without permission from the owner or artist. For more information about copyright, go to www.copyright.gov/help/faq. We explain how to find usable images on Flickr.com in Chapter 10.

Inserting documents using the Compose editor toolbar

Occasionally, you may want to offer your readers access to a document file (such as .pdf or .doc) that you've created on your computer. For example, if you're writing a post about creating a budget for a small business, you may want to offer a link to a sample budget in Microsoft Excel.

To include a download link for a document, follow these instructions:

1. **Click inside the Body text box where you'd like the link to appear.**

2. **Click the Insert File button on the Compose toolbar (the button looks like a document with a green arrow).**

   A pop-up window appears.

3. **Click the Browse button, and find the document you'd like to link to.**

4. **Click the Upload File button.**

   A new link appears in your post that says `Download [name of document]` (where `name of document` is the name of the document you're linking to).

Name the document you're using something descriptive that references its contents, because TypePad uses the name of the document in the link it creates. For example, name your document that describes the differences among dog breeds `dog_breeds.doc` instead of `dogs.doc`; a link that says `Download a list of dog breeds` is better than a link that says `Download dogs`.

Inserting files using File Manager

Any time you insert a file using the TypePad Compose editor toolbar (as shown in Figure 6-2), TypePad stores those files rather arbitrarily. For example, if you upload an image to your post via the Compose editor toolbar, that image is located at a URL similar to this one:

`http://typepadfordummies.typepad.com/.a/6a0115706537f9970c0120a56a4254970b-500wi`

Unfortunately, that kind of URL is hard to keep track of, and if you insert images into your posts frequently (we do!), it will be hard to find those files later if you need to reference them somewhere else on your blog or if you move your blog to another platform.

When you upload a file to File Manager (we explain how in Chapter 4), the item will have its own URL that reflects its placement in File Manager (instead of the arbitrary URL TypePad would assign it if you used the Insert button on the Compose toolbar). In the following examples, we've uploaded the same image two ways: using File Manager and using the Insert Image button.

File Manager URL: `http://typepadfordummies.typepad.com/type pad-for-dummies/images/castle.jpg`

TypePad URL: `http://typepadfordummies.typepad.com/.a/6a01157 06537f9970c0120a6c0802a970b-pi`

In the first example, we created a folder in File Manager called images and uploaded a picture of Cinderella's Castle from Walt Disney World. If we ever need to access that photo again, we know where it's located and can easily find it and insert it into another blog post.

In the second example, we used the Insert Image button from the Compose toolbar. The resulting URL is not intuitive and is not housed in File Manager. If we ever want to use that image again, we'll most likely have to reinsert it using the Insert Image button. This could be a problem if we no longer have the image on our hard drive or if we move our blog to another platform.

If you'd like more control of your filing structure so you can find your files easily, please review the topic of managing stored files in Chapter 4. Taking the time to upload your files into an intuitive filing system helps you find your stuff and makes it easier if you ever decide to migrate from TypePad (even if you're just upgrading to Movable Type). Instead of renaming all your image links, you can simply re-create your filing system on the new server or platform and move your files accordingly. You'll experience many fewer broken links or missing images. Uploading your files manually takes a few extra steps, but it's worth it in the long run.

Creating a link to a file using File Manager

The instructions for linking to podcasts, videos, or even documents are the same when you are uploading them to File Manager:

1. **Set up File Manager as suggested in the section on managing stored files in Chapter 4.**

   We suggest that you establish separate folders for images, podcasts, videos, and documents.

2. **Upload your file to the correct folder in File Manager.**

   See Chapter 4 for detailed instructions on how to upload files.

3. **Click the Link icon next to the file you want to reference.**

   A pop-up window appears with the HTML you'll need to make the link work.

4. **Copy this HTML and paste it into the HTML tab of the Compose editor.**

   Click back over to the Rich Text tab to preview how your link looks and make any changes. In particular, you may want to change the text of the link. You can do this by highlighting the text and typing the new text you want to use as the link text.

5. **(Optional) Preview your post to ensure that it appears correctly.**

6. **Publish your post as necessary.**

   You can save to draft, publish immediately, or set it to post at a future date.

Inserting an image using File Manager

Using File Manager to insert an image in your post instead of doing it using the Compose editor's toolbar requires you to use a little HTML. Don't worry — you use *very* little HTML, and the process is easy. These instructions explain how:

1. **Set up File Manager as suggested in the section on managing stored files in Chapter 4.**

   We suggest that you establish separate folders for images, podcasts, videos, and documents.

2. **Upload your file to the correct folder in File Manager.**

   See Chapter 4 for detailed instructions on how to upload files.

3. **Right-click the file name of the image you'd like to include in your post.**

   A menu appears.

4. **Choose Copy Link Location.**

   The URL for the image is saved to your clipboard.

5. **Paste the URL into the HTML tab of the Compose editor.**

   It should look something like this (but with your blog's info):

   ```
   http://yourblogname.typepad.com/blog_folder_name/images/image_name.jpg
   ```

6. **Edit that line to look like this:**

   ```
   <img src="http://yourblogname.typepad.com/blog_folder_name/image_
           name.jpg">
   ```

   You can read more about what that HTML code means and how it works in the section in Chapter 11 on how to include sidebar images on your blog.

7. **(Optional) Preview your post to ensure that it displays correctly.**

8. **Publish your post as necessary.**

   You can choose to save it as a draft, publish it immediately, or set it to post on a future date.

 You can align your image to the left or right of your text (and the text will wrap around it), or you can center your image. Just use these modifications to your HTML code:

Image aligned left (text wraps around the image):

```
<img style="float: left;" src= "http://yourblogname.typepad.com/blog_folder_
          name/images/image_name.jpg">
```

Image aligned right (text wraps around the image):

```
<img style="float: right;" src= "http://yourblogname.typepad.com/blog_folder_
            name/images/image_name.jpg">
```

Image centered (no text wrap):

```
<div align="center"><img src="http://yourblogname.typepad.com/blog_folder_name/
            images/image_name.jpg"></div>
```

Inserting video and audio files to your post

You can use the buttons on your Compose editor toolbar to easily share video or audio with your readers (see the buttons in Table 6-1). In Chapter 9, we fully address the subject of using multimedia in your blog.

Organizing Your Posts Using Categories

As we explain in Chapter 5, most bloggers use categories to organize content, making it easy for readers to browse your blog for related content. Also in Chapter 5, we show you how to use the links in the blog-level bar to edit or add to the default categories TypePad provides for all users. If you've already set up your categories the way you want them, it's simple to apply a category to the post you're writing. In the upper-right corner of the Compose editor, look for the box titled Categories, as shown in Figure 6-5.

After writing your post, click to select the boxes next to the names of the categories in which you'd like your post to appear (use the scroll bar to see them all). For your readers' convenience, choose as many categories as applicable. For example, if you were posting a review for a book about your favorite knitting patterns, you might choose both Books and Crafting as relevant categories (as shown in Figure 6-5).

In writing your post, you may discover that it doesn't fit it into any of your current categories. That's okay; you can either leave off the category altogether or (and this is more advisable) create a new, relevant category. To do this, you can either follow the steps we gave you in Chapter 5 or, more simply, click the Add a New Category link below the category box. Enter the name of the new category in the pop-up box that appears, and click Create.

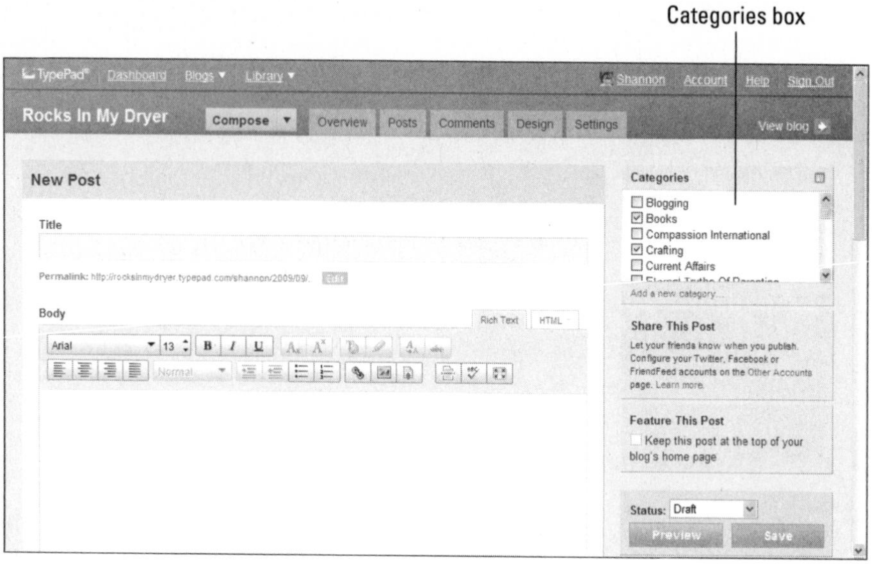

Categories box

Figure 6-5:
The
Categories
box in the
Compose
editor.

Be as specific as you can when naming categories, for your readers' convenience. Because there's no limit on the number of categories TypePad allows you to have, you might as well include as many as you think would be helpful. On the other hand, you don't want to be redundant. Having separate categories for, say, Food, Kitchen, and Recipes makes your category list less navigable.

Configuring Post Options

After you've written your post, you'll need to make a few decisions about how (and when) you want to it to appear. In this section, we explain the other features in the Compose editor so that you can control the timing of your post and the kind of feedback you'll allow on it.

Publishing, saving, or scheduling?

If you've written a post, you need to save it, of course. It's advisable to save your work often as you write, even when the post isn't yet finished. Fortunately, TypePad has an autosave feature that automatically saves your work. If you ever lose a post, try heading back to the Compose screen, where you will likely see a message (just below the blue blog-level bar) that you have an autosaved post. Click Recover, which should (we hope) restore your post from the last autosave.

The autosave feature is nice in an emergency, but you don't want to depend on it. Save your work, and do it often! Before you save, you have a decision to make: Are you ready to publish your post on your blog, or do you simply want to save it as a draft copy? At the bottom of the right sidebar in the Compose editor is a box that shows the status of your post (see Figure 6-6).

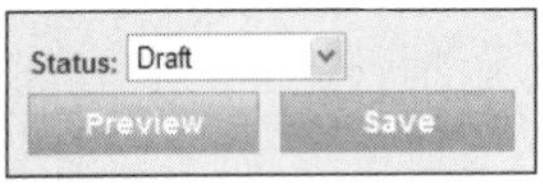

Figure 6-6:
The status box (set to Draft status) in the Compose editor.

Status: Draft

Preview   Save

In Figure 6-6, the status is set to Draft, which means that when this user clicks the Save button, the post is visible only to him, in his list of posts (see Chapter 5). The draft is not published on his blog. Choose the Draft option any time you're writing something that needs to be saved but is not ready for publication.

If you want to see how this post might look published on your blog, you can click the Preview button, below the status. Note that this option does not save or publish your work; it simply gives you a sneak peek of your work.

If you're ready to publish your post, use the drop-down menu in the status bar to change the option to Publish Now, as shown in Figure 6-7.

Figure 6-7:
The status box (set to Publish Now status) in the Compose editor.

Status: Publish Now

Preview   Publish

When you change the status to Publish Now, the buttons change to Preview and Publish (refer to Figure 6-7). Again, you can use the Preview button to see how the post will look when you publish it. The Publish button saves your post to your list of posts in the Dashboard and publishes it on the front page of your blog, ready for your readers' eyes.

Don't click Publish until you're sure your post is ready! You can always unpublish later by changing the status to Draft, but the change might not be reflected immediately, especially in feed readers. If you have any doubts about whether you're ready to publish, always choose Draft.

Even after you've published a post, you can still reenter the post to edit typos or change wording, and your saved updates will be reflected.

There is one more status option for your post: You can schedule it to post on a future date by choosing Publish On. (Note that this option is not available to TypePad users who have joined under the Micro plan.) When you click Publish On in the Status box, a small calendar appears, like the one shown in Figure 6-8.

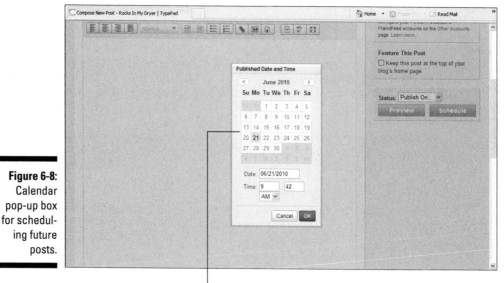

Figure 6-8:
Calendar
pop-up box
for schedul-
ing future
posts.

Calendar for scheduling posts

Use the arrow buttons to navigate through the calendar. Click the date (and double-check that the date you chose appears in the date field), set the time you want your post to publish, and then click OK. Your post is now saved and will publish on the date you requested. The post appears in the list of current posts (see Chapter 5) in sequential order, using the date you've scheduled it to appear, not the date on which you wrote it.

Changing the timestamp on your post

If you've written a post to be published in the future, and you've changed your mind about the date you want it to appear, simply reopen the post in the Compose screen (use the Posts tab to find it, as explained in Chapter 5). In the status bar, you'll see the date the post is scheduled to publish — this is referred to as a *timestamp*. To change the timestamp, click the date, and the calendar appears (refer to Figure 6-8). Simply choose the new date and click OK, and your post is rescheduled. If you don't want the article to post at all, you can change its status to Draft, as explained previously.

You can also change the timestamp to a currently published post in the same manner. It's probably not something you'll need to do very often, but if you do, simply click the date and change it to the date you'd prefer to have on the timestamp.

Displaying your comments

Occasionally, you may want to deviate from the usual way you allow your readers to interact with your post. If a post is generating an unusually high number of discourteous comments, for example, you may want to turn off or hide the comments for that post. Below the Body field in the Compose editor, look at the area titled Comments and TrackBacks. You may need to click the blue arrow next to the title Comments and TrackBacks to reveal this section, which looks like Figure 6-9.

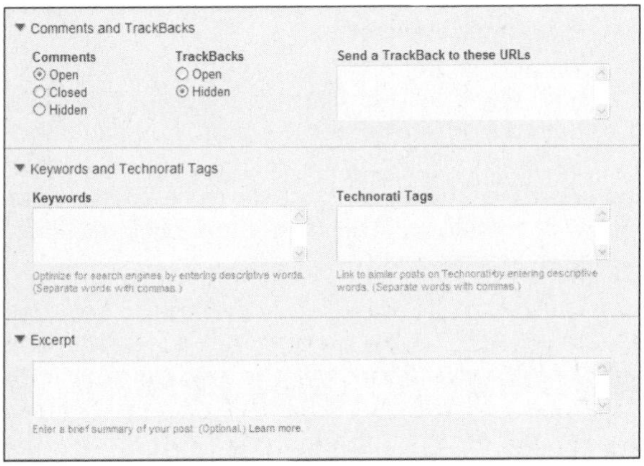

Figure 6-9: Comments and TrackBacks box in the Compose editor.

In this portion of the Compose screen, you have the option to adjust the kind of feedback you receive for this post. To keep the comments open and accessible (which is most likely your default setting), click to select the Open button.

To keep the comments section viewable but prevent further comments from being added (which you might do, for example, in the event of a contest or giveaway with a specific ending date), click to select the Closed option. TypePad shows a small message (it reads `The comments to this entry are closed`) at the bottom of your comment section.

If you do not want the comments section to appear at all, click to select the last option, Hidden. If you choose this option, there will be no Comments link at the bottom of your published post for readers to click and, therefore, no comment form for them to fill out.

Note that any changes you make in this section are applicable only to this particular post. If you want to change your default posting settings to apply to all your posts, you'll need to do so in the Setting tab in the blue blog-level navigation bar — but we discuss all aspects of comment management more thoroughly in Chapter 7.

Using trackbacks

Trackbacks are a useful way to let another blog or Web site know that you're linking to them or discussing them on your blog. You can send a trackback (if you're writing about another blog), or you can receive a trackback (if another blog is writing about you). It's a virtual heads-up, if you will. The trackback includes a link to the post discussing your blog so you can go see what the post says and maybe leave a comment.

We explain how to send trackbacks in Chapter 7, but for now, just know that if you open the Comments and TrackBacks section, you can choose to use trackbacks (click to select Open) or hide trackbacks (click to select Hide). If you're receiving many trackbacks that appear to be spam-related, you can hide trackbacks for a while and then turn them back on. That's usually enough to encourage the spammers to move on.

Setting keywords for your post

Below the Body field in the Compose editor, look at the area titled Keywords and Technorati Tags. You may need to click the blue arrow next to that title to reveal this section.

Assigning keywords and Technorati tags is a way to help search engines find your blog and determine whether its content is relevant to search queries. Technorati (www.technorati.com) is a blog search engine. If you're interested in seeing what other bloggers are writing regarding a specific topic, you can use keywords to search Technorati, and the site will return a list of blogs with relevant content. The difference between Technorati and a search engine such as Google is that Technorati searches only blogs, but Google indexes, or includes, everything (blogs, Web sites, video, and so on). See Chapters 1 and 5 for advice on how to choose keywords for SEO.

Customizing a post excerpt

Below the Body field in the Compose editor, look at the area titled Excerpt. You may need to click the blue arrow next to that title to reveal this section. Any time one of your blog posts is referenced in a feed reader or search engine, that post is accompanied by an excerpt, or short summary, of the post. Usually, this excerpt is pulled automatically from the first few sentences of your post (if your RSS feeds are set to short excerpts; you can find out whether you offer short excerpts or full posts via RSS by choosing Settings⇨Feeds from the blog-level bar).

If you'd rather have a say in how your blog's excerpt reads, you can type a custom excerpt in the Excerpt text box. Be aware, however, that typing a custom excerpt does not guarantee that search engines will use it; sometimes, search engines still pull excerpts directly from the content. Feed readers, though, use your custom excerpt, and what you write here may be more descriptive than a teaser from the actual post.

Featuring blog posts

Most bloggers have their blogs structured so that the most recent post is the one that appears at the top of their blog. Sometimes, though, especially in the case of an important announcement, bloggers need a post to remain at the top of their page for an extended time. A *featured post* (sometimes referred to as a *sticky post)* is one that remains at the top of the blog's front page, with newer posts appearing below it.

It's easy to turn a regular post into a featured post. In the Feature This Post section on the right side of the Compose screen, simply click to select the box. When you save the post, it is featured at the top of your blog until you deselect it as a featured post. (You can unfeature it by revisiting the post in the Compose screen, deselecting the Feature This Post box, and then saving. Featuring a different post also unfeatures any previously featured post.)

Featured posts are handy when you need them, but you'll probably want to use this tool sparingly. Readers are accustomed to seeing the most recent post at the top of your screen, and if you deviate from this too often, it can be confusing. Save your featured posts for when you really need to use them, such as to explain a change in your format or to announce some big news.

Using the Share This Post option

Below your list of categories in the right sidebar, you'll see an option to Share This Post. This is simply a way to let friends and peers on your social networks know that you've published a new blog post. If you've set up your TypePad account to include your other social media accounts (for example, Facebook or Twitter), you have the option to select which networks TypePad should send an alert to when you publish new content. After an account is selected, TypePad sends a link (via a Bit.ly link — discussed more thoroughly in Chapter 10) to the account that points back to your most recent post. The Bit.ly link helps you track who is clicking over to your blog from which social networks. You can track these stats from your blog's Overview tab. For help linking your TypePad account to your other social media accounts, see Chapter 4.

Editing Existing Posts

Most bloggers have several draft posts saved on their Dashboard. (Some of us have more drafts than published posts!) Any time you want to edit a post, visit the Posts tab in the blue blog-level bar. Your posts appear in the order in which they are published, scheduled to publish, or (if they're still drafts) the date on which they were written. Click the title of the post you want to edit, and you'll be taken directly back to the same Compose screen you used to write it in the first place. When you're finished, save the post as a draft or publish it.

Understanding the Difference between Posts and Pages

A post is the meat and potatoes of your blog. A post contains the story or information you're sharing with your readers. When you write a post, it shows up on the front page of your blog (usually at the top) and is pushed down the page as new posts are published. Posts are also listed in the Archives or Recent Posts link if you have those options in your sidebar.

A page is similar to a post in that

- ✔ You create a page in the TypePad Compose editor.

- ✔ Pages have the same design as posts (your TypePad theme is still in place, your blog's banner still shows, and so on).

- ✔ You can include multimedia elements such as video, images, and audio as well as text and links in a page.

Just like a post, a page has its own permalink. To share a page with your readers, though, you have to link directly to the page with a sidebar or navigation bar link or from within a post.

A page, although similar to a post, does have a few differences. A blog page does not publish to the front page of your blog, nor does it show up in a list of your archives or recent posts or in your RSS feed.

A page usually contains information that changes infrequently but needs to be readily available. For instance, you may use a page to display your About Me information (see Chapter 4). Or you may use a page to keep track of and share the list of books you're reading this year. A page is essentially information that you want to share with readers, but you don't need it to appear in the list of current or past blog posts.

To compose a page for your blog, follow these instructions:

1. **Click the down arrow next to the yellow Compose button, and select New Page.**

   A new page appears in your Compose editor.

2. **Compose your page as you would compose a regular blog post.**

   Don't forget, just like with a post, you can include text, images, video, and audio files (see Chapter 9 for instructions on how to use multimedia with your TypePad blog).

3. **To publish your page, click Save.**

   Unlike posts, pages can't be scheduled for later posting, so you don't see the Schedule button.

Be sure to make a note of your page's permalink so you can link to this page in your sidebar or from within another post.

That's it! You now know how to use the TypePad Compose editor to write a blog post. You can format your text, insert images into your post for interest, and create a page for extra information you want to share.

Remember, though, the important part is just starting. Trust us when we tell you that your posts improve the more you write — so get out there and get started! Also check out the sidebar information we include in this chapter for advice on what makes a great blog post.

Chapter 7

Interacting on Your Blog

*U*nlike other forms of writing, blogging is, at its core, a sort of dialogue between blogger and reader. No other venue offers writers such quick access to engaging a readership or puts such instant information and entertainment at a reader's disposal.

To many bloggers, receiving comments is an important part of the overall blogging experience. It's an instant dose of affirmation that what you've written has been read. Additionally, comments help build a community around your blog. The discussion generated in the comment section engages your readers and encourages them to come back. It stands to reason, then, that you'll want to manage those comments efficiently to invite people to contribute their thoughts.

In this chapter, we examine TypePad's commenting features, showing you how to manage existing comments and how to encourage your readers to leave even more. We tackle the not-altogether-pleasant subject of blocking commenters. And we discuss the topic of trackbacks — how to manage them at your own blog and how to leave them at others.

Don't let the subject of blog commenting discourage you. As much as we all enjoy the affirming feedback, it will take consistent work and nurturing of your blog before regular comments begin rolling in. Give it time.

Inviting Users to Comment on Your Blog

Ask various bloggers, and they'll probably tell you that they've experienced a curious phenomenon of blogging: A post that was an effortless, spontaneous afterthought will unexpectedly garner meaty and enthusiastic comments. Likewise, a painstaking, heartfelt post might sit completely ignored by commenters. If (or when!) it happens to you, shake your head and have a good laugh — chalk it up to being one of the great blogging mysteries!

Although it's true that comment patterns may be somewhat unpredictable, you can do a few things to encourage readers to step out of the woodwork:

- ✔ **Include a specific question in your post.** Pointedly ask readers what they think about your topic — they may just tell you!

- ✔ **Engage with readers in the comment section.** Thanks to threaded commenting (more on that in a moment), you can set up a direct and easy-to-follow dialogue with your commenters in the comment section. This may encourage them to comment more freely.

- ✔ **Respond to your comments.** If you choose not to respond to comments directly in the comment section, consider sending the commenter a private e-mail (TypePad makes this easy to do; we tackle this later in the chapter). If you receive a large volume of comments, it's unreasonable to expect that you could respond to every one. Respond to the ones you can — and it may eventually pan that every commenter receives a personal response from you.

- ✔ **Keep it simple.** If your readers have to jump through numerous hoops to leave a comment, they're less likely to do so. It may be appealing to ward off spammers with *CAPTCHA* (randomly generated word codes), but readers tend not to like that extra step.

- ✔ **Choose your topics wisely.** Again, it's not always easy to predict what topics will make your commenters speak up. But if a news story or an issue that's especially relevant to your readers pops up, offer your take — and ask for theirs. Let your blog be a place where people feel like they can be heard.

Avoid the temptation to beg for comments. Just like with traffic, garner comments because you've earned them with your good content, not because you tried to implement gimmicks. Occasionally doing a specific call-out for comments is fine, but if you do it every time, you might come across as needy.

Standard Commenting versus TypePad Connect

TypePad offers users two commenting formats. The first is the standard commenting format — the one that is automatically installed on your blog when you first sign up for a TypePad account. The second is a function called TypePad Connect — you have to manually select to apply it to your blog (more on that in a minute).

The basic functions of the two commenting formats are similar — both require that you make some decisions about the settings for the comment section. In this section, we explain the commenting features offered by both formats, as well as those that are unique to each one. This should help you determine which commenting format would work best for your blog.

For more information on TypePad Connect, visit www.typepad.com/connect. This commenting interface is available for installation by non-TypePad bloggers as well.

Options offered by both

First, let's walk through the features you'll find in both the standard commenting format and TypePad Connect.

Sign in

Either format lets you designate whether or not you will allow anonymous comments. If you do require that readers sign in, they'd be able to use their TypePad, Facebook, or Twitter account (if they don't have any of those, they'd have to offer some other form of identification, such as an e-mail address). It's a matter of preference — a few readers may bristle at this, but most would likely accept it as a standard blogging practice.

Comment moderation

Comment moderation means that new comments are not instantly published; instead, the blog owner must manually approve them first.

Autoclose

Autoclosing comments means that posts older than a designated length of time will automatically stop accepting new comments. You may want to do this to ward off spammers (who often seem inclined to leave their spam on older posts) and to keep the commenting energies focused on the freshest, most recent dialogues taking place at your blog.

CAPTCHA

CAPTCHA is a randomly generated verification code that keeps spammers from inundating you with junk comments. A CAPTCHA verification screen looks something like the one pictured in Figure 7-1.

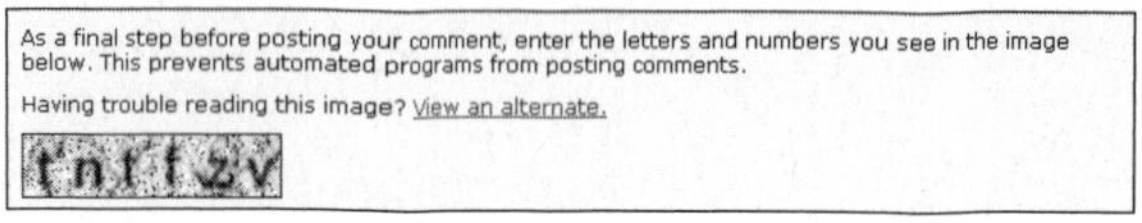

Figure 7-1:
A CAPTCHA
comment-
verification
module.

As a final step before posting your comment, enter the letters and numbers you see in the image below. This prevents automated programs from posting comments.

Having trouble reading this image? View an alternate.

Both TypePad commenting formats give you access to this tool, but you would want to implement it only if you are completely overrun with spam. (If you are, you should immediately submit a help ticket to TypePad — it has a good track record with spam management and is serious about not letting such comments through.) Most likely, any spam comments are going to be caught in TypePad's AntiSpam service (see antispam.typepad.com), meaning this CAPTCHA comment-verification screen will likely serve only to give your readers a frustrating extra step.

Allow HTML

If you choose to allow HTML, it means that bloggers can include simple HTML tags to give their comment a little pizzazz. For example, if you allow HTML, a commenter who says "I <i>love</i> this post!" will have their comment translated to "I *love* this post!" It's a good idea to give your readers this option.

Auto-link URL

With URL auto-links enabled, any commenter who leaves a full Web address in your comment will have that address automatically inserted as a hyperlink. It's an easy way to encourage the sharing of ideas among readers in the comment section.

Sort comment order

Both commenting formats let you decide in what order you'd like your comments displayed. The most common format is to post the oldest first, giving readers a beginning-to-ending look at the dialogue.

Userpics

If you enable the display of userpics, it means commenters with a TypePad account will have their picture appear next to their comment. It gives the comment section a more personalized feel.

Number of comments per page

In either commenting format, you select how many comments to display. Choosing a lower number means your page might load a little faster (especially for readers with slow connections). Choosing a higher number means your readers can follow the discussion with less clicking.

E-mail notification

One of the handiest commenting features (available in both formats) is the ability to have new comments e-mailed to you. This gives you instant access to your newest comments without having to sign in to the Dashboard. For many bloggers, enabling this option is a streamlined way to manage your community.

If you enable this option, your comments will be e-mailed to the e-mail address you have on file with your TypePad account.

Accepting or rejecting new comments

Although most bloggers encourage the leaving of comments, some bloggers prefer not to receive them. If you want to make it your standard setting not to allow comments on new posts or pages, both formats allow you to do so.

If you expect you'll allow comments on *some* posts (but not all of them), use the Compose Editor (see Chapter 6) to make the choice about including comments on each individual post or page.

How to leave a trackback

You manage your own incoming trackbacks from the Dashboard, but you may want to leave trackbacks for other bloggers as well. A trackback, as you may recall from Chapter 6, is a little ping that let's another blogger know you've written about him or her. To send a trackback, follow these steps:

1. **Grab the trackback URL you want to use (this is different from the URL of the post).**

   For a TypePad blogger, you can find the trackback URL at the top of the blogger's comment section, labeled Trackback URL for This Entry. Copy that URL, because you'll need it in a second.

2. **Write your post, linking (in the traditional way) back to the other blogger.**

At the end of your post, look in the Compose editor at the section below your post. The section is titled Comments and Trackbacks.

3. **Click the down arrow to expand the Comments and Trackbacks section.**

4. **In the box labeled Send a Trackback to These URLs, paste the trackback URL you copied in Step 1.**

5. **Save your post.**

   The other blogger will now receive notification of your trackback.

Remember that not all bloggers accept trackbacks. If you're looking around (unsuccessfully) for another blogger's trackback URL, he or she may not have the feature enabled.

Accept or reject trackbacks

A trackback (also discussed in Chapter 6) is a virtual nudge to other bloggers, giving them notice that you've blogged about them at your site (see the sidebar in this chapter). It's up to you if you want to accept them. They're a handy tool, but they tend to be an easy spam target.

What makes them different

Now that you've seen the basic functionalities allowed by both TypePad's standard commenting format and TypePad Connect, you need to know what makes them different.

Threaded comments

Threaded comments (a commenting setup that allows readers to respond directly to a comment, designated by a small indentation below the original comment) are available only in TypePad Connect. This is a helpful option, especially if you have a blog where robust conversation often takes place in the comment section.

An example of how threaded comments look is shown in Figure 7-2. You can see the indentation under the comment the reader is responding to. This threaded format makes it easier for others to reply to specific comments or follow a direct conversation (especially if you've enabled userpics).

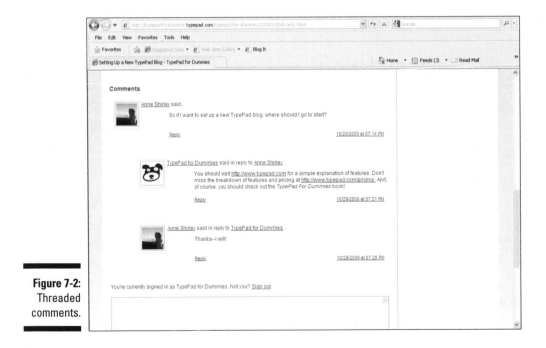

Figure 7-2:
Threaded
comments.

List (or unthreaded) comments have no indentations, as shown in Figure 7-3 — this can make it a little harder to follow the dialogue.

E-mailed responses posted in comment section

Although both commenting formats allow you to receive your comments via e-mail, TypePad Connect (not the default commenting format) gives you handy additional e-mail functionality. When bloggers receive a specific question in their comment section, they are often left wondering whether it's most efficient to reply to the commenter via e-mail or in the comment section. TypePad Connect allows you to do both at the same time. When a comment is e-mailed to you, replying to it will both send an e-mail directly to the commenter *and* post your answer in the comment section (visible to other readers). This feature can be an efficient time-saver.

Replying from the comment section

Still one more feature offered only by TypePad Connect is the ability to respond directly from your comment section. If you're scrolling through, reading your comments, and you see a comment that needs a response, click the small Reply link just below the comment (as shown in Figure 7-4).

When you click this link, your response is posted (in threaded format, if you've enabled it) directly on your blog, *and* it's e-mailed to the commenter.

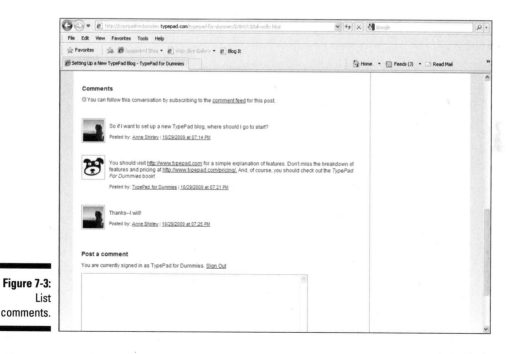

Figure 7-3:
List
comments.

Figure 7-4:
The Reply
link below
a TypePad
Connect
comment.

TypePad for Dummies said...

Drink lots of fluids! I hope your family gets to feeling better really soon. (Thank goodness for DVRs, right?)

Reply   *Thursday, October 29, 2009 at 09:38 PM*

Reply link

Comment sharing through social media

So far, we've told you about the options offered only in TypePad Connect, but there's at least one significant function that may make TypePad's standard commenting format appealing to you. Users of the standard commenting format can give readers the option to publish the comments they leave on your blog to their own Twitter and/or Facebook feeds.

If you enable this feature on the Settings tab (see next section), your readers will see the option shown in Figure 7-5 in the comment section.

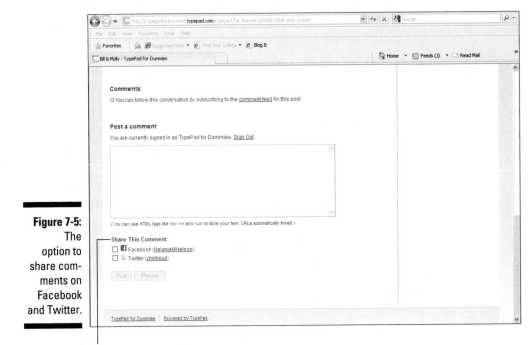

Figure 7-5:
The
option to
share com-
ments on
Facebook
and Twitter.

Comment-sharing option

To share his or her comments on another social media network, a commenter would simply select the appropriate box below your comment field (as shown in Figure 7-5) and then click the Post button. Her comment would then appear in her Facebook or Twitter feed or both (depending on which boxes she selected), along with a link to your original post.

Your readers do not need a TypePad account to participate in this social media comment sharing. If they sign in to your comment section using their Facebook or Twitter ID, they'll see the same comment-sharing options available at the end of the post. (For more on integrating social media with your TypePad account, see Chapter 10.)

Weigh your options, and decide whether TypePad Connect or the standard commenting format works best for you. Both offer powerful features, so you really can't go wrong.

Establishing Settings for Your Desired Commenting Option

After you've decided which of the two commenting formats suits you, you need to adjust your comment settings. To do this, you'll need to get to the Settings tab in the blue blog-level navigation bar. From the Dashboard, click the name of the blog in question. When the blog-level bar appears, choose the Settings tab, shown in Figure 7-6.

(Note the tab called Comments, also shown in Figure 7-6. This is where you can see a listing of all the comments you've received. We get to that tab later in the chapter. For now, we'll use the Settings tab.)

Look for the blue menu bar that appears on the left side of the screen. Click the Comments button, and you should see a screen that looks like the one in Figure 7-7.

Configuring settings for the standard commenting format

Unless you've already enabled TypePad Connect, the page shown in Figure 7-7 is the settings page for the standard commenting format — it's the one TypePad will use by default unless you specifically choose otherwise.

Comments tab   Settings tab

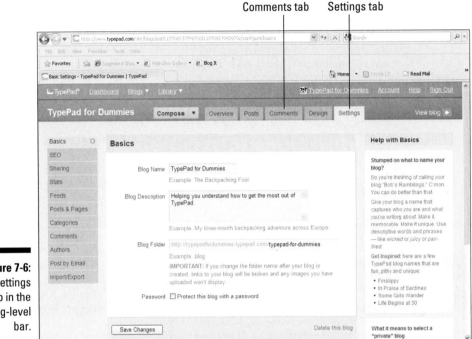

Figure 7-6:
The Settings
tab in the
blog-level
bar.

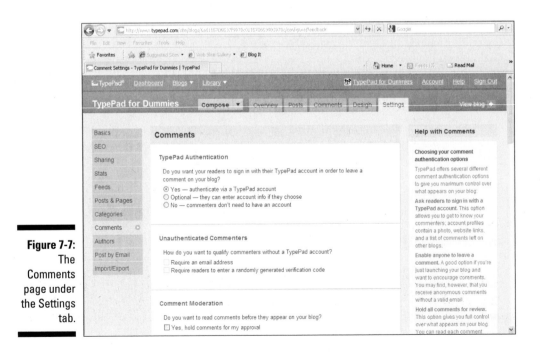

Figure 7-7:
The
Comments
page under
the Settings
tab.

If you've decided to keep the standard commenting format enabled on your blog, simply scroll down through the page shown in Figure 7-7. Refer to the previous section in this chapter for an explanation of each of the functions listed, and apply whatever settings will work best for you and your readers.

Configuring settings for TypePad Connect

If you've decided that TypePad Connect is the commenting format you prefer, you need to scroll down to the bottom of the page shown in Figure 7-7. At the bottom of the page, you have an option like the one shown in Figure 7-8.

Click the designated link, and TypePad Connect will be installed on your blog. If you change your mind and want to revert to the standard commenting format, look for the link at the bottom of the settings page, which reads Disable TypePad Connect Comments.

With TypePad Connect installed, you'll need to make your settings preferences by choosing Settings➪Comments Page. The page will look similar to the one in Figure 7-7, but your setting options will be worded a little differently and will be in a different order. Refer to the list of TypePad's commenting features explained earlier in this chapter.

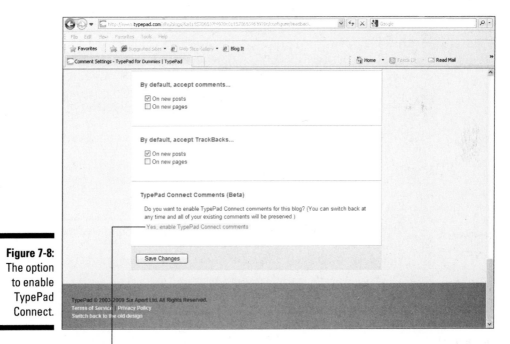

Figure 7-8:
The option
to enable
TypePad
Connect.

Click for TypePad Connect

Managing Existing Comments

Any time a new comment is left at your blog, it will join the list of comments in the Comments tab in the blue blog-level bar (refer to Figure 7-6). Click the Comments tab, and you should see a page that looks similar to Figure 7-9.

Taking action with your comments

When you click the drop-down button to the right of each comment (and designated in Figure 7-9), you have four actions you can take on that particular comment:

- ✔ **Publish:** If you've enabled comment moderation in the Settings tab, click this link to approve and publish each new comment. If you've previously unpublished a comment for some reason, you can click this option to republish it.

- ✔ **Unpublish:** If you've received a comment that you want to save in your account but make unviewable by other commenters, click the Unpublish button in the drop-down menu.

- ✔ **Delete:** If you want to delete a comment, click this button, but do so with caution — the action can't be undone. Unless you are positive you want the comment wiped out, your best bet might be unpublishing instead of deleting.

- ✔ **Mark as Spam:** Clicking this option identifies the comment as junk mail, which helps "train" TypePad's AntiSpam feature in how it filters spam at your blog. You're doing yourself (and other TypePad users) a service when you mark spam — honing the spam filter benefits us all.

In addition to the drop-down menu to the right of each comment, you can click the links below a comment:

- ✔ **Reply:** Clicking Reply takes you directly to the comment section, where you can leave a reply comment.

- ✔ **Edit:** Want to edit an existing comment? Click the Edit link, and you are taken to a page where you can make edits to the comment in question. If you don't have threaded comments, you might use this option to leave your own response directly on the comment needing a response.

- ✔ **View:** Clicking View takes you to the comment section, where you can see that particular comment in action.

Drop-down Action menu

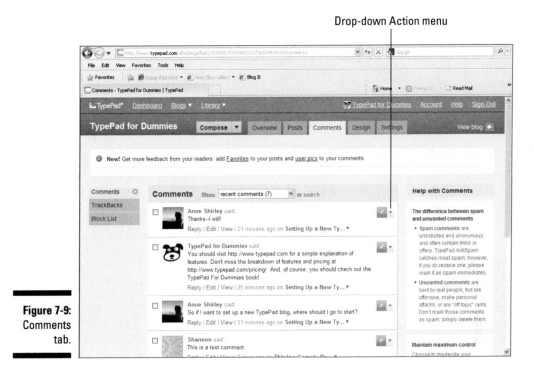

Figure 7-9:
Comments
tab.

Taking action with trackbacks

In the blue menu bar to the left of the Comments tab (refer to Figure 7-9), click the Trackbacks link. You're taken to a page that looks nearly identical to Figure 7-7, except that it lists the trackbacks you've received instead of comments. You have the same options (via the same drop-down menu) to publish, unpublish, delete, or mark as spam.

Blocking comments

It's a hard call for a blogger: choosing to block a particular commenter from leaving more comments at your site. It's a step most bloggers do not take lightly, but you may encounter times when it's necessary. If a commenter repeatedly stops by your blog for the sole purpose of personal attack or off-topic rants, it's *your* prerogative as the blog owner to block him or her.

To take this step, click the Block List link on the left side of the Comments tab (refer to Figure 7-9). The screen shown in Figure 7-10 appears.

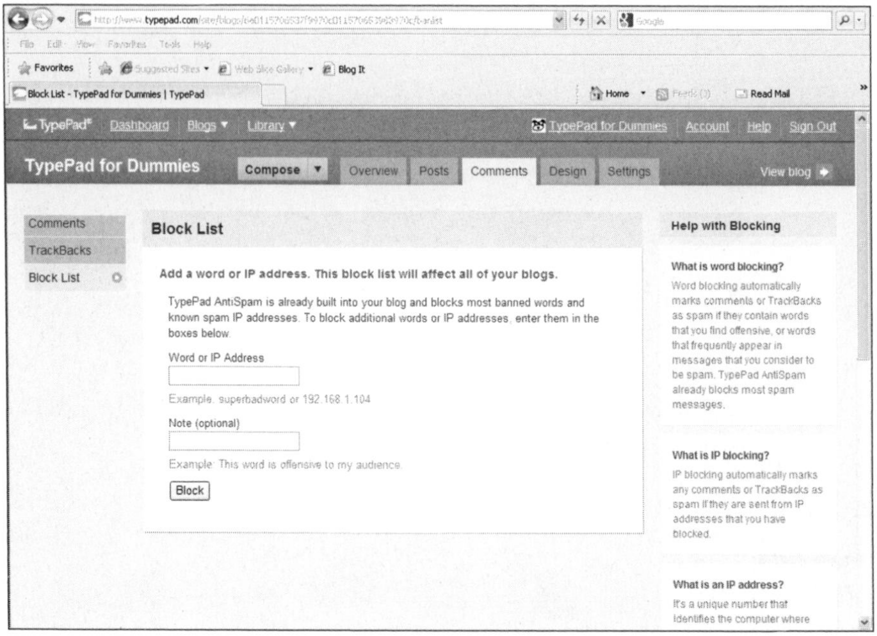

Figure 7-10:
The Block
List screen.

In the appropriate field, enter the IP address for the commenter you want
to block. (You can find the commenter's IP address by clicking the Edit link
under the commenter's name. When the Edit Comment screen appears, look
for the IP address on the right side of the page, under Additional Info.) When
you're finished, click the Block button.

You can also block comments containing certain words. TypePad's AntiSpam
feature automatically flags certain offensive words, sending them straight
to spam. But if you find a troublesome word getting through, enter it in the
appropriate field. When you're finished, click Block.

Use the Note field, if you want, to leave yourself a reminder about why this
word or IP address was blocked (such as "offensive word" or "commenter
sends political hate mail"). This field is optional.

You can block only an IP address. This will not prevent a difficult commenter
from leaving a comment using another computer at another location. Also
remember that although you can block an IP address from leaving a comment,
you cannot block the address from *viewing* your blog — this feature is not currently offered by TypePad.

Replying to your readers' comments

It's a good blogging practice to respond to as many of your readers' comments as is reasonable (see Chapter 18). The easiest way to do this is to have your comments e-mailed to you.

If you have the Emailed Comments option enabled, simply respond to the comment e-mail when it arrives in your inbox. In TypePad's standard commenting format, your response will go directly back to the commenter. In TypePad Connect, your response will go to the commenter *and* will be posted in your comment section — be sure you don't forget about this and say something too personal!

If you do not have the Emailed Comments option enabled, replying takes an extra step or two. One way is to respond directly in the comment section, leaving a comment of your own. If you want to reply via e-mail, pull up the Comments tab (refer to Figure 7-9). For the comment needing a response, click the Edit link. Copy the commenter's e-mail address, and paste it in a new e-mail.

Enjoy this communication with your commenters, whether it's via e-mail, Twitter, or the comment section. Most bloggers will tell you that the interaction with readers is a big part of the joy of blogging!

Part III

Adding Useful Elements to Your TypePad Blog

The 5th Wave   By Rich Tennant

"Look into my blog page Ms. Carruthers. Look deep into its rotating spiral, spinning, spinning, pulling you deeper into its vortex, deeper...deeper..."

In this part . . .

Ready to polish your blog? This part of the book points you toward some helpful tools to enhance your TypePad experience — tools such as multimedia, TypeLists, and social media integration. We also walk you through the fundamentals of TypePad blog design, showing you how to get just the look you want.

Chapter 8

Using TypeLists and Widgets

Most blogs have *sidebars* (the vertical columns on the sides of your main content column), and you'll display some important information there. What you choose to put in your sidebars has an effect on your blog's readability and usefulness. Many bloggers use their sidebars as navigation — they include links to different parts of their own blog or to other Web sites or showcase extra information (maybe what they're reading for next month's book club). As you find out in this chapter, TypeLists and widgets are easy ways to populate your sidebar.

As you consider whether to use TypeLists or widgets on your sidebar, it's important to note that there is a key difference in how TypePad archives them. If you remove a TypeList from your sidebar, the TypeList is still in your Library, so you can republish it to your sidebar later. If you remove a widget, it is deleted. If you decide you want to republish that widget to your sidebar, you have to reinstall it from the host site (we show you how to do that later in this chapter).

This chapter is closely related to the information in Chapter 11, which is all about using TypePad themes. The way you organize and present information in your sidebars visually affects any design you ultimately choose to implement. As you find out how to apply TypeLists and widgets, keep in mind that their ultimate aim is to make your blog more user-friendly for both you and your readers. In other words, you don't *have* to fill up your sidebars to the brim (and from a design standpoint, you really shouldn't). Choose the tools that serve your purpose, and ignore the ones that don't.

Understanding the Different TypeLists

Any time you want to add something to a TypePad sidebar, you'll do it using a TypeList, a simple yet powerful tool that is a much-loved feature among TypePad loyalists. A *TypeList* is TypePad's way of organizing sidebar information without requiring you to mess with your blog's template code. TypeLists allow you to display simple HTML (such as a text link to another blog) or complex coding (such as a search field) anywhere in your sidebar(s), all without ever having to alter your template code — everything happens behind the scenes.

TypePad uses four kinds of TypeLists. The kind of information you want to share with your readers determines which TypeList you use:

- ✔ **Link TypeList:** This TypeList allows you to post text links in your sidebar. You might, for example, use a Link TypeList to display your *blogroll* (the list of blogs you most frequently visit). You might also use it to create a "Best Of" section in your sidebar, pointing your readers to the favorite posts you've written. This kind of TypeList has endless applications.

- ✔ **Notes TypeList:** This is the TypeList you'll use when you'd like to include more complex code (whether written by you or a third party) in your sidebar (for example, a search field or an image). Any time you see a TypePad blog that has a graphic image in its sidebar (such as ad space), it has probably been placed there via a Notes TypeList.

  TypePad also has an Embed Your Own HTML widget in the Design portion of the Dashboard that does the same thing as a Notes TypeList. You can choose Design➪Content➪Categories (Widget)➪Modules (Embed Your Own HTML) to find that widget. See the section in this chapter titled "Using the Embed Your Own HTML widget."

- ✔ **Books TypeList:** Are you an avid reader looking for an easy way to share what you're reading, what you've read in the past, or just a list of your favorite books? You can use the Books TypeList for this. It's similar to a Links TypeList, but it has the additional functionality of allowing you to include your personal book ratings.

- ✔ **Album TypeList:** Want to share your love of music with your readers? The Album TypeList (similar to the Books TypeList) allows you to share everything from individual songs to entire albums (including how you rate them) with your readers.

Creating New TypeLists for Your Blog

Your TypeLists are stored in the Library, which you can find by clicking the Library link in the green account-level bar. Choose TypeLists from the drop-down menu, and you'll see a screen that looks like Figure 8-1.

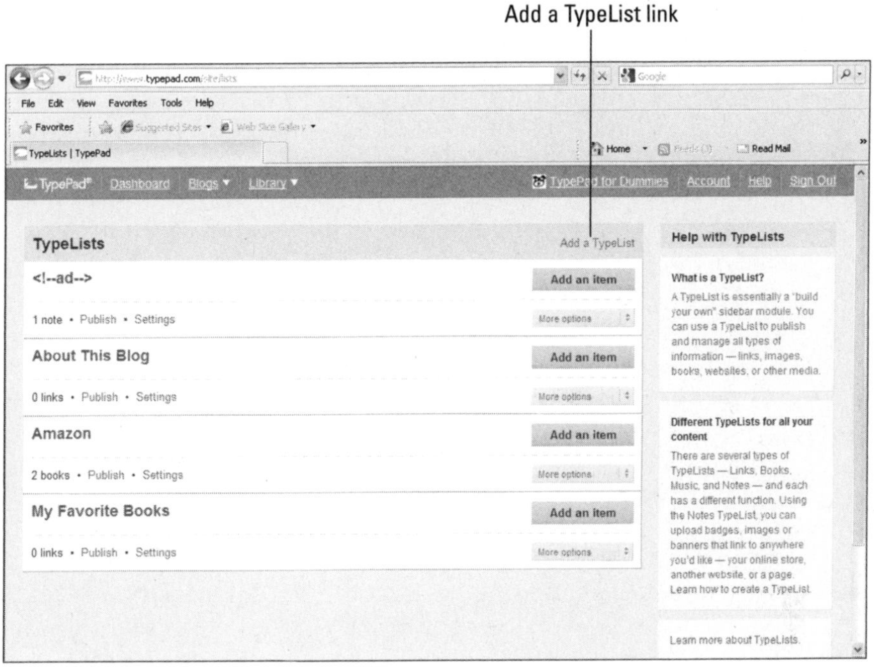

Add a TypeList link

Figure 8-1:
The
TypeLists
Library
page.

On this page, you see a complete list of all the TypeLists you've ever created for your account. If you have more than one TypePad blog in your account, you'll see all your TypeLists, from all your blogs, listed here. To create a new TypeList, simply click the Add a TypeList link, as designated in Figure 8-1.

This takes you to the Add a TypeList page, as shown in Figure 8-2.

The first item on this page asks you what kind of list you want to create. Using the drop-down menu, choose which of the four TypeLists suits your needs best. The specific steps for TypeList creation vary depending on which one you choose, so let's walk through each one.

If you want to create a list but do not want the list's title to be visible on your blog, name the list this way: `<!--InsertNameHere-->`, changing `InsertNameHere` to the name you want to use, of course. The characters on either side of the TypeList title ensure that the title is not visible to readers. This trick works with any TypeList.

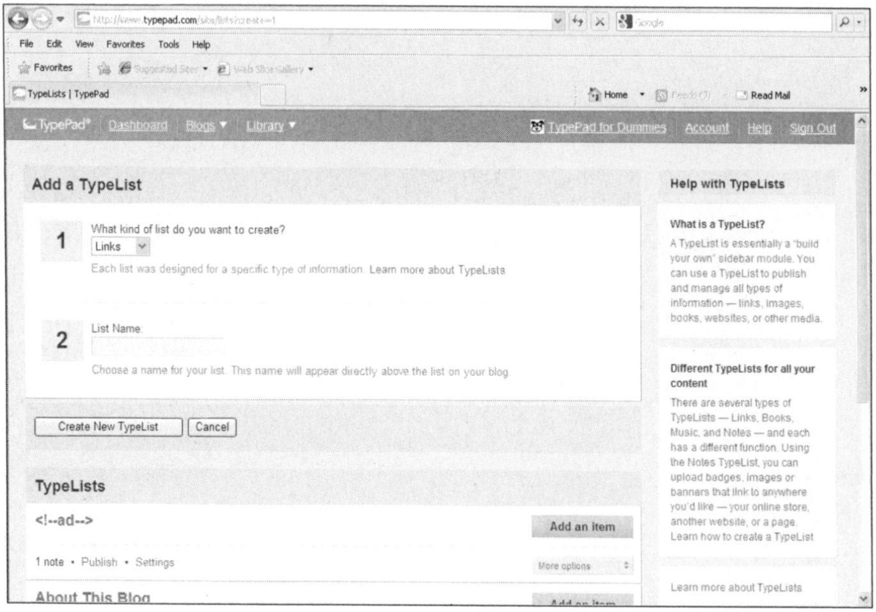

Figure 8-2:
Add a
TypeList
page.

Creating a Links TypeList

If you need a Links TypeList, follow these steps:

1. **From the TypeLists Library (refer to Figure 8-1), click Add a TypeList.**

   This takes you to the Add a TypeList page (refer to Figure 8-2).

2. **Choose Links from the drop-down menu.**

3. **Name your TypeList in the List Name field.**

   Note that the name you enter will appear on your blog, just above the list. See our tip in the preceding section if you'd like to hide the name of your list so that it doesn't appear in your blog's sidebar.

4. **Click the Create New TypeList button.**

   The Add Link page appears, as shown in Figure 8-3. Note that the name of the TypeList (in this example, My Favorite Soccer Sites) appears in the blue blog-level navigation bar.

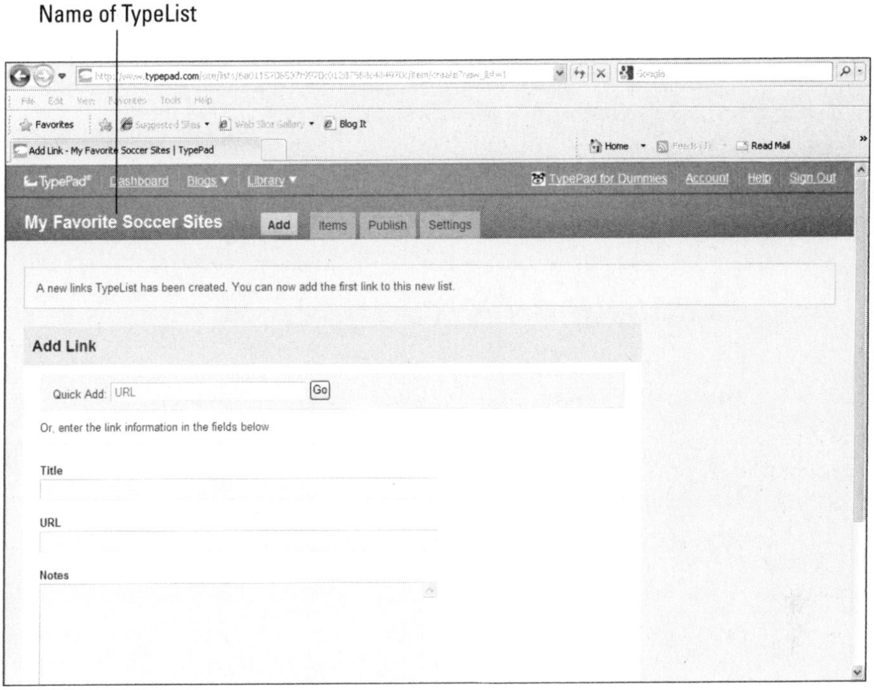

Name of TypeList

Figure 8-3:
Add Link
page.

5. **Add a link to your TypeList.**

    You can add a link to your Links TypeList in two ways:

    • Enter the URL in the Quick Add field (see Figure 8-3) and click Go. TypePad magically finds the title of the blog or Web site associated with the URL you type and populates the Title and URL fields in the Add Link page. (You can edit these fields later, if you like.)

    • Fill in the Title and the URL fields yourself. Note that whatever you put in the Title field is what readers will see listed in your sidebar.

6. **(Optional) Type a description of the link in the Notes field.**

    Depending on the settings you determine for your TypeList (we discuss your options later in this chapter), whatever you type in the Notes field may appear in your sidebar. Allowing your notes to appear in the sidebar is one way to offer a brief explanation of the link.

7. Click Save Changes.

A page appears that lists all the items you've added to this Links TypeList. To add another item, click the yellow Add button in the blue menu bar or use the Quick Add field.

To give you an idea of the finished product, Figure 8-4 shows a Links TypeList in a sidebar.

Creating a Notes TypeList

Need to add a graphic image, or any other piece of code, to your sidebar? Use the Notes TypeList. Here's how:

1. From the TypeLists Library (refer to Figure 8-1), click Add a TypeList.

The Add a TypeList page appears (refer to Figure 8-2).

2. Choose Notes from the drop-down menu.

3. Name your TypeList as you'd like it to appear on your sidebar.

See the tip in "Creating New TypeLists for Your Blog" about hiding the names of TypeLists if you'd rather not have the TypeList title show.

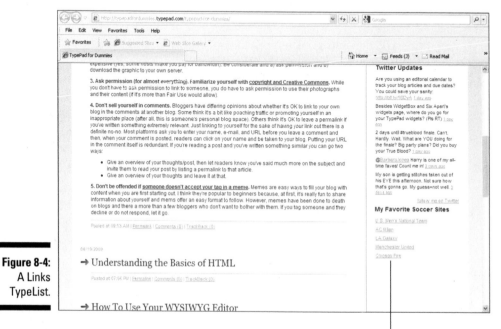

Figure 8-4:
A Links TypeList.

Links TypeList

4. Click the Create New TypeList button.

The Add Note page appears, as shown in Figure 8-5. Note that the name of the TypeList appears in the blue navigation bar.

5. (Optional) Give your note a label.

Whatever you type in the Label field appears above this note in your sidebar. If you don't want any text to appear above the note, leave the Label field blank, or see our tip in "Creating New TypeLists for Your Blog" about hiding the title of your TypeList.

6. In the Note field, enter the code you want to use in your sidebar.

For example, let's say you want to use a sidebar image that advertises the work of Compassion International. When you visit Compassion's blog, it offers a page with several sidebar images you can choose to display on your own blog. Below each image, Compassion's Web site lists the code you need to display the image (with a link back to Compassion International) on your sidebar. Highlight and copy that code (Ctrl+C on a PC; Command+C on a Mac). Paste (Ctrl+V on a PC; Command+V on a Mac) that code into the Note field.

After you've pasted the code into the Note field, saved your changes, and published your TypeList (which you'll do in a minute), your new TypeList would appear as shown in Figure 8-6.

Name of TypeList

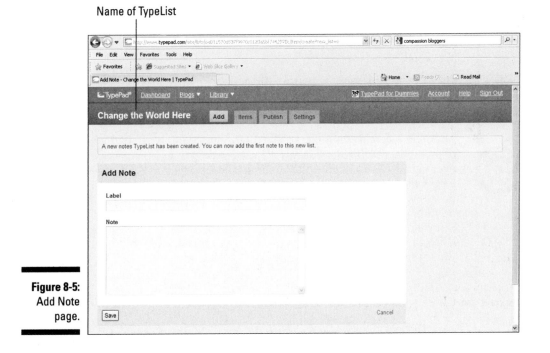

Figure 8-5:
Add Note
page.

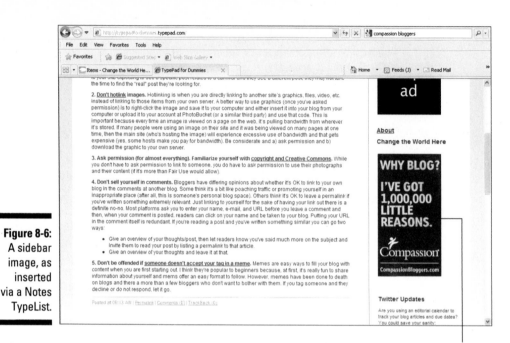

ad

Figure 8-6:
A sidebar
image, as
inserted
via a Notes
TypeList.

Image added via Notes TypeList

Want to add a sidebar image via a Notes TypeList, but you don't have
the code for referencing the image? You'll need to generate it yourself.
See Chapter 11 for instructions on including an image in your sidebar.

7. Click Save.

A page appears that lists all the items you've added to this Notes
TypeList. To add another item, click the yellow Add button in your blue
menu bar.

Although it is most common to use the Notes TypeList for adding code (in particular, images) to your sidebar, it's not the *only* thing you can use it for. If you
ever need to add a simple blurb of text to your sidebar — no links, no images,
just text — enter that text in the Note field, pictured in Figure 8-5. For example,
perhaps you want a small section in the top of a sidebar to offer a brief introduction: "Hi, I'm Rose. I'm a cancer survivor married to a dentist, and this blog
is my story. Thanks for stopping by." If so, enter that text (perhaps along with
a link to your full About page) via a Notes TypeList, and place it where you
want it to appear on your sidebar (see Chapter 11).

Adding a Books TypeList

If you want to use your sidebar to recommend a list of books, use a Books TypeList. If you have connected your Amazon Associate ID, Amazon Wish List ID, or both with your TypePad account (see Chapter 4), any books you include in a Books TypeList are automatically linked to Amazon (sorry, it doesn't link to any other store except Amazon). If you are an Amazon Associate, your Associate ID is included in the link, so you'll be rewarded for any purchases your readers make via your link. You can read more about the Amazon Associate program in Chapter 12. If you have not connected your Amazon Associate or Wish List ID to your TypePad account, don't worry! If you use Quick Add to include an item in your Books TypeList, that item is still linked to Amazon.com, but you won't get any affiliate credit.

Books TypeLists are not just for books! You can list any product offered at Amazon.com (including videogames, camera equipment, DVDs, and cookware) within a Books TypeList, and that product is treated just as a book is treated: TypePad generates a link to Amazon that includes your Amazon ID (if it's linked to your TypePad account).

If you would like to list items and link them to another store Web site, we encourage you to make a new List TypeList and link items directly to the Web site you'd like to share. For instance, if you're quite the cook and want to share cooking utensils and supplies from a local store, a List TypeList lets you do that.

When you're ready to create a Books TypeList, use these instructions:

1. **From the TypeLists Library (refer to Figure 8-1), click Add a TypeList.**

   The Add a TypeList page appears (refer to Figure 8-2).

2. **Choose Books from the drop-down menu.**

3. **Name your TypeList as you'd like it to appear on your sidebar.**

   See the tip in "Creating New TypeLists for Your Blog" for information about hiding the names of TypeLists if you'd rather not have the TypeList title show.

4. **Click Create a New TypeList.**

   The Add Book page appears, as shown in Figure 8-7. Note that the name of the TypeList appears in the blue navigation bar.

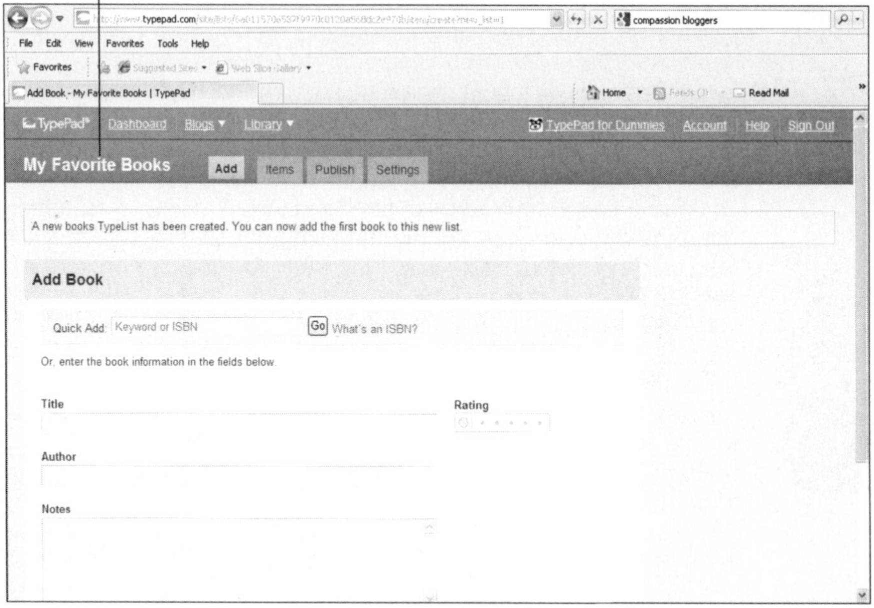

Name of TypeList

Figure 8-7:
Add Book
page.

5. Type the book (or other product) information.

You can enter the information in two ways:

- Use the Quick Add field to enter the title or ISBN (a ten-digit code by which books are uniformly identified — you can find it on the book's bar code). When you use the Quick Add field to search using a book's title, you are presented with a list of search results. Click to select the button next to the title that works best for you and then click the Choose Selected button.

- If you'd like to use specific information for your Books TypeList item, you can use the Title, Author, and Notes fields to type the book or product information you want to include in your TypeList.

When you enter information this way instead of using the Quick Add field, the resulting item in your list is not linked to Amazon or any other store; the item is simply a text list item. If you want your book or product to link to Amazon, be sure to use the Quick Add field.

The Edit Book page appears.

6. Confirm that the book title and author name(s) are correct.

If you'd like to make a change, simply click inside the relevant field and make any necessary changes.

TypePad lists the author name(s) before the book title in your Books TypeList. If you'd like to have the book title appear first, leave the Author text field blank.

7. (Optional) Give the book a rating, if you like.

If you give your item a rating, be sure to check the settings for this TypeList to ensure that you've chosen to share your ratings; otherwise your ratings won't show up in your sidebar. See "Managing settings for a TypeList," later in this chapter.

8. (Optional) Include your review or opinion of the book in the Notes field.

Use the TypeLists Settings tab to determine whether the rating, notes, and book artwork are visible to your readers (see "Managing settings for a TypeList," later in this chapter).

9. Click Save.

A page appears that lists all the items you've added to this Books TypeList. To add another item, click the yellow Add button in the blue menu bar or use the Quick Add field.

When you're finished, you can expect a completed Books TypeList to look similar to the one pictured in Figure 8-8.

Books TypeList

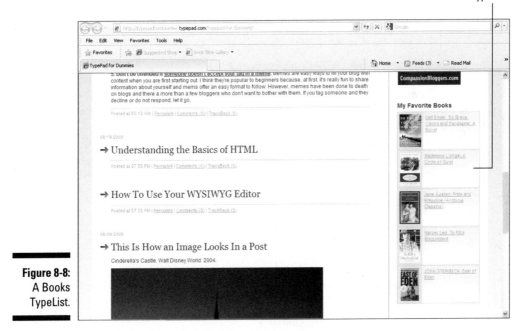

Figure 8-8:
A Books
TypeList.

Adding an Album TypeList

An Album TypeList is similar in concept to a Books TypeList. Both types list your favorites, with your personal star rating, and both link to these favorites at Amazon.com. If you've connected your Amazon Associate or Wish List ID to your TypePad account (see Chapter 4), the links are automatically generated to point to your Amazon associates account, which means you could generate some affiliate revenue if your readers make a purchase from your recommendation. Keep in mind that the only Amazon product an Albums TypeList allows you to list is CDs.

If you do not use the Quick Add feature to include an item in your TypeList, that item is not linked to Amazon.com; the item shows up in your list as an unlinked text item.

Here's how you set up an Albums TypeList:

1. **From the TypeLists Library (refer to Figure 8-1), click Add a TypeList.**

   The Add a TypeList page appears (refer to Figure 8-2).

2. **Choose Albums from the drop-down menu.**

3. **Name your TypeList as you'd like it to appear on your sidebar.**

   See the tip in "Creating New TypeLists for Your Blog" for information about hiding the names of TypeLists if you'd rather not have the TypeList title show.

4. **Click the Create a New TypeList button.**

   The Add Album page appears, as shown in Figure 8-9. Note that the name of the TypeList appears in the blue navigation bar.

5. **Type your album information.**

   You can add the album information in two ways:

   • Use the Quick Add field to enter the title of the album or the artist. When you use the Quick Add field to search for an album's title, you are presented with a list of search results to choose among. Click to select the button next to the album that works best for you and then click the Choose Selected button.

   • If you'd like to use specific information for your Albums TypeList item, you can use the Title, Author, and Notes fields to type the book or product information you want to include in your TypeList. Note that when you enter information this way, the resulting item in your list is not linked to Amazon or any other store; the item is simply a text list item. If you want your album to link to Amazon, be sure to use the Quick Add field.

   The Edit Album page appears.

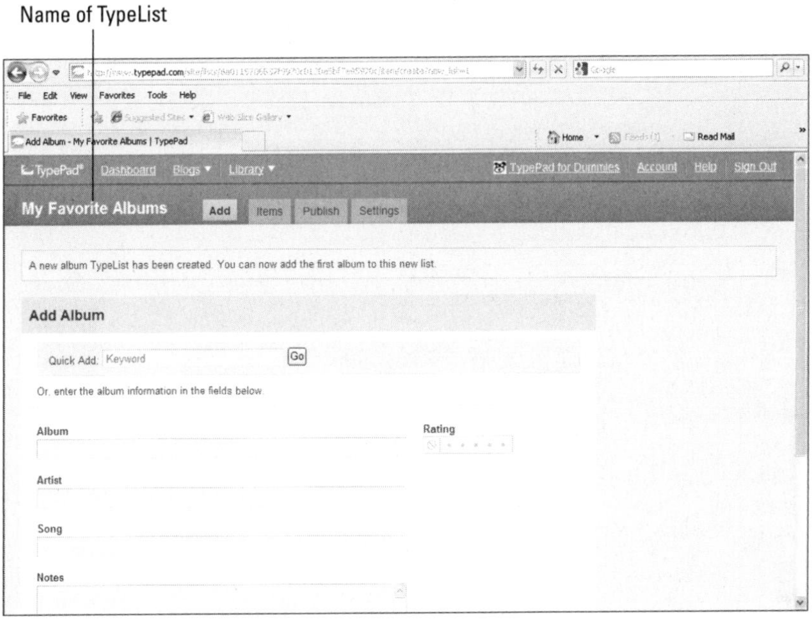

Name of TypeList

Figure 8-9:
Add Album
page.

6. **Confirm that the album title is correct.**

   If you'd like to make a change, simply click inside the Album field and make any necessary changes.

7. **Confirm or include the artist's name (if Quick Add didn't do it for you).**

   If you'd like to make a change, simply click inside the Artist field and make any necessary changes.

8. **(Optional) Give the album a star rating.**

   In a moment, we show you how to change your settings so that these notes and ratings are visible to your readers.

9. **(Optional) Include the name of a song from the album.**

   When you use the Quick Add field to search for an album, it's possible that TypePad automatically puts the album's title in the Song field. Click inside the Song field, highlight and delete the information, and then type the correct song title in the field (or leave it blank if you don't want to call attention to a particular song).

10. **Click Save.**

    A page appears that lists all the items you've added to this Albums TypeList. To add another item, click the yellow Add button in the blue menu bar or use the Quick Add field.

When you're finished, you can expect a completed Albums TypeList to look similar to the one in Figure 8-10.

Albums TypeList

Figure 8-10:
An Albums
TypeList as
it appears
in a blog
sidebar.

Editing and Configuring an Existing TypeList

If you want to make any edits to an existing TypeList, or adjust the way you've set a TypeList to display, start by revisiting the TypeLists Library (refer to Figure 8-1). From there, you can decide which parts of your TypeLists appear (for example, the Notes you included), search or edit your TypeLists, and publish or unpublish a TypeList.

Managing settings for a TypeList

TypePad allows you to establish settings for individual TypeLists, including things such as whether book or album art is displayed with each item and how many list items appear within the TypeList.

You can get to the TypeList Settings page in a couple of ways. From the TypeList Library (refer to Figure 8-1), either click the Settings link below the TypeList's name or click the TypeList's name and then click the Settings tab. Both links point you to the same place: the Settings page for that particular TypeList.

Depending on the kind of TypeList you're editing, the Settings page contains different information, as follows:

Notes: The Settings page for a Notes TypeList simply lists the name of the TypeList (if you want to change the name, type the new name in the designated field). The Settings page also gives you a spot to add a description of the TypeList. This is purely for your own reference; TypeList descriptions are not visible to readers. The description appears under the TypeList name on the main TypeList Library (refer to Figure 8-1), so it can jog your memory about what you've included here. Click Save Changes when you're finished.

Links: The Settings page for a Links TypeList allows you to change the name of the list or make notes to yourself in the Description field. Under the Display header, you can choose the number of list items you want visible on your sidebar. You can edit the order in which the list items are arranged by clicking the pull-down menu below Order and selecting your preference. The Link Titles field does not currently affect your TypeList. You can ignore this menu.

Show Header: Choose how (or whether) you want your Notes displayed:

- ✔ Selecting the Notes as Text option causes anything in your Notes field to be visible directly under the link.

- ✔ Selecting the Notes As Tooltip option causes anything in the Notes field to be visible only when the reader's mouse hovers over the link.

- ✔ Selecting the Do Not Show Notes option keeps your notes invisible to readers, but they are still viewable to you within your TypePad Dashboard.

Books and Albums: On the Settings page for both Books and Albums TypeLists, you can change the name of the list or make notes to yourself via the Name and Description fields. Under Display, choose how many list items to display in your sidebar. Under Order, use the drop-down menu to select how you'd like to arrange your list items. Under Show, decide whether you want the book or album artwork, your star rating, and your notes to appear in the sidebar next to the list item.

Editing a TypeList

You'll probably make changes to your TypeLists fairly often. For example, if you're using a List TypeList to manage your blogroll, you'll likely want to add and delete blogs from it as your blog-reading habits evolve over time.

- ✔ To make changes to the content of an existing TypeList, simply find that TypeList in your TypeList Library (refer to Figure 8-1). Click the TypeList you want to edit, and you'll see what you currently have listed in that TypeList.

- ✔ To remove an item from a TypeList altogether, click to select the check box next to its name and then click the red Delete button. The item is gone.

- ✔ To add an item, click the yellow Add button or use the Quick Add function (except for Notes TypeLists, which do not have Quick Add functions).

- ✔ To edit an existing list item, click its name, and you'll be taken to a screen just like the one you used to add the item originally. Edit as needed.

Publishing a TypeList

After you've created and saved your TypeList, you'll probably want to publish it on your blog. To publish it, head back to your main TypeList Library (refer to Figure 8-1) and click the Publish link below the TypeList's name. This takes you to a master list of all your blogs under your TypePad account. Click to select the box next to the blog(s) you want to add your TypeList to and then click the Save Changes button at the bottom of the page.

If you decide to remove a TypeList from a page, simply click to deselect the box next to the blog from which you want the list removed and then click Save Changes. To add an existing TypeList to another of your TypePad blogs, click to select the box next to that blog's name and then click Save Changes.

On the Publish page, note the Organize Content link below each blog's name. That link takes you *out* of the TypeList module and *into* the Design module — that's where all the TypeList arranging takes place. Because it's a completely different portion of the Dashboard, we tackle it in our chapter on blog design (Chapter 11).

Searching a TypeList

Need to find a particular item in your TypeList? TypePad gives you a way to do a search within a particular TypeList — a feature you're most likely to need if your TypeList is very long. Open the TypeList you want to search through, and you'll see a search field on the line below the blue tabs. Enter the text you're looking for (such as a blog title or an artist's name) and then click Search. The search results are displayed, and you can click the item you need.

Deleting a TypeList

Want to delete the TypeList altogether? Do this by clicking the gray More Options button in the TypeList Library and then selecting Delete This TypeList.

You don't have to delete a TypeList to keep it from showing up on your blog. You can simply unpublish it from your blog; it will still exist in your account. This is advisable, because you never know when you may want to reapply that particular TypeList to one of your blogs.

Finding Creative Uses for TypeLists

You can apply TypeLists to your blog in endless ways, so be creative. Maximize your use of this tool to get a great deal of information to your readers in a short space. To get you started in your inventive TypeList thinking, here are a few ideas to consider.

Product recommendations

You can use a Books TypeList or a Links TypeList to create a list of product recommendations. A fashion blogger, for example, might have a TypeList called Must-Have Fashion Pieces for Fall, whereas an outdoor-sports blogger might offer My Favorite Hiking Equipment. Use the Books TypeList to recommend Amazon.com items to readers, and be sure you've listed your Amazon Associates ID with TypePad. To recommend products that aren't sold at Amazon, consider using a Links TypeList so you can link the products manually to the store you plan to use.

Your favorite blogs

When you link to your favorite blogs, the list you make is referred to as a *blogroll*. It's an excellent way to engage in the blogging community by passing around your traffic to other bloggers. You do not need to get someone's permission to link to them, nor do you need their permission to remove their link from your list (though we can't guarantee that their feelings won't be hurt!). Consider calling your blogroll a Rotating Blogroll and then rotate new blogs through. Or offer a reciprocal blogroll, telling readers you'll link to anyone who links to you. (Watch it, though: Reciprocal blogrolls can get unmanageable quickly, especially if you have a lot of readers.)

If you have your heart set on offering your readers an exceedingly long and comprehensive blogroll, but you don't want to lose the valuable sidebar space, consider creating a page for your blogroll instead (see Chapter 6). Then you can link to that page from your sidebar via a graphic link, as discussed in Chapter 11.

Your favorite Web sites

Use a sidebar to point readers toward your favorite nonblogging Web sites (you could call it My Favorite Links, or something along those lines). A brief list of your favorite links can actually tell your readers quite a bit about you. Let's say, for example, that you list The Sound of Music Fan Club, Golf Digest, American Kennel Club, and This Old House. At a glance, a new reader now knows that you're a musical-theater-loving, golf-playing, dog-owning DIY-er!

Places to go

Especially if you blog often about restaurants or travel, consider adding a TypeList that points your readers to specific geographical places you've traveled to or those you recommend. You can even offer a brief explanation of each location in that link's Notes section (for example, "The best cheesecake you'll ever have!" or "Perfect spot for honeymooners").

Share more about your blog

Create separate pages containing helpful information about your blog (for example, a page with all your contact information, a page containing customer testimonials, or a page providing details for potential advertisers). Then create a Links or Notes TypeList, and list these items in one place — quick and easy information for your readers!

Other places readers can find you

These days, we all seem to have more than one spot online where readers can find us. We've shown you how you can aggregate all the locations on your TypePad Profile (see Chapter 3), but a quick list on your sidebar might be helpful for readers, too. For example, use a Links list (perhaps called "Where Else You Can Find Me" or "See Also"), and list all your social media accounts (Twitter, Facebook, Linked In, Flickr, and so on), as well as any other blogs or media outlets where you contribute.

As you can see, the possibilities for TypeLists go on and on. Always keep in mind that the point is to keep information clearly organized for your readers. Be descriptive in your TypeList titles, and keep them topical and frequently updated. For some examples of bloggers using TypeLists well, see Chapter 17.

Adding Blog Functions with Widgets

If you think TypeLists are awesome, wait until we tell you about widgets. A *widget* is a piece of code that adds a specific function to your blog (such as posting your tweets in your blog sidebar as you submit them to Twitter or showcasing your latest photos uploaded to Flickr). You can organize your widgets and determine how they flow with your TypeLists by using the Design tab (we discuss this more in Chapter 11).

Understanding widgets

Widgets are generally produced by a third party and are placed in your sidebar (not the main posting area). They are made up of JavaScript or HTML code that produces a specific function (such as providing a search engine for your blog). You can find a widget that pertains to just about any blog topic you can think of. For instance, you can find useful widgets that allow your users to add your blog to their feed reader with one click, or you can find less useful (but fun!) widgets for counting down the days until the next episode of *Lost.*

Most widgets are a point–click–install affair. By that, we mean that you find the widget you want to use and choose the TypePad option offered, and TypePad installs the widget for you. In most cases, you'll have to provide some basic information (such as your blog's URL) and work your way through a short setup process via an easy wizard. All in all, it's a painless and easy process.

Sometimes, though, you'll come across a widget that does not have automatic installation, and you'll have to do some work to get the widget on your blog. One example is the Etsy widget, which we mention in "Finding and activating new widgets." An easy wizard helps you set up the content of the Etsy widget, but you have to copy the JavaScript code and paste it into an Embed Your Own HTML widget (discussed in a minute) or a Notes TypeList (discussed earlier in this chapter).

If you're using Advanced Templates, you have to install all widgets by creating a new template module (see Chapter 14 for more information about using Advanced Templates).

Use widgets sparingly. It's easy to get carried away with the fun stuff you find, but remember that widgets are also a distraction. The more clutter you have in your sidebar, the harder it is for visitors to find what they're looking for. Depending on the number of widgets you use, they may also cause your blog to load slowly.

Using the Embed Your Own HTML widget

The Embed Your Own HTML widget allows you to quickly create a sidebar module, place it in your blog design, and save the changes to publish immediately. The Embed Your Own HTML widget and a Notes TypeList are essentially the same; they're just located in different places on your TypePad Dashboard.

You can find the Embed Your Own HTML widget by choosing Design➪Content➪Categories (Widget)➪Modules (Embed Your Own HTML). To use the module, follow these instructions:

1. **Click the Add This Module button.**

   The Custom HTML pop-up window appears.

2. **Type a new name in the Label field.**

   We suggest using a title that reflects the function of the widget. Remember, you can hide the title of the widget by using the following, changing `widget name` to the title you want:

   ```
   <!-- widget name -->
   ```

3. **In the HTML text field, type or paste the code you want to include.**

4. **Click OK.**

   The widget is saved and placed at the top of your sidebar. You can drag and drop the widget to arrange its order on your sidebar.

If you decide to unpublish the widget, it will be deleted, and you will not be able to access it again. To republish the widget to your sidebar later, you will have to rebuild it from scratch.

Finding and activating new widgets

TypePad offers more functionality for your blog through its Widget Gallery at www.sixapart.com/typepad/widgets (see Figure 8-11). The widgets listed change often; we encourage you to visit frequently to see what's new. Another place to find TypePad-friendly widgets is www.widgetbox.com.

After you've activated a widget by using the easy wizard, you'll see TypePad's Add a Sidebar Widget page (see Figure 8-12), which lists the blogs you have on your TypePad account and allows you to select which blogs you want to install the widget on. You can also customize the name of the widget.

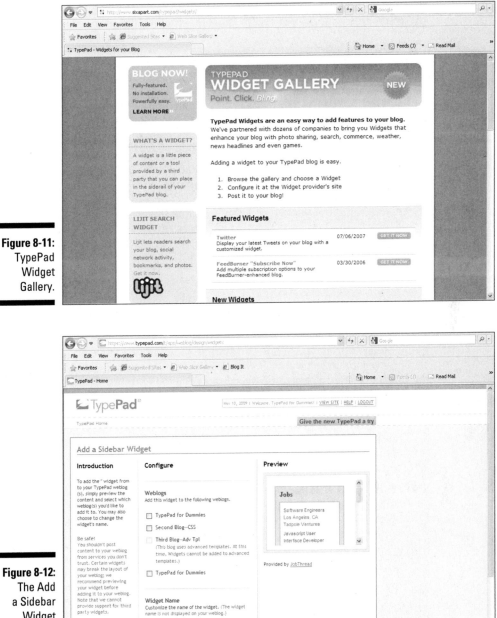

Figure 8-11:
TypePad
Widget
Gallery.

Figure 8-12:
The Add
a Sidebar
Widget
page.

After you select the blogs where you'd like to install the widget, click Add Widget. A new page appears, with the following link choices:

- ✔ **View Weblog:** Click this option to see how your blog looks with the new widget. Note that because you haven't ordered your content yet, the widget is probably at the bottom of your sidebar.

- ✔ **Change Content Ordering:** Click this option to visit the Content page in your blog's Dashboard. From here, you can use drag-and-drop content ordering (discussed in Chapter 11) to determine the order of your sidebar items, including your newly installed widget(s).

- ✔ **Return to (*Widget Site*):** The text replacing (*Widget Site*) depends on where you found your widget. For example, if you found your widget at TypePad, the link will say `Return to TypePad Widget Gallery`; if you found the widget at WidgetBox, the link will say `Return to WidgetBox`. You can click this option to return to the site and find more widgets to install.

- ✔ **TypePad Home:** Click this option to return to the main page of your blog's Dashboard.

If you're unsure what type of widgets you should include on your blog, we've come up with a short list to assist you. The following list explains how several popular widgets can help you and your readers use your blog more effectively by promoting your content to other social media sites, encouraging readers to subscribe to your RSS feed, and showcasing your affiliate marketing products (if you're an affiliate marketer) or Etsy items:

- ✔ **Share This (`sharethis.com/publishers/getbutton`):** Readers can quickly and easily share your article with social media and social bookmarking sites such as Twitter, StumbleUpon, Digg, and Facebook. We explain social media sites and how they can enhance your community and blogging experience in Chapter 10.

- ✔ **FeedBurner's Subscribe Now (`www.sixapart.com/typepad/widgets/publishing-tools/feedburner_subs.html`):** If your blog uses FeedBurner for RSS, this widget gives your readers a one-click option for subscribing to your blog's RSS feed.

- ✔ **Search field (`www.sixapart.com/typepad/widgets/search/`):** Readers will appreciate a way to search your archives for posts of yours they previously read and want to locate again. If you have an easy-to-find search field in your sidebar, you've made it that much easier for readers (and you) to find what they're looking for. Using a search field is much better than browsing endlessly through random archives or categories. We suggest trying out a few different search fields to see which one works best for your blog.

- ✔ **Etsy Mini (`www.etsy.com/mini_generator.php`):** Are you an Etsy vendor who wants to showcase your Etsy shop's items on your blog? Or are you just an Etsy junkie who likes to show off the cool items you find on Etsy? This widget allows you to build your own widget (don't worry — an easy wizard walks you through the steps) so you can display it on your sidebar. This widget doesn't offer automatic installation, though, so you'll have to copy the JavaScript code, paste it into a Notes TypeList, and then publish the TypeList on your blog's sidebar. Good thing we tell you how to do all that in this chapter.

- ✔ **LinkWithin (`www.linkwithin.com/learn`):** This attractive widget automatically links to related archived posts at the bottom of newly published posts. The idea is that if readers enjoyed one post, they may want to read more like it; this widget provides links to those related posts.

- ✔ **PopShops widget (`www.popshops.com/faq/typepad`):** If you are interested in affiliate marketing and have an account with PopShops, you can use its widget to earn commissions from Commission Junction, LinkShare, Google Affiliate Network, and ShareASale. (For more information about making money with your blog, see Chapter 12.)

Turning widgets off and on

Over time, you may find that a widget is no longer useful to your evolving blog. To disable a widget, just choose Design⇨Content to see your blog's content modules. Find the widget you'd like to disable, and click the red X in the top-right corner of the widget module. A pop-up window asks you to confirm that you really want to remove the module; click OK. Then scroll down the page and click Save Changes. You've removed the widget from your sidebar and have deleted it from your options. To reinstall it, you have to revisit the site where you found it and reinstall from scratch.

As you develop your blog and choose what information to share with your readers, we're sure you'll find this chapter, in particular, helpful. TypeLists and widgets are two of the easiest ways to enhance your blog quickly. The more you practice with TypeLists and widgets, the easier they become to create and manage — and the more you'll come to depend on them.

Chapter 9

Adding Multimedia to Your Blog

· ·

In This Chapter

▶ Setting up a new photo album

▶ Displaying a photo album in your blog

▶ Adding a podcast to your blog

▶ Using video on your blog

· ·

Multimedia includes all kinds of media, such as images, audio, anima-tion, and video. Given the interactive nature of the Web and blogs in general, multimedia options are perfect for encouraging reader response on your own blog.

Each of the four TypePad pricing levels offers you the ability to post images, audio, and video, but remember that files such as these require considerably more server space than a simple text blog post. If you plan to frequently post multimedia, you should be sure you're signed up with a TypePad pricing plan that suits your storage needs (see Chapter 2).

Keep in mind that a little multimedia goes a long way on a blog. Visiting a page that is heavily packed with video, sound, and moving graphics can be visually overwhelming, and it might drive viewers away. For example, a common pet peeve among blog readers is autoloading music (that is, blogs that automatically play music when you visit them)

If you're ready to use multimedia with your own blog, read on! We explain how you can use TypePad's photo album feature to showcase your personal images and how to use podcasting and video to make your blog more interesting.

Creating Photo Albums and Galleries

Photo albums are one way to showcase groups of photos without having to insert them individually into a single post. When you create a TypePad photo album, you're creating a virtual photo album similar to the tangible albums you may have at home. Virtual photo albums are particularly useful if

- ✔ You're a photographer who would like to show your talents grouped by genre.
- ✔ You want to document a particular process or event (such as a vacation, a home renovation, or your child's first year).
- ✔ You would like to share new items you've made (for instance, you're a craft blogger who wants to show off your newest projects).

We're sure you can think of a million other uses for incorporating photo albums — they're an excellent tool for sharing snippets of your life with readers.

Follow these steps to get a TypePad photo album up and running:

1. **Click the Library link on the green account-level bar.**

2. **Choose Photo Albums from the pull-down menu, as shown in Figure 9-1.**

   The photo album page appears. If you have existing photo albums, they're listed here.

3. **Click the Add a Photo Album link in the top-right corner.**

   The Add a Photo Album page appears (see Figure 9-2).

Library pull-down menu

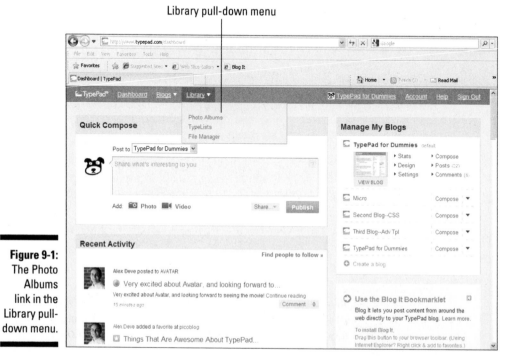

Figure 9-1:
The Photo Albums link in the Library pull-down menu.

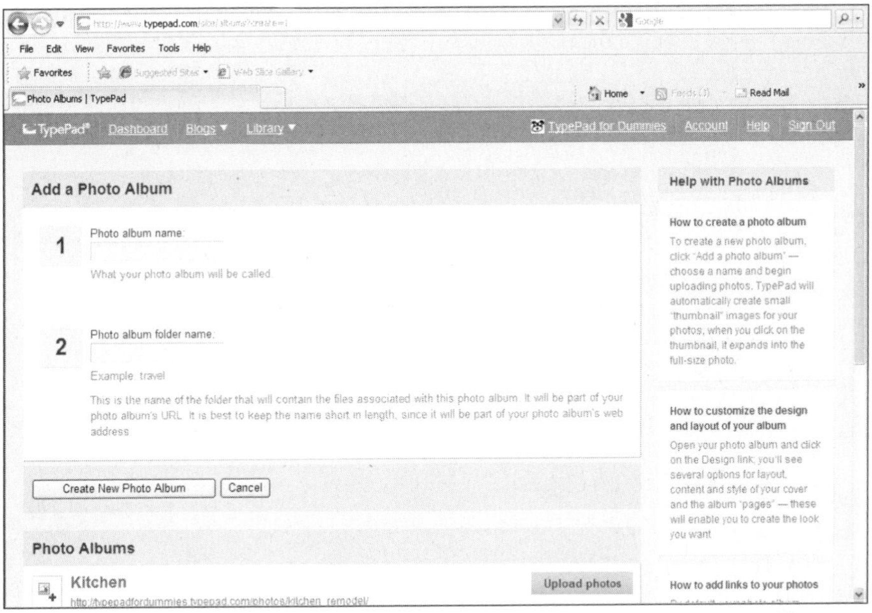

Figure 9-2:
Add a Photo
Album page.

4. **Click inside the Photo Album Name text box, and type the name of the photo album you're creating.**

   Note that as you type the name of your album, you're also creating a file folder (to be housed in File Manager for easy reference) with the same name. The name you choose for these items should be descriptive but short. The file name is part of your photo album's URL.

5. **Click the Create New Photo Album button.**

   The Upload New Photos page appears, showing a blog-level (blue) bar that reflects the name of the photo album you just made (as shown in Figure 9-3).

   This page has three tabs: Photos, Design, and Settings. We discuss each of these tabs shortly, right after we show you how to upload some pictures into this new photo album.

6. **Use the pull-down menu to select how many files you'd like to upload to this photo album.**

7. **Use the Browse button to find the files on your computer that you'd like to upload.**

8. **Click the Upload button.**

   The Photos page appears (note that this is the Photos tab on the blog-level bar). From here, you can delete photos (click to select the box next to each photo you want to delete and then click the red Delete button) or upload more photos to this album (click the Upload Photos link).

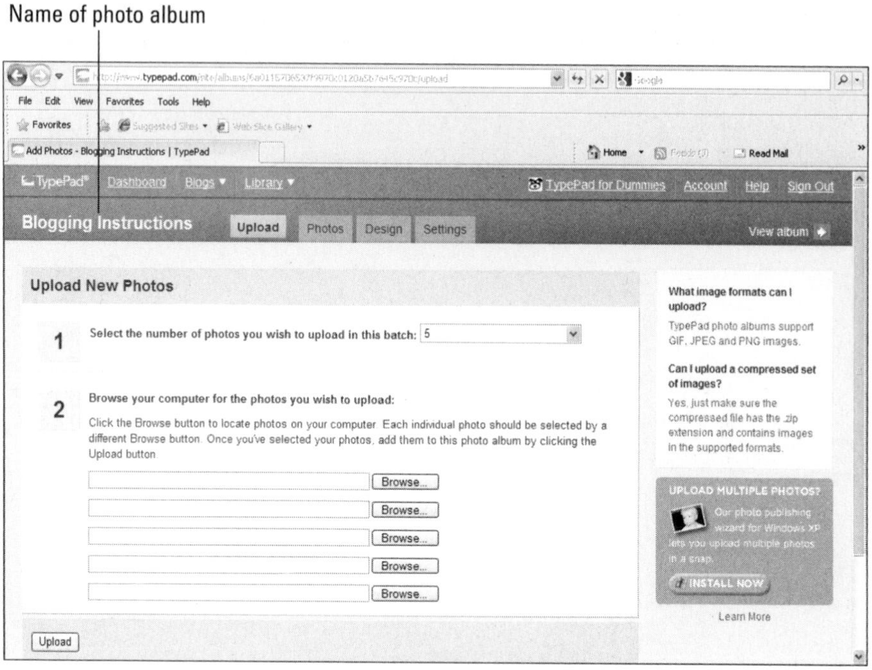

Name of photo album

Figure 9-3:
Upload
New Photos
page.

Choosing your photo album design

Now that you've created a TypePad photo album, you need to decide how you'd like that album to appear online. To do that, click the Design tab in your blue blog-level bar for the photo album you're working with (choose Library⇨Photo Albums⇨Your Album⇨Design tab).

The Design page appears with a list of four links in the left sidebar:

✔ Overview

✔ Layout

✔ Content

✔ Style

Let's discuss each of these in order.

Overview

From the Overview tab, you can change the layout, content, or style of your photo album (just click the related link). You can also apply a style from an existing photo album to the current photo album. To do that, use the pull-down menu to select the album whose design you'd like to use. Click the Use This Album's Design button to apply the settings.

Layout

Clicking the Layout link takes you to a page that looks like to the one in Figure 9-4.

This page allows you to choose how your cover page (the main page of your album) and your photo pages are displayed within your blog. You have several choices. Your cover page can display

✔ Thumbnails only (*thumbnails* are smaller versions of your original image; when clicked, a thumbnail usually links to the larger original image)

✔ Thumbnails with descriptions

✔ A photo with an explanatory paragraph (similar to an introduction to your album)

✔ No cover for your album (in which case your album just begins with your first photo)

Name of album   Design tab

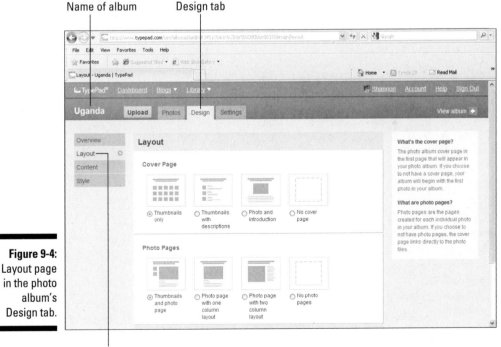

Figure 9-4:
Layout page
in the photo
album's
Design tab.

Layout link

You also have a few options for your photo pages:

- **Thumbnails and Photo Page:** This option shows a large photo with a thumbnail of the next (and previous, if applicable) photo in the left sidebar. The page includes text links to the next/previous photo, the album cover page, and the permalink for the displayed image.

- **Photo Page with One Column Layout:** This option shows a single image on the page with small text links in the top-right corner to the next or previous images. Any descriptive text appears below the image. (You can set descriptive text in the Settings tab, which we cover in a bit.)

- **Photo Page with Two Column Layout:** This option is similar to the preceding option but offers two columns instead of one.

- **No Photo Pages:** Instead of having a design attributed to your photo pages, readers click a thumbnail on the photo album cover and are taken to a page with just that image. There are no thumbnails of next/previous images or text links to next/previous images.

Content

Let's go back to the list of links on the left side of your photo album's Design tab. Click the Content link, and you see a page like the one in Figure 9-5.

Name of album

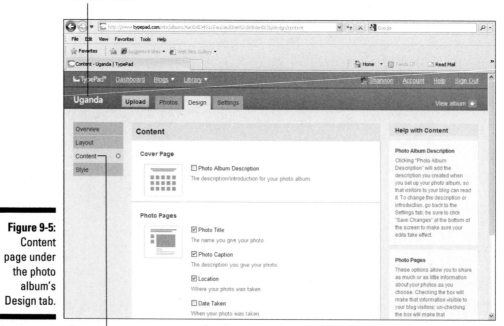

Figure 9-5:
Content
page under
the photo
album's
Design tab.

Content link

The Content tab is where you'll choose what content to include with each image as it's displayed. Click to select the box next to the options that fit your needs. You can choose

✔ Photo Title

✔ Photo Caption

✔ Location

✔ Date Taken

✔ EXIF Data

Don't forget to click the Save Changes button so you don't lose your changes.

Style

The last link under your photo album's Design tab is Style. Click the Style link to choose the look and feel for your album. Figure 9-6 shows an example of a Style page.

A *style* is sort of like the theme for your blog, but this style is applied only to your photo album. Use the pull-down menu to see how different themes look with your album. When you're happy with the look and feel, click the Save Changes button.

Name of album

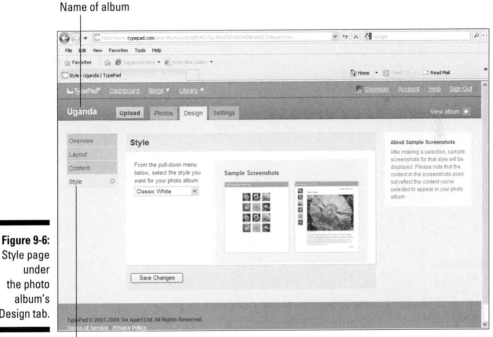

Figure 9-6: Style page under the photo album's Design tab.

Style link

Choosing your photo album settings

As you can with each part of your TypePad blog, you can establish specific settings for your photo album(s). To do that, click the Settings tab in the blog-level bar for the photo album you're working with (choose Library➪Photo Albums➪Your Album➪Settings tab). Figure 9-7 shows an example Photo Album Settings tab.

Basics

Within the Settings tab, you have the option of determining your album's name, description, cover images, privacy, and other things:

- ✔ **Name of Photo Album (required):** This text box shows the name you gave the photo album when you created it. You can change the album's name, but that change does not change the name of the folder where the album resides. This is a good thing, because even if you change the name of the album, any previous links to it still work.

- ✔ **Description/Introduction (optional):** If you'd like to include an overview explaining what an album includes (for example, vacation pictures or timeline of a kitchen remodeling), you can type that description here. We think it's handy to provide a description or an introduction to your photo albums because it gives your audience context for the images.

Name of album   Settings tab

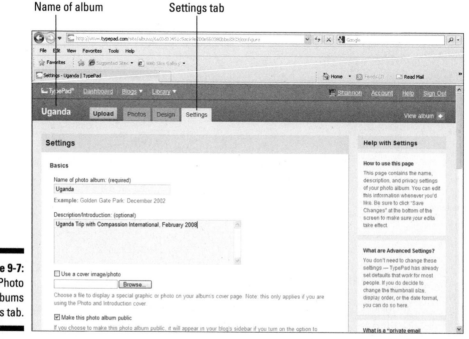

Figure 9-7: Photo Albums Settings tab.

✔ **Use a Cover Image/Photo (optional):** If you'd like to choose a specific image to be the virtual cover of your photo album, click to select this option, and then click the Browse button to choose the file you want to use as the cover image from your computer.

✔ **Make This Album Public:** If you'd like to share the contents of a photo album with the public, click to select the box next to this option. If you'd rather keep an album private, you can deselect the box next to this option.

Advanced

Scroll down below the Basics section pictured in Figure 9-7 to the section titled Advanced. These settings are set to defaults that generally work best with all photo albums. However, if you want to edit these defaults, you can do so.

Your photo album cover page settings are as follows:

✔ **Number of Columns to Display Thumbnails:** This is pretty much what it says: TypePad displays the thumbnails from an album on the cover page, and you can choose how many columns show.

✔ **Crop Thumbnails to Uniform Dimensions (Square):** If you'd like all the thumbnails in an album to be uniform, click to select the box next to this option.

✔ **Thumbnail Size:** Click to select which size (small, medium, or large) you'd like your photo album thumbnails to be.

✔ **Date Format:** Use the pull-down menu to choose the date format you'd like to display with your photo album.

✔ **Display Order:** Use the pull-down menu to choose the order in which you'd like to your album images to appear.

Your photo page settings are as follows:

✔ **Photo Size:** When readers click a thumbnail of an image in your photo album, they see a larger version of that image. The choice you make in Photo Size determines the size of that larger photo. Use the pull-down menu to choose whether you'd like your image(s) to appear small (350 pixels), medium (500 pixels), or large (640 pixels).

✔ **Date Format:** Use the pull-down menu to choose how you'd like the date to appear when someone views an image in your photo album.

✔ **Password Protection:** If you'd like to password-protect your images in an album, click to select this option. Then click inside the Username and Password text boxes, and type the information you want associated with this album's photo pages.

Just as you can post to your blog remotely (see Chapter 5), you can post photos to your albums remotely. This option is handy because you never know when you'll capture the perfect shot and want to share it with your readers. TypePad assigns you a random e-mail address to which you can send photos. The e-mail address is lengthy enough that you most likely won't be able to remember it off the top of your head (it's about 15 characters long and made up of both numbers and letters in a random sequence). If you plan to use the remote posting feature, it may be helpful to send yourself an e-mail with your TypePad mobile e-mail address as the message. If you want to be sure your mobile upload was successful, click to select the Send Me an Email Notification option when an e-mail message has been successfully posted.

If you've made any changes on the Settings page, don't forget to click the Save Changes buttons so your work isn't lost.

Optimizing images for the Web

When you choose to use images in your blog, it's worth noting that size matters. Both the physical pixel size and the digital size of your image have an effect on how quickly your blog's pages load. If a page takes too long to load, readers move on. If you'd like to make your photos and images as attractive to readers as possible and still have those images load quickly, you need to optimize them for the Internet before you use them in your blog.

Optimizing an image for the Web simply means compressing its digital data so the image file is smaller and loads faster. When you take a digital picture, for instance, a lot of noise is included in the digital file that isn't necessary for the picture to be viewed. You can clean out that noise, and thus make the file smaller, simply by choosing Save for Web in your graphic-editing software (such as Adobe Photoshop Elements or GIMP). If you don't have that option in your software, save the file in the appropriate format — JPG, GIF, or PNG — and choose the smallest file size in that format.

Our advice is to keep your image file size to less than 50KB. Of course, sometimes that's not possible. In some cases it may be worth it to post a larger file. One option would be to make a thumbnail of the image (perhaps 300 pixels by 300 pixels or smaller) and link it to the larger image. By optimizing your images, you'll be optimizing your site's download time.

Should I use JPG, GIF, or PNG? And what's the difference?

The three most common file formats for graphics are JPG, GIF, and PNG. Each of these file formats is best used for a specific kind of graphic: JPG is used for photographs, and PNG or GIF is used for everything else. Why? A JPG file can contain millions of colors, but GIF files can be saved only with up to 256 colors. PNG files were created to replace the GIF format and can be saved as 8-, 24-, or 64-bit images and are about 20 percent smaller than GIF images.

If you are posting digital photos, save your file as `.jpg`; if you're posting any other sort of image (such as line art, like a cartoon), save your file as `.png`.

Podcasting on TypePad

Podcasting is simply broadcasting audio files (for example, voice files, music files, or a combination) via the Internet. Sometimes people lump video in with podcasting, but in this section, we're talking about only audio podcasts; we discuss video in the next section.

Podcasting equipment

Podcasting is a fairly easy way to incorporate multimedia into your blog. All you need are a computer, Internet access, a microphone, and audio-editing software. Because you're reading this book, chances are high that you already have a computer and Internet access. The microphone you choose may cost anywhere from $20 to $200. Any time you're just trying something out, and you have to buy something, we suggest that you go for the midrange item. Why spend hundreds of dollars on something you may not pursue? However, if you decide podcasting is an integral part of your blogging adventure, it's a good idea to choose quality peripherals (such as your microphone). A good mic can make the difference between a so-so podcast and a phenomenal sensation that sweeps the land. Think about it: Do you want to listen to a grainy podcast with inconsistent sound levels? Neither does your audience.

If you're wondering which audio-editing software to use, we have a few suggestions for you:

✔ **Audacity** (`audacity.sourceforge.net`) is an easy-to-use, popular podcasting software option, and it's free. It's available for Windows, Mac, and even Linux. It saves your podcast to MP3 (the most popular format for podcasts)

✔ **Adobe Audition** (`www.adobe.com/products/audition`) is an option when you're ready to take things to the professional level. Professional podcasting software comes with a professional price tag, though. Be prepared to shell out about $350 for Adobe Audition.

✔ **GarageBand** (`www.apple.com/ilife`) is included with the Mac software iLife (Macs come with a 30-day trial of iLife). iLife is affordably priced and includes not only GarageBand, but also iPhoto, iMovie, iWeb, and iDVD.

When you've created and edited your podcast so that it's just right, you'll need to save it as an MP3 file, which is still the most popular format for podcasts. However, as we've noted, multimedia files of all kinds can be quite large. You can make your podcast file smaller by using an audio rate of 128 Kbps. You may even be able to use a smaller bit rate, but be sure to listen to the podcast and make sure it's not too *lossy* (that is, there's a noticeable degradation in the end sound quality).

Why podcast?

Podcasting can add a new dimension to your blog and draw in your readers. However, not every blog niche lends itself to podcasting, so consider whether your blog can benefit from a podcast. Here are some examples of how podcasting can benefit you and your readers:

✔ Your readers may enjoy downloading your podcast so they can listen to it at their leisure. A podcast is sort of like a portable blog post that your readers can download to their MP3 player, smartphone, or other portable device and listen to when it's convenient for them. If you upload your podcasts to iTunes, it's especially easy for your

readers to take advantage of this option. Read more about using iTunes for your podcasts at `www.apple.com/itunes/podcasts/specs.html`.

✔ Interviewing other people in your niche is interesting, and doing it via podcasting allows your readers to hear the inflections they may miss by reading a transcript of the interview.

✔ Podcasts are one more way to bring your audience into your community. You are providing a voice to go with your writing, sharing a new part of yourself.

You can link to podcasts from your blog and even upload them to iTunes. We assume that if you're interested in podcasting, you've already researched how to start podcasting, but you need our help to show you how to integrate your podcast with your TypePad blog. You can do so in a few ways.

Sharing audio files in your blog post couldn't be easier with TypePad. We explain how in the following instructions:

1. **Click the Insert Audio button on the Dashboard (it looks like musical notes).**

   The Upload an Audio File pop-up appears.

2. **Click the Browse button, and find the file you want to upload.**

3. **Click Upload File.**

   MP3 files appear as inline audio players, but other file formats (such as WAV) appear as links that ask the user to download the file so they can listen to it.

Linking from File Manager

When you include an audio file in your post by clicking the Insert Audio button, TypePad automatically places that file in the Files folder in File Manager. TypePad also places image and video files in the Files folder if you haven't manually uploaded the files to another folder yourself.

Using File Manager instead of the Insert Audio button allows you to decide where your files are stored within File Manager, which in turn helps you locate files easily. If you'd like more control over how your individual files are managed, we suggest that you forgo the Insert Audio button and use File Manager instead. We explain how to do this in the following instructions:

1. **Compose your blog post as usual, and save it as a draft.**

2. **Open File Manager (choose Library⇨File Manager).**

3. **Find the folder to which you want to upload your audio file, and open it.**

   See Chapter 4 for detailed advice on setting up an intuitive filing system.

4. **Click inside the Upload a New File text box (as shown in Figure 9-8) or click the Browse button.**

5. **Choose the file you'd like to upload, and click the Upload button.**

   The file is listed in File Manager.

6. **Click the Link icon next to the file you uploaded (the icon looks like a piece of chain link).**

   A pop-up window appears with the necessary code for inserting the link to this audio file within your blog post.

7. **Click inside the pop-up window, and select and copy the code.**

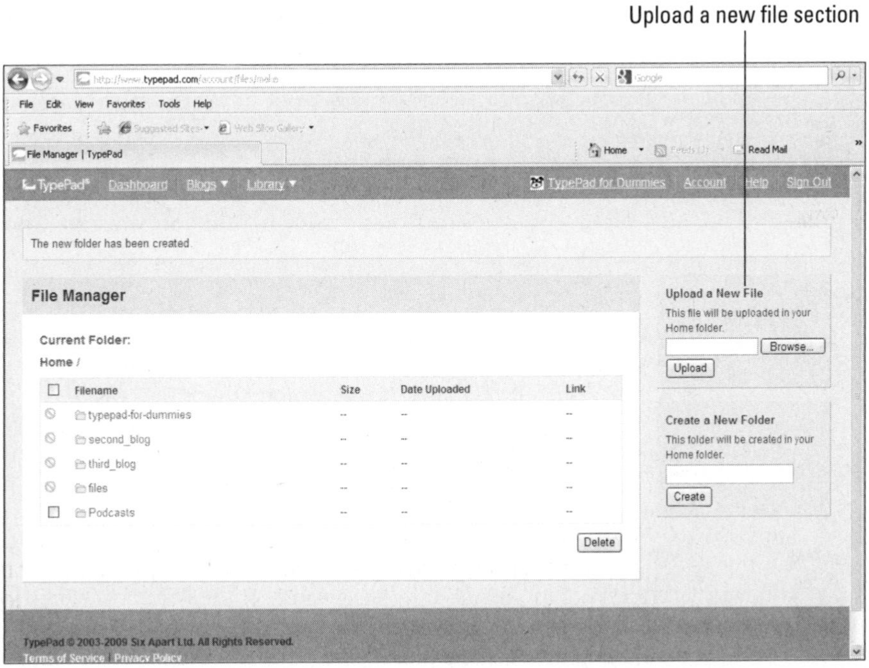

Upload a new file section

Figure 9-8: File Manager, showing Upload a New File section.

8. **Click the Close button.**

9. **Return to your blog post, and click the HTML tab.**

10. **Paste the link code where you'd like it to appear within your blog post.**

11. **Preview your post, and make changes as necessary.**

12. **Publish your blog post.**

   You now have a link to your audio file in your blog post. If you'd like the file to show as an inline audio player instead of a link, you need to use `<embed>` code (explained next).

Using `<embed>` code

To have your audio show up as an inline audio player instead of a link to download the file, you need to use `<embed>` code. Note that if you use the Insert Audio button on your Compose toolbar, TypePad automatically includes the `<embed>` code. But if you insert your audio file manually by using the File Manager method described previously, you have to manually insert the `<embed>` code into your post. The following instructions explain how to do that:

1. **Compose your blog post as usual.**

2. **Upload the file to File Manager, and create a link to the audio file (see the preceding section).**

3. **Click the HTML tab in the post editor.**

   Look for the following HTML code:

   ```
   <a href="http://blogname.typepad.com/weblog/files/podcastname.mp3">Download
           Testpodcast</a>
   ```

4. **Edit the code to look like this:**

   ```
   <embed src="http://blogname.typepad.com/weblog/files/audio.mp3"
           controller="true" autoplay="false" autostart="0" loop="false"
           height="50" width="150"></embed>
   ```

   This HTML code tells the browser to display a controller within your blog post that allows your readers to play the podcast. You can change the values of the HTML code to change the appearance and action of the controller. For example, you can change the height and width values to change the size of the controller. Or you can change the autoplay value to `"true"` if you'd like to have the controller automatically play the audio file when someone arrives at your blog.

   We strongly suggest you do not use autoplay music on your blog. Autoplaying audio is not only annoying and surprising to your visitors, but it's also a bandwidth hog and makes your blog load slowly.

5. **Save or publish your post.**

If you decide to host a podcast, it's up to you how you'll structure your show. Will you find theme music? If so, keep copyright issues in mind. Will you read your content from a script or speak off the cuff? Either option can be a great success; it ultimately boils down to your own style and comfort level. However you set up your podcast, plan! Even a few basic notes or a simple outline go a long way toward keeping you on track. For more information, check out *Podcasting For Dummies,* 2nd Edition, by Tee Morris, Chuck Tomasi, Evo Terra, and Kreg Steppe.

Adding Video to Your Blog

Video is one more way to share content with your readers. You can share a video you've made yourself or a video you found on YouTube (or another video-hosting site). With so many people (bloggers and nonbloggers alike) uploading and sharing content via sites such as YouTube, the process for sharing video on a blog has become simple.

When should you use video in your blog? Well, video is ideal if you are providing a tutorial. Although written instructions are always appreciated, seeing how to do something allows your audience to connect visually with your instructions. This can be helpful whether you're teaching your readers how to start a campfire, sew on a button, or insert video into a blog post! A video tutorial saves you from having to write lengthy step-by-step instructions, and it helps your readers understand better. All you need are a way to capture your video (a digital camcorder, a digital camera, or downloaded software) and the ability to upload your video to a video-sharing site.

Some bloggers offer their readers video posts in place of written text posts, addressing the camera (and, thus, their readers) on their topic of choice. Some readers love this, and others would prefer text — but you, we hope, know your readers best. If a video post would be well-received by your readers, give it a try. We encourage you to make a plan, though — a long, disorganized, rambling video is not putting your best foot forward.

Sharing video from a third-party site

Two of the most popular places to host shareable videos are YouTube (`www.youtube.com`) and Vimeo (`vimeo.com`). These two sites (and many others) make sharing their videos easy. For ease of understanding, we'll use sharing a video from YouTube in our instructions.

Visit YouTube, and find the video you'd like to share. On the page where you view the video, look at the bluish-gray square to the right of the video. That square contains information about the video, including two text boxes labeled URL and Embed, as shown in Figure 9-9.

Video-creation software and video-hosting sites

Video you share with your audience may be called different names: screencast, vlog, or video podcast. Each term essentially refers to the fact that it's video on your blog. If you're interested in trying your hand at a video blog, TechSmith has a few options that help you dip your toes in the video water:

- **Camtasia** (www.techsmith.com/camtasia.asp): This site is available for both Windows and Mac. You can sign up for a 30-day, fully-functional trial of the software. If you're happy with what you see, you can buy the software for $299.

- **Jing** (www.jingproject.com/features): This site is a good option if you just want to make short videos or try out vlogging to see if it's a fit. You can create screen captures or even create a short, five-minute video and share it immediately. Jing offers a free version as well as an affordable Pro version for $14.95/year.

Here's a handy tip: Save or convert your video to MP4 instead of using AVI. Making this conversion shrinks your video files, which gives you faster download time.

After you start vlogging, you have several options for hosting those videos so they don't take up room at your TypePad account. Here's a list of some hosting sites to check out. You'll want to read each site's policies on copyright, file size, privacy, adult content, and publicity to determine if the site is a good fit:

- **YouTube** (www.youtube.com): This site is probably the most popular of the video-hosting sites and allows you to make your own channel so all your videos are on a single page.

- **Vimeo** (www.vimeo.com): Vimeo allows you to post videos and create communities around them. You can also create a personal channel where you showcase all your videos.

- **NewBaby** (www.newbaby.com): This site is geared toward women sharing information, but it's not limited to women with new babies. In addition to videos with parenting tips, NewBaby hosts video on everything from fitness and exercise to finance and product reviews.

- **Blip** (blip.tv): Blip.tv is different from other video-hosting sites because it focuses on helping independent creators of episodic videos showcase their content.

- **Flickr** (www.flickr.com): Flickr is best known as an image-hosting site, but it also hosts videos.

At this point, you have a choice about how to share this video. You can simply provide your readers a link to the video (they click the link and watch the video at YouTube, not your blog), or you can embed the video in your post so viewers can see it at your blog, with no clicking away from your site required. Depending on which option you choose, follow the appropriate instructions in the next sections.

Figure 9-9:
Details
you need
to share a
YouTube
video.

Details required to share video pictured at left

Linking to or embedding a video

Whether you want to include a video in your blog post or just want to link
to the video (but not have the video appear in your blog), TypePad lets
you do that with ease. To begin, copy either the <embed> code (to show
the actual video in your blog post) or the URL information (to link to the
video but not show it in your post) at YouTube to the clipboard, and follow
these steps:

1. **Compose your blog post as usual, using the TypePad editor.**

   Include a description of the video you are linking to.

2. **Highlight the sentence(s) you want to use as the link to the video.**

3. **Click the Insert Video icon (it looks like a piece of movie film) on the
   toolbar.**

   The Insert Video pop-up window appears.

4. **Choose which option you want to use:**

 • **To link to the video (without showing it in your post):** Paste the URL of the video in the Link URL text box.

 • **To show the video in your post:** Paste the `<embed>` code into the Embed text field.

5. **Click Insert Video.**

6. **Save or publish your blog post as usual.**

Sharing video from File Manager

If you take your own video and would like to share it with your audience, your best bet is to set up an account at a video-hosting site and embed your videos in your blog from there, using the previous instructions.

If you'd rather host your video in TypePad File Manager, however, you have a few options. You can

✔ Upload the video file to File Manager

✔ Insert the video as a file

✔ Use `<embed>` code

Instructions for each of these options follow.

Link from File Manager

Uploading your video to File Manager and linking to it in a blog post allows you to decide where your file is stored in File Manager.

When you upload video to File Manager, it may take a while for TypePad to receive the video, depending on the file's size. Because of this delay, TypePad suggests hosting your video files on a video-sharing site. These third-party sites are optimized for serving video, so you'll be able to access your video sooner.

The following instructions explain how to upload and link to a video file from File Manager:

1. **Compose your blog post as usual, and save it as a draft.**

2. **Open File Manager (choose Library➪File Manager).**

3. **Find the folder to which you want to upload your audio file, and open it.**

4. **Click inside the Upload New File text box or click the Browse button.**

5. **Choose the file you'd like to upload and then click the Upload button.**

 The file is listed in File Manager.

6. **Click the link icon next to the file you uploaded (the icon looks like a piece of chain link).**

   A pop-up window appears with the necessary code for inserting the link to this audio file within your blog post.

7. **Click inside the pop-up window, and select and copy the code.**

8. **Click the Close button.**

9. **Return to your blog post, and click the HTML tab.**

10. **Paste the link code where you'd like it to appear within your blog post.**

    Notice that your post now shows a link that allows your readers to download your video. If you would rather have the video embedded within your post, please see the instructions below for using <embed> code.

11. **Preview your post, make changes as necessary, and then publish your post.**

Insert your video as a file

Inserting your video as a file automatically stores your uploaded file in a generic folder called Files in File Manager. Any files (video, audio, text, images, and so on) uploaded via the Insert File link on the Compose editor toolbar are stored in the same folder in File Manager. This could make it difficult for you to find your files efficiently.

To insert your video using the Insert File button from the Compose toolbar, follow these instructions:

1. **Compose your blog post as usual in the Compose editor.**

2. **Place the cursor where you would like to insert your file.**

3. **Click the Insert File icon on the toolbar.**

   The icon looks like a piece of paper with a green arrow on it (see Figure 9-10). A pop-up window appears.

Figure 9-10:
The Compose Editor showing the Insert File icon.

Insert File icon

4. **Click the Browse button, and find the audio file you want to include in your blog post.**

5. **Click the Upload File button.**

   TypePad inserts a link to the file within your post. If you would rather have the video embedded within your post, see the following instructions for using <embed> code.

Use <embed> code

If you plan to use <embed> code to embed an audio controller in your post, be aware that this requires you to change some HTML code within your post. The following instructions explain how to insert your video into your post by using <embed> code:

1. **Compose your blog post as usual.**

2. **Upload the file either to File Manager or via the Insert File button on the toolbar (see the preceding section).**

3. **Click the HTML tab in the top-right corner of the Compose editor.**

   Look for HTML code similar to this:

   ```
   <a href="http://blogname.typepad.com/weblog/files/movie.wmv">Download
           Testpodcast</a>
   ```

4. **Edit the code to look like this:**

   ```
   <embed autostart="0" src="http://blogname.typepad.com/ weblog/files/movie.
           wmv" height="XXX" width="XXX">
   ```

   This code tells the browser to display a video window in your blog post that allows your readers to play the video.

   You must change the height and width values to match your video. If you don't know these values, make your best guess and change the values as necessary. We usually start by using 300 for both the height and width.

5. **Save or publish your post.**

Experiment with the types of multimedia files that might be of interest to your readers. Whether you post video, audio, or photos, these additions can add an entirely new dimension to your blog community, giving you new and creative ways to connect with your readers.

Chapter 10

Exploring Social Media

· ·

In This Chapter

▶ Defining social media

▶ Integrating your social media accounts with your TypePad account

▶ Introducing important social media and social bookmarking sites

▶ Using social media to build community

· ·

*I*f you've read a single technology headline in the last three years, you've surely heard the phrase *social media* — it's the darling of the hour. As people look for more ways to connect to one another online, and as corporations enter the fray seeking to establish bonds with customers, social media is quickly becoming a cornerstone of the online experience.

In this chapter, we tell you what social media is, how it works, and how you can incorporate it on your TypePad blog. If you're a small-business owner, you might like the tips on enhancing your marketing efforts through social media.

Understanding Key Social Media Sites

Social media refers to the information sharing and gathering that takes place in relational, online forums. Blogs are a big part of social media, of course, but social media also encompasses interactive sites such as Facebook, Twitter, FriendFeed, and others. Any Web site that allows people to connect with one another and share information qualifies to sit under the social media umbrella.

And it's an umbrella that's growing. Every day, new sites join countless existing ones to provide people a place to build online community. An entire industry has been created as social media consultants advise bloggers and corporations on the best ways to navigate the social media waters. The bottom line? You can't be everywhere at once. Unless you plan to spend your every waking moment online (we don't recommend it!), you'll have to pick and choose which online communities are the best fit for you. In this chapter, we provide an overview of the key social media sites TypePad integrates into your blogging experience: Twitter, Facebook, FriendFeed, and Flickr.

As with any community — online or not — the more involved you are, the more people accept you as part of their group. As you offer items and comments to various social networking sites, you're building your credibility (as well as your brand). It's a good idea to promote others in your community more than you promote yourself. People tend to be put off if you're constantly tooting your own horn.

Adding Your Social Networks to Your Blog

TypePad is committed to harnessing the power of social media and handing the reins to its users. The redesign of TypePad in 2009 was centered largely on the goal of turning your blog into the hub of your online community. From your TypePad blog, you can reach out to your other networks (Twitter, Facebook, and so on). The new software developments are geared toward full control for the user.

In Chapter 3, we explain your TypePad Profile, a handy tool for aggregating your online presences into one central hub. Likewise, in Chapter 6, we explain how you can share your posts with Twitter, Facebook, or FriendFeed as you publish them. TypePad also allows your readers to share comments they leave at your blog with their own Facebook or Twitter communities (see Chapter 7 for an overview of your comment options). Built-in features like these allow you to streamline the management of your online community.

One of TypePad's goals is to make it easier to manage your online presence by integrating all your social media accounts. Although TypePad has always worked well with Flickr, now Six Apart has specifically integrated the most popular social media tools with your TypePad blogging account. TypePad allows you to

✔ Sign in using a third-party social media account such as Facebook or Twitter (your TypePad account recognizes it's you; a commenter can also sign in with his or her social media account to leave a comment)

✔ Share your newest post with your Twitter, Facebook, and FriendFeed communities (see Chapter 6)

✔ Insert links at the end of each post so your readers can share your post with social media sites (see Chapter 11)

✔ Connect your other social media profiles to your TypePad Profile (see Chapter 3)

Although your other social media accounts appear only as links in your TypePad Profile's page, those links are a handy way to share your information with readers who visit that page. Readers only have to click the relevant link to connect with you anywhere online.

The rest of this section defines and explains how some of the integrated social media communities (Twitter, Facebook, FriendFeed, and Flickr) work and how you can make the most of them as you build your social media community.

Twitter

Twitter (`twitter.com`) allows you to share your thoughts, ideas, and updates in 140 characters or fewer. It's evolved from a tool that allowed people to give short updates about their lives to a *microblog* (a short update or snapshot of time) tool used by millions to exchange ideas, promote brands and links, and make connections across the globe.

Setting up a Twitter account is easy. Just visit `twitter.com` and click the Sign Up Now button. You'll be asked for your full name, the username you would like, a password, and your e-mail address. Your Twitter username can be anything you like (as long as it's not already taken), but we suggest that you consider a few things when choosing your Twitter handle:

- ✔ **Shorter is better.** You get only 140 characters per tweet, and your username counts toward those 140 when someone addresses directly on Twitter (using the @ symbol directly in front of your username).

- ✔ **Promote your brand.** If readers and peers know you more through your brand than as your personal name, use the brand as your Twitter handle.

- ✔ **Promote yourself.** These days it's not uncommon for your brand to be *you*. If that's the case, see if you can secure your name as your Twitter ID. In fact, it's always a good idea to secure your name in as many online venues as possible, even if you're not active with that account. You just never know how things are going to work out, and it's nice to have that base covered.

After you create your Twitter account, you can start finding and following your friends who also have Twitter accounts. When you follow someone, you see their tweets and can respond if you like. If they follow you, they'll see your tweets as well. If you're following each other, you can also send a DM (direct message) or private messages to each other.

Twitter etiquette

Yes, even Twitter has best practices and accepted behavior. You'd be surprised at how much you can pack into 140 characters — and *how* you do it matters. Here's a list of Twitter dos and don'ts:

✔ **Do customize your Twitter Profile page.** Upload an avatar, share your blog's URL, write a bio. You can find advice about customizing your background by searching *customize Twitter profile* in your favorite search engine. A personalized profile shows that you're part of the community. You know who doesn't customize their profiles? Spammers. You don't want to be mistaken for one of them.

✔ **Do share ideas and thoughts.** Bring something to the table. When you find your online community, you'll soon see what interests them (and you). Add to that community by sharing links, re-tweeting interesting tweets, and commenting on what you're seeing. As we mention in Chapter 18, linking to items other than your own articles builds goodwill and community. Being a respected part of the community means sharing with the community and promoting others. If you're linking only to your stuff, people notice and lose interest quickly. Also, when you share a link, make a brief comment about it. People are more likely to click a link if it has context.

✔ **Do be interesting.** Twitter gets a bad rap (often deservedly so) for offering users trivial, useless information. A well-written tweet, whether it's funny, informative, or moving, *is* possible, though. Find clever ways to offer your followers something valuable or entertaining in a short space — it gets easier with practice.

✔ **Don't send an automatic DM thanking someone for following you.** (DM stands for direct message; it's essentially a private tweet.) Even if you are trying to be appreciative and are trying to let the person know you're glad they've followed you, resist the urge to send an automated "thanks-for-following-me" DM. Many in the Twitter community look at these DMs as spam. Some people may ignore it; others unfollow you for it.

✔ **Don't use your public Twitter stream for a private conversation.** Use the DM feature for conversations that go on for more than a tweet or two or that are private. Just as in blogging, your community doesn't have to be privy to *everything*.

✔ **Don't use Twitter as your personal advertising space.** It's okay to tweet your latest blog post, but just be sure it's not *all* you're tweeting. Twitter is a community, and it's all about the give and take. If you're always taking (promoting only yourself and your products), people start to ignore you.

As you start using Twitter, here are a few words you'll want to be familiar with:

✔ **Tweet:** A *tweet* is simply any message typed in Twitter. The message can be up to 140 characters long.

✔ **Twitter stream:** This is a list of the updates from other Twitter users. When you follow someone (that is, you keep track of their updates), any tweets they post show up in your twitter stream.

✔ **Re-tweet:** If someone likes what you've tweeted or wants to share a comment about something you've tweeted, that user may re-tweet your message with RT at the beginning. Here's an example of a re-tweet:

```
RT @chilihead I'm co-authoring TypePad for
Dummies with @rocksinmydryer! So excited!
```

The original Twitter page you see when you sign up doesn't offer a lot of functionality. You can't automatically shorten URLs (and those take up precious character count!), and you have to manually refresh your browser page to see if anything new has come up in your Twitter stream. Just about everyone who Twitters uses a third-party program to keep track of their Twitter community because, among other things, those applications allow you to shorten URLs and have one-click direct messaging. Here are a few Twitter applications you may want to try:

✔ HootSuite (hootsuite.com)

✔ PowerTwitter (addons.mozilla.org/en-US/firefox/addon/9591)

✔ TweetDeck (tweetdeck.com)

✔ Twhirl (www.twhirl.org)

You can share pictures, video, and even music via Twitter if you have the right applications. These are the ones we've found to be popular:

✔ Share pictures via Twitpic (twitpic.com) or Flickr (www.flickr.com/help/sharing/#953361)

✔ Share videos via Vidly (vidly.com/?twitvid) or Twiddeo (beta.twiddeo.com)

✔ Share music clips via Blip.fm (blip.fm) or Twt.fm (twt.fm)

Still looking for more tips, tricks, and best practices for Twitter? Check out TwiTip.com.

Facebook

Facebook (www.facebook.com) is a social network offering personal and business profile pages, fan pages, and group pages. You can share pictures, video, Web links, and personal updates via your profile or page.

Facebook is the largest social network going right now. Why is it 300 million strong? Like all good social media, it allows you to customize and filter the information you view based on your interests and the recommendations of your friends.

To set up a Facebook account, go to www.facebook.com and complete the short sign-up form. Next, complete your profile information, which is one of the most important things you can do when you are using social media. At a minimum, you should include a picture of yourself and some basic information (your interests, a link to your blog, and so on). Deciding whether you want your page to be primarily personal, business, or a combination of the two determines what information you share.

When your profile is complete, start looking for friends. Point your browser to www.facebook.com/find-friends to use your e-mail contacts to find potential Facebook friends, or use the search feature to find people you know or companies you're familiar with.

As your Facebook community grows, you may find yourself overwhelmed with the amount of information streaming through your news feed. The key to managing any social media presence is knowing how to manage your information. In the following sections, we tell you how to manage your news feed with lists and untag yourself in a photo.

Managing your news feed with lists

When you have several hundred friends, your news feed can be a jumble. You may miss useful news, links, or updates. One way to control what information you see and when is to create and assign lists to your friends. Depending on how you use your Facebook account, you may have both personal and professional contacts. You may want to start by creating lists for family, friends, professional colleagues, and so on.

To create a new list, follow these instructions:

1. **Sign in to Facebook, and go to your Home page.**

   Note that your Home page is different from your Profile page. Look at the top of your page, and click the Home link to make sure you're on the right page.

2. **Click the More button under the left column to reveal more news feed options.**

3. **Click the Create New List link at the bottom of the expanded left column.**

   A pop-up window appears.

4. **In the text field, type the name of the list.**

   You can name your list whatever you like (for example, family, friends, or professional contacts).

5. **Click the name or profile picture of the people you want to include in this list.**

   You can either scroll down the list and choose people or do a quick search for specific friends using the search field.

6. **Click Create List.**

A new Facebook List appears in the left column. Now, instead of sifting through your news feed, you can click a specific list to see what those people have shared recently.

You can repeat these instructions to create as many lists as you like.

Untagging unflattering or unprofessional photos

When you share photos with your Facebook community, you have the opportunity to tag photos with the names of others who are in the picture. Of course, this means others can also tag you in their photos. When you are tagged in someone else's photo, that photo appears in your Photo tab, and your entire Facebook community can see it (as well as the communities of anyone else tagged in that picture). Sometimes, photos surface that you'd rather not be openly associated with. If you'd like to untag yourself in a photo, follow these instructions:

1. **Open the picture in which you're tagged.**

You can usually find it by going to the Photos tab in your Facebook profile. The top of the Photos page shows all the photos in which you've been tagged. Click to open the photo you want to untag.

2. **Click the Remove Tag link under the photo.**

You are no longer tagged in that photo, and no one can re-tag you later.

Of course, those photos are still out there, and people could search for a specific photo (especially if they know someone in the picture with you and that person's tag is functional). To keep others from searching for photos of you, you'll need to configure your Facebook preferences as follows:

1. **Use your cursor to hover over the Settings link on your Facebook profile.**

A menu appears.

2. **Choose Privacy from the menu.**

The privacy setting page appears.

3. **Click the Profile link.**

Your profile settings page appears. Find the option labeled Photos Tagged of You.

4. **Choose Customize from the Photos Tagged of You pull-down menu.**

The Photos Tagged of You pop-up window appears, asking "Who can see this?"

5. **Click to select Only Me.**

6. **Click OK.**

Facebook can't stop others from posting pictures of you and tagging you in those pictures. However, by setting your privacy options as just shown, the tag that shows up in the picture does not link to your Facebook profile.

FriendFeed

FriendFeed (friendfeed.com) allows you to track your many social networking accounts from a single place in real time. In addition, you can include items for your social networking sites such as Facebook, Twitter, Flickr, your blog, Delicious, Google Reader, YouTube, or even Amazon. Whatever you post on the networks you share with your FriendFeed account automatically shows up in your FriendFeed stream as well.

When an item appears in your FriendFeed stream (whether from you or a friend), you can "like" or "share" or "comment" on that item. You can even have a real-time conversation via chat about a topic.

FriendFeed has several applications you can use to streamline your FriendFeed use:

✔ BuddyFeed ($2.99) is available from the iTunes App Store. It allows you to track your FriendFeed stream by using your iPhone or iPod touch.

✔ FriendFeed offers several widgets you can include on your blog's sidebar. You can find these at friendfeed.com/embed. Use a Notes TypeList or the Embed Your Own HTML widget (see Chapter 8) to include one in your blog.

✔ FriendFeed Notifier (friendfeed.com/settings/notifier) allows you to access your FriendFeed account directly from your computer's desktop.

Publishing Flickr photos on your blog

Flickr.com is a photo and video-sharing Web site. Flickr is linked to your Yahoo! ID, if you have one, and it takes only a minute to register. After you've registered with Flickr, you can start uploading your photos and videos to your account and editing them if necessary (Flickr partners with Picnik for photo editing). Then you can start sharing those photos with friends and family or with everyone (you can set the level of privacy you want through your account page). You can also join groups related to your own interests.

Another feature Flickr offers is tagging your photos with Creative Commons (creativecommons.org) information to let others know how you're willing to share your photos. You can determine whether you want a photo to have all rights reserved or if you're okay with people using your photo as long as they give the proper attribution. You can choose among several options when using Creative Commons.

If you are looking at Flickr to find images you can use on your site, you need to check the Creative Commons license of the image before you use it. It's illegal to use images without the permission of the owner. If the image doesn't have a Creative Commons license associated with it, you have to contact the owner directly to ask permission to use the image.

Flickr allows you to group your photos into sets or collections. *Sets* are individual groups of photos (such as Trevor & Ewan's Playground Adventure or Disney World 2004). A *collection* is a selection of sets (or other collections) that relate to a broader theme (such as family or travel).

If you already have your photos loaded to Flickr and prefer to use those for your blog instead of uploading them to TypePad File Manager, you can do that. Flickr simply requires that you post a link back to Flickr any time you link a photo from its site (www.flickr.com/guidelines.gne).

You can use Flickr photos on your blog in three ways:

✔ Cut and paste the HTML related to a specific photo into your TypePad blog post.

✔ Link your blog to your Flickr account and write a post in Flickr that posts to your TypePad account.

✔ Embed a Flickr slideshow in your post.

We tell you how to achieve each of those options next.

Post Flickr pictures via TypePad

Posting Flickr photos on your TypePad blog is a simple process. We think it's easiest if you have two tabs open in your browser: one opened to your Flickr account and one opened to the TypePad post you're working on. Then follow these steps:

1. **Find the photo you want to use via Flickr.**

   Remember that if the image is not yours, you must have permission to use it from the owner.

   You should see a page similar to the one in Figure 10-1. You know you're on the correct page if you see the toolbar above the photo. If you don't see the toolbar, click the photo until you do.

Figure 10-1:
Use this
toolbar to
generate
the HTML
for your
photo.

Slideshow button

2. Click All Sizes on the toolbar.

A new page appears with your picture and several size options above it (as shown in Figure 10-2).

3. Click the photo size that works with your blog.

A new page appears that shows you how big the image will look.

We prefer to use either Small or Thumbnail. We've found that anything larger sometimes doesn't fit within the content column of our blogs.

You have two HTML options:

- Complete HTML to embed the photo in your post. To use this option, continue to Step 4.

- A simple URL you can use to link a word to the photo. To use this option, continue to Step 5.

4. To use the HTML option to embed the photo in your post:

a. Copy the HTML `<embed>` code.

Click inside the box to highlight the code and then press Ctrl+C (PC) or Command+C (Mac) to copy the code.

    b. **Return to your TypePad post, and click the HTML tab.**

    c. **Paste the code into your post.**

    d. **Click the Rich Text tab to see how your photo appears in your post.**

    e. **Save and publish your post as usual.**

      You're finished; you don't need to continue past this point.

5. **To instead use a URL to link a word to the photo:**

    a. **Copy the URL, and return to your TypePad post.**

    b. **Highlight the word(s) you want to link to the photo.**

    c. **Click the link icon in your post toolbar (it looks like a piece of chain link).**

    d. **Paste the URL you copied at Flickr into the URL field in the pop-up Link Options box.**

    e. **Click OK.**

    f. **Save and publish your post as usual.**

Size options

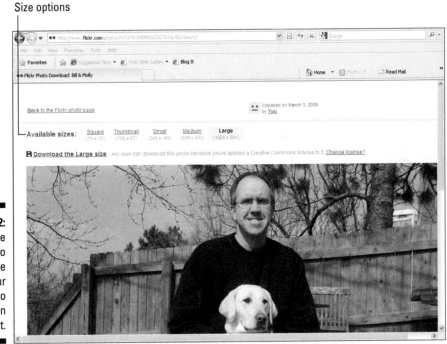

Figure 10-2:
Use the size options to determine how your photo appears in your post.

Post Flickr pictures through Flickr

It's easy to upload a photo to Flickr and blog about it immediately without having to open your TypePad account. You just need to associate your TypePad blog with your Flickr account. To do that, follow these instructions:

1. **Sign in to your Flickr.com account.**

2. **Click the arrow next to You in the Flickr navigation bar.**

   A larger pull-down menu appears.

3. **Choose Your Account from the menu options.**

   Your account page appears. You see four navigation tabs: Personal Information, Privacy & Permissions, Email, and Extending Flickr.

4. **Click the Extending Flickr tab.**

   Find the Your Blogs section of the Extending Flickr page.

5. **Click Configure your Flickr-to-blog settings.**

   The Your Account/Blogs page appears, with information on linking your blog to Flickr.

6. **Click Set Up Your Blog.**

7. **Choose TypePad from the pull-down menu.**

8. **Enter your TypePad username and password.**

   Flickr must have this information to link your TypePad and Flickr accounts.

9. **Use the pull-down menu to choose which blog you want to associate with your Flickr account.**

10. **Click Next.**

    The Confirm Your Details page appears.

11. **Type your blog's URL in the text box labeled URL.**

    You can use the TypePad address (for example, `http://typepad fordummies.typepad.com`) or your own domain (for example, `www.myblog.com`) if you've mapped it to your TypePad blog (see Appendix A for instructions on how to map your domain).

12. **Click All Done.**

    Your blog is now linked to your Flickr account, and you can include photos on your blog quickly and easily.

Now you're ready to write a blog post, insert your picture, and post it to your TypePad account. The following instructions tell you how.

If you've set the Creative Commons license of your photo to None (which means all rights reserved), your photo will not show up in your post. You need to change the Creative Commons license to something more flexible to use the Blog This Photo options. You can find out which Creative Commons license is right for you at `www.flickr.com/account/prefs/license` (we like the Attribution-NonCommercial-NoDerivs option).

1. **Find the photo you want to use via Flickr.**

   You should see a page similar to the one in Figure 10-1. You know you're on the correct page if you see the toolbar above the photo. If you don't see the toolbar, click the photo until you do.

2. **Click Blog This on the toolbar.**

   A pull-down menu appears.

3. **Choose the name of the blog you want to post the picture to.**

   The Blog This Photo page appears, as shown in Figure 10-3.

4. **Type the title of the post in the Title text box.**

   If you've titled your photo, that title may automatically appear in the Title box. You can simply replace it with the title you'd like to use. The text in this box is the title of your post.

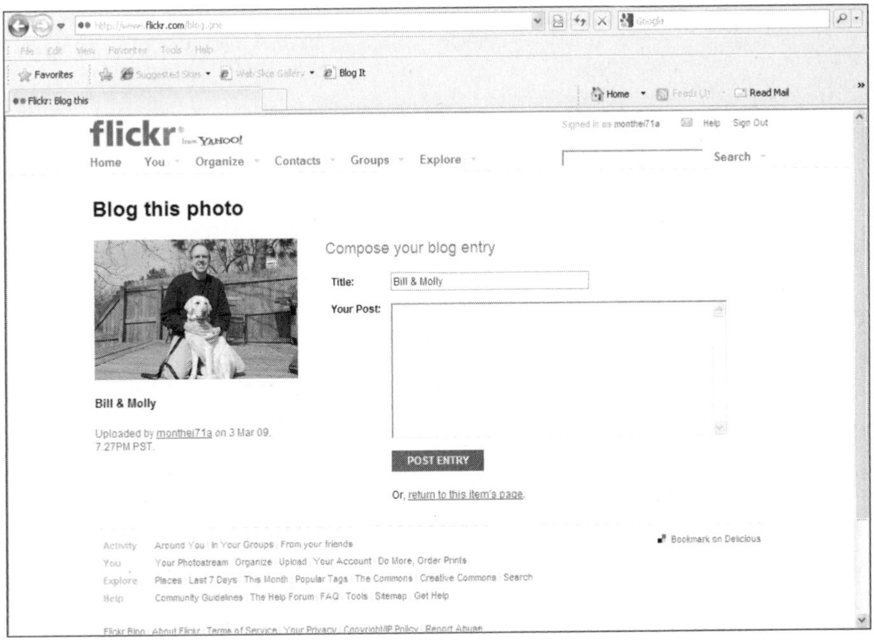

Figure 10-3:
The Blog this photo page at Flickr.

5. **Click inside the Your Post text box, and begin typing your post.**

6. **Click Post Entry.**

7. **Visit your blog to see your post.**

   If you visit your TypePad Dashboard, you'll see that this post is listed in the Posts tab.

Display a Flickr slideshow within a post

If you have several photos you'd like to share in your blog post, it may be easier to share a slideshow with your audience. It's an easy process; just follow these instructions:

1. **Choose the set, collection, or photo group you want to share.**

2. **Click the Slideshow button.**

   (The slideshow button is labeled in Figure 10-1.) A slideshow of your pictures starts, as shown in Figure 10-4.

3. **Click the Share link in the top-right corner.**

   Two HTML options appear:

   • **Grab the URL allows you to link to the slideshow.**

     You can do this by copying the URL, returning to your TypePad post, and highlighting the words to link. Then click the link icon in your post toolbar (it looks like a piece of chain link), and paste the slideshow URL in the URL box. Click OK.

   • **Grab the embed HTML allows you to embed the entire slideshow directly in your blog post.**

     Just copy the embed code, return to your TypePad post, and click the HTML tab. Paste the <embed> code, and publish as usual.

Use Flickr applications

Sometimes, of course, you don't need to embed a photo in a post. You just want to show off what you're sharing on Flickr. In those instances, a simple widget can help you out. Here are two you may like:

✔ The Flickr widget by Roy Tanck (www.roytanck.com/get-my-flickr-widget) displays a rotating selection of your Flickr photos based on your Flickr RSS feed.

✔ With the Flickr Badge generator (www.flickr.com/badge.gne), you can choose an HTML badge or an Adobe Flash badge.

Share link

Figure 10-4:
A sample
Flickr slide-
show and
available
links.

Using Bit.ly Links to Track Social Media Traffic

As we explain in Chapter 6, when you publish a new blog post, you have
the option of sharing that post immediately with your Twitter, Facebook,
and FriendFeed communities. When you do so, TypePad uses bit.ly (a third-
party URL shortening company) to track the links sent to Twitter, Facebook,
and FriendFeed. Bit.ly keeps track of each time one of those links is clicked and
provides some basic statistics on those clicks. Understanding which social media
community is clicking your links consistently can help you determine which
audience(s) you should focus on when disseminating certain information. For
instance, if you notice that each time you post about volunteering at the veteri-
narian's office, you receive more clicks from your Facebook community, you may
want to consider posting even more information regarding volunteering, animal
rescue, animal training, or general pet ownership tips on your Facebook fan page.

Although TypePad can tell you how many people have clicked your bit.ly link,
you'll need to click over to the bit.ly Web site to see a true representation of

how your communities are using your links. To see an overview of your bit.ly statistics, follow these instructions:

1. **In TypePad, click the name of the blog whose stats you want to view.**

   The blog navigation bar for that blog appears. The Overview tab is open by default. On the Overview tab, you see a graph of your blog's traffic. Below that graph, you'll see a link that says Social Media Optimization: Bit.ly Traffic. Figure 10-5 shows you exactly where that link is.

2. **Click the Bit.ly Traffic link.**

   The Real Time Bit.ly Traffic page appears and looks similar to Figure 10-6. This page lists all the posts you've shared (the titles link back to the posts at your blog), via bit.ly links, with your social media communities.

3. **Click the URL under Bit.ly Info to see your bit.ly statistics.**

   Note that when you click this link, you leave the TypePad site and move to the bit.ly Web site, which displays a page with traffic statistics for the post you chose. Figure 10-7 shows an example of a bit.ly statistics page. You have an overview of how many clicks the link received. You can also view clicks, referrers, and location (the geographic locations of your readers when they clicked over) based on current information, the past week, or even the past month.

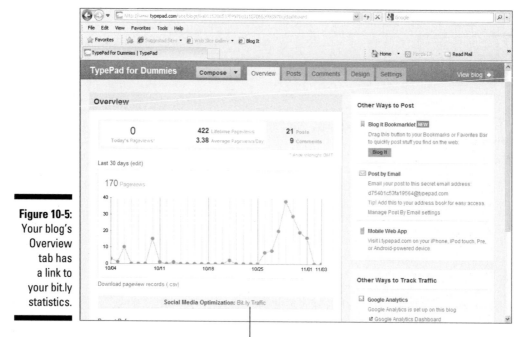

Figure 10-5: Your blog's Overview tab has a link to your bit.ly statistics.

Bit.ly Traffic link

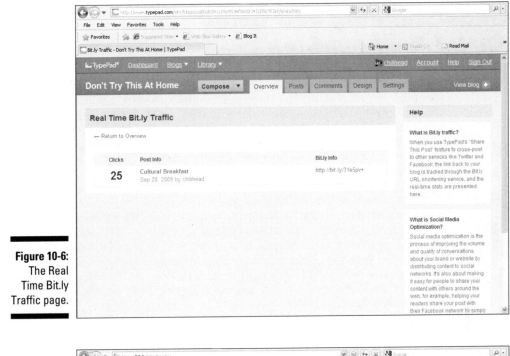

Figure 10-6:
The Real
Time Bit.ly
Traffic page.

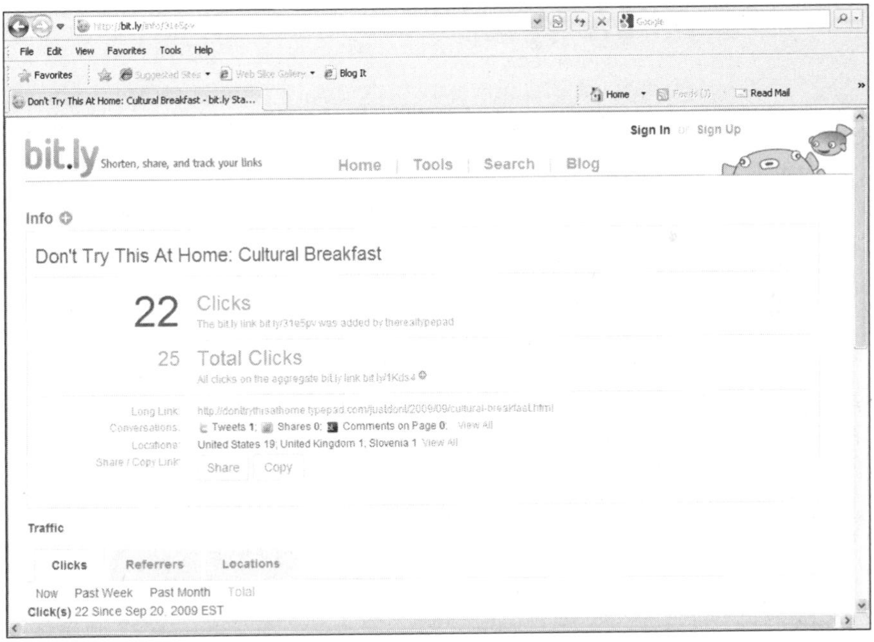

Figure 10-7:
The bit.ly
Web site
provides
more
detailed
traffic sta-
tistics than
the TypePad
overview.

Understanding and Using Social Bookmarking

Social media, as you can well imagine, is vast. It includes more than tools that push information out to others (for example, sharing your newest post URL with your Twitter community). Social media includes tools that pull media to you based on your interests and keep track of the things you like. Those types of sites are called *social bookmarking sites.* Although there are many, we'd like to draw your attention to a few that we have found most valuable.

Any time your blog is included in a social bookmarking site, you're bound to benefit from a spike in traffic. However, be aware that this traffic is what's known as *drive-by traffic.* The people visiting your site are temporary readers and may or may not subscribe to your RSS feed or return to read your updates. It's your job (and not an easy one) to engage them enough to subscribe to your feed and become regular readers. How? At the risk of repeating ourselves: Produce great content; have an engaging, clean design; and make your RSS subscription button easy to find.

StumbleUpon

As you surf the 'net, it's easy to get into a rut and return to the same sites over and over. StumbleUpon (www.stumbleupon.com) strives to make finding relevant information not only easy, but also interesting. The premise of StumbleUpon is simple: It finds sites you like based on the interests you share in your StumbleUpon profile.

The interesting thing about StumbleUpon is that it learns from your behavior and adjusts the kinds of sites it offers you accordingly. StumbleUpon uses an algorithm to keep track of the Web sites or blogs you like and don't like. Then, based on your preferences (both from your profile and your votes), you see more sites that are relevant to your interests.

To use StumbleUpon, you sign up for an account and choose your interests (such as technology, books, crafts, and writing — don't worry; you can add or delete interests if they change). Then you install the StumbleUpon toolbar (www.stumbleupon.com/download.php) in your Web browser. The StumbleUpon toolbar (shown in Figure 10-8) allows you to do two main things:

✔ **Browse random sites based on your interests.** Just click the Stumble link on the toolbar, and you're surfing.

✔ **Vote on the sites that you like best or are relevant to your interests.** Just click the thumbs-up icon in the toolbar to show that you like a site.

You can also use the StumbleUpon toolbar to share links with your friends or bookmark your favorite sites in your StumbleUpon account.

If one of your articles is *stumbled* (that is, someone gave it a thumbs up), the result can be a spike in traffic. You may see hundreds of visitors over the course of 24 hours after the initial stumble. We haven't met a blogger yet who doesn't appreciate the increase in readers (even if the increase is temporary).

It may be tempting to stumble your own posts frequently to enjoy that boost in traffic as often as possible. In a word, don't. StumbleUpon notices if your blog is constantly being stumbled and assumes you're trying to game the system, either by stumbling your own articles or asking people to stumble them for you. The result is that you'll be penalized, and your link won't show up as often. As with everything online, moderation is key. If you're particularly proud of an article, don't be afraid to ask a friend to stumble it for you. Just save that favor for the really good articles.

StumbleUpon toolbar

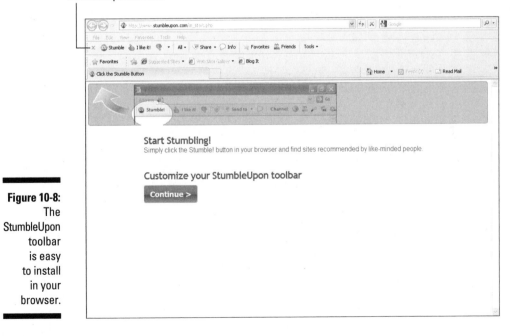

Figure 10-8:
The
StumbleUpon
toolbar
is easy
to install
in your
browser.

Kirtsy

Kirtsy was born out of the need for a social bookmarking site that caters to women. The women who created Kirtsy.com were aiming to create the female version of Digg (described next). Kirtsy's four founders work with a team of about 20 editors to find the most interesting stories online as they relate to women. Those stories are listed on the Kirtsy site and then readers have the option of voting stories up or down. The more votes a story gets, the longer it stays on the front page.

If you're interested in a specific topic, you can search the top stories (submitted by both the editors and readers just like you) in several categories: arts and entertainment; design and crafts; family and parenting; fashion and style; food and home; Internet and technology; mind, body, and spirit; travel and leisure; and politics, world, and business.

To use Kirtsy, just create an account by clicking the Join Kirtsy! link at the top of the page and following the wizard's instructions. After you're a registered member, you can submit a story to Kirtsy (and then invite your online community to vote it up), find an interesting story to read (look at Kirtsy's home page or search one of the categories), or vote a story up or down. To vote *for* a story, just click the title of the article. You'll be taken to the article's site so you can read it. If you like it, great. If you don't, and you want to take back your vote, just return to Kirtsy and click the Un-Vote link by that article.

You can vote on several articles a day at Kirtsy, but you can vote on only a single article once per day. For example, you may choose to vote up (and read) several articles on the Kirtsy home page. You can't vote for a story more than once a day, though, so even if you click over to an article a second time, your vote still counts only once. But you can always return tomorrow and vote again!

Digg

Digg.com may be the most well-known social bookmarking site going these days. Like the other social media or social bookmarking sites we've discussed in this chapter, Digg.com is a place to find news, blog posts, images, and even video from anywhere on the Web. All the content featured at Digg is submitted by the Digg community.

After something is submitted, the rest of the community determines its value: They either vote it up (digg it) or vote it down (bury it). If something receives enough votes, it makes it to the front page of Digg.com. It's notoriously difficult to make it to the front page of Digg, but if you do, your blog will enjoy the craziness of tens of thousands of hits in a single day. You'll definitely be on the map if you make it to the front page of Digg. If you want to be part of the Digg community, register an account with Digg and jump into the conversation. Then, just like at the other social bookmarking sites, you can start building your Digg community. Look for people you've connected with on Twitter or Facebook or via your Gmail account. You can even choose the topics you're most interested in reading about.

Those in the Digg community don't like to see others promoting only their own stuff. If you want to be a part of the community, make sure you're offering interesting items from other people as well. And don't forget to join the discussion! Offer your comments about a particular item.

Delicious

Delicious allows you to tag, save, and share articles you find useful or interesting, or just want easy access to. Sure, you could bookmark an item in your browser, but sites like Delicious allow you to share your favorites with your community and see what your friends are sharing as well.

To start using Delicious, register for an account by visiting `delicious.com` and clicking the Join Now! link in the top-right corner of the page. After you have your account established, install the Delicious toolbar so you can easily tag and save links as you find them. You can find links to the toolbar within Delicious help: `delicious.com/help`. The Delicious toolbar installs three small buttons on your browser toolbar. Table 10-1 provides an overview of each button.

Table 10-1		Delicious Toolbar Buttons
Button	*Button Name*	*What It Does*
	Delicious	Links to your Delicious account page
	Sidebar	Opens a sidebar in your browser so you can quickly search or browse your Delicious bookmarks
	Tag	Opens a window that lets you tag and save a Web page in your Delicious bookmarks

If you'd like to share your links with your blog readers, it's easy. Just follow these instructions to install the Delicious widget on your sidebar:

1. **Sign in to your Delicious account.**

2. **Click the Settings link in the top-right corner of the page.**

   The Settings page appears. Scroll down until you see the Blogging header.

3. **Click Linkrolls.**

   The Linkrolls page appears. Scroll down until you see Display options.

4. **Set your display options as you see fit.**

   Some of the options include editing the title of the Delicious widget, sorting links by date or alphabetically, and determining how many links to display.

5. **Click the link under the code text box: If You Use TypePad You Can Add This Linkroll to Your TypePad blog.**

   The TypePad widget page appears.

6. **Click to select the box next to the blog(s) on which you want to install the widget.**

7. **Click Add Widget.**

   The widget is now on your blog's sidebar. You may want to visit your blog's Content area in your Dashboard to arrange the order of your sidebar content.

We've touched on some of the most important social media and bookmarking tools available to you right now. You may not want to use all of them immediately or even at the same time. In fact, we suggest that you don't use them all at once. Our advice is to try out your options and see what works best for you. In the end, you may decide that social media tools just add noise to your blogging endeavors. Or you may find that integrating Twitter and Facebook add a new dimension to your community. Remember that you have time to try things out and make changes as necessary.

Chapter 11

Finding and Using a TypePad Theme

*T*he appearance of your blog makes an instant and important impression on your readers. Ideally, your overall design should be a reflection of your content, complementing and highlighting what you're offering your readers. If you have impeccable content and a brilliant overall blogging concept, but your design is difficult to navigate or hard on a reader's eyes, that reader may be hesitant to stick around.

In this chapter, we tackle the fundamentals of TypePad blog design. We talk about the general rules to consider as you make decisions about your blog's appearance. We also show you how to apply any one of TypePad's numerous themes. Within each theme, you have the freedom to change a wide variety of settings and preferences, including the order and setup of your sidebars and whether you'll use a text or a custom graphic header — we show you how to do both.

After you have a working understanding of these simple design functions, you may be interested to find out how you can tweak your design using *CSS* (Cascading Style Sheets), a subject we explain more fully in Chapter 14.

Grasping Basic Design Principles

Before we explain how to apply and adjust your TypePad design, it would be helpful to understand a few basic design principles that help you put your best visual foot forward. Of course, your own preferences are a big factor — it's *your* blog, after all, and you can design it how you choose. But if your aim is to attract new readers, sticking to some time-tested design principles will serve you well. Refer to the design principles in this section as you use the rest of this chapter (and Chapter 14) to make decisions about your blog's appearance.

Consider your voice

As you blog, you are surely developing a distinct voice and tone. Let your design be a visual reflection of your content's voice. A blog on global finance, for example, should communicate refinement and professionalism, whereas a highly creative craft blog might communicate whimsy and lightheartedness. See Chapter 17 for some good examples of blogs that have implemented designs that reflect their content well.

Be consistent

Have one visual cue that makes people think of your blog — a logo, perhaps, or a specific color scheme. Find ways to keep that design element recurring throughout your blog — it helps solidify your brand identity and is pleasing to a reader's eye. For example, do you use overlapping squares in your custom header design? Find a way to incorporate overlapping squares into your sidebar images or in other graphics you use throughout your site.

Use color well

Color is always a powerful visual tool, of course. Most often, designers recommend that bloggers stick to a specific color palette, using two or three foundation colors to keep your look unified. Other colors may appear in your site, of course, especially if you use photos or graphics frequently in your posts. But consistent use of the same color scheme will give your blog professional polish. When choosing a color scheme, consider using a color wheel to help you choose colors that complement one another. You can find a great color wheel tool at `www.sessions.edu/ilu/ilu_1.asp`.

Incorporate change wisely

When you spend a lot of time at your own blog, you naturally will want to freshen things up sometimes. Be careful, however, that you don't tweak your design so often that your readers never know where to find things or are never able to form a mental picture of your blog's voice. If you're itching for a fresh look, find subtle ways to implement change (a slightly modified color scheme, perhaps). If you *do* need a complete design overhaul (and occasionally you will), walk your readers through the redesign in a post, and do what you can to make them feel at home.

Make your posts easy on the eyes

The format of the text within your posts is very important. Be sure you've set your fonts to a size that is large enough to be readable. (Not sure if yours is? Find a friend who requires reading glasses, and ask him to test it for you!) Also, keep in mind that a light-colored font (such as white) on a dark-colored background (such as dark blue or black) tires out a reader's eyes more quickly than the more traditional dark font on a light background. Last, keep your paragraphs short (ideally, no more than five to seven sentences), and use a blank double space between paragraphs — that blank space gives the eyes a brief moment of rest.

Minimize the clutter

When you configure your sidebars, keep in mind that less is more. Sidebars that are overly cluttered with graphic images and text will draw the eyes away from the most important part of your blog: your main content column. When you *do* post graphics (such as ads) in your sidebar, try to keep their sizes uniform. Consider rounding up as many of your sidebar items as possible and placing them on a separate page (see Chapter 6). For example, if your blog has won multiple awards, you don't have to post all those award images on your sidebar — instead, create an Awards page containing all those images, and link to the page from your sidebar.

Keep things moving left to right

Remember, especially in Western cultures, our eyes are naturally inclined to move from left to right. For this reason, consider placing the most important information on the left side of your blog — together with your header design, it's probably what people will notice first. Additionally, we recommend that you keep the body of your posts aligned left. TypePad gives you the option to center your entire post, and it may work occasionally for short, poetic works or lists of links. Overall, though, our eyes aren't fond of reading chunks of centered text for extended periods of time.

Locating and Navigating the Design Tab

Anything related to the creating, editing, or managing of your blog design takes place in the Design tab. To get there, sign in to your TypePad account; from the main Dashboard, click your blog's name in the list of blogs on the right (as a shortcut, you can click the Design link under your blog's name). In the blue blog-level bar, click the Design tab. The page that opens looks like the one in Figure 11-1.

The page shown in Figure 11-1 will be our home base for the rest of this chapter, so let's start with an overview of its primary elements. Throughout the chapter, we examine each one further.

Overview

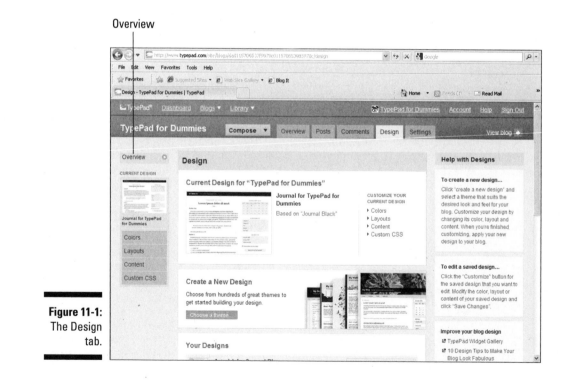

Figure 11-1:
The Design
tab.

In the top-left corner of the Design tab, note the small button called Overview. This button will be very helpful to you as you navigate the Design tab. Any time you want to go back to the main Design tab, click that Overview button to be returned there instantly. Be sure you save your work first, though!

If you are signed up under the Micro pricing level, most of this chapter will not be relevant to you — your design customization options are limited.

Your current design

The design you have currently applied to your TypePad blog is clearly displayed at the top of the Design tab — in two places, actually. As shown in Figure 11-1, you can see which theme you have currently applied by looking in the vertical menu bar on the left side of the page, as well as the Current Design box at the top of the page. Using whichever of the two you'd prefer (both offer identical information), you can click the links to view and edit the following elements of your design:

- ✔ **Theme Builder:** This button is visible only if you are using the *Theme Builder*, TypePad's tool for generating a more custom look without delving into code (see the corresponding section later in this chapter). Clicking this button takes you directly to the Theme Builder.

- ✔ **Colors:** This button is visible only if you're *not* using the Theme Builder and if you're using a theme with editable colors (not all themes have them). Click this button to change the color scheme of your TypePad theme.

- ✔ **Layouts:** A Layout refers to the "bone structure" of the content on your page — how many columns your blog will have and where each one will be. To edit your current layout, simply click the Layouts button.

- ✔ **Content:** This button takes you to the page where you determine which content will appear in each section of your blog. Clicking here will allow you to rearrange and edit to your heart's content (see the corresponding section later in this chapter).

- ✔ **Custom CSS:** For TypePad users with the Pro Unlimited level or above, you can click this button for access to the field where you can customize your CSS. We explain custom CSS further in Chapter 14.

Create a new design

Below the Current Design box is a box labeled Create a New Design. This is the starting point any time you want you start a new design, whether you're using a TypePad theme, the Theme Builder, or Advanced Templates (see Chapter 14). We come back to this box shortly.

Your designs

Moving farther down the page, you'll see a box titled Your Designs. This is a list of all the designs you've created for all your TypePad blogs, and it's the starting point for going back to make edits to these designs. For more information, see the last section in this chapter, where we explain this box further.

Finding and Applying a TypePad Theme

Now that we've established the lay of the land for the Design tab, it's time to move on to the fun part: playing around with the dozens of TypePad themes available to users. With only a few simple clicks, you can easily change the entire look of your blog, using the professionally designed themes offered by TypePad.

As we work our way through the rest of the design process in this chapter, it's important to note the difference between applying a design and saving a design. *Applying* a design means that you are choosing it as your current design, making it instantly viewable to your readers. *Saving* a design does not apply it to your blog — it simply means that the design will appear in your list of designs (the Your Designs box in the Design tab), making it available to you in the future to edit and apply later (should you choose). With this in mind, browse, experiment, and save confidently in TypePad's design interface, making sure that you *apply* a new design only when you're absolutely ready.

Browsing the available TypePad themes

To get started with a new theme, look at the front page of the Design tab (refer to Figure 11-1). In the box titled Create a New Design, click the green Choose a Theme button. You are taken to a page that allows you to browse through available themes. It's a page that looks similar to the one in Figure 11-2.

Listed in the main column, you'll notice several themes to choose among. To test-drive a theme, click it and then click the Preview button on the right (see Figure 11-2). This gives you a sneak peek of how your own content will look with the chosen theme, as shown in Figure 11-3. In this example, we've chosen to preview the Magnetic theme.

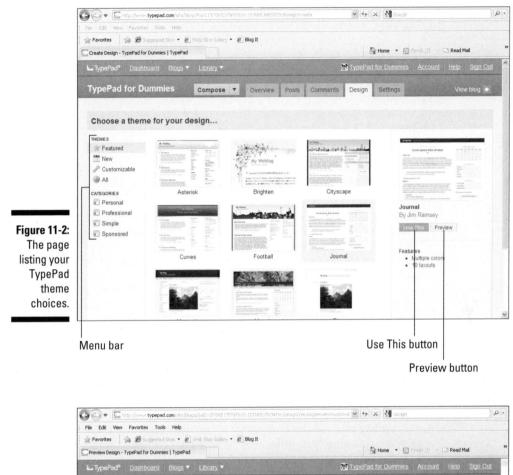

Figure 11-2:
The page listing your TypePad theme choices.

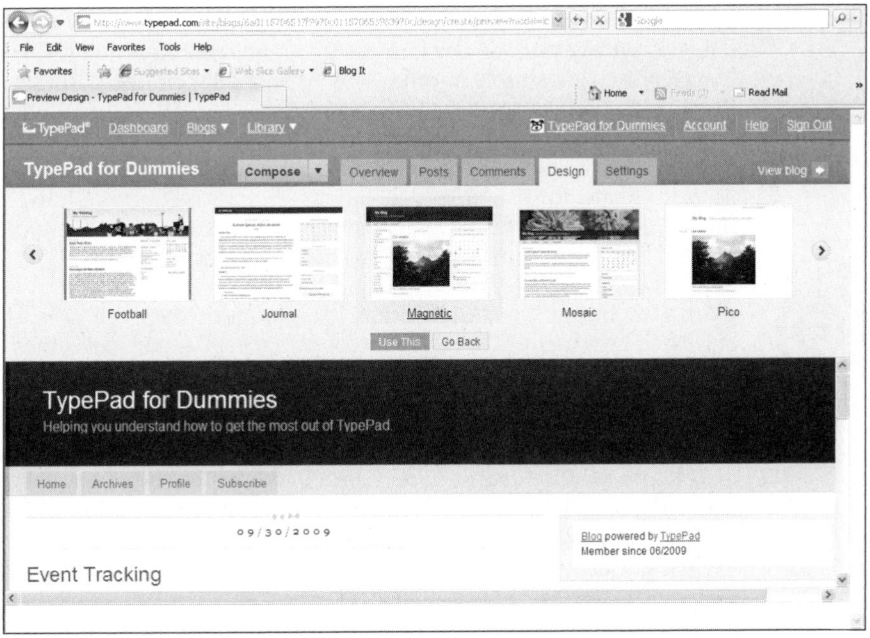

Menu bar

Use This button

Preview button

Figure 11-3:
Theme pre-view page.

Click any theme option to see it applied. If you want to save the design, click the Use This button. To go back to the list of themes, click Go Back.

TypePad offers so many theme choices that it's sorted them in the vertical menu bar on the left (refer to Figure 11-2). Clicking each item in this menu gives you a wide variety of theme choices in the page's main column, broken down this way:

- ✔ **Featured:** These themes rotate regularly, giving TypePad a chance to showcase its current featured design options.

- ✔ **New:** These themes are the ones most recently added to TypePad's theme collection; click this menu button often if you want to see your newest design options.

- ✔ **Customizable:** If you want to step out on your own, you don't have to choose one of TypePad's standard themes. Clicking the Customizable link gives you two options: Theme Builder and Advanced Templates. The Theme Builder option gives you a chance to build your own theme without muddying your hands in code. (We explain the Theme Builder option more fully later in this chapter; for now, we'll just address the predesigned themes.) Clicking Advanced Templates will allow you full control over your TypePad design, but extensive coding knowledge is required. We explain Advanced Templates in Chapter 14.

- ✔ **All:** As you might expect, clicking this menu option will cause every available TypePad theme to appear, making this the easiest way to compare all your options at once.

Next in the menu, TypePad offers you a different way to sort your design choices, letting you see the choices grouped by style, such as Personal and Professional. It's simply another way to sort your options, but you'd still most likely be best served by browsing using the All button.

Some of the themes have special customization options worth noting. In the Mosaic theme, for example, you can insert your own image into the header design. And the Cityscape theme lets you choose among 20 city skylines around the world to feature in your header design.

Click a theme and then look in the right column, under Features. Here, you'll see listed how many layouts and color schemes this particular theme supports.

Applying your chosen theme

After you've browsed the TypePad themes thoroughly and have chosen the theme that suits you best, click the Use This button on the right side of your screen (refer to Figure 11-2).

Clicking Use This does not *apply* your design to your blog; it only *saves* the design to your account, making it editable later.

The screen that appears next will vary, depending on the theme you choose. If you've chosen a theme with customizable colors, you may first be asked to choose the color scheme you'd like to use. Other customizable themes (such as Cityscape and Mosaic — see the preceding section) will ask you for your customization preferences. The Chroma theme (the only one available to Micro users) will ask you to select the photo you'd like to include in the banner. Still other themes will ask you to choose your design's layout (see next section). Whichever screen appears for you next, make your selections.

Before moving on to the next screen, be sure to take note of the options at the bottom of your screen, pictured in Figure 11-4:

✔ To apply your new design to your blog (remember, this makes it instantly viewable by your readers), scroll down the page, select Apply This Design to [Your Blog's Name], and then click Save Changes. Your new design is applied to your blog, and your readers can see it.

✔ If you're not ready to apply your design but want the option of playing around with it later, simply click Save Changes, and the design will be saved and listed on the front page of your Design tab using the name of the theme and the name of your blog (for example, Magnetic for Don's Cycling Blog). You can rename this specific design later; for instructions on renaming a design, see the last section in this chapter.

Figure 11-4:
Your options for saving and apply-ing a design.

As you experiment with applying new themes, always look for a Save Changes button at the bottom of the screen. Click this before you proceed to keep from losing your work.

Selecting the Layout of Your Theme

With your theme in place, you need to decide what kind of layout you'd like to use. As we explained, your *layout* refers to the quantity and positioning of your columns. Ten layouts are available, though not every TypePad theme supports each one. The Brighten theme, for example, supports five layouts, whereas the Curves theme supports all ten. Be sure you've chosen a theme that supports the layout you prefer.

To see your layout options, click the Layouts button (shown in Figure 11-1) in the left menu bar. You'll be taken to a page that shows you all the layouts supportable in your chosen theme. In Table 11-1, we describe each of the ten TypePad layouts.

Table 11-1	Available TypePad Layouts	
Layout Image	*Layout Name*	*Layout Description*
	Two Column Right	The content column is on the left, and the sidebar (containing the TypeLists, widgets, ads, and so on) is on the right.
	Two Column Left	The content column is on the right, and the sidebar is on the left. Both of the two-column options offer pleasing, simple designs, but keep in mind that our eyes tend to start on the left side of the page and move right. In light of this, this layout may not place *quite* as much focus on the main content column as the preceding design.
	Three Column Right	The content column is on the left, with two sidebars to the right. This layout is quite visually pleasing, especially if you can manage to keep the sidebars clutter-free, because it keeps the sidebar information grouped on one side of the page.
	Three Column	The content column is in the center, with a sidebar on each side. Both this layout and the next one provide the most sidebar real estate if you have a large quantity of sidebar information to share with your readers.

Layout Image	Layout Name	Layout Description
	One Column	The simplest of all the blog layouts, this one has no sidebars (typical sidebar information is listed at the bottom of the page). This type of format keeps the focus on your content, but it might not be quite as navigable for your readers as the traditional blog design, which usually contains at least one sidebar. The typical sidebar content is placed below your posts.
	Artistic	This layout (and all the others that follow) is a *mixed media layout,* meaning that it's used by bloggers who want to highlight their photos. The artistic layout places the main content column to the left, and the most recent photo has a high-profile spot to the right. The other recent photos are listed horizontally below the most recent photo.
	Calendar	In this layout, the photos are published in a calendar format, with the images appearing in the calendar date on which you posted them. Any additional sidebar content appears below the calendar.
	Three Column Mixed Media	The main content column is in the center, the sidebar is on the left, and the most recent photographs appear on the right.
	Four Column Mixed Media	The most recent photos appear on the left, the main content column appears in the center, and the two sidebars appear together on the right. This layout lets you present a significant amount of information to your readers at first glance. If you choose this layout, you may want to be particularly mindful of keeping the sidebars and header design tidy and streamlined so your readers aren't visually overwhelmed.
	Timeline	Similar to the calendar, in this layout the main content column is on the left, but readers have easy access to the most recent photos on the right.

If you're a photo blogger interested in using one of the mixed media layouts, you should know that your photo album images (see Chapter 9) do not automatically appear in your layout. The layout photos appear only when a blogger inserts a photo into an actual post. If you want a photo to appear in both your photo album *and* in your mixed media layout, you'll need to publish them in both places.

Choosing and Ordering the Content Modules on Your Blog

With the structure of your blog in place, you'll need to decide which elements you'd like to have appear on your blog and where you'd like them to go. TypePad refers to these page elements as *modules,* or page components, each with a specific function. For example, your list of blog categories is a module, as are your post title and an Amazon.com widget.

TypePad's drag-and-drop content layout editor makes the choosing and ordering of page modules an intuitive process. To get to this helpful tool, choose the design you want to edit and then click the Content button in the menu bar on the left side of the Design tab. You'll be taken to the drag-and-drop editor, which looks like Figure 11-5.

Selecting the modules to include

Let's start with the top half of the drag-and-drop editor, just below the bar labeled Content in Figure 11-5. You use this portion of the drag-and-drop editor to select which modules you want to include on your page.

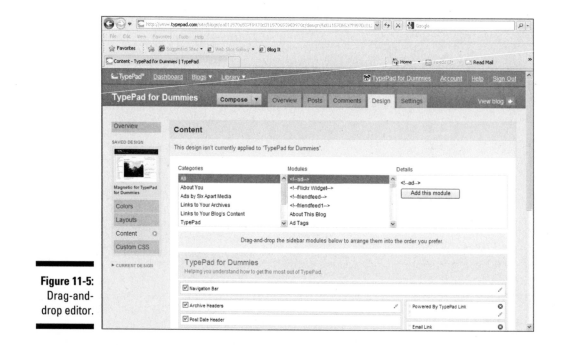

Figure 11-5: Drag-and-drop editor.

The box labeled Categories contains a long list of (not surprisingly) *categories.* Note that these are categories of page modules, as opposed to the blog post categories discussed in Chapter 6. Every page module offered by TypePad falls under one of the listed categories. When you click a category, a new list of modules related to that category appears in the Modules box, immediately to the right. Click any of the modules, and you'll see, in the Details box, an option to Add This Module, as shown in Figure 11-6.

Click the Add This Module button, and that particular module appears in the bottom portion of the drag-and-drop editor. In the next section, we show you how to rearrange these modules to your preferences. Before we get to that point, though, let's examine what type of modules you can expect to find in each category:

- **All:** Clicking the All category, as you might expect, causes every available module to appear in the Modules box, making it the simplest way to see what all of your module options are.

- **About You:** The modules that appear in the About You category are the most personal ones — they're the modules readers can best use to find out about and interact with you. For example, the Follow Me module is a sidebar button that allows other TypePad users to track your activity within their own Dashboard (see Chapter 4). The TypePad Profile module will insert a sidebar link directly to your TypePad Profile.

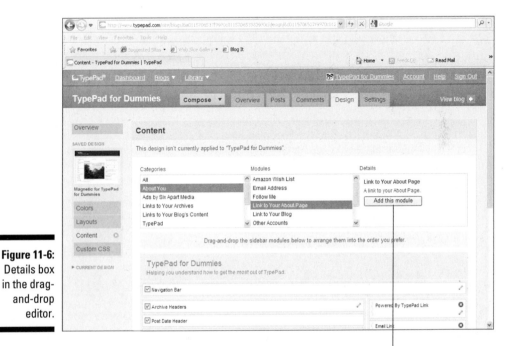

Figure 11-6:
Details box in the drag-and-drop editor.

Click to add module

✔ **Ads by Six Apart Media:** As we explain in Chapter 12, Six Apart Media is TypePad's ad network, and using this module gives you a quick way to insert your Six Apart Media ads. (Note that you still have to go through the signup and approval process described in Chapter 12.)

✔ **Links to Your Archives:** These modules will help your readers browse through your older posts in a wide variety of ways. Category lists and clouds, for example, give readers access to your categories, and the daily, weekly, and monthly archives arrange your content by its publish date. The most common format for presenting your archives is monthly; you probably shouldn't choose daily or weekly unless you are posting several times a day.

✔ **Links to Your Blog's Content:** This category offers still another way for readers to interact with your content. Modules such as Recent Comments and Recent Posts keep readers current with the topics addressed at your blog in the past few days or weeks.

✔ **TypePad:** This category has only a couple of options: It allows you to add a module telling readers you're a TypePad user, and it allows you to point your readers to posts being written on other TypePad blogs.

✔ **Widgets:** Widgets are third-party tools that you and your readers may find handy. See Chapter 8 for more information on widgets, and browse through all the ones available to you by clicking in the Modules box.

✔ **Your Feeds:** If you enjoy aggregating content for your readers from other valuable resources, you may find the Your Feeds category especially helpful. Clicking Add This Module will take you a pop-up screen where you can enter the URL of any site with an RSS feed. Then you'll be asked to choose how many of the site's most recent updates you'd like to list in this particular sidebar module (choose between five and ten). Click OK, and that site's most recent updates will appear in this module on your sidebar.

✔ **Your Photo Albums:** When you click this category, you'll see all your photo albums listed in the Modules box. Sharing your photo albums in your sidebar is an easy and organized way to share your photos with your readers; it's also an alternative to using the mixed media layouts explained earlier in this chapter. For more about TypePad photo albums, see Chapter 9.

✔ **Your TypeLists:** Click this category to see a list of all the TypeLists you've created. Select which ones you'd like on your sidebars — see Chapter 8 for more on TypeLists.

Arranging the modules on the page

Now that you've chosen which modules will appear on your blog, you need to arrange their positions on the page. You'll do this in the bottom half of the drag-and-drop editor, which will look something like the one pictured in Figure 11-7.

Click to edit module

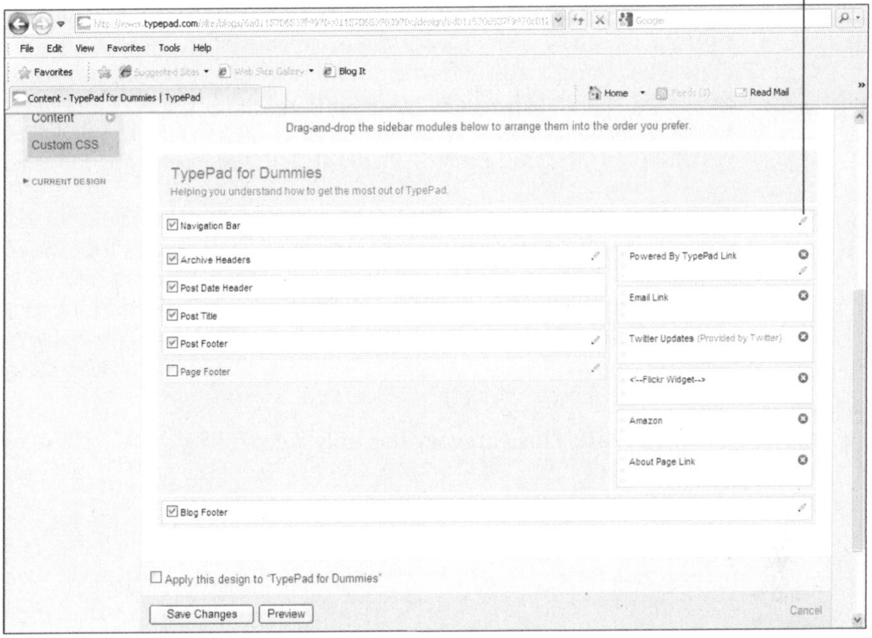

Figure 11-7:
Bottom half
of the drag-
and-drop
editor, for
arranging
the position
of your page
modules.

If you have chosen a mixed media layout, you will not be able to use the drag-and-drop feature. You can still choose which modules appear on your blog (as described in the previous section), but you cannot rearrange the modules' order.

You arrange four primary page elements via the drag-and-drop editor:

- Sidebar(s)
- Horizontal navigation bar (if you choose to use one)
- Main content column (where your posts appear)
- Blog footer

Your blog header is a significant page element, of course, but it's not addressed in this screen. (If you have a custom header, it's managed in the Theme Builder, which is described addressed later in this chapter.)

In the remainder of this section, we break down each of those four primary page elements and show you how to arrange and edit each one.

Sidebars

To rearrange the order of the modules currently placed in your sidebar, simply click and drag the module to its desired position. If you've changed your mind about including a particular module, click the red X in the module's top-right corner. Clicking this X only removes the module from your page; it doesn't delete it from your account (for example, clicking the X in a photo album in your sidebar simply means that photo album is no longer displayed, but it's still safe and sound in your Photo Album Library). The *exception* to this is if you've added any widgets to your sidebar — they're not saved anywhere in your account, so deleting them from your sidebar means you'll have to rebuild them from scratch if you ever want to reinsert them.

Some of the sidebar modules have a yellow pencil on the right side. When you see that little pencil (refer to Figure 11-7), it means that the module can be edited. Click the pencil, and a pop-up screen appears, letting you make edits as you'd like. For example, the Powered by TypePad Link module is editable — when you click the pencil, the screen shown in Figure 11-8 appears.

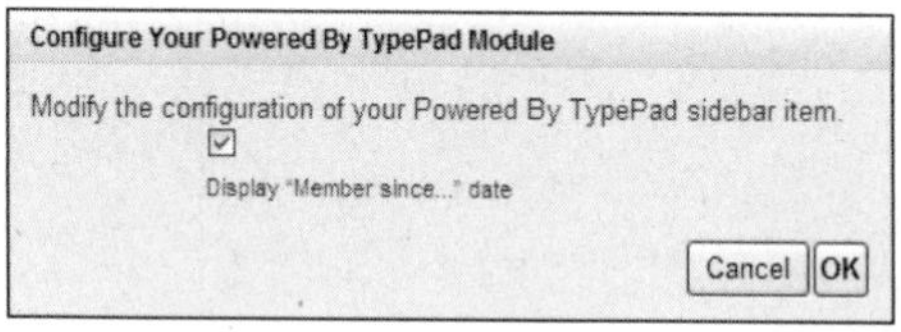

Figure 11-8:
Pop-up
screen for
editing a
page
module.

Configure Your Powered By TypePad Module

Modify the configuration of your Powered By TypePad sidebar item.

☑

Display "Member since..." date

Cancel | OK

In this example, you can choose whether or not you'd like to display `Member Since [date you joined TypePad]` with your TypePad link.

Keep your eye out for these little yellow pencils. Not all modules have them, but if one does, feel free to experiment with the formatting for that particular module, getting it set up in a way that's most convenient for you and your readers.

Navigation bar

A horizontal navigation bar is a powerful tool for a blogger. By default, the navigation bar appears below the header and gives a prominent spot to whatever information you choose to include there. Applied to a blog, a horizontal navigation bar looks like the one pictured in Figure 11-9.

If you want to include this navigation bar on your blog, simply click to select the Navigation Bar module. Just selecting the module isn't enough, though; you need to fill it in with the information you'd like to have in your blog's navigation bar. To do this, click the yellow pencil on the far right side of the module. This takes you to a screen containing a list of ten blank fields, like the one shown in Figure 11-10.

Navigation bar

Figure 11-9:
A horizontal navigation bar on a TypePadblog.

You have two options for the way you want to set up the navigation bar. You can use simple text links, or you can use graphic images as the links for a more custom look. We give you both sets of instructions.

Navigation Bar Configuration

Enter up to ten links to display in your navigation bar.

	Title	URL
1	Home	http://typepadfordummies.typepad.com/ty
2	Archives	http://typepadfordummies.typepad.com/ty
3	Profile	http://profile.typepad.com/6p0115706537f!
4	Subscribe	http://typepadfordummies.typepad.com/ty
5		
6		
7		
8		
9		
10		

Cancel OK

Figure 11-10:
The pop-up window for editing the navigation bar.

To insert text links into the navigation bar, follow these steps:

1. **In the pop-up window shown in Figure 11-10, enter in the Title field the title for the link you want to create.**

   Whatever you type here will appear on your blog exactly as you enter it, including capitalization. Consider keeping the titles as short as possible; if you don't, they may drop down onto a second line.

2. **In the right field, enter the complete URL to which the text or image should link.**

3. **Click OK.**

   The navigation bar is now saved using text links.

To insert image files into the navigation bar, follow these steps:

1. **Save the image file(s) you want to use in the navigation bar to TypePad File Manager.**

   You may need to experiment with image widths to get the navigation bar looking just the way you want. The correct image width depends largely on how many links you want the navigation bar to include (they can be wider if you have only a few or shorter if you have several). We recommend that you begin with a 100-pixel-wide image and adjust up or down as needed.

2. **In File Manager, right-click the name of the image you just uploaded, and choose Copy Link Location from the menu.**

3. **Navigate to your blog's Design tab.**

4. **Click the Content tab in the left sidebar.**

5. **Find the Navigation bar module, and click the yellow pencil.**

   When you click the yellow pencil on the right side of the navigation bar module, a pop-up window like the one in Figure 11-10 appears.

6. **In one of the Title text fields, type the following HTML:**

   ```
   <img src="http://blogname.typepad.com/images/navicon1.jpg">
   ```

   Be sure to change the URL to match the one you noted in Step 2.

7. **Type the URL you want the image to link to in the URL text field.**

8. **Repeat Steps 1–7 as necessary until you have the navigation bar the way you want it.**

9. **Click OK.**

   The navigation bar is saved using text links.

If you choose to use the navigation bar, consider using it to highlight the most important information on your site. Some good uses for this bar include the following links:

- ✔ **About Me:** Include a link to your About Me page (see Chapter 4 for several About Me page options).

- ✔ **Contact:** Include a link to the page containing your contact information and e-mail policies (see the section on managing e-mail issues in Chapter 18).

- ✔ **Blogroll or other links:** If you've listed your blogroll (or a list of other favorite links), include a link to that page here. If you want to introduce a charity or other cause to your readers, you can include a link here.

- ✔ **Other business(es):** If you own another business (an Etsy shop, for example) you're highlighting through your blog, place a link front and center in your navigation bar for quick access.

- ✔ **Facebook, Twitter, and so on:** If you don't want to clutter your sidebar with modules pointing to your other social media accounts, you can offer a direct link to your Facebook page, Twitter feed, and so on directly in your navigation bar.

- ✔ **Greatest hits:** Many bloggers like to keep a page listing the favorite posts they've written (Greatest Hits, Best Of, My Favorite Posts — name it however you like). This is a great way to quickly acquaint new readers with your writing. If you've composed such a page, consider including a link in the navigation bar.

Be creative as you decide which pages to link to, and use this high-profile navigation bar as a tool to point your readers toward valuable information.

You can make some edits to the appearance of the navigation bar by making some simple tweaks to your CSS code — see Chapter 14 for instructions.

Main content column

This important column contains the meat of your blog. You can't rearrange the order of the modules in this column, but you can select which ones you'd like to use and (on some of them) edit the formatting via the yellow pencil button. Here's an explanation for each of these modules:

- ✔ **Archive headers:** When your readers look through your sidebar and click a month in your archives or a category name, an *archive header* appears at the top of their page to remind them which date or category they're viewing. You can edit the format of these archive headers by clicking the yellow pencil and choosing your desired format from the drop-down menu. If you deselect the option, no archive header will appear.

- ✔ **Post date header:** This option simply means that the date your post is published will appear at the top of your post. Deselect this option if you don't want a date to appear. If you use the Theme Builder (see the upcoming "Using the Theme Builder" section), you can format the size, font, and alignment of the post date header.

- ✔ **Post title:** Selecting this option means that the title of your post will be visible at the beginning of each post. Because it's standard blogging practice to include a title, we recommend that you select this option. If you ever want to omit a title from a post for some reason, simply leave the title field blank in the Compose editor when you write the post.

✔ **Post footer:** TypePad allows you to put an automatic footer at the end of each post — click the yellow pencil to see your editing options in the pop-up window. Select the details (such as time, date, and author's name) you'd like to include in each footer.

The post footer pop-up window also allows you to place buttons or links at the bottom of each post, making it easy for your readers to submit the post to various social networking sites. (For more on how TypePad integrates with social media sites, see Chapter 10.) You can list the prompts as text or as graphic buttons. Applied to a blog, the page footers should appear similar to the one in Figure 11-11.

✔ **Page footer:** Similar to the post footer, this is the footer for your blog's pages (to understand the difference between posts and pages, see Chapter 6). Unlike the post footer, you do not have the option to add footer details such as author's name and time. You can, however, add the same social networking options as those in the post footer.

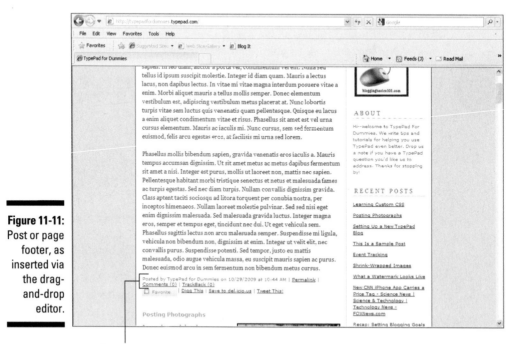

Figure 11-11:
Post or page footer, as inserted via the drag-and-drop editor.

Post footer

Blog footer

The blog footer is the information that appears at the bottom of the screen. Unless you've set up your blog to be short (having only one post at a time on the first page), the footer may not be noticed by that many people. You might want to include really important information elsewhere. But if you do want to include something on the footer, click the yellow pencil and edit similarly to the way you edited the navigation bar, earlier in this chapter. You can select the Advanced button if you know HTML coding and want to insert information this way.

Using the Theme Builder

Thus far in this chapter, we've largely addressed the use of TypePad's standard themes. Some of them have customizable color schemes, and of course, you can customize the layouts of any of them. But what if you want a more customized design? You can use Advanced Templates and Custom CSS (see Chapter 14) to make as many changes as you want, but both options require that you deal with HTML and CSS coding, and that's not a route all bloggers want to take. Enter the Theme Builder, a powerful tool for customizing your blog *without* delving into your code.

To walk through the Theme Builder functions, let's start at the beginning and create a new design. From the Design tab, click the Choose a Theme button. On the menu of theme choices in the left column, choose Customizable. Select the Theme Builder and then click the Use This button on the right. This takes you directly into the Theme Builder, which is shown in Figure 11-12.

The Theme Builder addresses your customized design in four distinct parts (Banner, General, Posts, and Sidebar Modules), giving each one its own section. Under each of these sections, you see a specific part of your design broken down even further (under the Banner section, for example, are the Text or Image subsection and the Background and Border subsection). Next to each subsection, click the up-and-down arrow button (refer to Figure 11-12) to expand the section fully. Be sure you expand each section as you work your way down the page.

Drop-down arrows

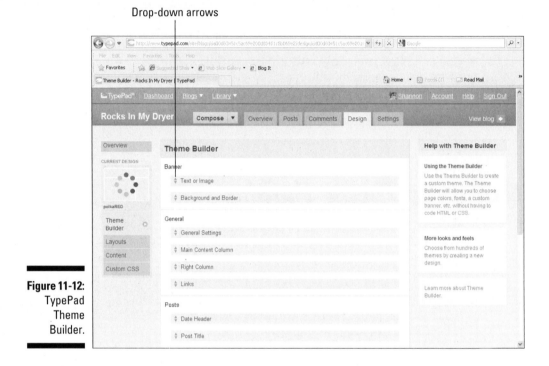

Figure 11-12:
TypePad
Theme
Builder.

Banner

The page *banner* (or *header* — the words are used interchangeably, but they mean the same thing) is integral to your overall design — it's likely the first thing a reader notices about your blog. Using the Theme Builder, you can fully customize the way the blog header appears or even replace it with a custom-designed banner that's representative of your blog's brand and voice.

Text or Image subsection

The Banner section's first subsection lets you customize the appearance of the font in the blog's banner. To customize a simple text header, follow these steps:

1. **Expand the Text or Image subsection, using the up-and-down arrow button.**

2. **For the Text/Image option, click to select the button next to Text.**

3. **In the Text Color field, enter the hexadecimal (hex) code for the color you'd like to use, or click the color tool to browse through your choices.**

   For more on hex colors, see the related sidebar in this chapter.

Creating your own graphics

Looking for a custom header or sidebar buttons, but don't want to pay a designer? Finding out that the fundamentals of graphic design might not be as hard as you think. Many beginning designers (and many experienced ones, too!) use desktop software such as Adobe Photoshop (or its simpler sister product, Photoshop Elements) or Corel Paint Shop Pro. You can even use some online services such as Picnik (`www.picnik.com`) and GIMP (`www.gimp.org`). Sites such as these allow you to generate JPG, GIF, or PNG graphic images, which are the building blocks for customizing your site to look the way you want. For additional information, do a Google search on your chosen graphics program to find out what books or online tutorials are available.

4. **In the remaining four sections, specify which alignment, style, font, and size you'd like to use for the text.**

5. **Click Preview at the bottom of the page to see if these changes suit you.**

6. **Click Save Changes to save these changes to your blog.**

If you're looking for a little more personalization than just a tweaked font, consider using a custom banner at the top of your blog page. A custom banner involves more work, but it's worth it because it can speak volumes about your blog.

When you (or your designer) create your custom banner, be sure you make it the appropriate width. To do this, calculate the total pixel width of your layout. It involves a little math, but it's nothing too hard: Simply add the column widths of the main content column, right column, and left column (if applicable) as you set them up in the General section of the Theme Builder page. That number is your total layout width. From this number, subtract 30 (TypePad automatically inserts a 15-pixel border around your image, so you'll need to allow for 15 pixels on the both the left and right). The resulting number is the correct pixel width for your banner image. Here's an example of this formula in action:

	400 pixels for the center column
	200 pixels for the right column
	200 pixels for the left column
=	800 pixels layout width
–	30 pixels (15 for each side)
=	770 pixels, the appropriate banner width

You can choose any height for the banner image — it automatically adapts to your layout. (Keep in mind, however, that a tall banner pushes your content farther down the page. For this reason, you probably shouldn't choose a height much taller than 300 pixels, and less is even better.)

If you use TypePad's default About Me page (see Chapter 4), you'll notice that it's a one-column page (regardless of whether you're using a two- or three-column theme for your regular blog). This makes a difference if you want to apply your blog's theme to TypePad's default About Me page, because your banner may be too large to fit in the main column. To get around this issue, we suggest duplicating your design, making a second banner that's 30 pixels smaller than your original banner and inserting it into your About Me page. However, you can save yourself the hassle by simply avoiding the default About Me page and either using your Profile (see Chapter 3) or creating a custom blog page (see Chapter 4).

Here's how to insert a custom banner:

1. **Create an image file (JPG, PNG, or GIF), and save it on your hard drive.**

   See the sidebar titled "Creating your own graphics" in this chapter if you need help creating an image from scratch. Also, be sure you follow the instructions earlier in this section to generate a banner that's the correct width.

2. **Return to the Design tab.**

   Click the name of the saved design you want to add the banner to.

3. **Click Text or Image to show options.**

4. **Next to Text/Image, select the button next to Image.**

   A different set of options appears.

5. **Click the Browse button to search your hard drive files for the image you created in Step 1.**

6. **Scroll to the bottom of the page, and click the Save Changes button.**

   You must save your changes before you can preview your new banner in your blog design. Note that clicking Save Changes doesn't apply the new design to your blog; it just saves the theme for you.

7. **Click the Preview button to see how your banner will look in your blog's new design.**

8. **If you're ready for your design to go live and your readers to see the changes you're made, select the Apply This Design to [*your blog's name*] option.**

   If you aren't ready for the changes to be live yet, you can access this new design from your list of designs on the main Design tab.

Understanding hex codes

A hex code is a six-digit code the Internet "reads" to understand exactly which color you want to use. The hex code for black, for example, is #000000, a bright seafoam green is #a7f7cb, and a bold purple is # 9107f2. There are other codes for communicating colors to your computer, but the hex code system is the one used by TypePad. Search for *hex color scheme* to find several free tools to help you generate your own hex codes for your design.

Hiring a professional designer to create an overall blog design might be cost-prohibitive, especially if you're a hobbyist blogger. But hiring a designer simply to create a custom header is generally much less expensive — you'd simply need to communicate to him the exact dimensions you want to use, using the formula just described. See Chapter 14 for more advice about hiring a designer.

Background and Border subsection

Let's move to the next portion of your Banner section in the Theme Builder: Background and Border. Click the up-and-down arrow button to expand this section and reveal your options. You are first asked to customize the background color for the header. This background color refers to the 15-pixels-wide border that TypePad automatically inserts around your banner image or (if you're simply using a text header) the background color that appears behind the header text. In the designated field, choose the hex code you'd like to use or click the color wheel button to view all the color options. For best results if you're using a custom banner, try using the identical background color of your banner image.

The next field asks you what type of border you'd like to use. We know this is a little confusing, because the previous field referred to the 15-pixels-width border around your custom banner. *This* border, however, refers to a different one — it's the small, hairline-width border you can insert in a variety of formats (solid, dashed, or dotted) around the banner. The most common use for this border is to insert only a bottom border or to omit the border (choose None). Use the drop-down menus to format the banner border, and click the Preview button at the bottom of the page — experiment until you get the look you want.

In the last field, you simply designate the color of the border (if you've chosen to use one). Choose one that complements your overall color scheme, and again, experiment until it suits you.

General

Moving down the Theme Builder page, we come to the General section, where you format column widths, background colors, and link colors for your entire blog. Use the up-and-down arrows to expand each subsection, and let's walk through them one at a time.

General Settings subsection

Using the first field under General Settings, select the background color for the area that borders your entire blog. To see this in action, see the sample TypePad blog in Figure 11-13. In this example, the background color is set to black, and the backgrounds of all the columns are set to white.

In the second two fields under General Settings, you can choose if you want to have a border around your entire page, and if so, what style and color you want that border to be. Be advised that any border you put around your entire page will not be especially visible — you might simply want to choose None from the drop-down menu and move on.

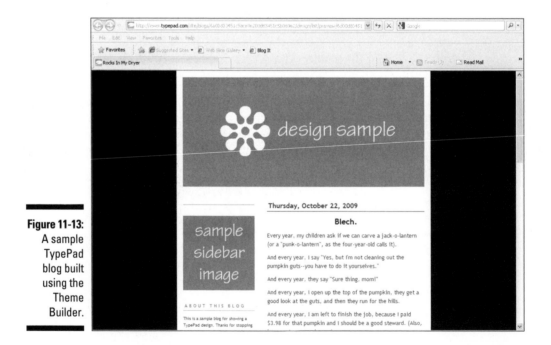

Figure 11-13:
A sample TypePad blog built using the Theme Builder.

Main Content Column subsection

In the fields under Main Content Column, choose first which pixel width you want this column to be (if you've inserted a custom banner using the steps earlier in this chapter, you should already have a number in mind). You can choose one of the pixel-width options listed in the drop-down menu, or you can choose the fluid-pixels option. *Fluid* means that your page width will adapt to the browser and screen size of each individual reader. Each column-width setup provides a different look for your blog; experiment and click the Preview button at the bottom of the page to see which column-width setup suits your preferences.

Next, determine what background color you'd like to use for this column (remember, a light background is much easier on the eyes). You can also specify whether you'd like a border around this column and what color and format you'd like that border to take. In the sample shown in Figure 11-13, the background color for the column is white, and the border is solid left.

Right Column and/or Left Column subsection

If you've selected a multiple-column layout for your blog, you'll have a subsection under General for *each* sidebar. Within this subsection, you need to determine the width of the column (again, keeping in mind the width of your custom banner, if you've used one), the background color, and the border format for each of these sidebar columns. In the sample shown in Figure 11-13, the background color for the left column is white, and no border has been applied.

Links subsection

In the Links subsection, you choose how you want to display the links that appear within your posts (though not within your sidebars — we get to those in a minute). Four kinds of links are listed, and you need to make a decision about the appearance of each. Not sure what the different link types are? Here's a quick rundown:

- **Normal link:** This is any link that has not been recently clicked.

- **Visited link:** If a reader clicks a link in your post, visits the new Web site, and then returns to your page, the visited link appears in the color you assign it here.

- **Hover link:** If a reader hovers his or her cursor over a link on your page but doesn't click, that link switches to the color you assign here.

- **Active link:** When a reader clicks a link, it's active. The act of clicking the link changes the color of the link to the color you specify here. After the link has been clicked, though, it's considered a visited link and will change to the color you specified in the Visited Link field.

If you want outgoing links to appear in a different color from your primary font color (and this is advisable), insert the hex code you want to use (click the color wheel button if you need some ideas).

Last in this subsection, decide if you want your links to be bold, underlined, both, or neither. It's entirely a matter of personal preference, but it's highly advisable that you have at least one way to set apart your links from normal text, whether you use a different color, an underline, or a bold font (or some combination of the three).

Posts

The Posts section in the Theme Builder is where you make decisions about the font, color, and appearance of the text in and around your blog posts. Under each subsection (Date Header, Post Title, Post Body, Post Footer), the options are identical — they're pictured in Figure 11-14. Once again, we walk you through each of the four subsections.

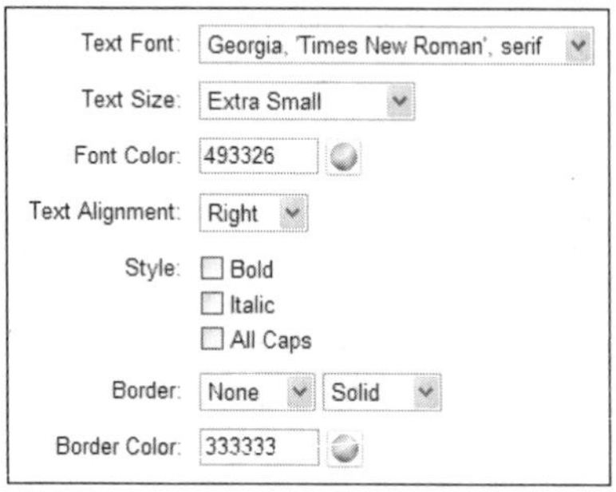

Figure 11-14:
Options in
the Theme
Builder's
Posts
section.

Text Font:	Georgia, 'Times New Roman', serif
Text Size:	Extra Small
Font Color:	493326
Text Alignment:	Right
Style:	☐ Bold ☐ Italic ☐ All Caps
Border:	None / Solid
Border Color:	333333

Date Header subsection

If you've chosen to display a date header on your blog (a decision you make in the Content portion of the Design tab), use the drop-down menus shown in Figure 11-14 to select the font, text size, and color of the date header. As you experiment with your options, you'll see the sample text in the box change, giving you a quick preview.

In addition, you must decide how you want the date header aligned. Experiment and see which way is most pleasing to you. Also decide if you want the date header bold, italic, and written in all caps. Again, use your best judgment to decide which look is best for blog.

You may want to use a border to set apart the date, and you can choose among a variety of options in the drop-down menu.

Post Title subsection

Make your selections for the appearance of your post title. Generally, the post title is the most noticeable and prominent element of a blog post, and it's standard to set it apart with a different alignment, color, size, or some combination of the three.

Use a border, if you like, to further set the title apart, but be careful about the overuse of borders in your main content column. Generally, one or two borders in the post area of a blog is all that's advisable; if you use more, it starts to get visually cluttered.

Post Body subsection

Again, choose how you'd like your text to appear, this time for the body of your post. The post body is the heart of your content, and you want it to look its best — select a size and color that are easily readable. In the post body, you might want to steer clear of centered text, which works well in date headers and post titles but can make the post body hard to read.

Post Footer subsection

If you've chosen to display a footer, you'll format it in the Post Footer subsection. Generally, the post footer is given a lower profile than the rest of the items in your main content column. You might want to make the font smaller and lighter than the other elements — just be sure it's still readable.

As you set up the Posts section of the Theme Builder, you will notice that you have the option to set each element to a different font. You *can* do it, but you probably *shouldn't* do it — using the same font for all the items in your posts is visually pleasing. To set apart elements such as footers and titles, consider using other methods, such as color and alignment.

Sidebar modules

The last section of the Theme Builder is titled Sidebar Modules; as you might guess, you use this section to format the text, images, and links that appear in your sidebar(s). If you have multiple sidebars, the choices you make in this section apply to all of them.

Before we go further, see Figure 11-15 for a close look at a sample TypePad sidebar — this will make it easier to understand what sidebar element each of these subsections addresses.

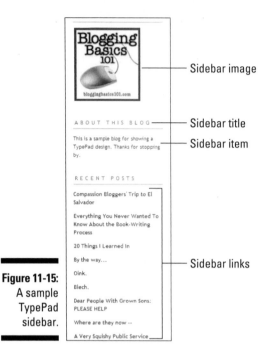

Sidebar image

Sidebar title

Sidebar item

Sidebar links

Figure 11-15:
A sample
TypePad
sidebar.

Sidebar Title subsection

A sidebar title, as designated in Figure 11-15, refers to the titles of your TypeLists (see Chapter 8). Using the fields and drop-down menus, decide what font, colors, alignments, and borders you want to use in your sidebar titles. In the sample shown in Figure 11-15, a bottom border is applied, and the text is aligned left, with a bold, all-caps font.

It's common for bloggers to make the font in their sidebars smaller than the font in their main content column — if you do this, be sure the text is still easy to read!

Sidebar Items subsection

The Sidebar Items subsection deals with the text in your sidebar that is not a title. If, for example, you have a Notes TypeList that serves as a welcome statement (such as the one in Figure 11-15), that text would be formatted in this subsection.

Use the fields and drop-down menus to make your style selections just as you've done throughout the Theme Builder.

Echoing our advice in the preceding section, consider making your font choice uniform throughout your blog. It's advisable (though certainly not required) for the titles and text in your sidebar to be the same font that you used in your main content column.

Sidebar Images subsection

You will likely place some images in your sidebar — perhaps you'll use a personal photo or a graphic banner. If you want a border to appear around these images, you'd use the fields and drop-down menus in the Sidebar Images subsection to edit the format of your border.

Depending on the types of images in your sidebar, keep in mind that applying a border may interfere with the appearance of your images. Play around with your options in this subsection, and do several previews, making sure you've selected an option that highlights your sidebar images best.

Sidebar Links subsection

You use the Sidebar Links subsection to customize the appearance of your sidebar links, just as you did with your post links in the General section of the Theme Builder. Insert the hex codes into the fields next to each of the four types of links (refer to the "Links" section, if you need a refresher).

Your sidebar will likely contain many more links than your posts contain. Be sure you've selected hex codes that complement your design — you may even want to use the identical hex codes you used for your post links.

Inserting an Image into Your Sidebar

Including a sidebar image on your blog is an excellent way to promote another Web site, blog, or product. Sidebar images are usually fairly small (a common size is 125 pixels by 125 pixels, but the size ultimately depends on your own blog's theme and design), and you can set them up to link to another Web site or blog.

You upload a graphic or an image to your TypePad account and use simple HTML to *reference* (or show) the image and link it to the other site. TypePad offers two ways to insert a sidebar image: You can use a Notes TypeList or an Embed Your Own HTML widget (both are addressed in Chapter 8). Both options offer identical results. The only real difference (and it's a notable one!) is that the TypeLists can be saved in your Library even when they're not in place on your blog. This gives you the freedom to publish and unpublish your TypeLists freely without having to re-create them from scratch. The Embed Your Own HTML widget, on the other hand, cannot be stored if it's not in use. As long as it's installed on your sidebar, your code is in place. If you remove the widget from your sidebar (using the drag-and-drop content editor), the widget is deleted, along with the code it contains.

Keeping the storage difference in mind, our best recommendation is to use the Notes TypeList to insert sidebar images. If you still want to proceed with the Embed Your Own HTML widget, however, we give instructions for it (and the Notes TypeList) in the next two sections.

Inserting a sidebar image using a Notes TypeList

To insert a sidebar image using a Notes TypeList, follow these steps:

1. **Upload your graphic or image to File Manager.**

2. **Click the image file name.**

   A new browser tab opens and displays the image.

3. **Copy the URL in the address bar.**

   This is the URL where your image resides on the TypePad server. You'll need it for your HTML code in a minute.

4. **Go to your TypeLists Library, and add a new Notes TypeList.**

   (For detailed instructions, see "Creating a Notes TypeList" in Chapter 8.)

5. **Add the following HTML in the Notes field:**

   ```
   <a href="http://www.blogname.com"><img src="http:// URL_you_copied_in_
           step_3.jpg"></a>
   ```

   Referring to the sample code in this step, change the first URL (`http://www.blogname.com`) to the address of the site you want the image to link to; change the second URL (in the `<img src>` code) to reflect the address you copied in Step 3.

   In a moment, we explain exactly what that HTML code is doing. For now, proceed to Step 6.

6. **Click Save.**

7. **Publish your new TypeList to your blog.**

Inserting an image using the Embed Your Own HTML widget

Using the Embed Your Own HTML widget is the other method for inserting an image in your sidebar. The following instructions explain how to do it:

1. **Upload your graphic or image to File Manager.**

2. **Click the image file name.**

   A new browser tab opens and displays the image.

3. **Copy the URL in the address bar.**

   This is the URL where your image resides on the TypePad server. You'll need it for your HTML code in a minute.

4. **Go to your blog's Content area (located under the Design tab).**

5. **Choose Widgets from the Categories menu.**

6. **Choose Embed Your Own HTML from the Modules menu.**

7. **Click Add this Module in the Details box.**

   The Custom HTML pop-up window appears.

8. **Type the following HTML in the HTML field:**

```
<a href="http://www.blogname.com"><img src="http:// URL_you_copied_in_
        step_3.jpg"></a>
```

   Referring to the sample code in this step, change the first URL (`http://www.blogname.com`) to the address of the site you want the image to link to; change the second URL (in the `<img src>` code) to reflect the address you copied in Step 3.

   Change the first URL (in the `<a href>` code) to the address of the site you want the image to link to; change the second URL (in the `<img src>` code) to reflect the address you copied in Step 3.

   In a moment, we explain exactly what that HTML code is doing. For now, proceed to Step 9.

9. **Change the Label name, if you like.**

10. **Click OK.**

    Your new widget module appears at the top of your sidebar. You can reorder it as necessary.

Understanding the sidebar image HTML

As you know, computers don't just *know* what to do; humans have to *tell* them what to do. We convey those instructions by using computer code to speak their language. Now, we realize that people assume you have to be crazy smart and super nerdy to know how to code. Well, some coding *is* involved and takes years to learn, but other coding, such as simple HTML, is easy and can be learned quickly. To start you on your way, we will explain the HTML you just used in your Notes TypeList.

The Notes TypeList you just created needs to tell the browser to show an image in your sidebar and link it to another Web site or blog. We did all that with two sets of HTML parameters: `<a href>` and `<img src>`.

In the example

```
<a href="http://www.bloggingbasics101.com"><img src="http://"URL_of_image.
          jpg"></a>
```

we start with `<a href="URL">` and end with `</a>`. Those two tags — `<a href="URL">` and `</a>` — go together. The first one opens the command (it tells the browser to pay attention because we're giving it instructions to link somewhere). The `</a>` ends the command and tells the computer we are finished with those instructions. In this case, the command is that we want to link to another blog, so we replace the URL between the quotes with the URL of the blog we want to link to (we use Melanie's blog, Blogging Basics 101, as an example):

```
<a href="http://www.bloggingbasics101.com">
```

Note that the URL is within quotes. This is important. The quotes are another part of the instructions for the browser. If you leave out the quotes or use smart quotes (curly quotes) in HTML, it won't work because the browser software won't recognize the command.

Now, because `<a href="URL">` `</a>` is the code for a link, you want to make sure you have text or an image that is a link. We need to put something (in this case, an image) between the two pieces of code so the reader has something to click for the link to work. To use an image, we have to tell the browser which image to use and where to find it. That HTML code looks like this:

```
<img src="URL_of_image.jpg">
```

You can tell that `img src` is shorthand for image source (or where the image is located). To call the correct image, you tell the browser which image you want to use. We did that in Step 3 (in the "Inserting an image using the Embed Your Own HTML widget" section) when we clicked the image and copied the URL.

So now you understand a little bit of HTML code. You know that this code

```
<a href="http://www.bloggingbasics101.com"><img src="http://"URL_you_copied_in_
          step_3.jpg"></a>
```

is telling the browser to pull a specific image (`<img src="http://URL_you_copied_in_step_3.jpg">`), link it to Blogging Basics 101 (`<a href="http://www.bloggingbasics101.com">`) and then stop the command after the image is pulled and linked (`</a>`).

Managing Existing Designs

There is no limit to the number of designs you can save in your TypePad account, so feel free to add and experiment with new looks, saving them for editing or applying later. When you are ready to go back and take a look at a design you've saved, visit the Design tab, and scroll to the bottom of the page. You'll see a box that looks similar to the one in Figure 11-16.

Every TypePad design you've created (for this particular blog or any other blog under the same account) is listed in this box, saved under the name of the theme, unless you've renamed it.

Customizing a saved design

To make change to an existing design, click the Customize button to the right of the design's name (refer to Figure 11-16). A drop-down menu appears, giving you the option to choose the Theme Builder (only if it's a Theme Builder design), Colors (only if it's a theme with editable colors), Layouts, Content, and Custom CSS. Choose any one of these options, and you'll be taken to the corresponding page; simply follow this chapter's editing instructions for that particular function.

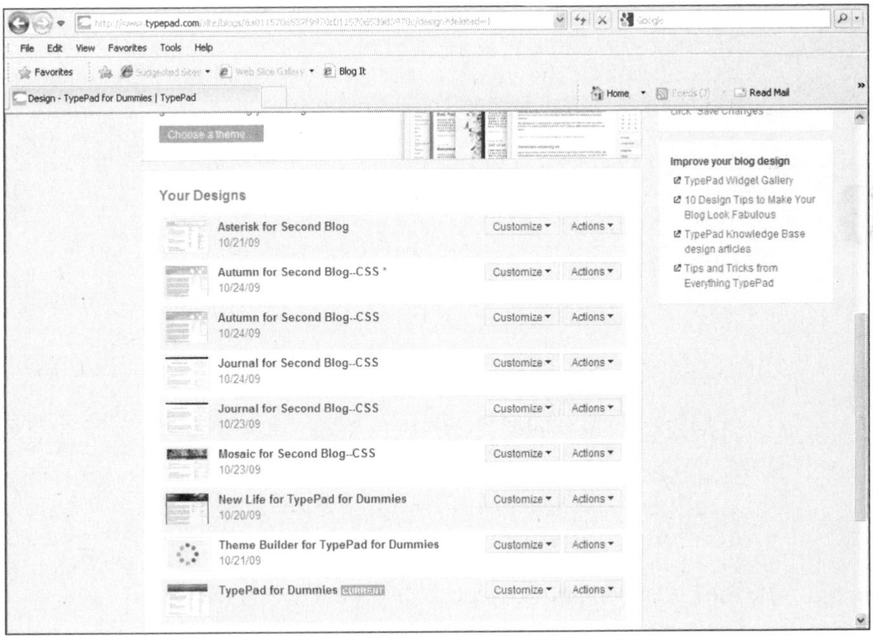

Figure 11-16: Your Designs box in the Design tab.

Taking other actions on a saved design

You may need to take a broader action on a particular design, and clicking the Actions button to the right of your design's title (refer to Figure 11-16) gives you a drop-down menu of available actions. The menu contains four or five options, depending on whether it's a currently applied design. Let's walk through each one.

Apply

Selecting the Apply option instantly applies the design to your blog. Choose this option only when you're sure it's the design you want to use!

Preview

The Preview option is just what it sounds like; when you click here, a new window opens, offering you a peek at how the design will look on your blog. It's always a good idea to preview a design before you apply it. When you're finished with the preview, simply close out the preview window, and you'll still be at the Design tab.

Rename

By default, TypePad names your saved designs by the name of the theme. If you're managing multiple designs, this might make it hard to keep them straight. Click Rename to give the design a name that makes sense to you. When you choose this option, you'll see the design name change to two blank boxes, like the ones pictured in Figure 11-17.

The top box is where your design's name should go. To change the existing one, delete what is currently in the box, and add the new name. Whatever you type in the bottom box will appear below the design's title in your design list. You can leave the bottom box blank, or you can use it to leave yourself a note regarding the design (such as "apply in August" or "designed by John").

Duplicate

The Duplicate option is a useful feature. Click this option, and TypePad will make an identical copy of the selected design, saved under the name `Copy of [original design name]`. This lets you duplicate a design you like, tweaking only the small elements that may need work. It prevents you from having to rebuild another version of the design from the ground up. This may be especially helpful for bloggers who like to change out their header design (perhaps seasonally) but want to keep their sidebar information in the same spot.

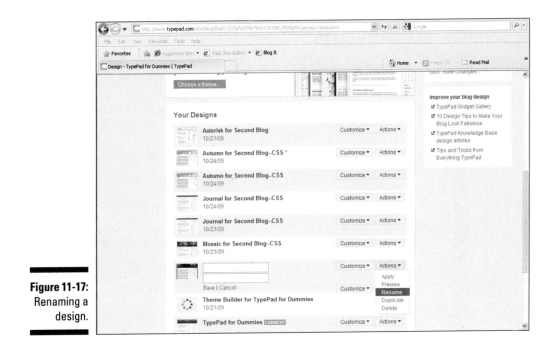

Figure 11-17:
Renaming a
design.

After you've duplicated a design, you can rename or edit it using the steps previously given in this chapter.

Delete

The Delete option allows you to delete one of your saved designs. Note that it does *not* delete the blog, only the design. You will see this option in the Actions drop-down menu only if the design is *not* currently applied to a design in your account. This handy safety measure keeps you from accidentally deleting a design you're using! If you don't see the Delete option, it means that you've applied the design (perhaps to a different blog under your same account). If you still want to delete the design, you'll need to find where it's applied and apply a different theme, and only then can you delete it.

Because TypePad lets you store as many saved designs as you like, you don't have to do a lot of deleting. But if you find that your old designs are cluttering up the Design tab, and you're positive that you'll never use them again, deleting them might be a good way to simplify.

This chapter has given you a ton of information to chew on — the subject of blog design is a big one! The bottom line is that you shouldn't be afraid to experiment, especially on the designs that aren't currently applied to your blog. Jump in and learn the ropes by trying out the features in the Design tab. Refer to the resources in Chapter 16 for additional help.

Part IV
Taking Your Blog to the Next Level

The 5th Wave   By Rich Tennant

MCSE TCP/IP TESTING

"I assume you'll be forward enough thinking to allow .dog as a valid domanin name."

In this part . . .

If you're ready to blog like a pro, this part of the book helps you show your readers that you mean business. We tell you how to monetize your blog and how to customize your design further with custom CSS or Advanced Templates. If you already have a blog and want to import your content to TypePad, this part shows you how.

Chapter 12

Making Money with Your Blog

*I*t's the million-dollar question (no pun intended): "How can a blogger turn his blog from a hobby into a business?" If you've invested a lot of time and creative energy in churning out a top-notch blog, it's understandable that you'd want to see some return on that investment. Do a Google search on *making money with my blog,* and you'll likely encounter sites that tell you how you can make many thousands of dollars monthly with blogging. You'll probably encounter others who bemoan how hard it is to earn even a hundred bucks a month. You'd be wise to enter the world of professional blogging with your eyes open and your expectations realistic, realizing that many successful bloggers don't earn enough to consider it a full-time primary income. But it's not a bad part-time job, especially if it's something you'd be doing anyway, for free!

Entire books have been written on the subject of blog *monetization,* or earning income on your blog, so one chapter won't be enough to cover every angle of the subject. We can, however, give you an overview of how many bloggers are accomplishing this, especially as it relates to TypePad blogging. Professional blogging is a lot of work, whether you use an outside ad service, sell ads yourself, or use TypePad's in-house ad network. But TypePad has several tools in place to make things simpler.

The rules for making money with your blog

If you choose to work with marketers and advertisers, you must understand that you have an ethical and legal responsibility to your readers to disclose all relationships related to compensation (including product reviews). This isn't just our opinion; the FTC (Federal Trade Commission) has handed down specific guidelines for how bloggers and advertisers disclose their relationships (www.ftc.gov/multimedia/video/business/endorsement-guides.shtm). If you are accepting products for review or being paid in any way for a post, you must disclose that to your audience. Don't be overwhelmed by this, because the solution is simple: Be entirely transparent, and disclose anything that might be construed as compensation. Transparency is your friend; it will help keep your blogging integrity intact and may save you a legal headache or two.

Understanding How You Can Make Money with Your Blog

When it comes to blog monetization, you need to keep in mind one important (if slightly harsh) truth: Earning income requires traffic. If your content is stellar and your concept is marketable, but no one is reading you, you'll be hard-pressed to find advertisers willing to pay you for advertising. The most important first step in monetizing your blog is to manage a blog that invites a readership. You can do this by regularly offering valuable content (see Chapter 6) and participating robustly in the online community (see Chapter 1). After you have a solid traffic base, you'll begin to attract advertising interest.

Keep in mind, too, that blogging for income is a business. You'll need to keep good records and talk with your tax professional about what your tax implications might be. (While you're at it, ask that same professional what blog-related expenses, such as a computer and monthly Internet access, you can deduct — you might be surprised!)

If you're new to blogging, you may be wondering how it's even possible for a blog to generate income. Entrepreneurial bloggers are finding ever more creative ways to earn money, but their efforts usually fall under these four categories: selling ad space, participating in an affiliate ad program, getting paid for posts, and using their blogs as a springboard for other paying jobs. We describe each of these in this section.

Sidebar advertisements

Magazines, as you well know, include with their content plenty of advertisements to generate revenue. You can do the same by selling ad space on your blog, placing ads wherever your design and personal inclination allow.

Install advertisements the same way you'd install any other image on your sidebar: by using either a Notes TypeList or an Embed Your Own HTML widget. See detailed instructions for both methods in Chapter 11.

Figure 12-1 shows how a blog might look with an advertisement in the sidebar (in this example, the advertisement reads Sample Ad).

You can use an outside ad network — a service that sells the ads for you, keeping a percentage of earnings (usually between 40 and 60 percent) in exchange for selling your ads. The ad network gives you a snippet of code to place on your blog's sidebar. Then the ad network rotates the ads through the designated space, using the code you placed there.

Sidebar ad

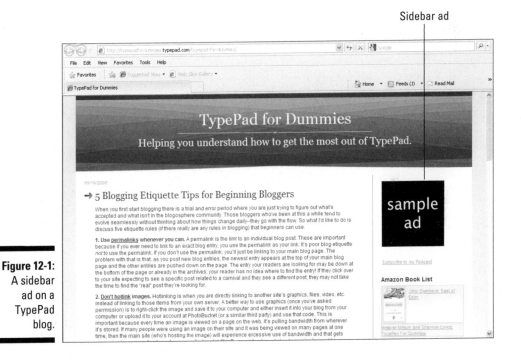

Figure 12-1:
A sidebar
ad on a
TypePad
blog.

You are paid based on the number of *impressions* (or page visits) you receive. This advertising model is referred to as *CPM*, which stands for *Cost Per Mille* (that's *mille* as in *thousand*). Do a Google search for *CPM ad networks*, and you'll find plenty of networks you can contact for more information about the services they can offer. Some ad networks are highly selective, offering spots only to bloggers of a specific niche or traffic range; others are open to anyone. Each network's terms vary widely, so be sure to read the fine print about what percentage of revenue you'll receive.

Some other outside ad services (Google AdSense is a well-known example) follow a *CPC*, or *Cost Per Click*, model, which means you are paid only when the ad on your blog is actually *clicked*, not just *viewed*. Again, try a Google search for *CPC ad networks* to begin your comparison.

Usually (but not always), CPM advertising is more profitable for bloggers than CPC advertising.

Affiliate advertising

An affiliate advertising model is one in which you sign up with a company as someone who refers readers to that company or its products, either through a graphic ad in your sidebar or a link somewhere on your blog. That company then assigns you a specific identification code that you include in your links for tracking purposes. Under this system, when one of your readers clicks your link to that company and buys something, you receive a small commission on that purchase. This model tends to work best for people who are frequently blogging about products related to their niche.

Probably the most well-known example of affiliate advertising online is Amazon.com. In fact, TypePad offers an Amazon widget (`www.sixapart.com/typepad/widgets/commerce`) that helps you post your Amazon favorites on your blog and earn income if one of your readers makes a purchase from your link (note that you have to have your Amazon Associate or Wish List ID connected to your TypePad account to be paid for reader purchases; see Chapter 4 to make sure your accounts are linked). For an example of how this widget might look on a sidebar, see Figure 12-2.

Here's an example of how affiliate advertising might work. Suppose you're a food blogger, and you establish affiliate accounts with several online stores that sell high-end cooking products. If you post a tutorial on the right way to cook a roast, you can include links to several roasting pans through your affiliate accounts, earning income if a reader purchases something.

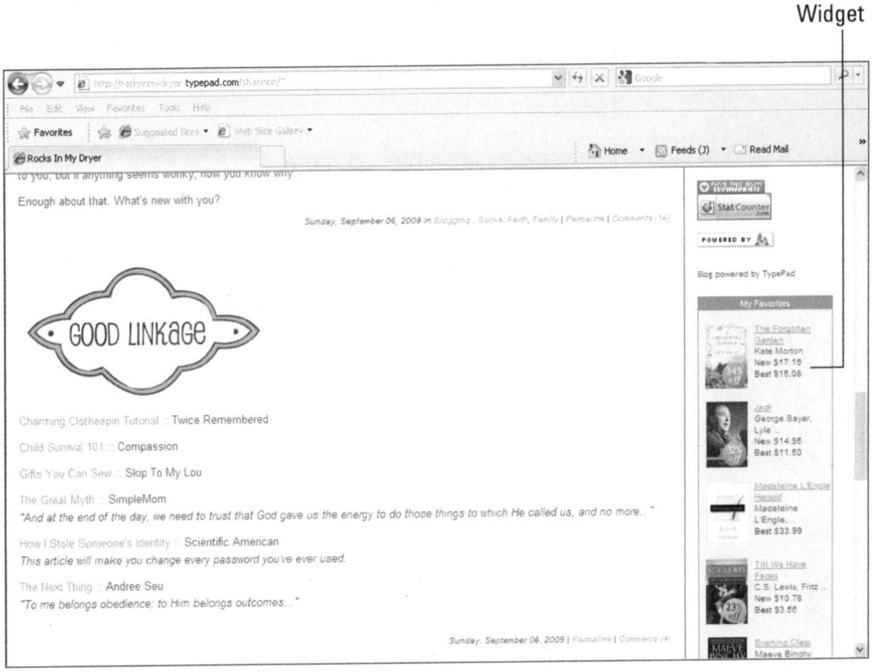

Widget

An Amazon.com widget on a TypePad sidebar.

Figure 12-2:
An Amazon.
com widget
on a
TypePad
sidebar.

In affiliate advertising (as in all advertising), your integrity is important. If you want your readers to be able to trust you, don't use your posts as a clearinghouse for every imaginable link to every conceivable product, on the slight chance that you might earn a small commission. Instead, link only to products you'd actually recommend (with or without the commission). Let your readers know that they can count on you to link only to products and companies you trust.

Paid blog posts

Some bloggers generate revenue by charging companies a fee to blog about their product. Bloggers do this either through a direct arrangement with the company or by signing up with an outside service that makes such arrangements. PayPerPost (payperpost.com) is one well-known example; Izea (izea.com) is another. This topic has become a contentious one in the blogosphere: Should bloggers consider themselves objective journalists who would never put their opinion up for sale? On the other hand, aren't bloggers entitled to charge a fee to generate a post and earn some income for their hard work?

The issue is surrounded by some murky ethical waters, so tread carefully as you determine what would suit your own conscience best. Especially if you're new to blogging, you might want to spend a little time observing and learning within the blogging community before making a firm decision on the issue.

It is also common for companies to approach a blogger with an offer of a free product in exchange for a review of that product (and the company may or may not offer a fee for the blogger's time). Especially once you've established a solid record of traffic on your blog, you can be certain these offers will begin rolling in. As we said earlier in this chapter, you'd be wise to make decisions about the direction of your blog with the best interests of your readers in mind. Don't agree to review a product just because it's free; on the other hand, if it's a product your readers may legitimately find interesting, your honest opinion may be of real value to them.

Whatever path you choose, remember that readers want to be able to trust the bloggers they read.

If you do accept payment for a particular post, or if you receive a free product, the new FTC guidelines require you to disclose this fully to your readers. It's a good idea to set firm standards for yourself in this area, and you can post those standards clearly on your About Me page or a separate page devoted to your disclosure policies (see Chapter 6 for instructions on creating a page).

Other projects

You may never be a blogger who earns thousands each month in advertising revenue, but you might be surprised what other doors blogging can open for you. A top-notch blog with good traffic can lead to endless opportunities, particularly if you're an expert in a particular area. If you have aspirations of developing a freelance writing or photography career, think of your blog as a portfolio to show to potential clients. Do you want to be an interior decorator? Write a great blog on home décor, develop a following, and use your blog as a launching pad for your design business. Let your blog be the online place where you hone skills that you can market in the real world.

Making Your Blog Attractive to Advertisers

No matter what approach you take with blog advertising (such as using an ad network or selling ads yourself), you can do several things to encourage companies to advertise with you:

✔ **Establish good traffic.** We've said it once, but it's worth saying again: Advertisers are most interested in blogs that have a lot of readers. Companies want to maximize their ad revenue by getting their ads in front of as many eyeballs as possible. Work hard at establishing a reputable, interesting, entertaining, well-read blog, and the advertising dollars are more likely to follow.

✔ **Place ads in prime spots.** Companies are less inclined to spend money on ads buried far down on your page. The closer an ad is to the top of your page, the more desirable it is, and the more you can reasonably charge for it. Most companies prefer ads that are above the fold, which is ad-speak for the part of your blog design that is viewable without any scrolling down required. (*Above the fold* is a holdover term from newspaper days when articles or advertisements were identified as either above or below the fold of the newspaper.)

✔ **Keep it clean (at least mostly).** There are exceptions, of course, but most companies are hesitant to buy ad space on blogs that use excessive profanity or post adult content.

✔ **Write often.** Companies prefer to buy ads on blogs that are updated regularly. In fact, many ad networks accept only bloggers who commit to updating their blogs at least twice a week (or some other set minimum). Especially if you sell your own ad space, consider planning, when possible, for extended posting absences — you can either charge lower rates or remove the ads.

✔ **Be professional.** If you're serious about blogging professionally, treat it as you would any other small business. That means you should correspond promptly, keep good records, and follow through on your commitments. If you sell an ad and then forget to run it, you're disrespecting the advertiser and harming your professional reputation.

✔ **Be honest.** Don't inflate your own statistics to sell an ad. Companies are making decisions based on what you tell them, so be a good steward of their trust (and their advertising dollars!). For more on this, see the section in this chapter about creating your own media kit.

Using TypePad's Own Advertising Program

In the spring of 2008, Six Apart (TypePad's parent company) decided to use its large existing network of bloggers to enter the arena of blog advertising, and Six Apart Media was born. Partnering with Adify (a service that serves as the engine, technologically speaking, of the ad network), Six Apart Media may be especially appealing to TypePad bloggers who like the idea of staying under the Six Apart umbrella with access to the Six Apart technical support they've grown to count on.

Six Apart is growing its ad network by using an in-house sales team. Participation in the network is open to bloggers on all blogging platforms (not just TypePad). One interesting feature offered is the ability of participating bloggers to set their own CPM rates, an option not all CPM-based networks offer.

Any blogger can join Six Apart Media by visiting www.sixapart.com/advertising. Click the Bloggers and Publishers link; this takes you to the page that allows you to get started. There are currently no minimum traffic requirements, but this page lists a few basic requirements that *are* in place, including updating weekly and not posting any adult content. Click the Apply Now button, and type your information in the appropriate text boxes. After your application is approved, Six Apart contacts you with further instructions, usually within a matter of days.

You should note that participating in the Six Apart Media ad network requires you to have an account set up with Adify, a step that Six Apart explains more fully in the e-mail informing you of your acceptance to the program.

For more information, visit the Six Apart Media blog (vip.typepad.com), which offers many helpful posts and webinars explaining how you can maximize your blog revenue with Six Apart Media. In particular, check out its help page (vip.typepad.com/help) for assistance with the application process, ad placement, and ad tags. You can also contact Six Apart Media's support team directly at VIP@sixapart.com.

When you have your Adify account in place, click the Help link in the top-right corner of the Adify Dashboard (not the TypePad Dashboard) for more help navigating and managing your account.

Running Your Own Advertising Campaign

As companies grow more eager to advertise in the blogosphere, many bloggers are selling their own ad space, eliminating the middleman ad network and thus keeping 100 percent of their revenue. This option works best for bloggers who have already established a solid track record of good blog statistics. Selling your own ads is not a difficult thing to manage, though it does require a willingness to keep good business records of the ads you have scheduled to run and the payment you've received. You'll need to have a strong familiarity with managing how and where to put graphic images or links on your sidebar using TypeLists.

You can wait until businesses approach you to ask about buying an ad on your blog (and if your traffic is significant, they probably will). But if you're a go-getter, don't hesitate to knock on some doors and try to sell your ad space to companies. Small to midsize businesses are probably more likely to respond than large corporations, which generally funnel their advertising dollars through ad networks. Keep in mind that you'll want to approach companies that are especially relevant to your target audience. If you're writing a blog that covers U.S. men's soccer, for example, a sporting-goods store might be interested in an ad. A company that sells handmade diaper bags? Probably not.

Create a media kit

If you decide you want to try to sell your own advertising, you must have a *media kit,* or a list of details that tells potential advertisers everything they need to know about your blog. Prepare a document containing those details and e-mail it to advertisers upon request. Or, on a TypePad blog, it is even more efficient to accumulate this information on a permanent page (see Chapter 6). When you approach an advertiser (or it approaches you), you can give the advertiser the permalink to your media-kit page. A distinct advantage of hosting your media kit on a page is that you can update it as needed, knowing that advertisers always have access to the most current information.

Be specific, thorough, and professional in your media kit, and include the following information:

- ✔ **Branding:** Visually, your media kit and your blog should have a similar look and feel (logo, colors, tone, and so on). This is another distinct advantage to hosting your media kit on a page — the header at the top is actually your blog header.

- ✔ **Elevator pitch:** Imagine that you have 60 seconds to explain to a stranger what your blog is about. You'd want your answer to be catchy, descriptive, and accurate (for example, "Bringing you the latest and greatest information about U.S. men's soccer"). Include your elevator pitch at the beginning of your media kit.

✔ **Explanation of your blog's topic or niche:** Expand a little more on what you write about, why it's an important part of the online dialogue among others in the same niche (or blog topic), and why you are a good candidate for an ad buy.

✔ **Traffic statistics:** Being entirely honest, give an accurate report of your blog traffic. Potential advertisers have the right to expect full disclosure from you in this department, and communicating accurately may end up leading to a long-standing business relationship. Some of the figures you might want to include are the monthly unique visitors or page views and the total number of feed subscribers. You can also share your Google PageRank, Technorati rank, and Alexa page rankings, if you're so inclined.

Providing plenty of meaty statistics requires that you have access to more than just the statistics provided in the TypePad Dashboard; consider using a third-party statistics service (discussed in Appendix B).

✔ **Traffic interpretation:** This is especially important if you write a blog that's targeted to a geographical area. For example, if you live in Chicago, and you're trying to sell a blog ad to the deli down the street, the deli owner may not be especially impressed that you have thousands of daily visitors from around the globe. But if the statistics counter tells you that you have substantial viewers in your Chicago community, the deli might see great value in an ad.

✔ **Demographics:** Consider taking a confidential survey of your readership, using an online survey service (free and paid options are available — do a Google search for *blog survey* to find options that may work for you). Marketers may want to know more specifics about your readership (gender, income, marital status). Proceed carefully, though — some readers may (understandably) see this as an intrusion. Be clear about your reasons for the survey and how you plan to use the data you collect.

✔ **Advertising sizes/options, rates, and guidelines:** What size(s) of advertising do you offer (for example, 125×125, 120×600)? Are your rates weekly, monthly, or both? Will you give clients a discount if they book longer ad times? Explain all these policies in your media kit. Also let advertisers know if you accept animated advertising, whether you issue refunds, and under what circumstances refunds are granted.

✔ **Payment:** Be clear about how and when you expect payment. Using PayPal (www.paypal.com) or another online payment system is especially helpful, because those companies generally offer easy-to-use invoices that make recordkeeping much simpler.

Set your prices, terms, and conditions

Determining the amount you'll charge for an ad is tricky. No universally accepted formula exists for generating this rate; most bloggers base it on a comparison with what other bloggers in their niche are charging, combined with a good, old-fashioned gut instinct. It will likely take you a few months to settle on an ad rate that is profitable for you and reasonable to advertisers, so expect some trial and error.

Because you have to start somewhere, here's a suggestion: Investigate an ad network that interests you or one that is widely used by other bloggers in your niche. Find out what CPM range it offers — it can vary widely from a few pennies to $20 per thousand page views. Use that number to calculate a beginning price point for your own ads. For example, let's say you settle on a CPM rate of $3. If you receive ten thousand page views per month, that's ten separate thousand-click increments. Ten times a $3 CPM equals $30, so you could charge $30 per month for a moderately-sized sidebar ad (less for a smaller ad, more for a larger one). Your best bet is to start on the more modest end of the pricing spectrum; then, if your ad space sells like hot cakes, you'll know you can gradually move your prices up.

Again, it would be valuable to install third-party traffic-interpretation software such as Google Analytics (www.google.com/analytics) on your TypePad blog. Google Analytics allows you to track *click-throughs* (the number of times readers click a particular link or ad you put in front of them). Tracking click-throughs allows you to show value in advertising and help yourself sell more ads down the road. We discuss using third-party statistics software more fully in Appendix B.

Advertising on your blog is a personal decision. Many bloggers want to focus on writing and their community without the worry of making money. On the other hand, if you can make a few bucks doing something you love, why not? The key is to disclose your policies and be transparent with your readers. Let them know what they can expect from you right up front.

If you decide that advertising is something you'd like to try, we've given you several options to choose among. Take a few months to try out those options to see which one is a fit with you and your blog. If you're serious about blogging professionally, treat it as you would any other small business: Do it well, and do it with the best interest of your customer (reader) in mind.

Chapter 13

Importing, Exporting, and Archiving

In This Chapter

▶ Importing an existing blog to TypePad

▶ Backing up your TypePad blog

*J*ust about every blogger contemplates migrating his or her blog at some point. It's not uncommon for bloggers to start a blog on one platform and then, after they're comfortable with the nuances of blogging, decide that a different platform better suits their needs. It may be that they would like to have more control over their blog and template code, or would like to have advertisements on their blog and their current platform doesn't allow those. This chapter walks you through the steps of importing content from an existing blog to your TypePad blog and shows you how to export and archive your TypePad blog.

We encourage you to refer to Chapter 4 and our discussion about setting up an intuitive filing system. Taking the time to set up a filing system that makes sense to you helps you find files as easily and quickly as possible.

Understanding TypePad's Import and Export Options

Importing or exporting a blog simply means you're moving existing blog content from one blogging platform *(exporting)* to another blogging platform *(importing)*. When you export blog content, you create a file that contains all of your blog's post content and comments. You use that file to import the content to your new blog platform.

Note that neither your blog's template code nor your actual images are included in this export file. The export file you create is a stripped version of your blog that includes only basic HTML markup and content, image links, and reader comments. You must move any images, podcasts, and video files manually.

Exporting and importing a blog is rarely painless: You'll most likely experience broken permalinks, missing images, and possibly missing comments (among other issues). To make this process less of a headache, it might be a good idea to consider from the start how you'll set up your file structure for uploaded images, documents, video, podcasts, and the like. After your new file structure is in place, you'll be able to import or export your blog to a new platform (such as TypePad, Movable Type, or WordPress) more easily because you can set up a version of that filing system on your new blog platform or server and move your files (for example, images, videos, or podcasts) directly into their relevant folders. A little planning on the front end may save you some headaches down the road.

Importing an Existing Blog to TypePad

Before you import an existing blog from another blogging platform to TypePad, you need to export the content of that blog. Each blog platform has its own method of exporting content, but it's usually as simple as finding the export option and then saving a file to your computer. Then you upload or import that file to the TypePad blogging platform. The instructions in this section assume that you have already exported your blog's existing content and have saved the export file (or you have the URL for the file).

TypePad allows you to import blog content to its platform from another TypePad blog, Movable Type, WordPress.com, or WordPress WXR file (generated from your WordPress.org blog). If you would like to import your Blogger blog to TypePad, you can find specific instructions for that migration at `help.sixapart.com/tp/us/blogger_import.html`.

To import blog content to a TypePad blog, you have to set up an initial TypePad blog (see Chapter 5). After you've established your new blog, you can find TypePad's import/export options by clicking Settings⇨ Import/Export on the blog-level bar. This takes you to a screen like the one in Figure 13-1.

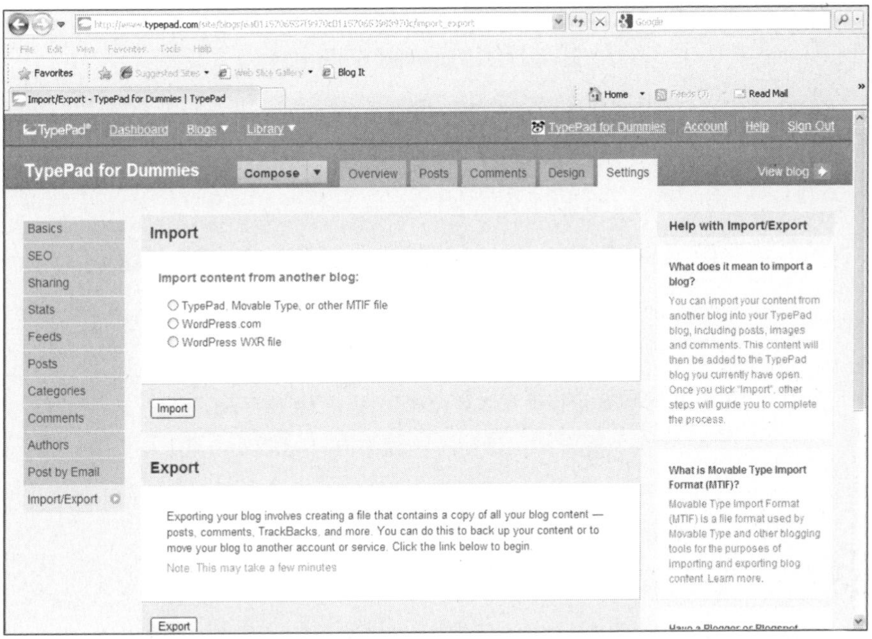

Figure 13-1:
Import/
Export
page, on
your blog's
Settings tab.

Importing a TypePad or Movable Type blog

If you have a TypePad or Movable Type blog that you want to merge with your current TypePad account, you can definitely do that. Remember that you still need to create an export file of the blog (which we discuss later in this chapter) before you can import it into your current account. These are the instructions for importing an existing TypePad or Movable Type blog:

1. **Click to select the TypePad, Movable Type, or Other MTIF File option.**

2. **If you want to upload the file from your computer:**

   a. **Click to select Upload File from Your Computer.**

   b. **Click the browse button to find the file.**

   c. **Click the Import button.**

3. **If you want to import from a Web address:**

    a. **Click to select Import from a Web Address.**

    b. **Click inside the Import URL text box, and type the necessary URL.**

    c. **Click the Import button.**

Importing a WordPress.com blog

When you are ready to move your WordPress.com blog to TypePad, you can follow these instructions:

1. **Click to select the WordPress.com option.**

2. **Type your WordPress.com information in the text boxes provided.**

    You'll need your URL, username, and password.

3. **Click the Import button.**

Importing a WordPress.org blog

If you'd like to import your WordPress.org blog to TypePad, you can use these instructions:

1. **Click to select the WordPress WXR file option.**

2. **If you want to upload the file from your computer:**

    a. **Click to select Upload File from Your Computer.**

    b. **Click the Browse button to find the file.**

    c. **Click the Import button.**

3. **If you want to import from a Web address:**

    a. **Click to select Import from a Web Address.**

    b. **Click inside the Import URL text box, and type the necessary URL.**

    c. **Click the Import button.**

Now that you've transferred your existing blog to your TypePad account, you can view the blog by clicking the View Your Blog link. Your blog probably won't look the same as it did on your previous blog platform. You'll need to do some tweaking.

Many bloggers choose to keep their previous blog up and running (allowing readers to leave comments, and so on) while they work on perfecting their blog's new look. You can choose a new template or re-create your previous template, tweak the category or tag lists, ensure that your images are still showing up, check your permalinks to make sure they still work, and set up a new RSS feed. Then, when you have everything just the way you like it, tell your readers your new blog URL, and give them your new RSS feed so they can subscribe to your new blog's updates.

Creating an Export of Your TypePad Blog

People export a blog not only because they want to move their existing blog from one blog platform to another, but also to archive their blog's content. That way, they can restore the content if it's ever lost or compromised.

Archiving your blog content is a crucial, if mundane, part of blogging. *Archiving* your blog refers to the simple process of exporting your content and saving it in a place different from your TypePad account (for example, on your computer or an external hard drive). Although server failures and hacking attacks are a rare occurrence with TypePad-hosted blogs, it's always wise to make a backup, just as you should for anything you produce on your computer. In the unlikely event of a system failure or hacking attack, your exported file can be retrieved and imported back to TypePad to restore the missing information.

When you export your TypePad blog, you create a file that houses your blog's post content, image links (not the images themselves) and permalinks, and reader comments. You can use this file for two purposes: to export your TypePad blog to another blog platform or to restore your blog if anything happens to it. To export or archive your TypePad blog posts, follow these steps (from the same Import/Export page pictured in Figure 13-1):

1. **Scroll down the page, and click the Export button.**

   Depending on the size of your blog, it may take several minutes for the export to complete.

2. **When prompted, save the export file to your computer or external hard drive.**

To save yourself time when looking for blog-related files, you may want to make a specific folder on your home computer where you keep ideas, graphics, or export files related to your blog.

Chapter 14

Tweaking Your TypePad Theme with Custom CSS or Advanced Templates

. . . .

In This Chapter

▶ Discovering the difference between custom CSS and Advanced Templates

▶ Using simple CSS to customize your blog template

▶ Changing the fundamental design of your blog with Advanced Templates

. . . .

*I*f you have a TypePad Pro Unlimited account, TypePad offers you two ways to customize the look and feel of your blog beyond what is offered in regular templates: custom CSS and Advanced Templates. Both options allow you to change aspects of your blog (often referred to as *page elements* or *modules*) with CSS. *CSS* stands for *Cascading Style Sheets* and is similar to HTML in that it defines how a browser reads your Web pages (or, in this case, your blog's pages). You can use the custom CSS or Advanced Templates option to change everything from the color scheme of your template (including your background and link colors) to the font of your entire blog to using a custom banner. You can even build a new template on your personal tastes.

Any time you'd like to change the look of your blog, we strongly suggest that you make a test blog first so you can tweak everything and get it just right before you show it to your readers. After you have everything just the way you like it, you can apply the new template to your main blog.

To use custom CSS or Advanced Templates, you need a basic understanding of CSS and how to use it. Although we point you to a few CSS resources later in the chapter, we assume that you already have that basic understanding or are willing to make some mistakes and get your hands dirty in your CSS. We are not providing a complete CSS tutorial here. The instructions we provide in this chapter are basic tweaks; if you try them and understand how they work, you can work your way up to more advanced changes.

This chapter includes instructions for using customized colors in your blog design. To choose a customized color, check out `ColorPicker.com`. You select a color that suits your design, and the Web site tells you the hexadecimal value for the color so you can insert it in your CSS. (The *hexadecimal value* is the #number used by your browser to determine what color to display; for example, #2485C5 is the hexadecimal value for a specific shade of blue.) Using the same hexadecimal value in any custom design images (such as your banner) and for your post header and links ensures a more cohesive look. Two basic hex codes you'll want to know are white (#ffffff) and black (#000000). For a further explanation of hex codes, see the related sidebar in Chapter 11.

Choosing Custom CSS or Advanced Templates

TypePad's custom CSS option allows you to change elements of your blog design (for example, your blog's background color) without having to find and change specific codes. You can simply insert a snippet of CSS into the custom CSS text box and click Save to see the fruits of your labor. By using custom CSS instead of Advanced Templates, you are able to continue to take advantage of the drag-and-drop features in your blog's Content area, choose specific layouts, and so on.

If you choose to enable Advanced Templates, you lose the ability to organize your content via the drag-and-drop method offered on the main Design tab for your blog. You can only add sidebar content, change style elements, and change your design/layout by manually opening the relevant template in your Advanced Templates and inserting the appropriate code yourself.

You should use Advanced Templates when you want to do more than a little tweak. If you want to truly change the fundamental actions and design of a basic template, Advanced Templates allows you to do that.

Any CSS you include (either via custom CSS or Advanced Templates) overrides your blog's existing default stylesheet. Additionally, if you change the base template for your blog, you'll have to reenter your custom CSS information. For example, if you switch from the Asterisk theme (after you've tweaked your custom CSS or Advanced Templates) to the Curves theme, you'll find that your custom CSS isn't automatically transferred to the new theme. You have to do that manually.

Using Custom CSS

The custom CSS option allows you to control how your blog looks without having to work with the actual CSS, HTML, or XML files. Instead of working directly in those documents, you can quickly add simple CSS commands via the custom CSS option under the Design tab in your blog-level navigation bar. In this section, we provide instructions on how to make some basic changes to your current blog template with the custom CSS option.

To use the custom CSS feature, click your blog's Design tab and then click the Custom CSS tab in the left sidebar. The Custom CSS page appears, and you see a large, blank text area like the one in Figure 14-1. That blank field is where you type your custom CSS commands.

Your blog is made up of page elements and modules. Each *element* contains a part of your blog. For instance, your posts are an entry element, your comments are a comment element, and so on. *Modules* are parts of an element. For example, your sidebar element may have several modules in the form of TypeLists or widgets.

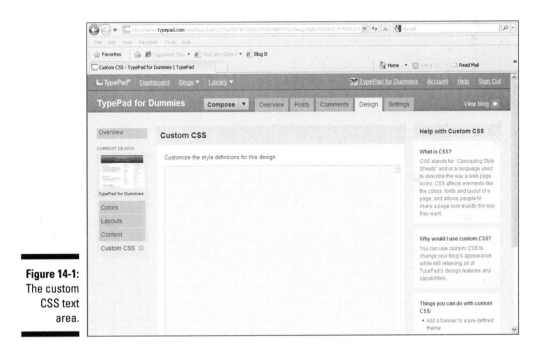

Figure 14-1: The custom CSS text area.

As you use your custom CSS option to enhance your blog's design, you'll need to know how TypePad references each of these elements via CSS. For a complete overview of TypePad's default CSS page structure, please go to `help.sixapart.com/tp/us/custom_css.html`. That Web page provides

- A page structure overview
- An explanation of page elements (for example, containers, banner, and columns)
- CSS examples for manipulating content modules (such as TypeLists and archives)

After you're familiar with how your TypePad theme works with CSS, we want to show you how to do a few things to customize your blog. In this section, we explain how to

- Use a custom banner instead of the default template banner
- Add a background image to your blog (or just change the background color)
- Remove the default border around your banner
- Tweak your navigation bar (if you're using one)
- Change the post header font, size, and color so it better matches your design
- Change the width of your columns

Using your own banner

Most bloggers like to customize the look and feel of their blog to represent themselves or their brand. An easy way to do that is to use a custom banner instead of the default banner from your blog's template. A *banner* is simply your header image, picture, or title at the top of your blog's page. As you can see in Figures 14-2 (before) and 14-3 (after), a custom banner can be an important element of your blog's brand. Your banner is one of the strongest elements people associate with you and your brand.

Figure 14-2:
This is an
example of
a TypePad
blog (www.
pensieve.
me) without
a custom
banner
installed.

Figure 14-3:
This is
the same
TypePad
blog
(/www.
pensieve.
me) with
a custom
banner
installed.

For best results, choose a template with the same background color as your custom banner, or make your banner the same color as your blog template's background. That way, if your banner doesn't quite fit, it's less noticeable.

The simplest way to insert a custom banner is to do it via the Theme Builder, using the steps we offer in Chapter 11. But the custom banner can be inserted using custom CSS as well. If you want to do it this way, follow these steps:

1. **Save the image file you want to use as your banner to TypePad File Manager.**

   See Chapter 4 for advice on setting up an intuitive filing system.

2. **In File Manager, click the name of the image you just uploaded.**

   A new browser window opens to show the image. Make a note of the URL in the address bar of this tab or window, because you'll need this URL in Step 5.

3. **Click your blog's Design tab.**

4. **Click the Custom CSS tab in the left sidebar.**

5. **Type the upcoming CSS in the text field.**

   Note that you need to make two changes to the following code:

   a. **Change the background URL to reflect the URL you noted in Step 2.**

   b. **Change the height value to reflect your banner's height in pixels. You can use a free graphics program such as GIMP to check this value (see Chapter 11 for more information on photo-editing software).**

In the following code, we've inserted explanations about what the code does, but that's just to help you understand how it works. You'll need to type the entire code block (without our explanations) in the CSS field.

The following code tells the browser what image file to use as your banner. Note that the banner does not repeat:

```
#banner
{
background: url(http://sampleurl.com/image.jpg) no-repeat;
height: 200px;
}
#banner-inner { overflow: visible; padding: 0; }
```

This part of the code tells the browser to put the banner flush with the top-left corner:

```
#banner-header
{
position: absolute;
left: 0;
top: 0;
width: 100%;
height: 100%;
margin: 0;
padding: 0;
}
```

The following code tells the browser not to let the default blog title and description show up over your banner.

```
#banner-header a
{
display: block;
left: 0;
top: 0;
height: 199px;
text-indent: -1000em;
}

#banner-description
{
overflow: hidden;
width: 0;
height: 0;
margin: 0;
padding: 0;
text-indent: -1000em;
}
```

   6. **Click Save Changes.**

Changing your blog's background

If you'd like your blog's background color to reflect your personality or brand a bit more, you can either change the color or add a background image.

If you would just like to change the color of your blog's background, you can do that by typing the CSS below in the custom CSS text box. Remember to change the hexadecimal value (#000000) to the color you want to use.

```
body {
background: #000000;
}
```

To make the background even more interesting, you may choose to use an actual image. Figure 14-4 shows how you might use an image as your blog's background.

When choosing a background image, be sure it's not too busy. Your goal here is to add interest but not distract from your content. A good choice is a light crosshatch pattern or a subtle color gradient that gradually flows from dark to light as a reader scrolls down the page.

Follow these instructions to add a background image behind your content areas:

1. **Save the image file you want to use as your blog's background to TypePad File Manager.**

2. **In File Manager, right-click the name of the image you just uploaded, and choose Copy Link Location from the menu.**

   You'll need this URL in Step 5.

3. **Click your blog's Design tab.**

4. **Click the Custom CSS tab in the left sidebar.**

Figure 14-4: This TypePad blog (www. pensieve. me) has used cus- tom CSS to install a decora- tive striped background image.

Subtle striped background

5. **Type the following CSS in the text field, changing the URL to reflect the URL you noted in Step 2:**

```
body {
background: url(http://sampleurl.com/image.jpg);
}
```

6. **Click Save Changes.**

You may want the background image to repeat. If that's the case, choose one of the following repeat options, and change your custom CSS to reflect the relevant code.

Repeat horizontally and vertically

```
body {
background: url(http://sampleurl.com/image.jpg);
background-repeat: repeat
}
```

Repeat horizontally

```
body {
background: url(http://sampleurl.com/image.jpg);
background-repeat: repeat-x
}
```

Repeat vertically

```
body {
background: url(http://sampleurl.com/image.jpg);
background-repeat: repeat-y
}
```

No repeat

```
body {
background: url(http://sampleurl.com/image.jpg);
background-repeat: no-repeat
}
```

Removing the border around your custom banner

When you insert a custom banner (using custom CSS or the Theme Builder as described in Chapter 11), TypePad automatically inserts a 15-pixel border around your banner image. (Refer to Figure 14-3; because the background is set to white, you can clearly see the white border in the example.)

If you want to remove that default border, you can make the adjustment in your custom CSS by following these steps:

1. **Create a resized banner image.**

   In Chapter 11, we explain that you should subtract 30 pixels from your layout width to use a custom banner (for example, an 800-pixels-wide layout should use a 770-pixels-wide banner to allow for the border). If you're going to eliminate the border, however, you'll need to resize the banner without that 30-pixels allowance (for example, an 800-pixels-wide layout would use an 800-pixels-wide image).

   While you're using your graphics editor (such as Adobe Photoshop or GIMP), make a note of the exact pixel height of your banner, because you'll need it in a few steps.

2. **Insert the newly resized banner image, using either custom CSS (as described earlier in this chapter) or the Theme Builder (described in Chapter 11).**

3. **Click your blog's Design tab.**

4. **Click the Custom CSS tab in the left sidebar.**

5. **In the custom CSS field, insert the following code, replacing 225 with the *exact* pixel height of your banner image that you noted in Step 1:**

   ```
   #banner {
       background-position: 0px 0px;
       height: 225px;
       }
   ```

6. **Preview the changes.**

   If you've correctly sized your new banner, you should see an adjusted design with the 15-pixel banner border removed, as shown in the sample blog in Figure 14-5.

7. **Save your changes.**

Fine-tuning your navigation bar

In Chapter 11, we tell you how you can insert (or omit) a horizontal navigation bar in your TypePad blog by using the drag-and-drop editor in the Content portion of your design. If you've decided to use a navigation bar, your default navigation bar looks like the one in Figure 14-6.

Figure 14-5:
Banner
image with
default
15-pixel
border
removed
via CSS.

Default navigation bar

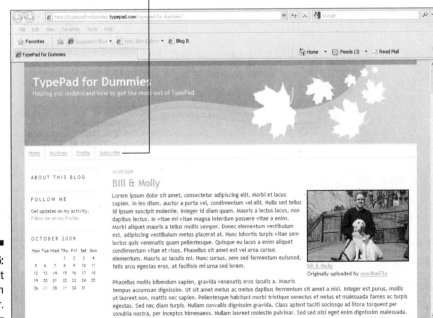

Figure 14-6:
The default
navigation
bar.

To make the navigation bar fit better with your blog's look and feel, you can change the colors, add borders, change the font, and more. CSS uses something called classes to define these changes. A *class* defines the style of a page element — in this case, the navigation bar. The CSS classes you'll want to know are

✔ **nav-list:** This is the container for the entire navigation bar.

✔ **nav-list-item:** This class addresses individual navigation items.

✔ **nav-list-item a:** This is the class for navigation links.

To show you how you can change your `nav-list` CSS to blend better with your theme design, we'll change our navigation bar from the default (refer to Figure 14-6) to the one shown in Figure 14-7.

To change your navigation bar modules, follow these instructions:

1. Click your blog's Design tab.

2. Click the Custom CSS tab in the left sidebar.

Custom navigation bar

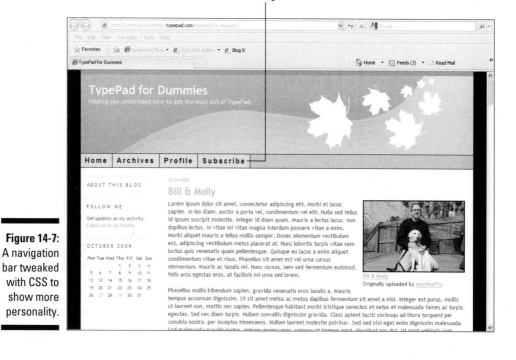

Figure 14-7:
A navigation bar tweaked with CSS to show more personality.

3. Type the following CSS code in the text box:

```
.nav-list
{
background-color: #FABC07;
border-top: 1.5px solid #000000;
border-bottom: 1.5px solid #000000;
}

.nav-list-item
{
background-color: #FAEB07;
border-right: 1.5px solid #000000;
}

.nav-list-item a
{
text-decoration: none;
color: #000000;
font-family: Arial, sans-serif;
font-size: medium;
font-weight: bold;
letter-spacing: 3px;
}
```

4. Click Save Changes.

We encourage you to play with this code and change the colors, spacing, font, and so on. If you're not fluent in CSS, the best way to learn is to change small things and see what happens. Pretty soon, you'll know exactly how to change the things you want to change!

Changing the font, style, and color of the post heading

It's possible to define the size, font, and color of several page elements via the custom CSS option. Doing so can help reinforce your brand as it meshes with the look and feel of your blog. For instance, if the primary color of your design (including your logo, which is part of your brand) is green, you may want to make your post heading that color instead of the default black. A little custom CSS can help you achieve that.

The individual post heading (or title) of a blog article is defined by three CSS classes. The first class, `.entry-header`, tells the browser how to display the post heading. In the following code (which we took from one of our own test blogs), the `.entry-header` class tells the browser to display the post title in a 22-pixel, black (#000), Georgia, Times New Roman, serif font. When an individual post is displayed (that is, when someone uses a permalink to find a post), that is how the post title appears.

```
.entry-header {
        color: #000;
        font-family: georgia, 'times new roman', serif;
        font-size: 22px;
}
```

The next class, .entry-header a, tells the browser how to display a linked title. In the following sample CSS, we are telling the browser to display a linked post header as dark green (#08AB2F). Because the font family and font size values are not included in this CSS, the browser defaults to the preceding CSS, which is a serif font at 22 pixels. Because post titles on the main page of a blog are automatically linked to the post's permalink, this is how the post header displays on your front page.

```
.entry-header a {
        color: #08AB2F;
        text-decoration: none;
}
```

The final class, .entry-header a:hover, tells the browser how to display the text if a reader mouses over the title. The following sample CSS tells the browser to underline the post header when a reader mouses over the title:

```
.entry-header a:hover {
        text-decoration: underline;
}
```

To change how the post header appears, simply change the necessary values. For instance, if the default font for your post header is a 22-pixel, black, serif font, but you'd like it to be a 30-pixel, blue, sans-serif font, type this CSS in your custom CSS text box:

```
.entry-header {
        color: #2485C5;
        font-family: arial, helvetica;
        font-size: 30px;
}

.entry-header a {
        color: #2485C5;
        text-decoration: none;
}

.entry-header a:hover {
        text-decoration: underline;
}
```

Changing column widths

You may find that your dream design doesn't have quite the same dimensions as the TypePad theme you've chosen. One way to get around that issue is to change the width of your columns with custom CSS.

Following are some examples of the basic CSS you might use to change the width of your columns. To start, find a layout in this section similar to what you are currently using. The CSS under the relevant layout is what you will use in Step 4 of the instructions later in this section.

Two-column, sidebar on the right

```
.layout-two-column-right #container { width: 800px; }
.layout-two-column-right #alpha { width: 550px; }
.layout-two-column-right #beta { width: 250px; }
```

Two-column, sidebar on the left

```
.layout-two-column-left #container { width: 800px; }
.layout-two-column-left #alpha { width: 550px; }
.layout-two-column-left #beta { width: 250px; }
```

Three-column, main content in the middle of two sidebars

```
.layout-three-column #container { width: 800px; }
.layout-three-column #alpha { width: 140px; }
.layout-three-column #beta { width: 520px; }
.layout-three-column #gamma { width: 140px; }
```

Three-column, with both sidebars on the right

```
.layout-three-column #container { width: 800px; }
.layout-three-column #alpha { width: 520px; }
.layout-three-column #beta { width: 140px; }
.layout-three-column #gamma { width: 140px; }
```

Figure 14-8 and the following list explain how the columns in your design reflect the code:

✔ #container is the total width of the content area. It includes all columns. The width of the container is the sum of the column widths: #alpha + #beta + #gamma = #container.

✔ #alpha is the farthest-left column in the content area.

✔ #beta is the next column to the right of #alpha.

✔ #gamma is the next column to the right of #beta.

Alpha   Beta   Gamma

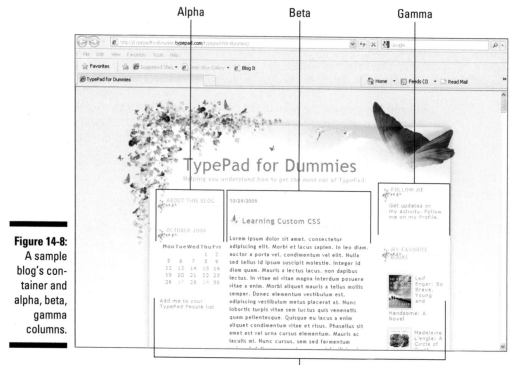

Figure 14-8:
A sample
blog's con-
tainer and
alpha, beta,
gamma
columns.

Container

You can change the width of the columns by changing the width value in the CSS code. Because all TypePad themes are different, it's impossible to give one solution that fits all blogs. We can provide only an overview of what to try; then you'll have to play around with values until you figure out what works for your theme. For instance, one theme may have padding included in its stylesheet. *Padding* is white space around the page element (in this case, possibly a sidebar) so it doesn't bump into the next element. When you change the values of the columns, you may discover that they don't look as you thought they would. This is most likely because the theme has padding.

To change the width of your columns with custom CSS, follow these instructions:

1. **Click your blog's Design tab.**

2. **Click the Layout in the left sidebar.**

    Determine which layout you are using (two-column right or left, three-column, one-column, and so on).

3. **Click the custom CSS link in the left sidebar.**

   You see the custom CSS page.

4. **Type the relevant CSS code (listed earlier in this section) in the text box.**

   For instance, if you were using a three-column layout with the content between two sidebars, you would type the following in the text box:

   ```
   .layout-three-column #container { width: 800px; }
   .layout-three-column #alpha { width: 140px; }
   .layout-three-column #beta { width: 520px; }
   .layout-three-column #gamma { width: 140px; }
   ```

   Change the width values to reflect your needs.

5. **Click Save Changes, and preview your blog.**

   If you aren't happy with how the changes appear, change the width values until you like the way the layout looks.

CSS and Advanced Templates resources

This chapter offers instructions for changing your blog's basic style elements using custom CSS or Advanced Templates. If you're interested in finding out even more about coding, we can point you in the right direction.

There's plenty more to know about CSS — it's a huge topic that's been written about at length elsewhere. For some additional information, consult the following:

✔ TypePad Knowledge Base: Add custom CSS (`help.sixapart.com/tp/us/custom_css.html`)

✔ *CSS For Dummies,* by Richard Mansfield

✔ *HTML, XHTML, & CSS For Dummies,* by Ed Tittle and Jeff Noble

✔ Do a Google search for *CSS tutorial*

TypePad's Knowledge Base offers several pages for you to use as references as you learn how to apply Advanced Templates to your blog:

✔ Tag documentation (`developer.typepad.com/tags`): This page gives you the correct reference name for each of your blog's page elements (for example, MTBlogName references your blog's name as it is in your blog's Settings tab).

✔ Template Tag Syntax (`help.sixapart.com/tp/us/template_tag_syntax.html`): This page explains how TypePad uses tags and how to tell if a tag in your template is an HTML tag or at TypePad tag.

✔ TypePad One (`www.typepad.com/one`): This page offers tips, tricks, and video to help you make the most of your TypePad blog.

We suggest choosing a base theme that has few graphic elements. As you change the column widths on graphic-heavy themes, sometimes the graphics disappear because the content fields are now larger than the area allotted to the graphics. Using a theme with fewer graphic elements may limit your frustration as you define your template with custom CSS tweaks.

Using Advanced Templates

The Advanced Templates option, like the custom CSS option, is available to TypePad users with accounts at the Pro Unlimited or Business Class level. The Advanced Templates option allows you to edit your blog's template code directly in the relevant CSS, HTML, or XML file. You can control every part of your blog's structure (for example, design, HTML, and layout) via these files.

The Advanced Templates feature is desirable if one of the following is true of you:

- ✔ You like to have control of your own templates.
- ✔ You want to try to build a custom blog template from scratch.
- ✔ You are importing an existing blog from another platform to your TypePad account.

Installing Advanced Templates

To enable Advanced Templates, click the name of the blog you want to work with and then follow these steps:

1. **Click the Design tab.**
2. **Click Choose a Theme.**
3. **In the left sidebar, click the Customizable link.**
4. **Click the Advanced Templates option.**
5. **In the right sidebar, click the Use This button.**

It's important to note that although you've chosen the Advanced Templates option, it's not yet applied to your blog. After you've finished creating your design with Advanced Templates, and you're ready to display it to your readers, you finish applying it as follows:

1. **Return to the Design page.**
2. **Scroll down to the list of Your Designs, and find Advanced Template Designs.**

3. Choose Apply from the Actions pull-down menu.

The Asterisk template is the default template for Advanced Templates. Now that you've applied Advanced Templates, your blog looks like the design shown in Figure 14-9.

Hiring and working with a designer

If you like the idea of customizing your blog's design but don't feel you have the necessary design or coding skills needed to do that, you may want to consider hiring a designer. But will you hire a graphic artist or a programmer? You may need both. Or, if you're just doing some simple image insertion, your graphic artist may be able to do that for you. Before you hire either, we'd like to give you some advice on hiring and working with designers and programmers so you're both happy with the outcome.

Check his work. Your first step in choosing a designer is looking carefully through his portfolio — does he regularly produce designs for others that suit your own tastes? Be sure to ask for references, especially if you're investing a significant amount of money in the process.

Know what you want. The "I'll know it when I see it" or "You're the expert; I'll go with whatever you say" approach rarely works. The designer isn't familiar with your tastes or needs, and it's a pretty good bet that whatever she comes back with won't be what you had in mind. Instead, have a clear idea of the goals you want to meet with your site and the brand you want to convey to your audience.

Be sure the person has experience with TypePad. Whether your designer will be installing a simpler design (using the Theme Builder) or a more complicated one (with Advanced Templates), you may want to be sure he has experience installing designs in TypePad blogs.

Share examples. When you discuss your needs with your designer, help her share your vision by showing her examples of what you do and don't like. Be specific about the elements you'd like to see in your own design. After the designer understands your tastes, she can offer advice about what may or may not work together.

Understand the value of Web design services. Whether a designer is coding your design, creating custom images for your design, or both, you should be aware that the designer is using specific skills and spending time on your design. Be prepared to pay for that special skill set. As with everything else, you get what you pay for.

Be clear about what you expect the designer or programmer to do. Some designers will create and install your custom images in your blog; others only create the images. Programmers, on the other hand, don't always create the highest-quality graphics, but they can install anything you give them. When you're talking with your designer or programmer, be sure you explain exactly what you need. After you've both agreed on the scope of the project, any changes later will cost you money. Being clear about expectations at the beginning of the process will help you avoid unexpected costs later.

You can find a list of TypePad-savvy designers at www.typepad.com/one/typepad-services.html.

Figure 14-9:
The default
Asterisk
Advanced
Template
design.

To begin editing your blog's templates, click the Templates link. The Templates page appears and lists all the individual files for your blog's Index Templates, Archive Templates, and Template Modules.

Understanding your templates

Although we assume that if you're ready to use Advanced Templates, you probably have an understanding of CSS, HTML, and XML, we think it's a good idea to know how your templates are organized. Here, we give you a brief overview of the index templates and the template modules; we don't discuss the archive templates because those are fairly self-explanatory (for example, Category Archives is the template for your archives arranged by category). Most of the work you'll do in Advanced Templates will occur in an index template or one of the template modules.

Index templates

✔ **Archive Index template (`archives.html`):** This template determines how your archives page looks. It calls each archive module and displays it in the correct order and within the established design parameters.

✔ **Atom template (`atom.xml`):** This template contains the XML information needed for your Atom RSS feed.

- ✔ **Main Index template (`index.html`):** As its name states, this is the main template file for your blog. It references the other templates and modules, and ensures that those items are shown in the correct order (and with the correct design elements) when your blog is displayed.

- ✔ **RSS 2.0 template (`rss.xml`):** This template contains the information needed for your RSS 2.0 feed.

- ✔ **RSS template (`index.rdf`):** This template contains the information needed for an RSS 1.0 feed.

- ✔ **StyleSheet (`style.css`):** This template contains the information needed for your overall styles.

- ✔ **Theme stylesheet (`asterisk-style.css`):** This stylesheet assigns specific values to your banner, background, link color, headings, and so on. If you just want to tweak the Asterisk theme to showcase your style, this is the file you'll want to start with.

- ✔ **Create new index template (link):** You can tweak the existing `index.html` to customize your blog page elements, or you can create a new `index.html` with your own coding and parameters.

If you choose to make a new `index.html` file, we encourage you to do the following:

- ✔ **Create a test blog.** This way, you can tweak your code without bothering your readers. It's always better to make mistakes in private. Also, you'll have the freedom to test ideas and play with code. A test blog simply ensures that your testing and tweaking are private until you're ready to take them public.

- ✔ **Copy the original `index.html` file.** Save the copy somewhere else, such as a text document on your hard drive. Then if things don't work as you planned, you will have that code as a backup.

- ✔ **Rename `index.html`.** We suggest you save your work-in-progress `index.html` as something other than `index.html` until you're ready to test it — that way, you won't overwrite your original `index.html` file.

- ✔ **Double-check your copies.** When you're ready to test your `index.html`, double-check that you have the original `index.html` copied and saved somewhere else so you can go back to it if necessary.

Template modules

Modules are the items you'll use when you want to add sidebar items to your blog, because you can't do that via the drag-and-drop Content option under Design. Modules are referenced in the Main Index Template (`index.html`) like this:

```
<$MTInclude module="module-name"$>
```

Where `"module-name"` reflects the actual module name, such as `"user-photo"`.

By default, the Asterisk theme calls the following modules in this order:

```
<$MTInclude module="user-photo"$>

<$MTInclude module="about-page"$>

<$MTInclude module="category-cloud"$>

<$MTInclude module="monthly-archives"$>

<$MTInclude module="elsewhere-grid"$>

<$MTInclude module="subscribe-to-feed"$>

<$MTInclude module="powered-by-typepad"$>
```

You can change the order of these modules (which changes the order in which they appear on your sidebar), or you can delete modules (you can include them again later, if you change your mind). You can also include other modules simply by creating a new line referencing the module you want to include on your sidebar.

Here is a short explanation of each sidebar module:

- **about-page:** This module provides a text link (it says simply About) that links to your About Me page (see Chapter 4).

- **calendar:** This module shows a calendar with dates linked to the posts published on that day. If a reader clicks a linked date, he or she sees a page listing all posts published on that date.

- **category-cloud:** This module lists each category you assign to your posts. Frequently used categories appear with a larger and heavier font.

- **category-list:** This module provides a simple alphabetical list of the categories you use for your posts. Unlike in the category-cloud module, no weight is associated with frequently used categories in the category-list module.

- **elsewhere-grid:** This module shows clickable icons linked to the other social media accounts you have associated with your TypePad account. See Figure 14-10 for a comparison of the elsewhere-grid and elsewhere-list modules.

- **elsewhere-list:** This module is similar to the elsewhere-grid module, but it not only shows clickable icons, but also includes your associated ID for the other social media accounts you've shared with your TypePad account. See Figure 14-10 for a comparison of the elsewhere-grid and elsewhere-list modules.

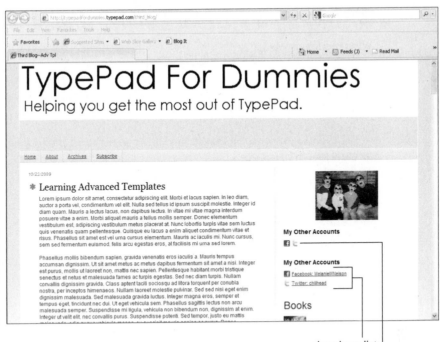

Figure 14-10:
The
elsewhere-
grid and
elsewhere-
list modules.

elsewhere-list

elsewhere-grid

- ✔ **monthly-archives:** This module simply provides a clickable list of the last few months. When a reader clicks a month, he or she sees a page listing all the posts published in that month.

- ✔ **navigation-bar:** This module creates the navigation bar for your blog. Later in this chapter, we explain how to include specific page links in your navigation bar and where to place the navigation-bar module in the Main Index Template (`index.html`).

- ✔ **powered-by-typepad:** This module shows a box in your sidebar that says (*name of your blog*) powered by TypePad on one line and Member since (*date you signed up*) on the next line.

- ✔ **recent-comments:** This module provides a list of the most recent comments posted to your blog.

- ✔ **subscribe-to-feed:** This module provides a link for subscribing to your blog's feed.

- ✔ **create new template module:** If you would like to customize your blog even further, you can create a new template module here and reference it as needed in your index template. You use this option to add a widget or TypeList to your blog's sidebar.

Installing a custom banner image

Although the Asterisk template is nice, you're probably using Advanced Templates because you want to make your blog's design personal. As we state in the section on custom CSS, using a custom banner is an important step toward that autonomy. To include a custom banner in your advanced template design, follow these instructions:

1. **Upload your custom image to File Manager, and make a note of its URL.**

2. **Click your blog's Design tab.**

3. **Click the Templates tab in the left sidebar.**

4. **Open the Theme Stylesheet (asterisk-style.css).**

5. **Find the banner code.**

   The banner code will start with a line that looks like this:

   ```
   /* banner styling */
   ```

6. **Replace the existing banner code with the upcoming code.**

   In the following code, you need to replace `background: url (http://url.com/image.jpg)` with the URL you noted in Step 1. You also need to change `height: 200px;` to reflect the pixel height of your custom image.

   ```
   #banner
   {
   background: url(http://url.com/image.jpg) no-repeat;
   height: 200px;
   }
   #banner-inner { overflow: visible; padding: 0; }
   #banner-header
   {
   position: absolute;
   left: 0;
   top: 0;
   width: 100%;
   height: 100%;
   margin: 0;
   padding: 0;
   }
   #banner-header a
   {
   display: block;
   left: 0;
   top: 0;
   ```

```
height: 199px;
text-indent: -1000em;
}

#banner-description
{
overflow: hidden;
width: 0;
height: 0;
margin: 0;
padding: 0;
text-indent: -1000em;
}
```

7. Click Save Changes.

Changing the navigation bar

To make changes to your navigation bar, go to the Templates page, scroll
down to the Template Modules list, and click the navigation-bar link. This
opens the navigation-bar template code so you can edit it. The navigation-bar
module code looks like this:

```
<div id="nav">
<div id="nav-inner">
<ul class="nav-list pkg">
  <li class="nav-list-item"><a href="<$MTBlogURL$>"><$MTTrans phrase="Home"$></
          a></li>
  <li class="nav-list-item"><a href="<$MTUserSiteURL$>about.html"><$MTTrans
          phrase="About"$></a></li>
  <li class="nav-list-item"><a href="<$MTBlogURL$>archives.html"><$MTTrans
          phrase="Archives"$></a></li>
  <li class="nav-list-item"><a href="<$MTBlogURL$>atom.xml"><$MTTrans
          phrase="Subscribe"$></a></li>
</ul>
</div>
</div>
```

Following are instructions for some popular navigation-bar tweaks: including
deleting links and using icons instead of text as navigation links.

Including additional links in your navigation bar

The default links in the navigation bar are

✔ Home (links to the main page of your blog)

✔ About (links to your About page; see Chapter 4)

> ✔ Archives (links to your Archive page)
>
> ✔ Subscribe (allows readers to subscribe to your blog's RSS feed)

To include additional links in your navigation bar, open the navigation-bar module, and insert a new list item (`<li>`) that looks like this:

```
<li class="nav-list-item"><a href="http://sampleurl.com">Sample Text</a></li>
```

Change `http://sampleurl.com` to the URL you want to link to, and change `Sample Text` to the link text you want to display in the navigation bar.

You can include as many list items as you deem functional. Just remember that your navigation bar shouldn't be so cluttered or confusing that readers can't find their way around your blog.

Using icons as your navigation bar links

Text links are fine and dandy for many blogs, but if you'd like to integrate your navigation bar into your overall design, you may want to have custom icons appear as your navigation links.

To use custom icons, you'll need to create them yourself or commission them from a designer. If you're very lucky, you may have a friend who has GIMP or Photoshop and is willing to help you with this task. After you have created your custom icons, upload them to File Manager (see Chapter 4 for more advice on setting up an intuitive and useful file structure). Make a note of the URL of each image, because you'll need those URLs in the upcoming Step 2.

To have your custom icons appear in your navigation bar as links, follow these instructions:

1. **From your blog's Templates page, scroll down to the Template Modules list, and click the navigation-bar link.**

2. **Replace the `<$MTTrans phrase>` items with the following image reference:**

   ```
   <img src="http://sampleurl.com/imagename.jpg">
   ```

   Remember to replace `http://sampleurl.com/imagename.jpg` with the URL of the image you want to use.

3. **Repeat as necessary for each navigation icon and link.**

Adding widgets and TypeLists in Advanced Templates

When you choose to use Advanced Templates to control your blog's design, you give up the option to use the drag-and-drop function in the Content area of the Design tab. Because that's the place you'd normally go to include a widget or TypeList in your blog's sidebar, you have to add those items manually in the correct template file. We explain how to do that in this section.

In the following instructions (both for widgets and TypeLists), you'll need to create and name a new template module. If you give your module a title with more than one word, you must hyphenate the title. For example, use *my-favorite-books* instead of *my favorite books*.

Adding a widget

As you might remember from Chapter 8, a widget is simply a piece of third-party code that performs a specific function (for example, showing your latest tweets from Twitter or providing a search engine for your blog). If you weren't using Advanced Templates, you'd be able to insert the widget into your sidebar via a simple wizard. Because you want the control of using Advanced Templates, however, to insert a widget into your sidebar, you have to do two things:

  ✔ Get the actual code for the widget.

  ✔ Create a new module for the widget.

You can include a widget in your sidebar by using Advanced Templates in two ways. The first method is to create a new sidebar module with the code embedded directly in the module template (instructions next). The second method is to create a Notes TypeList for the widget and then create a new sidebar module (instructions are shown later in this section).

Follow these instructions to create a new template module with the code embedded directly inside:

  1. **Click the Create New Template module link.**

     The Create Template Module page appears.

  2. **Type a name for your new module in the Template Name text field.**

  3. **Paste the widget code in the Template Body text field.**

  4. **Click Save Changes, and return to the Templates page.**

     Your widget is now saved as a module, but you need to include it in your Main Index Template so it shows up in your sidebar.

5. **Click to open the Main Index Template.**

6. **Look for this notation:**

```
<!-- include sidebar module content here -->
```

The modules listed under that notation vary, depending on what you are currently displaying in your sidebar. The order in which the modules appear in this list is the order in which they will appear on your sidebar. See the "Template modules" section of this chapter for further explanation.

7. **Insert a new line of code for the module you just created.**

Your new line of code should look similar to this (but with `"name-of-new-module"` replaced the name of the module you created):

```
<$MTInclude module="name-of-new-module"$>
```

The code doesn't have to go at the end of the sidebar list. You can place it in the order in which you want it to appear in your sidebar. For instance, if you want it to appear after your About page link but before your category cloud, you would insert your new sidebar module after the about-page module and before the category-cloud module so it looks like this:

```
<$MTInclude module="user-photo"$>

<$MTInclude module="about-page"$>

<$MTInclude module="name-of-new-module"$>

<$MTInclude module="category-cloud"$>
```

8. **Click Save Changes.**

Adding a TypeList

If you're using Advanced Templates, you can easily include a TypeList in your sidebar. Just follow these instructions:

1. **Click the Create New Template Module link.**

The Create Template Module page appears.

2. **Type a name for your new module in the Template Name text field.**

3. **In the Template Body text field, type the appropriate code for the kind of TypeList you want to use.**

You must change `"TypeList Name"` to reflect the name of the TypeList you want to use. For example, if you've created a TypeList called *My Favorite Drive Shaft Songs*, replace `"TypeList Name"` with that title. You don't need hyphens between the words in the new title.

Links TypeList code

```
<h2>Links</h2>
<ul>
<MTList name="TypeList Name">
<li>
<a href="<$MTListItem field="url"$>" target="_new">
<$MTListItem field="title"$></a>
</li>
</MTList>
</ul>
```

Notes TypeList code

```
<h2>Notes</h2>
<ul>
<MTList name="TypeList Name">
<li>
<$MTListItem field="note"$>
</li>
</MTList>
</ul>
```

Books TypeList code

```
<h2>Books</h2>
<ul>
<MTList name="TypeList Name">
<li>
<a href="<$MTListItemURL$>"><$MTListItemImage$></a>
        <br />
<$MTListItem field="title"$> <br />
<$MTListItemRating$>
</li>
</MTList>
</ul>
```

Albums TypeList code

```
<h2>Albums</h2>
<ul>
<MTList name="TypeList Name">
<li>
<a href="<$MTListItemURL$>" title="<$MTListItem
        field="artist"$>">
<$MTListItem field="album"$> </a> <br />
<$MTListItem field="notes"$>
</li>
</MTList>
</ul>
```

By default, the TypeList code tells the browser to use a bulleted list for each list item in a TypeList and looks similar to this (this example is for a Book List):

```
<h2>Books</h2>
<ul>
<MTList name="TypeList Name">
<li>
<a href="<$MTListItemURL$>"><$MTListItemImage$></a>
<br />
<$MTListItem field="title"$> <br />
<$MTListItemRating$>
</li>
</MTList>
</ul>
```

If you would like the list to appear without bullets, modify the code to look like this:

```
<h2>Books</h2>
<MTList name="My Favorite Books">
<p>
<a href="<$MTListItemURL$>"><$MTListItemImage$></a>
<br />
<$MTListItem field="title"$> <br />
<$MTListItemRating$>
</MTList>
```

Notice in the preceding code, we simply removed the `<ul>` and `</ul>` tags and the `<li>` and `</li>` tags. We left the `<MTList>` and `</MTList>` tags. We added a `<p>` tag after `<MTList name="My Favorite Books">`.

4. **Click Save Changes, and return to the Template page.**

You've created your new module. Now you need to include it in your Main Index Template so it appears in your sidebar.

5. **Click to open the Main Index Template.**

6. **Look for this notation:**

```
<!-- include sidebar module content here -->
```

The modules listed under that notation vary depending on what you are currently displaying in your sidebar. The order in which the modules appear in this list is the order in which they appear on your sidebar. See the "Template modules" section of this chapter for further explanation.

7. **Insert a new line of code for the module you just created.**

Your new line of code should look similar to this (but with `"name-of-new-module"` replaced by the name of the module you created):

```
<$MTInclude module="name-of-new-module"$>
```

The code doesn't have to go at the end of the sidebar list. You can place it in the order in which you want it to appear in your sidebar. For instance, if you want it to appear after your About page link but before your category cloud, using the code example from Step 6, you would insert your new sidebar module after the about-page module and before the category-cloud module so that it looks like this:

```
<$MTInclude module="user-photo"$>

<$MTInclude module="about-page"$>

<$MTInclude module="name-of-new-module"$>

<$MTInclude module="category-cloud"$>
```

   8. **Click Save Changes.**

Changing your picture

By default, the user-photo module references the photo from your TypePad Profile (discussed in Chapter 3). If you'd like to make the image on your blog different from the one on your TypePad Profile, you can do so by changing the code in the user-photo module as follows:

   1. **Upload the photo or image you'd like to use to File Manager.**

   2. **In the File Manager list, click the name of the file you want to use.**

      A new browser window or tab appears, showing the photo or image.

   3. **Make a note of the URL in the address bar.**

      You will need this URL in Step 6.

   4. **Go to the Templates page, and scroll down to Template Modules.**

   5. **Click user-photo.**

      You see this code:

```
<!-- user photo -->
<MTUserIfPhoto>
<div class="module-photo module">
  <div class="module-content">
    <img src="<$MTUserPhoto$>" alt="<$MTTrans
        phrase="My Photo"$>" />
        </div><!-- .module-content -->
</div><!-- .module-photo .module -->
</MTUserIfPhoto>
```

6. Change the code to look like this:

```
<!-- user photo -->
<MTUserIfPhoto>
<div class="module-photo module">
  <div class="module-content">
    <img src="http://sampleURL.com/photo.jpg" />
        </div><!-- .module-content -->
</div><!-- .module-photo .module -->
</MTUserIfPhoto>
```

Remember to change `http://sampleURL.com/photo.jpg` to reflect the URL for your image (see Step 3).

7. Click Save Changes.

Deleting or replacing the post-title asterisk

The default template for Advanced Templates is the Asterisk theme. You may want to get rid of the default asterisk icon that appears by each of your post titles, or you may want to replace it with a customized icon you've made. This is a fairly easy change. Just look for the following code in the `asterisk-style.css` file:

```
.entry {
 background-image: url(/.shared-typepad/themes/walt/theme-asterisk_white_wide/
          post-ornament.png);
```

Then change that code to look like this to remove the asterisk icon:

```
.entry {
 background-image: url(none);
```

If you'd like to make your own icon and upload it to File Manager, you can replace the asterisk icon with your custom one. To do that, change the original code (as mentioned) to look like this (changing the URL to reflect the URL for your icon):

```
.entry {
 background-image: url(http://url.com/image.jpg);
```

If you choose to make a custom icon, we suggest starting with a 20-pixels-by-20-pixels image. If it's too big or too small for your needs, you can change the size as necessary.

Part V
The Part of Tens

The 5th Wave
By Rich Tennant

"I'm not sure a fantasy sports blog about professional wrestling would work. Professional wrestling is already a fantasy sport."

In this part . . .

*W*e give you some top-ten lists in this part of the book. First we share our favorite blogging tips, and then you discover where to find TypePad resources. Next, you get ten pointers for being a well-mannered blogger. Finally, we point you toward ten bloggers who are making TypePad work very well for them.

Chapter 15

Ten Tips and Tricks

Looking for some quick ways to add a professional polish to your blogging experience? In this chapter, we give you ten tricks of the trade for blogging. A few are technological in nature, pointing you to some specific tools you can integrate with your blog. Others are more general pieces of advice that should move you further down the road toward professional success. But all are worth considering to help you blog your best!

Set Reasonable, Measurable Goals

Although suggesting that you set reasonable and measurable goals may seem like an elementary piece of advice, it's a principle that's easily overlooked. Many people begin blogging as a hobby, only to see their blogs gradually evolve into a business. Others plan to blog professionally from the start, but they set such ambitious goals that they're quickly frustrated. Whether you're a hobby blogger or aspire to be a professional blogger, sit down and make some realistic goals regarding traffic, income, and your personal blogging habits. Keep your goals incremental enough that you don't lose heart!

As you set your blogging goals, consider the following:

- **Concentrate on subscribers, not page views.** Increasingly, readers are following their favorite blogs in feed readers. Your number of subscribers is probably a much more stable and accurate picture of your blog's following than your actual traffic. Consider that your blog's traffic can be drastically affected by even the smallest factor, such as taking a week off or a big news event (for example, an election) that grabs readers' focus. These same events, however, are not likely to change your number of subscribers, making your number of subscribers a more reliable benchmark. In addition, many of your subscribers opt to read your articles within their feed readers rather than click over to your site. It's quite likely that the number of people reading your articles is higher than what your stats indicate. (Of course, this depends on whether you've enabled full or partial feeds in your blog's settings; see Chapter 5.)

  You still need to be aware of your page views — advertisers, especially, want to know those numbers, because they more accurately represent how many eyeballs are seeing your ad space (see more on third-party tracking software in Appendix B). But for *your* purposes — gauging what is, we hope, a steadily growing influence — that subscriber number is the one to watch.

- **Keep in mind general blogging trends.** Certain traffic and income trends seem to hold true for most bloggers, so figure them into your goals. For example, traffic tends to slow down in late December and late summer. Conversely, corporate interest in buying ad space tends to ramp up before gift-buying holidays (such as Christmas and Mother's Day). Don't be discouraged by a traffic dip that everyone else is experiencing too!

- **Consider internal, not external goals.** Ultimately, you can't control others' reading habits. Instead of constantly gauging your own subscribers, income, or page counts, gauge what you *can* control. Set a goal to blog once a day for 60 days, for example, or aim to write for an hour a day. Your good discipline will be reflected in the quality of what you publish, which will, with any luck, translate into increased traffic over the long haul.

- **Consider what motivates you.** We've met several bloggers who choose a niche based on how much money they thought it would make instead of how much they loved the topic. If you're setting goals for a niche that doesn't interest you, it's likely you'll lose interest quickly. Not only will your blogging experience be less enjoyable, but also, you definitely won't be achieving your goals.

✔ **Be explicit about how you'll know you've achieved each goal.** If one of your goals is to make money with your blog, try to refine that or even set tiered goals. Perhaps your first goal can be to sell two $25 ads on your sidebar, a second-tier goal can be to have enough monthly income to take your significant other to a fancy restaurant for dinner once a month, and a third-tier goal could be to save enough income from your blog to buy an original Salvador Dali painting. Each goal is tangible, and you can recognize it when you achieve it. At the same time, the goals are broad enough that you have to consider how you'll meet them. The goal is a challenge, but then, most goals are, aren't they?

Use an Editorial Calendar

Many bloggers write their posts on a whim, posting and publishing in one fell swoop whenever inspiration hits. That's fine, of course — some of our own best posts are the ones we wrote on the spur of the moment.

As your blog grows in scope, though, you may find you need some help planning what to write about and when. This is especially true if you write for multiple blogs (either your own or others for which you're a contributor). Enter the editorial calendar: a plan that lays out where you're writing, what you're covering, and when it all takes place. The calendar can help you remember weekly writing assignments (such as regular features at your own blog or regular contributions you've committed to at another one). You can look ahead and make sure your editorial calendar makes allowances for events in your personal calendar, too, which can help you keep your sanity in check! Additionally, an editorial calendar keeps you from duplicating your efforts, which is especially important if you're generating content for which you're being paid — advertisers or employers need to know they're getting the best and freshest you have to offer.

Your editorial calendar doesn't have to be elaborate — it may simply be some scrawled notes in your personal day planner. If you plan better with pen and paper in hand, consider keeping your editorial calendar on a wall calendar or a pocket calendar (the latter has the benefit of being portable, so you can jot down post ideas when you're on the go). Plenty of online resources allow you to print calendar pages as well, such as WhichTime (www.whichtime.com) and ePrintableCalendars (/www.eprintable calendars.com).

If online calendars are more your style, you have numerous options to choose among, such as Google Calendar (`google.com/calendar`). Or you can use offline calendar software (iCal for Mac users or Microsoft Outlook) that comes bundled with your computer. A bonus is that Google Calendar, Microsoft Outlook, and iCal can all sync with your smartphone so you can add ideas on the fly. Other options (not all of them free) include 30 Boxes (`30boxes.com`), Annomate (`www.annomate.com`), and BraveNet Calendars (`www.bravenet.com/webtools/calendar`).

Keep Solid Records

Because most of us don't make vast sums of cash from blogging, it would be entirely too easy to assume that the small dollar amounts don't matter in the eyes of the Internal Revenue Service. That's a foolish mistake — earning income from your blog makes you a business, no matter how small (see more on monetizing your blog in Chapter 12).

Treat your blogging revenue as legitimate small-business income. Keep a file folder or three-ring binder that holds all your receipts for business-related purchases. You'll want to talk more with a tax professional about this, but do realize that many of your blogging-related expenses (computer, Internet access, business cards, and so on) might be tax deductible, at least in part. You'll never know until you ask your accountant! (You might also check out *Taxes 2010 For Dummies,* by Eric Tyson, MBA; Margaret A. Munro, EA; and David J. Silverman, EA.)

You might also set up a separate bank account for your blogging income, just to keep it separate from your primary personal account. We suggest that you keep a running spreadsheet of your income and save your receipts. As with all tax-related issues, it's best to err on the side of keeping too *much,* not too little. You can always toss later.

The more you take yourself seriously as a professional blogger, the more your readers will too!

Submit Your Site to Directories

As the blogosphere grows, more and more directories are popping up to serve as clearinghouses, pointing readers toward blogs they might find interesting. If you do a Google search on *blog directories,* you'll see just how many you have to choose among. Some of the most well-known blog directories are

✔ Alltop (`alltop.com`)

✔ Blog Catalog (`www.blogcatalog.com`)

✔ Blogarama (`www.blogarama.com`)

✔ Blogged (`www.blogged.com`)

✔ BlogTopsites (`www.blogtopsites.com`)

✔ MyBlogLog (`www.mybloglog.com`)

You certainly don't need to list your site with every online directory. You could spin your wheels indefinitely looking for the latest and greatest new directories, and many of them may not even offer you that much traffic. Do a little poking around and find the ones that seem most reputable to you. In particular, which ones are listing blogs you trust and enjoy?

If you're writing a niche blog geared at a specific audience, one possibility is to do a Google search for a directory in that particular niche (for example, *sports blog directory*). Listing your blog in a directory aimed at a more specific audience might yield better results.

Technorati , pictured in Figure 15-1, was one of the first search engines dedicated to searching blogs as opposed to searching the entire Web.

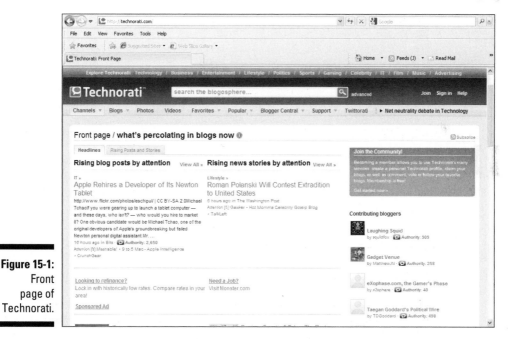

Figure 15-1:
Front
page of
Technorati.

Technorati is a directory that not only lists your blog, but also measures your blog's *authority* (the number of blogs that link to you). To get started at Technorati, you need to *claim* your blog, which simply means you need to let Technorati that know your blog is out there and that you're the owner (you can do this by visiting `technorati.com`.). You can find the steps for claiming your blog by clicking the Support link at the top of Technorati's home page (refer to Figure 15-1).

Use the Blog It Widget

If you're the type of blogger who frequently likes to post about news stories, videos, or other current events, you are going to love TypePad's Blog It widget. This simple little tool is a button that can be installed on your browser's toolbar. Whenever you see a story you'd like to blog about, the button helps you instantly compose a post, right on the spot. Here's how you install it:

1. **Visit TypePad's Blog It page at `www.typepad.com/features/ blogit.html`.**

    The page looks similar to the one in Figure 15-2 — look for the blue Blog It button.

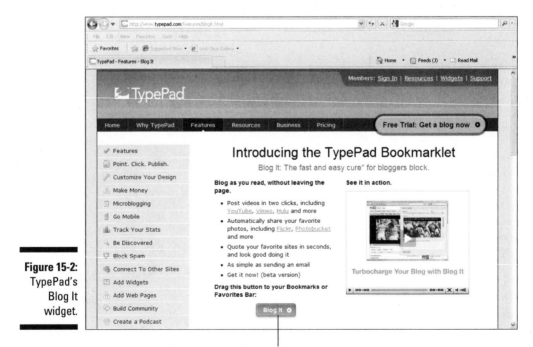

Figure 15-2: TypePad's Blog It widget.

Click and drag to toolbar to install

2. **Place the cursor over the Blog It button, and then click and drag it up to the browser's toolbar.**

   The Blog It button is now installed on your browser toolbar or menu bar, and you're ready to see it in action!

After you have the Blog It widget installed in your browser, use the following instructions to use the widget to quickly and easily compose a post. These instructions assume that you are currently looking at a page in your browser that you'd like to share with your blog readers:

1. **Use your cursor to highlight the part of the article that you want to share with your readers.**

   If you do not highlight a specific portion of the article, Blog It automatically assumes that you would like to use the first paragraph of the article.

2. **Click the Blog it link on your browser's toolbar.**

   The Blog It editor appears as a pop-up window, as shown in Figure 15-3.

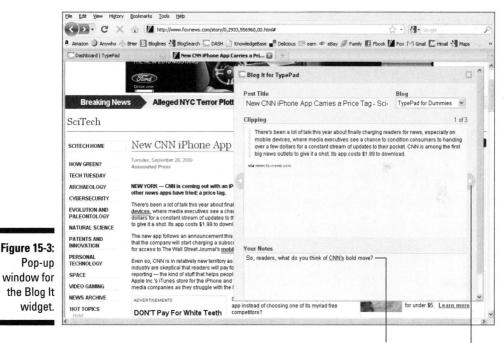

Figure 15-3:
Pop-up window for the Blog It widget.

Your comments on the story

Arrow for changing clipping

3. Change the fields in the Blog It window as necessary.

- Post Title: By default, Blog It uses the title of the original article you are referencing. You can change the title, if you want.

- Blog: Use the pull-down menu to choose which of your TypePad blogs you want to post this article to.

- Clipping: This text field shows you which part of the original article will appear on your blog. If you'd like to edit this text, click inside the Clipping text box, and it immediately switches to HTML view. When you've finished editing, click OK.

If you don't like the default clipping, you can click the arrows designated in Figure 15-3 for a different clipping option. Or you can close the Blog It widget and highlight the part of the article you want to include on your own blog.

- Your Notes: Click inside this text box, and type your commentary on the article. This text will appear below the clipping of the original article. You can include simple HTML tags (for example, a link) as necessary.

4. Click Publish Now.

The excerpted article and your commentary (if you included any) appear on your blog with a link to the original story. Figure 15-4 shows an example of how it may appear.

If you've written your text, but you're not quite ready to publish, simply click Edit in TypePad. You'll be taken to your blog's Compose editor so you can either make edits to the post or save it as a draft.

Figure 15-4: A published TypePad post using the Blog It widget.

Blog Offline with Windows Live Writer

Windows Live Writer (available to Windows users only — sorry, Mac owners) is a free, downloadable tool you can use to write your blog posts offline. It's always handy to compose your blog posts in your platform's Dashboard, but when you're working somewhere without Internet access, you may need a backup tool. Figure 15-5 shows a sample blog post being composed offline in Windows Live Writer.

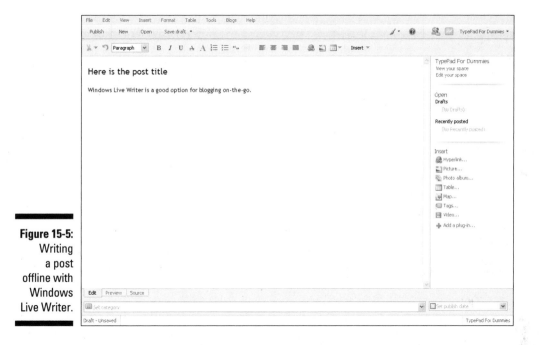

Figure 15-5:
Writing a post offline with Windows Live Writer.

You may be interested in this tool especially if you have multiple blogs on different platforms (such as TypePad and Google Blogger). Because Live Writer is compatible with a variety of blogging platforms, you can post to more than one blog (on multiple platforms) from only one Dashboard. You can also use Live Writer to easily tweak photos with special effects.

Download this tool at `download.live.com/writer`. For a helpful tutorial on Live Writer, see `www.viddler.com/explore/remarkablogger/videos/20`.

Post via Your Phone

There may be times when it makes sense to blog on the fly. You can't always be at your computer to blog — sometimes you're out there living life, and bloggable stuff happens! To make sure you're ready when the spontaneous blogging urge strikes, e-mail your post from your phone (if your phone has e-mail capability). You can also download one of the following TypePad applications that's compatible with your smartphone:

- **Blog It for iPhone (`http://everything.typepad.com/blog/2008/06/back-in-april-w.html`):** Free. If you love your Blog It widget (discussed earlier in this chapter), you'll be happy to know you can use that same widget with your iPhone. Just open Safari on your phone, go to the Blog It page (`blogit.typepad.com`), and choose Add to Homescreen (which installs the Blog It icon on your iPhone). Now you can use the Blog It widget directly from your phone for those gotta-blog-it-now moments.

- **E-mail:** Free. TypePad assigns each account a unique e-mail address so you can send a post via e-mail to your account. Chapter 5 explains how to find your unique TypePad e-mail address and use it to post to your blog from your phone.

- **Shozu for BlackBerry (`www.shozu.com/portal/tour.do?refid=typepad`):** $4.99. Shozu allows you to upload photos and video to your TypePad blog as well as to other social media sites, such as Facebook, Twitter, YouTube, and Picasa.

- **TypePad for iPhone (`www.apple.com/webapps/productivity/typepadforiphone.html`):** Free. Upload blog posts and photos just as easily as if you were sitting at your computer at home. This app also lets your friends know you've posted by automatically updating your Twitter account.

- **TypePad Mobile (`www.sixapart.com/typepad/tmdownload.html`):** Free. If you have a Palm OS, Windows Mobile 5, or Symbian Series 60 smartphone, you can download TypePad Mobile and update your blog or photo albums directly from your phone.

Protect Your Writing

The issue of copyright is a serious one in the blogosphere. The things you write on your blog are your intellectual property, and they are automatically protected under copyright law whether or not you explicitly display a copyright symbol and notice.

Unfortunately, being a published writer (whether in print or digitally) means that you run the risk of someone stealing your words. It's frustrating, and it's happened to most experienced bloggers. Be aware of your rights and legal status (a good starting point is `www.copyright.gov/help/faq`).

One common copyright infringement that takes place in the blogosphere is the practice of scraping. *Scraping* is when other bloggers place all or part of your post at their blog (often, but not always, via automated methods) with the hope of drumming up some revenue via the ads on their blogs. It's illegal, and it's unpleasant, especially if you find your content scraped at a site that hosts objectionable material. You can try contacting the site's owner to ask him or her to remove your content. If that doesn't work, try contacting the company that hosts the blog (such as Google Blogger or TypePad). If you still can't make any headway, you can seek legal counsel.

To help curb scraping, some bloggers issue a *partial feed,* meaning that they send out only an excerpt to readers via feed readers. Because scrapers often use feed readers to cull their content illegally, this might offer you some protection. Be aware, however, that there are some significant disadvantages to offering a partial feed; most notably, readers tend to find full feeds more convenient.

Your best bet is to make it clear to readers that you're serious about your copyright. You can include a copyright blurb in your blog footer (see Chapter 11) or in your sidebar (by using a Notes TypeList, explained in Chapter 8) like the one pictured in Figure 15-6.

Figure 15-6:
A copyright notice in a TypePad sidebar.

COPYRIGHT © 2005-2009
rocks in my dryer

Include the copyright symbol, of course, and be sure to add the years in which you've been producing content on your blog. You can even spell it out further, if you like (that is, "No material on this site may be reproduced in written or digital form without the author's consent"). It's no magic bullet, but there's some value in making yourself clear. If you ever *do* find yourself having to enforce your copyright, at least you'll be able to point the offender to your up-front expectations.

Still another option is to participate at Creative Commons (`creative commons.org`), a nonprofit organization that provides legal tools to content producers. It allows you to spell out conditions under which you *are* willing to share content, as well as the conditions under which you *aren't*. Visit the Creative Commons FAQ link for more details.

For other valuable information on copyright protection, visit CopyScape (`www.copyscape.com` (it's a site that allows you to search and see if your page has been copied by someone else) and Plagiarism Today (`www.plagiarismtoday.com` (a helpful source of information for many Web-based copyright issues).

Ultimately, copyright issues are legal issues. If someone has infringed on your copyright, your best and surest course of action is to consult an attorney experienced in copyright enforcement.

Protect Your Images

Just as it's frustrating to see your content at someone else's blog, it's frustrating to see your images at another Web site. Whether your images are your livelihood or something you simply share with your readers as a record of your life, it's never pleasant to discover that people are using your content for their own gain. This is especially true if they aren't attributing the work to you or didn't ask your permission. Unfortunately, you can't stop this online theft from happening completely, but we can offer a few solutions to help deter it.

Use a watermark

A traditional *watermark* is an image, a pattern, or text that appears on your image to show ownership. Figure 15-7 shows a TypePad post containing an image *without* a watermark (the image on the left) and one *with* a watermark (the image on the right).

A watermark is an easy way to mark your images with your copyright, trademark, or brand so anyone viewing them knows they belong to you. You can use your own image-editing software to create a customized watermark, or you can use an online tool (such as Water Mark Tool, `www.watermark tool.com`) to help you. If you choose the latter, you'll upload your image to the Web site (the image must be less than 200KB), generate a watermark with their tools, and then save the altered file to your computer so you can upload it to File Manager.

If you don't have Adobe Photoshop, you may want to check out GIMP (www.gimp.org or www.picnik.com).

A *digital watermark* includes digital information within the image's original digital file. You can include information such as author, copyright, or date. Whereas a traditional watermark is a clearly visible part of an image, a digital watermark is not. A digital watermark converts the information to digital noise that is read by digital-watermark software. To use a digital watermark, you need to have the necessary software. Digimarc (www.digimarc.com) is one option that works with Photoshop as a plug-in. Digimarc embeds the watermark noise in your files and then tracks the watermark so you can see how your images are being used. Because a digital watermark is invisible to human eyes, this is not so much a deterrent to people who are using your images without permission as a way to track those images and claim your ownership if they are taken.

There is no foolproof method for avoiding content theft. If someone is determined to use your content, they'll find a way. Even if you're using a digital watermark, someone can take a screen shot of your image, crop it, and use it; the digital watermark will no longer be associated with that file. If you don't want to risk someone using your content, don't put it online.

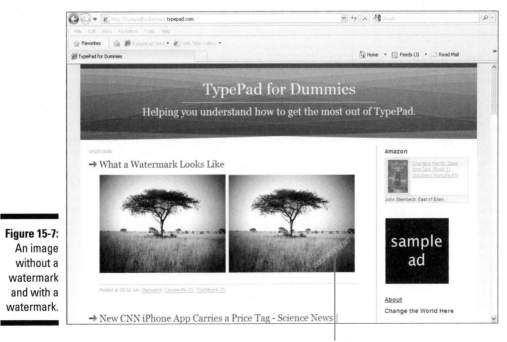

Figure 15-7:
An image without a watermark and with a watermark.

Watermark

Shrink-wrap your images

Shrink-wrapping your images is sort of like putting your images under glass so that if visitors right-click an image to save it to their computer, they're saving just the glass (in this case, a transparent image file).

To shrink-wrap your image, you'll need to make a transparent image file. After you have your transparent image and the image you want to show (which we refer to in these instructions as your *viewable image)*, you can build a simple table with HTML code (see the following instructions) to shrink-wrap the viewable image. What you're doing with the table is making the viewable image the background and then placing a transparent image on top of it. If people try to right-click to view, copy, or save the viewable image, they get only the transparent image (because it's on top).

Any professional image-editing software (such as Photoshop) has the ability to create a transparent image. However, that software is pricey. We suggest downloading GIMP (`www.gimp.org`), which is free and fairly robust — and allows you to make transparent images.

The following instructions show you how to make a transparent image with GIMP:

1. **Open GIMP, and create a new file.**

   The Create New Image pop-up window appears.

2. **Set the width and height to 10 pixels each.**

   The size is not important, because you'll be changing it to match the size of the visible image when you make your HTML table (which we'll get to after we show you how to make the transparent image).

3. **Click the + next to Advanced Option.**

   A submenu appears.

4. **From the Fill With pull-down menu, choose Transparency.**

   You can ignore the rest of the choices. You don't need them for this image.

5. **Click OK.**

   The main window appears, showing your new image. Don't worry if it doesn't look transparent right now.

6. **Choose File⇨Save As, and name your image.**

   We usually name our images something like `dot` or `clear`.

7. **Choose where you want to save the image on your computer.**

8. **Click the + next to Select File_Type (By Extension).**

   A submenu appears.

9. **Scroll down the menu, and choose PNG Image.**

10. **Click Save.**

Now that you have a transparent image, it's time to make a table in your TypePad blog post and shrink-wrap your viewable image. Go ahead and sign in to TypePad, and then upload your transparent image and your viewable image to File Manager. Make a note of the URL of each image, because you'll need those URLs for your HTML table.

To make your HTML table, follow these instructions:

1. **Create a new post.**

2. **Click the HTML tab so you are in HTML view instead of Rich Text view.**

3. **Carefully type the following HTML code in your post, with the appropriate changes:**

   ```
   <table><tbody><tr><td background="http://URL_for_viewable_image"><img
           src="http://URL_for_transparent_image" height="---" width="---"
           /> </td></tr></tbody></table>
   ```

   Change `"http://URL_for_viewable_image"` to the appropriate URL from File Manager for the image you want your readers to see.

   Change `"http://URL_for_transparent_image"` to the appropriate URL from File Manager for your transparent image.

   Change `height="---" width="---"` to reflect the height and width of your viewable image. For example, you may size your viewable image to 380 pixels by 500 pixels. Your code would reflect that: `height="380" width="500"`.

   By assigning height and width values to the transparent image that match the viewable image, you are essentially hiding the viewable image behind the shrink-wrap (or transparent image).

   If you aren't sure what pixel dimensions you need, open the image you want to show your readers in GIMP (or other image-editing software), and view the image size. Make sure that the dimensions are in pixels, and make a note of the height and width so you can insert those values into your table.

4. **Finish writing your post, if necessary.**

   5. **Save your post as a draft.**

   6. **Click the Preview button.**

      A new window appears, with your post and your picture.

   7. **Right-click your image, and choose View Image.**

      You should see a blank page. If you do, your table is working, and your image is shrink-wrapped. If you don't, look carefully at your HTML table, and ensure that it is exactly like the code in Step 3.

   8. **Save and Publish your post when you're satisfied that your image is shrink-wrapped.**

Shrink-wrapping your image is time-intensive when you first try it, but the process becomes more efficient as you gain experience.

Many visual artists protect themselves further by not including high-resolution images of their work, making them less worth stealing. But as we state earlier, if you're worried about people stealing your content, don't put it online. Even shrink-wrapping your images isn't 100 percent effective — a determined thief will just take a screen shot of the image and use it anyway. However, precautions such as watermarking and shrink-wrapping are enough of a deterrent for most people.

Offer E-Mail Subscriptions

In Chapter 5, we tell you more about your RSS feed and how readers who subscribe to your blog can receive regular updates in their feed readers each time you publish new content.

Not all blog readers use feed readers, though, and you have another option for delivering your content quickly and conveniently to your readers: e-mail subscriptions. Offering an e-mail subscription simply means that readers who choose this option receive your most recent post in an e-mail format, directly in their inbox, every time you publish. Many blog readers find this to be a convenient tool, so it's a common courtesy to offer them the option — especially because it's so easy to set up!

You may have already burned an RSS feed through FeedBurner (and if you haven't, it's easy to do — just follow the steps in Chapter 5). After you've *burned a feed* (which simply means that you've connected your feed to FeedBurner), you can easily offer the option of an e-mail subscription by following these steps:

1. **Sign in to your FeedBurner account.**

   A list of your currently burned feeds appears.

2. **Click the name of the blog you want to add an e-mail subscription option to.**

3. **Click the Publicize tab at the top of your screen.**

   A list of several services appears on the left side of your screen.

4. **Click Email Subscriptions (it's in the list of links in the left sidebar).**

   A screen explaining e-mail subscriptions appears, as shown in Figure 15-8. (A message at the bottom of the box tells you whether this service is active or inactive.)

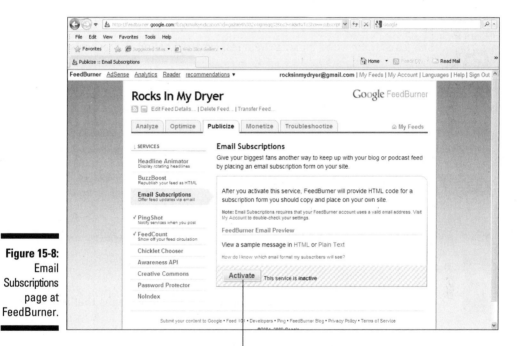

Figure 15-8:
Email
Subscriptions
page at
FeedBurner.

Click to activate

5. **Click Activate.**

   A Subscription Management page appears, as shown in Figure 15-9, giving you the code to insert in your blog's sidebar. If you scroll down the page, you see the option Use as a Widget in TypePad.

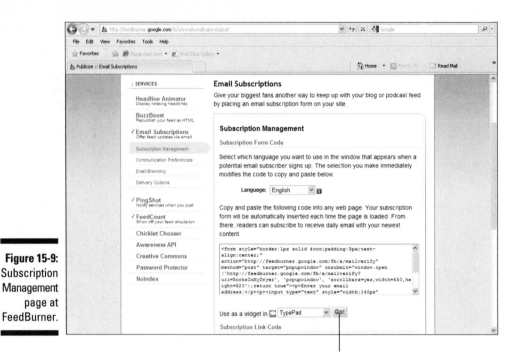

Figure 15-9:
Subscription
Management
page at
FeedBurner.

Click to install as a TypePad widget

6. Click the Go! button next to the Use as a Widget in TypePad option.

A new browser tab or window opens, with the Add a Sidebar Widget page in TypePad.

7. Click to select the name of the blog you want to add the widget to.

You should add the widget only to the blog whose feed you're offering in e-mail format. If you'd like to include e-mail subscriptions to your other blogs under your TypePad account, you'll need to repeat these steps separately for each blog.

8. (Optional) Change the widget name.

The default name for your widget (visible in your TypeLists) is *Subscribe via email.* You can change this name, if you want.

9. Click Add Widget.

The widget is installed on your blog. To arrange the widget in your sidebar, visit the Design tab on the Dashboard. For instructions on rearranging your sidebar contents, see Chapter 11.

Always subscribe to your own feed (both through e-mail and through a feed reader) so you can see how it looks!

Chapter 16

Ten Places to Find TypePad Resources

*W*e hope that this book is giving you plenty of solid information for maximizing your TypePad experience. But we all know that technologies can change rapidly, and TypePad, in particular, is going through a season of frequent updates. You'll want to have access to sources beyond this book for finding the latest and greatest about TypePad. This chapter gives you ten helpful online resources. Visit all these sites often (many offer RSS feeds) to stay abreast of the offerings by TypePad. Especially with TypePad's frequent rollout of new features, having access to these sites will help you keep your blog on the cutting edge.

In Chapter 2, we explain that TypePad is not developed by an open-source community. This means that most new TypePad features are developed not by the community of users but by Six Apart, at the corporate level. This isn't necessarily a bad thing. It's what puts TypePad in a position to offer such stellar technical support: All the features are created and managed by Six Apart staff, so they're the ones who are in the best position to do the instructing. As a result, huge numbers of TypePad resources don't exist outside the Six Apart umbrella — most of the resources we list in this chapter have some affiliation with TypePad.

Here's an extra resource for you: visit *TypePad One* (www.typepad.com/ one). It's a resource page that aggregates helpful TypePad tips from all over the support network, including many of the sites listed in this chapter.

Everything TypePad Blog

`everything.typepad.com`

Everything TypePad is the official TypePad blog written by TypePad team members. On this frequently updated site, you'll find posts ranging from where the Six Apart group will be (maybe the same blogging conference you're attending!) to updates on new TypePad features to instructions on how to implement new things on your blog (such as a custom footer). If you're wondering what the TypePad community is doing, this is where you'll find out. On the front page of the blog (see Figure 16-1), note the black navigation bar across the top of the screen. In particular, look for the Browse the Archives link.

Browse the archives

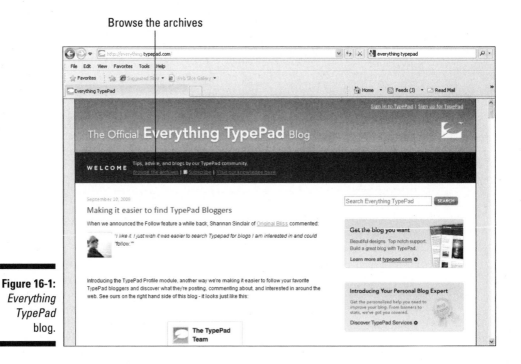

Figure 16-1:
*Everything
TypePad
blog.*

Clicking Browse the Archives takes you to a list of categories covered by *Everything TypePad*. Browse to your heart's content, but three categories in particular deserve your special attention:

- The Videos category points to the video tutorials included on the *Everything TypePad* blog. Let's face it — it's nice to have step-by-step instructions, but seeing how to do something can be really helpful too. The videos listed also include the step-by-step instructions in a written format.

- Additionally, be sure to visit the Live Events category. TypePad uses live events to engage its community, hosting seminars (both online and in person). If you'd like to know when the next seminar is and what the topic will be, this is the place where you can find out.

- The Tips and Tricks category offers you suggestions for fine-tuning your use of TypePad features. In particular, you'll find helpful CSS shortcuts for tweaking your design, including detailed and plain-English coding instructions.

Six Apart Status Blog

`status.sixapart.com`

The *Six Apart Status* blog is a simple blog with an important purpose: letting you know whether any systemwide glitches or failures affect your ability to publish posts, receive comments, and so on. During times of technical difficulties (which don't occur very often), Six Apart uses this blog to publish real-time updates to users, keeping you updated on how long outages might last.

Any time you're experiencing unusual glitches in your TypePad service (such as posts failing to show up after they're published or reports from readers that they can't leave comments), visit the *Six Apart Status* blog to find out if there's a bigger issue than just the one at your own blog.

If there are no reports of system abnormalities (in other words, if the post for the day looks like the one in Figure 16-2, reporting that TypePad is up), you know that your technical issues are smaller in scope and can likely be solved if you submit a help ticket.

If there are reports of systemwide issues, however, these issues are clearly addressed in the posts at the *Six Apart Status* blog. Even though outages like these are frustrating, there's at least some assurance in knowing that the problem is out of your hands. Check back in at the status blog until the problem is resolved.

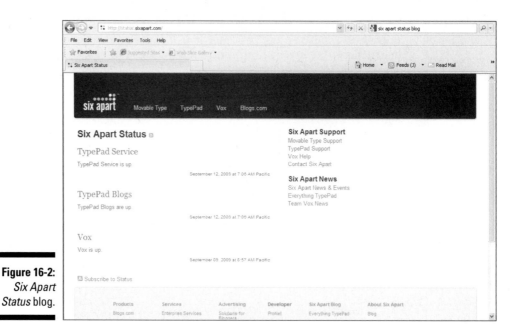

Figure 16-2:
*Six Apart
Status* blog.

TypePad Small Business Center

`typepad.com/small-business-blogs/`

The *TypePad Small Business Center* offers a list of resources for small-business owners who want to use TypePad to engage in the blogosphere. Included on the site is a current list of free business-related Webinars hosted by TypePad, such as the one shown in Figure 16-3. These Webinars (helpful to all bloggers, not just those who own small businesses) walk TypePad users through a wide range of topics, including helpful screen shots and step-by-step instructions.

Additionally, the right column of the *TypePad Small Business Center* provides links to other small businesses successfully running blogs via TypePad. Also included (under the Good Tools for Small Businesses header) are links to non–Six Apart small-business resources that users may find interesting, including invoicing, scheduling, and marketing resources (note that some of these resources charge a fee).

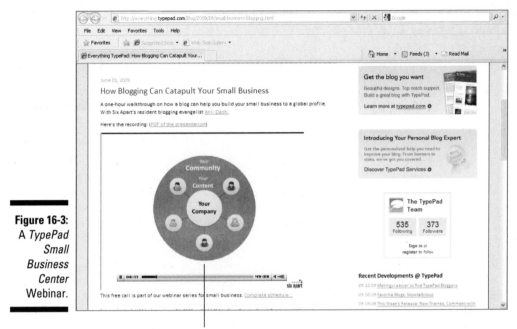

Figure 16-3:
A *TypePad*
Small
Business
Center
Webinar.

A TypePad Webinar

TypePad Beta Blog

`http://beta.typepad.com`

TypePad frequently rolls out new features, which generally go through a period of beta testing first. If you want to access TypePad's most cutting-edge tools, consider joining the team of beta testers (`http://beta.typepad.com/blog/join.html`). When you do, your account will automatically be updated with the beta features. The *TypePad Beta* blog explains the updates you see as a beta tester, including information about known technical issues. Be sure to click the Browse the Archives link for a full listing of topics covered.

Remember, the *TypePad Beta* blog is for beta testers only — when new features are rolled out to the entire user base, the features are announced on the *Everything TypePad* blog.

Six Apart Professional Network

www.sixapart.com/pronet

If you are a lover of all things code-related, you might be interested in the *Six Apart Professional Network*. This is a mailing list for people who want to roll up their sleeves and dig deeply into coding (for both TypePad and — even more heavily — for its sister product, Movable Type).

Subscribing to this e-mail list (which can be consolidated into a once-daily digest form) gives you access to the dialogue among designers and programmers about the most intricate, behind-the-scenes coding taking place on Six Apart blogs. At the very least, joining this list provides you access to people who already have these skills in place and might hire out their services, should advanced blog design and implementation be services that you need.

The *Six Apart Professional Network* generally does not provide tutorials to people wanting to learn coding; it assumes that you have a strong set of coding skills already in place.

TypePad Services

www.typepad.com/one/typepad-services.html

TypePad Services is a high-level set of services available to bloggers for a fee. *TypePad Services* reviews your current blog, makes suggestions on how to make it better (on wide-ranging blogging issues such as design, search engine optimization [SEO], community management, and so on), and then helps you implement the proposed changes. Services begin at around $250 — a pretty penny, to be sure, especially if you blog only as a hobby. It might be a more reasonable expense for a professional or corporate blogger, considering that this amount is comparable to what you might expect an outside consultant to charge. Click the See More Customer Reviews link to see what *TypePad Services* clients have to say about the service.

Get Satisfaction TypePad User Forum

getsatisfaction.com/sixapart/products/sixapart_typepad

A *forum* is an online meeting place where you can discuss a specific topic (in this case, of course, TypePad). The *Get Satisfaction TypePad user forum* is hosted at Get Satisfaction, a forum host for numerous corporations seeking to engage with customers. Here, you can visit TypePad's forum, where you can engage with other TypePad users in problem solving and idea sharing. Topics appear in list format on the front page of the forum (see Figure 16-4).

Forum topic

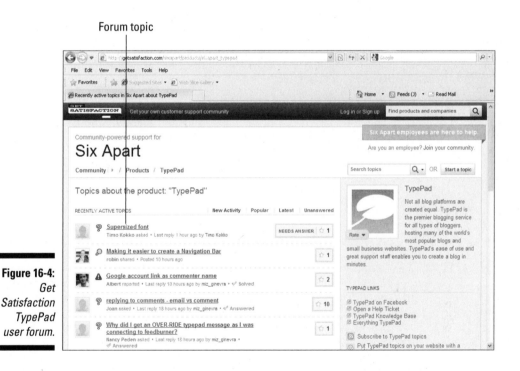

Figure 16-4:
Get Satisfaction TypePad user forum.

To the right of each topic, you see the number of responses already generated by that question or issue. Whether you are a new blogger or a seasoned TypePad user, you are welcome to ask questions, answer them, or browse through other conversations taking place.

Engaging in forum conversations and answering questions is an excellent way to build your reputation as a knowledgeable expert in a particular niche. This may in turn drive interested readers back to your own site. Even if you're a beginner, don't be afraid to jump in with both feet. Forums are typically great places to meet people with similar interests.

Six Apart's Twitter Feed

`twitter.com/sixapart`

Six Apart has joined the ranks of corporations that are effectively harnessing the power of Twitter with their customers. (For those not familiar with Twitter, it's a social networking site that creates real-time interactions with other users in 140-character blurbs, as shown in Figure 16-5. For more information on Twitter, see Chapter 10.)

Six Apart's Twitter feed is managed by team members, who frequently tweet links to the most late-breaking TypePad information throughout all their support sites. Frequently, TypePad staff use this Twitter feed to interact one-on-one with their tweeting customers. Send out a tweet to @sixapart and see what happens — you might be surprised at the response!

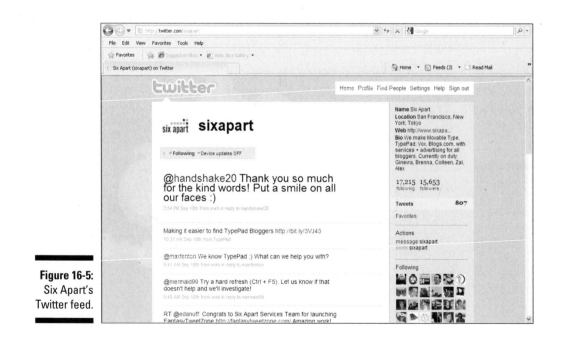

Figure 16-5:
Six Apart's
Twitter feed.

Blogging Basics 101

www.bloggingbasics101.com

In the interest of full disclosure, we should tell you that the *Blogging Basics 101* blog is written and managed by one of the authors of this book, Melanie Nelson. This site (shown in Figure 16-6) is geared to beginning bloggers, reassuring them right up front that there are no stupid questions.

Each post is presented in an easy-to-follow question-and-answer format and gives simple, nonoverwhelming instructions to bloggers on a wide range of blogging issues from the most simple ("How do I start a blog?") to the more involved ("How do I make a scroll box for HTML code?"). Answers are heavy on practical, numbered steps and light on confusing technical jargon. TypePad-related questions are frequently addressed (as are those related to Blogger and WordPress), and there is much coverage of TypePad's recent systemwide overhaul.

Figure 16-6:
Blogging Basics 101 blog.

Build a Better Blog

`www.buildabetterblog.com`

Build a Better Blog (shown in Figure 16-7) is a treasure trove of general blogging advice, especially if you're aiming to earn income at your blog (either by selling ad space or by using your blog to market an existing business).

Figure 16-7:
Build a Better Blog.

The author, Denise Wakeman, is an online marketing advisor who uses *Build a Better Blog* to coach business bloggers on social media strategies. Although it's helpful to bloggers at all platforms, TypePad bloggers may find it especially interesting. *Build a Better Blog* is itself a TypePad blog, and there are often posts on TypePad features, especially as they relate to business bloggers (see the TypePad Tips category in the blog's sidebar).

Chapter 17

Ten Bloggers Using TypePad Well

*I*t's helpful to read all the Web sites and books you can about how to make a great TypePad blog (for a list of some good resources, visit Chapter 16), but at the end of the day, some of your best tips will come from watching others do it successfully. Whether you're a new or an experienced blogger, stay engaged in others' blogs, and pay attention to what technologies and concepts are working well for your blogging peers.

In this chapter, we point you to ten TypePad bloggers who are representative of the best TypePad has to offer. They provide their readers with the whole package — a readable design, excellent content, an interesting title, and successful implementation of other great TypePad features. Most of the bloggers we've highlighted are using designs and blogging concepts that the average TypePad user can apply. These designs are workable, streamlined, and (most importantly) lead you directly into the content. As you look at what these TypePad bloggers are doing well, see what you can glean from them as you polish your own TypePad blog.

We've listed some good blogs for you, but it's easy to find more:

✔ TypePad regularly highlights great bloggers at their Everything TypePad blog (`http://everything.typepad.com`); click the Browse the Archives link, and then choose the Best of the Bloggers.

✔ Do a Google search on *typepad.com. This pulls up all searchable Web sites that end in the typepad.com prefix, which means most of the sites listed will be TypePad blogs. Also search *blogs.com (the suffix used by the earliest TypePad bloggers).

✔ Visit Blogs.com (`http://blogs.com`), a Six Apart–owned site that aggregates great bloggers from around the blogosphere (both TypePad and non-TypePad bloggers).

Allsorts

`http://allsorts.typepad.com`

There's no mistaking the tone of Jennifer Harris's blog *Allsorts* — it's visually communicated the instant you visit. Harris, a children's book illustrator, uses *Allsorts* as a gathering place for her love of crafts and art, and her blog design is as fun-loving and whimsical as her posts. In her right sidebar, she has made her blog supremely browseable by including a graphic link to each category. You can do this using a Notes TypeList or the Embed Your Own HTML widget (see Chapter 8).

Although it's a personal blog, Harris has been effective in allowing it to showcase the best of her work, encouraging visitors to click to her main site, her Twitter feed, her Etsy store, and her photo blog.

Harris is an accomplished seamstress, frequently posting tutorials for her projects on her blog. In the lower-right corner, she has included links to each of those tutorials, a valuable service to her faithful readers. If you regularly write highly informative posts like these (and they're popular with readers), consider following Harris's model of keeping the posts right at your readers' fingertips.

Career Hub

`http://www.careerhubblog.com`

Career Hub (shown in Figure 17-1) is managed by Louise Fletcher, president of Blue Sky Resumes (`http://www.blueskyresumes.com`). *Career Hub* aims to coach people through the job hunting process, offering concrete advice from a wide variety of expert guest authors.

Fletcher says she specifically chose TypePad for its ease of use and its accessibility to multiple guest authors, many of whom have never blogged before but have found TypePad to be quite user-friendly. Also, she appreciates how easy it is to tweak a design in TypePad (see Chapter 11): "We don't have a programmer, so we need something we can do ourselves," she says.

Figure 17-1:
Career Hub.

In the middle of the right sidebar of *Career Hub* (you may have to scroll down), note the graphic link to their free e-books. *E-books* are simply books (often PDF documents) written in digital form, and they're a smart tool for giving your readers solid value from your site. Bloggers sometimes use e-books as a free gift to readers, to establish their own value as an expert, and to encourage loyalty among their readers. Other bloggers sell their e-books and the e-book becomes a tool for blog monetization. "Free e-books are a great way to get your name out there. We have offered four of them now and each one has brought us additional PR and traffic from other bloggers and Web sites. The key to success is writing a book that adds real value for your readers," Fletcher advises. "Don't make the book overtly promotional because no one cares about you — they care about their own needs. Write a book that addresses key issues faced by your target audience. That's what will draw attention and traffic."

As a professional networker, Fletcher has solid advice for people wanting to harness the power of social media: "Social networking is just like in-person networking — you have to give to get. Building relationships takes time and effort but it's well worth it, so I think the most important advice I could give job seekers about using social media is to look for ways to help others. Don't just throw up a new blog or a Twitter page and expect everyone to be thrilled about it! They won't care until they see you adding value."

The professional-looking layout of *Career Hub*, designed by Fletcher's husband, Phil, is proof that even something as simple as the consistent use of a single main color (in this case, gold) adds a pleasant visual effect to a blog's presentation.

Eat Local Challenge

http://www.eatlocalchallenge.com

Eat Local Challenge (shown in Figure 17-2) is managed by blogger Jennifer Maiser and is an excellent example of how the blogosphere can be harnessed to promote social causes. In this case, Maiser's site encourages people to explore the health, environmental, and economic benefits of eating locally-produced food.

TypePad was a natural choice for Maiser, who had been writing a personal blog at TypePad since its earliest days (2003). She had always been drawn to its simplicity, saying that "the brilliance of using TypePad for the platform for this site is that the software and the hosting never got in my way. Rather, it supported everything that I needed the *Eat Local Challenge* to represent."

Figure 17-2: Eat Local Challenge.

Used by permission of www.eatlocalchallenge.com

The front page of the *Eat Local Challenge* is clear in its mission. The right sidebar (under "About This Site"), constructed via a Notes TypeList, tells new readers at first glance everything they need to know about the cause. Maiser has cleverly provided links to several significant posts, helping readers instantly gather the information they need. Included is a link to the post "Read Our 10 Reasons to Eat Local." Maiser points to that post as a significant turning point in promoting the cause: "It was attention-getting, concise, and something that the press could easily reprint and point to," she says. "It's been reprinted in over 100 publications, including online, traditional print, and industry publications. I was able to concisely summarize a concept that, at the time, was not talked about very much — and the public came to read it."

Maiser has also wisely placed a high-profile widget in the upper-left sidebar that helps people find a local farmer's market. This demonstrates how a well-placed, highly relevant widget is a powerful, albeit simple, tool.

Maiser has advice for bloggers seeking to use the blogosphere to highlight a social cause: "You have to have a complete passion for the cause that you're promoting," she advises. "Along the way, you'll be asking a lot of people to do a lot of different tasks to support your cause. Asking people to go out of their way for you is super simple if you are passionate about what you're doing and have a conviction about your cause. It will show, and people will organically gravitate to you."

Economist's View

http://economistsview.typepad.com

Mark Thoma, Ph.D. is an economist at the University of Oregon, and he writes the blog *Economist's View*, shown in Figure 17-3.

As an academic, Thoma has found TypePad blogging to be a valuable tool in his teaching. He videotapes his class lectures and uploads the video to TypePad. Also, Thoma says, "I use blogs for my classes, so the ability to only show certain posts (by tag) and the ability to organize material into categories has been beneficial."

In addition to writing his own economic commentary, Thoma uses his blog to point readers to valuable information elsewhere, a feature readers appreciate. "It's become a place that people use to find other material, a home base or hub," he says. He accomplishes this by organizing his sidebars efficiently, sharing various blogrolls via Link TypeLists (see Chapter 8).

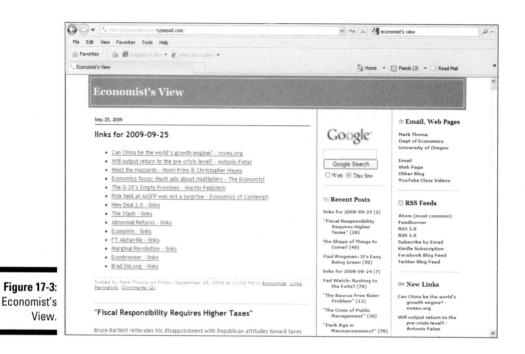

Figure 17-3:
Economist's
View.

One of Thoma's favorite TypePad features is located in the standard template tools within TypePad's Design tab (see Chapter 11). He chooses the Your Feeds module to aggregate content from several of his favorite sites.

Thoma's design is simple, befitting the academic, professional tone of his site. "The idea is to focus on the content," he explains.

Finslippy

http://www.finslippy.com

Finslippy, shown in Figure 17-4, is the personal blog of Alice Bradley, an accomplished diarist — her blog reads like a honed and polished memoir. Blogging since 2004, Bradley has established her voice in the blogosphere by publishing posts that follow a distinct narrative thread — a clear beginning, middle, and end (see more on the subject of polishing your posts in Chapter 6).

Bradley's blogging voice is consistent throughout her site. Even the About page (see the link in the upper-right corner) is entertaining, while still communicating important facts about her site: She humorously warns readers that she might not be able to answer all her e-mail and that she doesn't participate in product reviews.

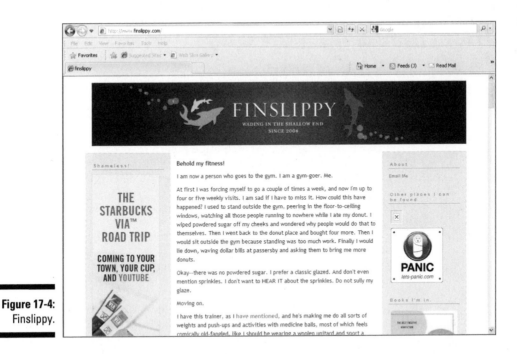

Figure 17-4:
Finslippy.

Finslippy's understated design allows her writing to be the true focus. Her header is a nod to the unusual name of her blog, a story you'll find via a link on her About page. (We show you how to insert a custom header on your own blog in Chapter 11.)

Bradley has managed to use her blog as a starting point for a successful writing career. "I'm at this amazing stage now where I don't pitch stories; typically, editors come to me, or already know me through my blog," she says. "Many of my happiest writing assignments have come from editors who discovered my blog and then contacted me. It really helps establish expectations on both ends. I can say, essentially, this is who I am, and this is how I write."

For other bloggers hoping to launch a writing career via their blogs, her advice is to keep expectations realistic. "I will say that this took a while," she explains. "I wouldn't say that anyone should create a blog and expect editors to flock to them. It was a few years. Still, before that started happening, I could still pitch stories and direct editors to my blog, and it did help quite a bit."

Your high school English teacher probably told you that the best way to become a good writer is to read good writers, and the same principle holds true in blogging. Like most readers, you'll probably seek out informative, topical blogs about your hobbies or political leanings, but keep an eye out for bloggers producing literary-quality content as well.

Hey There's a Dead Guy In the Living Room

`http://heydeadguy.typepad.com`

Admit it: That title caught your attention, didn't it? Ours too! This is a perfect example of a how a noticeable, catchy title pulls a reader in from the very start. This group blog, shown in Figure 17-5 (and often dubbed "Hey Dead Guy" by readers) is administrated by mystery writer Jeff Cohen.

Hey Dead Guy is aimed at a specific niche: those interested in crime fiction. Regular contributors to the blog include authors, an agent, a publisher, and a publicist, and they cover the crime-writing process from the birth of an idea all the way through publication and marketing. This is a perfect example of *niche blogging*, which is a blog that is specific to a particular market or audience.

Jeff Cohen explains TypePad's appeal: "Simplicity is key for us — we're not technological wizards, and we're a diverse group from two different countries. So the ability to navigate and create easily is absolutely essential for us, and TypePad does that nicely."

Figure 17-5:
Hey There's a Dead Guy In the Living Room.

Notably, *Hey Dead Guy* is making excellent use of TypePad's multiple authors feature. The right sidebar lists all the blog's contributors, and Cohen says that each blogger commits to write regularly on a predetermined day. Cohen, as the administrator, has given each blogger Junior Author status (see Chapter 5), though he reports that the process is much more "democratic" than that. All their decisions are made as a group, and, he says, "The other authors simply put their posts up either to publish on their designated date or as a draft, and I schedule them to publish on time. I don't "edit" or change their copy in any way."

Cohen acknowledges that writing a group blog is a true commitment, not to be entered into lightly. The key, he says, "is to find people who really do want to participate every week (or every day, or whatever your schedule might be). Make sure they understand what's involved, and hash out any questions ahead of time."

Note, too, that they've incorporated a simple but descriptive graphic header (refer to Figure 17-5) — the body outline visually (and humorously) reinforces the blog's title. Any user with at least a Plus account can insert a custom header like this one to a TypePad theme (see Chapter 11 for instructions).

Money Saving Mom

http://www.moneysavingmom.com

Money Saving Mom, managed by Crystal Paine, is one of the leading frugality blogs on the Web(see Figure 17-6). Blogs on frugal living are wildly popular, as people look for creative ways to save money at home. As a frugality expert, Paine was understandably drawn to TypePad's pricing at first. "The biggest selling point for me is that you do not need to purchase additional hosting," she says. "I've talked to many bloggers who are paying quite a large sum of money each month for their hosting services. Me? I just pay the $15.95 monthly Typepad fee. Aside from paying my yearly fee for my domain name, I have no other Web site fees incurred."

Paine's site has seen such success because of the frequent and valuable updates she offers readers, posting coupon codes, sales, and other offers for the frugal-minded shopper. She runs her blog with a high degree of professionalism — it's her business, not just her hobby.

Also a homeschooling mother of three, Paine acknowledges that balancing the demands of a successful, time-sensitive blog requires setting some boundaries. "There are a thousand opportunities out there in the blogosphere and it's easy to feel as if we must capitalize on every one lest we miss out on something. Stop, take a deep breath, and remind yourself again that *you can't do it all,*" she cautions. "You can't read every blog, respond to every comment, answer every question, blog on every topic you want to, participate in every blogging meme...but you can sure wear yourself out trying!"

Instead, Paine has balanced these demands by staying organized. "Over time, I've learned that what works best for me is to blog in blocks. I have two three-hour blocks of time in my weekly schedule which are reserved for blogging," she explains. "I try to write at least a few posts during these times, in addition to working on other blogging-related projects and answering e-mails. I'm a busy stay-at-home homeschooling mom with three little children, so I've found it is a huge help to have posts prewritten and scheduled to run throughout the week — especially on those days when I'm feeling quite brain-fried!"

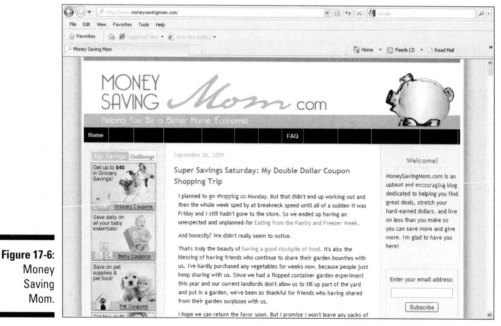

Figure 17-6:
Money
Saving
Mom.

Used by permission of Money Saving Mom, LLC

Raisin Toast

http://raisintoast.typepad.com

Raisin Toast is the blog of artist Susan Vaughn, who uses her blog to document her family's personal life and promote her artwork. *Raisin Toast*, shown in Figure 17-7 uses Advanced Templates (see Chapter 14), a skill Vaughn taught herself through trial and error.

"It took me a year to get up enough nerve to switch to Advanced Templates," she says. "As soon as I realized I could have a test blog with Advanced Templates, I thought I would try to figure it out. I did a lot of reading in their Knowledge Base, sent the customer support lots of questions, and little by little learned a lot about HTML, CSS, and JavaScript. I was determined to learn and build a better blog — one that I was proud of and a reflection of me — but I couldn't afford to pay someone to help me. I am a perpetual student, and when I get determined to do something, I usually don't let up until I've got it under my belt."

Figure 17-7:
Raisin
Toast.

Take note of the way Vaughn uses graphic images in her sidebars (such as Homepage and My Opus) to make readers want to click and discover more of her site. After many years of hosting her online gallery at an expensive artist portfolio platform, she was pleased that her newfound confidence with Advanced Templates allowed her to move the gallery (`http://raisin toast.typepad.com/vaughn_fine_art`) to her TypePad blog (and for no additional fee, because it's hosted under her main *Raisin Toast* account). She has sold pieces and had others commissioned as a result of tying in her artwork with her personal blog.

Vaughn urges other bloggers not to shy away from rolling up their sleeves and gaining the necessary skills to take their blog to the next level: "It really is limitless what you can do. It just takes a little time and a desire to learn if you want to figure it out on your own."

Smart Dog

`http://smartdog.typepad.com`

Smart Dog, pictured in Figure 17-8 is the blog of dog trainer and small business owner Laurie Luck, CPDT. Luck owns Smart Dog University (`http://www.smartdoguniversity.com`), and she uses *Smart Dog* to give her instant connections with potential clients. "Blogging has been an essential and integral part of my marketing efforts," Luck says. "No one wants to work with someone without knowing what they'll get. The *Smart Dog* blog has brought Smart Dog University into the homes and offices of potential clients. With the blog, I'm able to show people who I am, what kind of work I do, how I can help them, and let them into the world of a dog trainer and service dog raiser. Before people call me, they have an idea of what they'll be getting. We're starting off as acquaintances — friends even! — not strangers."

Wisely harnessing relatively simple technology, Luck frequently incorporates regular video (hosted at YouTube), into her blog posts. This gives potential clients an upfront view of her dog-training skills and techniques, and it's a valuable selling point. She advises video bloggers to keep video posts short (a minute or two, ideally), and says they don't have to invest in expensive equipment. "I'm using a $160 video camera and a point-and-shoot camera with video," Luck explains. "Super easy, super affordable."

Luck explains that her experience has shown that video blogging is not only affordable but simple: "You don't have to be a video editor to post good videos. With the free software that came with the cameras, I'm able to do everything I need. And the feedback I get from people — along with the increase in visitors when I post video — indicates that [readers] really like my posts that include video."

Figure 17-8:
Smart Dog.

For more on integrating video with your TypePad blog, see Chapter 9.

HELLO My Name Is Heather

http://HELLOmynameisheather.com

You'd be hard-pressed to find a blog with a stronger visual punch than designer Heather Bailey's blog, *HELLO My Name Is Heather,* shown in Figure 17-9. A fabric designer and entrepreneur, Bailey successfully runs her blog as a hub for her other online ventures, including a site selling hair accessories and an online fabric shop.

Although it's a personal blog, *HELLO My Name Is Heather* offers readers glimpses into the creative lifestyle that fuels Bailey's business — an effective marketing tool for any small business seeking to establish connections with customers. Another great tool employed at Bailey's blog (you'll need to scroll down to see it) is the lower-right sidebar titled "Your H.B. Creations." Readers use Flickr to submit their own items produced from Bailey's tutorials and products — they simply insert their uploaded photos into the photo streams Bailey has already set up. This wise use of social media has helped artistic readers find one another *and* highlight Bailey's products — a brilliant entrepreneurial stroke! As you employ social media at your own blog, follow Bailey's lead: Don't just help your readers find *you*, help them find *each other*.

Figure 17-9:
HELLO My
Name Is
Heather.

Used by permission of www.HELLOmynameisHeather.com

Chapter 18

Ten Blogging Etiquette Tips

*I*n the first chapter, we discuss the importance of participating in the blogosphere with courtesy and respect. In the strange world of cyberspace, we usually don't have the benefit of interpreting one another's facial expressions or other nonverbal communication. We have to determine others' intent based on what they say and how they conduct themselves. It's an interesting dynamic, and this makes it an exciting time to be a blogger — we're all out there learning as we go, doing our best to represent ourselves well based entirely on a cyberimpression!

The issue of blogging etiquette frequently comes up when bloggers get together to talk about tools of the trade. This can be especially frustrating to a new blogger, who may wonder how to decipher what the ground rules are. In truth, no firm ground rules exist. Most of us just do our best and exhibit the same commonsense courtesy we'd exhibit (and expect from others) in the real world. Additionally, you beginners shouldn't worry — there's a learning curve to this, and nearly all of us made some mistakes along the way.

However, you can follow a few widely accepted practices to be a well-mannered blogger, and this chapter shares ten of those practices with you. We're not so bold as to consider ourselves the final arbiters of what is and isn't socially appropriate in the blogosphere, but we think that these ten tips are surefire ways to let the blogging world know you intend to play nice.

Link Frequently and Accurately

Linking often to other good posts around the blogosphere (we tell you how to do it in Chapter 6) is a good blogging practice for many reasons. For starters, it spreads around traffic to your blogging peers; as in most cases, benefiting others has a way of benefiting you. Giving your readers links to good posts elsewhere is a valuable service to them as well. The blogosphere is a big place, and none of us can possibly see it all — sharing the best of it with your readers establishes you as a valuable resource.

As we explain in Chapter 6, you should never cut and paste a blogger's entire post in your blog — that's copyright infringement (for more on this, visit `www.copyright.gov`). But you can link to other posts freely, and when you do, consider these things:

- ✔ **Use brief excerpts when quoting.** It's fine to quote other bloggers, as long as you use only brief excerpts of their words and give full credit to them (including a link to the posts being quoted).

- ✔ **Whenever possible, use permalinks.** A *permalink* is a link to a specific blog post, as opposed to the more generic front page of a blog. To give you an example, a link to the front page of a blog might look like this: `http://typepadfordummies.typepad.com`. A permalink to a specific post on the blog, however, would look like this: `http://typepadfordummies.typepad.com/typepad-for-dummies/2009/08/understanding-the-basics-of-html.html`.

  Permalinks are helpful to your readers, especially, because frequently updated blogs have content regularly moving off the front page. A permalink helps a reader go directly to the post in question. To find the permalink of an article so you can link to it, just click the title of the post you want to include. Then look in the address bar of the browser to see the permalink. You can copy that URL and use it as a link within your post.

- ✔ **Avoid hotlinking.** *Hotlinking* is linking directly to the graphics, documents, video, and so on belonging to another site. Hotlinking is easier to explain with an example. Let's say you'd like to help tell people about a specific blog (Blog A). You contact the blog owner and ask her for a sidebar button that you can display on your blog with a link to her site. She responds with the URL for the button: `http://blogA.com/images/button.png`. Note that the image is housed on her server (that just means she uploaded it to her blog platform provider). If you use this URL as your image source, you'll be pulling bandwidth from her server each time someone views a page on your blog that shows the image. Why? Each time a blog page is viewed, the server keeps track of what files are being pulled (or shown) to the reader. Each time a file is shown, it uses bandwidth. Depending on the size of the file and how much traffic a blog experiences, you could be pulling a lot of bandwidth, and that can cost the original blog owner money (because many server providers require you to stay within a certain bandwidth limit or be charged for the overage).

To avoid the hotlinking issue, save the button to your own computer, and upload it to your own server (in this case, TypePad File Manager). Then follow the instructions in Chapter 9 for using an image as a sidebar item.

✔ **Communicate when you link.** Technically, you don't need another blogger's permission to link to her in a post or in your sidebar, but it's still a nice courtesy to let her know you did it. Who knows — a well-placed link might make the person's day! If you want to let another blogger know you've linked to her, you can send a quick e-mail or use trackbacks (we show you how in Chapter 7).

Many bloggers successfully host link round-ups at their sites regularly, either as a feature in their main column or on their sidebar. This is an easy way to share the best of the blogosphere with your readers, and it's a feature they'll likely appreciate and depend on. Figure 18-1 is an example of a link round-up hosted at Shannon's blog, *Rocks in My Dryer*.

In Chapter 10, we tell you more about how to integrate some social bookmarking services (such as `delicious.com`) at your blog and why doing so is an excellent way to share good links with your readers.

Figure 18-1:
A regularly published link round-up at a TypePad blog.

Don't Overly Promote Yourself in Someone Else's Comment Section

Be careful about overly hyping yourself, especially in the comment section of someone else's blog. Not all bloggers may agree on this point, but it's generally not advisable to use a comment section to give a sales pitch about yourself. The blog where you are commenting is someone else's space, after all, and a misplaced sales pitch can come across as traffic poaching or (even worse!) spam. When you leave a comment at someone else's blog, you are likely leaving a link to your blog in the comment form. If another reader wants to click over to your blog, he'll click your name — it's not necessary for you to invite him. Figure 18-2 shows you how it looks when you leave a comment on a TypePad blog — if you sign in to leave a comment (always advisable), you're automatically leaving a link.

Figure 18-2:
A TypePad
comment.

Commenter's name, linked to blog

If you're reading a post on a subject about which you've written, it *is* considered appropriate to offer the writer a link back to your original, on-topic post.

Here's an example of the kind of comment most bloggers are happy to receive: "Good luck with your bathroom remodel — it looks like you're making good choices so far. I went through the same thing a couple of months ago and learned some surprising stuff about grout; if you want to read more about it, you can see my post at `http://url.com`."

Here's an example of a comment that doesn't work as well: "Funny post about your gall bladder. Hey, stop by my blog and see how I've lost 50 pounds while running marathons, and while you're at it, check out my giveaway for my free book that I'm also selling. Signed, Joe from *Joe's Blog, The Blog about Running Marathons*" (with links scattered throughout the comment).

The second comment may seem like an extreme example, but you'd be surprised how often comments like these crop up. We know you get the general idea: Be discreet and respectful. If your link is relevant, include it; if you have a hint of doubt, leave it out.

Don't Ask for Reciprocal Links

A *reciprocal link agreement* involves two or more bloggers agreeing to link to each other. Sometimes reciprocal link agreements work, but often, they don't — bloggers who host reciprocal blogrolls often find that the list is so long and unwieldy it's rarely used by readers. Unless a blogger specifically publishes a reciprocal blogroll, avoid the temptation to contact him and ask him for a link. It puts the blogger in an awkward position, and it has the added consequence of making the requester sound a little desperate.

Instead of concerning yourself with reciprocal links, focus your energy on writing excellent content. Because most bloggers are eager and willing to link to good posts (see the first item in this list), a well-written post has a way of getting noticed. Build community and traffic based on your own quality work — it's not the fastest and easiest route, but it's the surest.

Give Others the Benefit of the Doubt

You know what the hardest (and most rewarding) part of blogging is? The relationships and community you build online. On one hand, you're constantly "meeting" new people when they comment at your blog or you comment at theirs. You start to feel as if you know them. On the other hand, you haven't actually met that other blogger, and she has a separate life outside her blog. The result is that sometimes, the lines of the relationship are blurred. You may start to expect a certain level of response or camaraderie from bloggers (or they from you).

The place this usually shows up is when a blogger is tagged for a meme. A *meme* (it rhymes with *dream*) is basically a quiz, survey, or list that a blogger completes and posts on her blog. When you first start blogging, memes are an easy way to generate content for your site and share a bit about yourself. The way a meme stays alive is that the blogger who participates in the meme then *tags* (or invites) several other bloggers to also answer the meme (usually asking for a link back to her blog). The problem occurs because many seasoned bloggers (and some new ones) are not interested in memes, but not responding to a tag appears rude. And that's where the relationship thing comes into play. If you feel like you're good friends with this blogger who has never actually met you (or vice versa), you can feel awkward.

We can offer a few solutions to this dilemma:

- ✔ When you post your meme and tag other bloggers, be clear in your tag that you will not be offended if the bloggers don't want to play along.

- ✔ Don't expect a response, and don't be upset if you don't receive one. You should know that some bloggers would rather ignore a request than have to confront the request with a "No, thank you."

- ✔ Participate in as many memes as you like and then either don't tag anyone or, alternatively, invite everyone who reads to play along and let you know how to find their posts by leaving a comment on your original meme post. This option allows you to invite everyone and invites them to post a link to their blog if they play.

It's possible that you may never encounter a meme or the awkward social dance that goes along with declining one. However, these virtual relationships show up in other instances as well. For example, if you are always commenting on someone's blog, but that person never return the favor, don't be offended. The blogger may not be as engaged as you are or may not have time to comment, or some other unknown factor may be in play. That's the key right there: You just don't know. Most bloggers are doing the best they can to engage in the blogosphere in a way that is meaningful to them, so it's a good idea to cut one another a little slack.

In short, try not to take things too personally or read too much into what you see. We know it's a tempting thing to do in the blogosphere, where we don't always have as much context for interpreting other people's actions. Instead, shrug it off, and preserve your sanity in the process.

Leave Comments Freely at Other Blogs

Lurking isn't quite as ominous as it sounds; it simply means that you read a blog without letting the blogger know you're there. It's not inherently rude to lurk at a blog. Most of us lurk at blogs from time to time — maybe we don't feel we have much to contribute to the conversation, or we think the bloggers already get so many comments they'd never notice ours, or maybe we're just plain busy. That's all understandable, so don't feel guilty about lurking from time to time.

There's another side to that coin, though. You are likely well aware of how encouraging a good comment is at your own blog, so don't hesitate to leave comments (at least occasionally) at the blogs you most enjoy. Those blogs are, after all, providing you something valuable enough that you keep going back to read. Even a quick "This post was just what I needed today" or "You always crack me up" might make the day of the person on the other side of that computer screen.

Similarly, consider responding to the comments you receive on your blog, a subject we discuss more in Chapter 7. You simply may not be able to respond to them all, but you can probably respond to *some*.

Be Up Front Where Products Are Concerned

If you're blogging about a product, a trip, or another service you received for free, you should fully disclose this to your readers (see Chapter 12 for more on this topic). Failing to disclose a corporate relationship is more than just bad manners — it's also bad business and harms your credibility. Especially if your blog is a personal one, readers may assume that the products you write about are a personal preference, not a paid endorsement, so be honest with them either way. Always be up front with your readers in this department. If you accepted payment for a post or received a product for free, let them know.

It's wise to have a policy in place on the subject of product-related blogging. Use the steps in Chapter 6 to compose a page with your product policy, and keep it easily accessible to readers (for example, provide a direct link to the policy from your home page). At the very least, include a brief statement of disclosure in your post (for example, "Wiley Publishing sent me a complimentary copy of the new book *TypePad For Dummies,* and I've been eager to tell you about it.") They'll appreciate your honesty. Figure 18-2 shows an example of a disclosure page on a TypePad blog.

For more tips on generating a disclosure policy, or to have one prepared for you, visit www.disclosurepolicy.org.

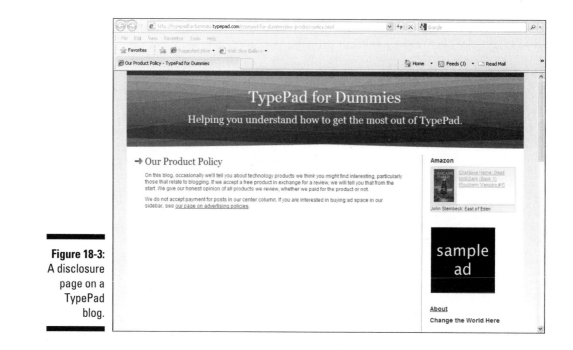

Figure 18-3:
A disclosure page on a TypePad blog.

Consider the Privacy of the People You Blog About

Remember that your blog is *your* story — be careful if you start making it someone else's. If your neighbor tells you a funny story about the night he got locked out of his house in his underwear, think twice before telling that story to the rest of the world on your blog.

Before you write anything substantial about someone else, get his or her permission. Or, at the very least, consider concealing the person's name and other identifying features. It would certainly be a shame to harm a real-life relationship because of a momentary lapse in online judgment.

In particular, be especially sensitive where children are concerned — both your own and others'. If you blog about your son's birthday party, for example, be aware that the other parents might not be comfortable having their kids' photos on your blog. And remember that the adorable little two-year-old in your house will someday be an eighteen-year-old who may not want his prom date Googling stories about his potty training.

Consider Your Readers' Best Interest

Your blog is likely governed by your preferences and love of blogging. This is natural, but it's still polite to consider your readers' preferences too. They are, presumably, visiting your blog for a specific purpose (to be entertained, inspired, educated). Just as most of us tend to clean up the living room and wipe down the sinks for company, there's nothing wrong with putting a good face forward to the readers who stop by your home on the Web. Here are a few things you can do to give consideration to your readers:

- ✔ **Give their eyes a rest.** Are you inundating readers with tons of visually distracting, blinking graphics? Are you using a font size that causes squinting? People might stop coming by if your design isn't visually welcoming. Go easy on their eyes!

- ✔ **Don't autoload music.** As we mention in Chapter 9, it's generally not advisable to have music automatically streaming when someone visits your blog. If you'd like to share your current playlist with your readers, offer a widget on your sidebar that they can operate. Let it be their choice. If your readers are listening to their own music on their computer, and a click to your blog brings your tunes also blaring through their speakers, they won't be pleased.

- ✔ **Install a search widget.** Consider installing a search bar in your blog so that readers can find your old posts easily. They'll appreciate that you're trying to save them time. See more on this in Chapter 8.

- ✔ **Be discerning with product reviews.** As companies approach you about doing product reviews (and they surely will if your traffic is steadily growing), accept only the products that are of true interest and value to you and your readers. It's okay to tell a corporation that you don't want to try its free toilet-bowl cleaner, especially if you think that a post on the subject would waste your readers' time. Use your own time — and your readers' time — well.

Manage the E-Mail Issue Well

Blogging can generate lots of e-mail for a blogger — we understand this all too well! Readers write to you, and they likely hope for a response — you should find a polite and professional way to handle this issue. Of course, we'd never advise that you sacrifice all your personal time by answering e-mails in the name of politeness; like everyone else, bloggers need to find ways to set healthy boundaries.

Taming the e-mail beast is a struggle for many of us, but you'll be saving your own sanity and enhancing your professional reputation if you have a streamlined way to manage it. Here are a few ways to do it:

- **Make your e-mail address easy to find.** E-mail can be overwhelming, but the solution is *not* to bury your e-mail address! Keep a link to your e-mail address front and center at your blog so readers have an easy way to reach you. You can include it in a TypeList that references other details about your blog (see Chapter 8), or list your e-mail clearly on your About Me page (Chapter 4). It's bad manners to waste your readers' time by forcing them to dig around for a way to reach you.

- **Explain your e-mail ground rules.** You know how we like policies, and e-mail is no exception. If you and your readers both know what to expect, feelings are less likely to be hurt. An e-mail policy may be especially helpful if you are increasingly inundated with e-mail as your blog's traffic grows. Consider setting up a separate page (called Contact or E-Mail), and give it a high-profile position on your sidebar. This contact page gives you a place to politely explain how much you appreciate receiving e-mails from readers, but you're not able to respond to each one. That's rarely a boundary bloggers are thrilled to set, but it's sometimes necessary, and readers usually understand. Figure 18-4 shows an example of a well-implemented contact page that includes a simple explanation of the blogger's policy.

- **Consider an autoreply e-mail.** Many Web-based e-mail services such as Gmail offer an autoreply (sometimes called a vacation response). You could have an autoresponse sent to people who contact you, offering a brief and polite thanks and an explanation of your e-mail policy. Opinion is split on this subject — some bloggers think the autoreply e-mail is a lifesaver, but others are concerned that it's intrusive. That's ultimately a matter of your own inclination.

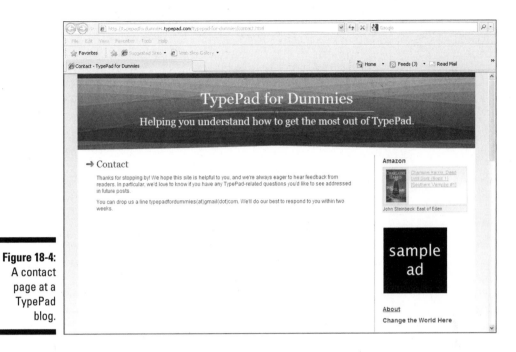

Amazon

John Steinbeck: East of Eden

sample ad

About
Change the World Here

Figure 18-4:
A contact page at a TypePad blog.

If you're having a hard time keeping up with e-mail, your readers may be having that same issue. Consider whether you want to add to their e-mail box with an automated message for every comment they leave you or whether you'd like to save the autoresponses for readers who send you private e-mail. Of course, we think it's perfectly okay to skip the automated e-mails, too.

✔ **Offer a Frequently Asked Questions (FAQ) page.** Especially if you blog on a subject that offers frequent and specific information to people (for example, on blogging advice, frugality, or home improvement tutorials), you may find that you receive the same e-mail questions over and over. If you find this to be the case, consider setting up a Frequently Asked Questions page (instructions for page setup can be found in Chapter 6). You can offer readers answers to commonly asked questions — it's helpful to the reader, and it might cut down on your e-mail! Figure 18-5 shows how TypePad blog *Money Saving Mom* (www.moneysavingmom. com) has implemented a FAQ page.

Used by permission of Money Saving Mom, LLC

Figure 18-5:
The FAQ
page at
*Money
Saving
Mom.*

Think Before You Post

It's what your mom told you, and we'll tell you too: Keep your cool, and think before you speak (or, in this case, post). Blogs feel fairly anonymous, and it's entirely too easy to pop off an angry reply, post, or comment from the safety of your solitary computer screen. Avoid that temptation by saying only things online that you'd say in person. Remember, too, that spoken words are more easily forgotten; the things you say online are in writing, preserved indefinitely.

If you find yourself on the receiving end of some online nastiness, know that blogging shouting matches are seldom productive or resolved. Engaging with people who are bent on stirring up trouble (especially if they're remaining anonymous) may backfire. Move on as best you can, and focus that frustrated energy into a creative blogging burst!

Participating in the blogosphere is an exciting social dynamic, and like the rest of us, you'll learn the social rhythm better as you move along. Keep your eyes peeled, and watch how experienced bloggers engage in the community. When you look for ways to extend courtesy, you'll likely find your own blogging experience enriched.

Appendix A

Domain Mapping

*W*hen you decide it's time to take your blog to the next level — meaning that you're serious about blogging, and you want it to show — purchasing your own domain name is an important step toward that goal. And after you secure your domain name, you'll need to map the domain to your TypePad account.

We just threw some serious phrases at you: *domain name* (which is the `.com`, `.net`, `.org` URL you purchase) and *map the domain* (which simply means that you want one URL to point to another; for example, you want `your blog.com` to point to `yourblog.typepad.com` so your readers don't see the TypePad reference in the URL). We know it sounds intimidating, and truth be told, this isn't a task for a blogging newbie who isn't comfortable with servers.

However, if you've been blogging for a while, are comfortable with your experience, and are eager to discover something new, we encourage you to buy your own domain name and map it to your TypePad account. Before you buy your domain name, though, we think it's prudent to consider how that domain name fits in with your blog's branding and your overall goals for your blog. Next, you need to know if the domain name is available for purchase and, if it's not, consider how that affects your blog's brand. If everything falls into place nicely, and you've purchased your domain name, the final step is connecting it to your TypePad account so the domain name, not the default URL, shows up in the address bar.

Many companies exist to help you buy your domain name. We include those that TypePad links to via the Account⇨Domain Mapping link:

- ✔ GoDaddy (www.godaddy.com)
- ✔ Network Solutions (www.networksolutions.com)
- ✔ PairNIC (www.pairnic.com)
- ✔ Yahoo! (smallbusiness.yahoo.com)

Understanding Domain Names

A *domain name* is the unique address, owned by you (not a third party), for your blog or Web site. When you own a domain name, that address does not include the name of the blogging platform you're using. For example, when you start blogging with TypePad, the URL for your blog is http://your blogname.typepad.com. Notice that you have .typepad.com at the end of your blog's URL. That tells everyone you're using TypePad as your blogging platform. The actual domain name for your blog is typepad.com, and the domain is not owned by you; it's owned by Six Apart (but Six Apart doesn't own your content).

When you buy your own domain name (which should match the name of your blog; see Chapters 1 and 3) and map it to your TypePad account, your URL will be www.*yourdomainname*.com, where *yourdomainname* is the name of your domain.

Why is having your own domain name important? Like it or not, your domain name says a lot about you and your blog. The main reasons for owning your domain name are validation, branding, and marketing.

Validation

The blogging community as a whole views using .com (or .net, .us, .me, .org, and so on) instead of the generic yourblogname.typepad.com as more professional. If your blog has the name of your blog platform in it (yourblogname.typepad.com), it's a sure tipoff that you're not as serious as some others out there or that you're a beginner. Owning your own domain name validates you as a serious or professional blogger. After you're perceived as professional, you'll have better luck with your peers and with advertisers. Having said that, there is always an exception to the rule, and many bloggers are perfectly happy with their default platform URLs.

Branding

Owning your domain name is one more way to reinforce your personal blog brand. If you don't own the domain for your brand, it's possible that someone else can buy it and use it. If a potential reader or vendor finds your competition instead of you, it could cost you a subscription or a sale. Or, worse, how will you manage it if the person who owns the domain that people associate with you is hosting content you don't want associated with you or your brand? Finding and buying the domain name early in your blogging career (even if you haven't mapped it to your TypePad account) leaves you in control of your brand.

Marketing

For us, the most reasonable argument for owning your own domain name is marketing. In other words, owning your domain name helps readers find you. If people know the name of your blog but not the actual URL, they can make an educated guess that your URL is your blog's name with `.com` or `.net` at the end. If they type that in their browser's address bar and find you, you've saved them a Google search and some guesswork. If they type it and see an error, will they think to type **blogname.typepad.com**? Probably not. They may not even be aware of that option. Save your readers (and yourself) the hassle, and make your blog easy to find with a domain name.

Choosing a Domain Name

It's a good idea to consider your domain name when you're naming your blog. When you're thinking of names for your blog, do a domain-name search for that name and, if it's available, buy it (you can map it later, but at least you'll own it). If the name is not available, consider how important it is for your blog's name and URL to match. Can you get a version of your name that makes sense? One of our personal blogs, *Don't Try This at Home*, has a URL of `www.donttryit.com`. It's not the best match but it was the closest available option. Ideally, you should name your blog from the very start based on the URLs that are available. (In reality, most bloggers — including us, when we started out — aren't thinking that far ahead!)

The most popular suffix is .com, followed by .net. Although .com is most desirable, both are fine. It's not a bad idea to buy both, if they are available, to protect your brand. Should you buy .net if .com isn't available? Opinions are varied on this one. One of our personal blogs, *Rocks in My Dryer,* is housed at rocksinmydryer.net, and that's always been sufficient. If you are purchasing the URL for a blog and have serious aims at turning it into a recognizable brand and business, you might want to settle for nothing less than .com. If it's not available, you can try to buy it later — though you might have to shell out big bucks. If that's not an option, you may simply have to head back to the drawing board for a new name.

Searching For and Buying Your Domain Name

You'll want to start the domain-buying process by finding out if the domain name you want is even available. To do this, simply visit any of the companies listed in this section; all of them allow you to search for your domain without making a commitment to buy anything. At the very least, this gives you an idea of what is available. When you've nailed down the URL you want to purchase, and you're ready to commit, choose the service that suits you best. This section helps you do just that.

When choosing where to register and purchase your domain name, keep in mind that TypePad requires that your *registrar* (the company you buy your domain from) supports custom *DNS services,* which means that you have access to and control over the DNS records for the domain(s) you purchase. (*DNS* stands for *domain name server.*) You must also be able to create and change your A, MX, and CNAME records. Check the FAQ or support page of the registrar you'd like to use to see if it supports those TypePad requirements. Alternatively, you can contact TypePad's support team, and they'll be happy to help you figure this out.

So many companies exist from which to buy your domain that pricing is competitive. Some companies offer domains as low as $5 per year, but the standard price is about $10 per year for each domain name. If you're paying more than that, definitely start shopping around!

If you buy your domain name via one registrar but find a better deal with another registrar, you can switch your registrar and still maintain ownership of your domain name. Make sure to read your registrar's terms of service to see if you're required to stay with that registrar for a minimum number of months.

Before you choose a domain name registrar, read the fine print for each option. For instance, at the time this book was printed, Yahoo! charged only $1.99 for the first year of your registration, but that price can be as high as $34.95 per year after your initial term expires!

GoDaddy

GoDaddy and TypePad are tightly integrated and have worked together to make buying and mapping your domain to TypePad as painless as possible. In fact, TypePad even has a page on the GoDaddy Web site (www. securepaynet.net/default.aspx?prog_id=447133; see Figure A-1) where you can search for a domain name, manage your GoDaddy purchases and account, and change your DNS (which we discuss a little later).

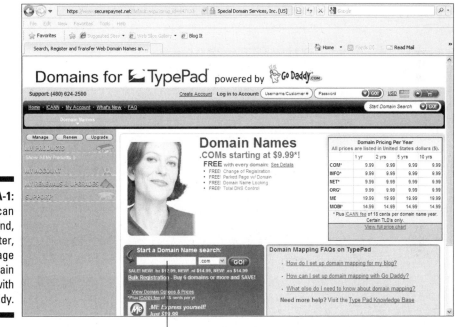

Figure A-1: You can find, register, and manage a domain name with GoDaddy.

Search box

To search for a domain name using GoDaddy, follow these instructions:

1. **Click inside the search box, and type the domain name you're searching for.**

2. **Click the Go! button.**

   You see a page similar to Figure A-2 that tells you whether your domain is available for purchase. The page lists any options that are also available for that domain name (such as `domain.tv`, `domain.info`, and `domain.biz`) and how much those options cost. If your domain is available, the box beside it is selected for purchase, and you are ready to check out. If you'd like to purchase any of the related domain names, simply click to select the box for that name or extension.

   If `.com` and `.net` are both available, we suggest that you buy them both. Those are the two most popular extensions for Web sites and blogs. Owning both protects your brand and prevents confusion with other bloggers.

   If the domain name you want to purchase is not available, you can do another search until you find a domain that is available.

3. **Click the red Add and Proceed to Checkout button.**

4. **Complete the checkout process with GoDaddy by providing the necessary information.**

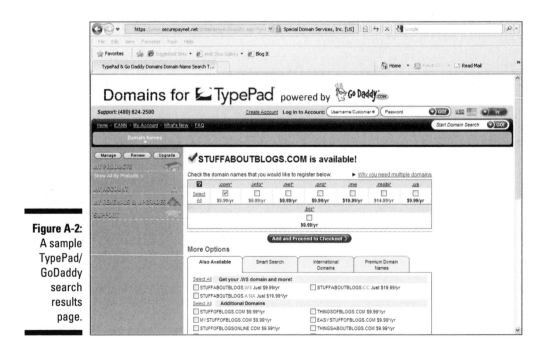

Figure A-2:
A sample
TypePad/
GoDaddy
search
results
page.

Network Solutions

Network Solutions is another registrar that allows you to search for and purchase a domain name. As you can see in Figure A-3, you can search for your domain name in the large text box at the bottom of the screen. You have the option of searching multiple extensions at one time, which is handy.

To search for domain name availability at Network Solutions, visit its Web site (www.networksolutions.com) and then follow these instructions:

1. **Click inside the search box, and type the domain name.**

   Do not type the extension (such as .com).

2. **Click to select the extensions you'd like to search for related to your domain name.**

   We advise you to search for at least the .com and .net versions of your domain name. Those are the most common extensions for blogs and Web sites.

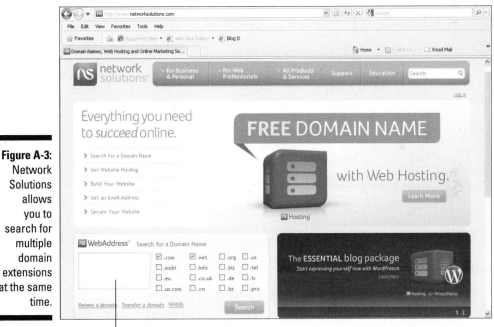

Figure A-3:
Network
Solutions
allows
you to
search for
multiple
domain
extensions
at the same
time.

Search box

3. Click the green Search button.

You see a page similar to Figure A-4 that shows you whether the domain name you searched for is available or not. Unavailable items are surrounded by a gray box; available items are surrounded by a green box.

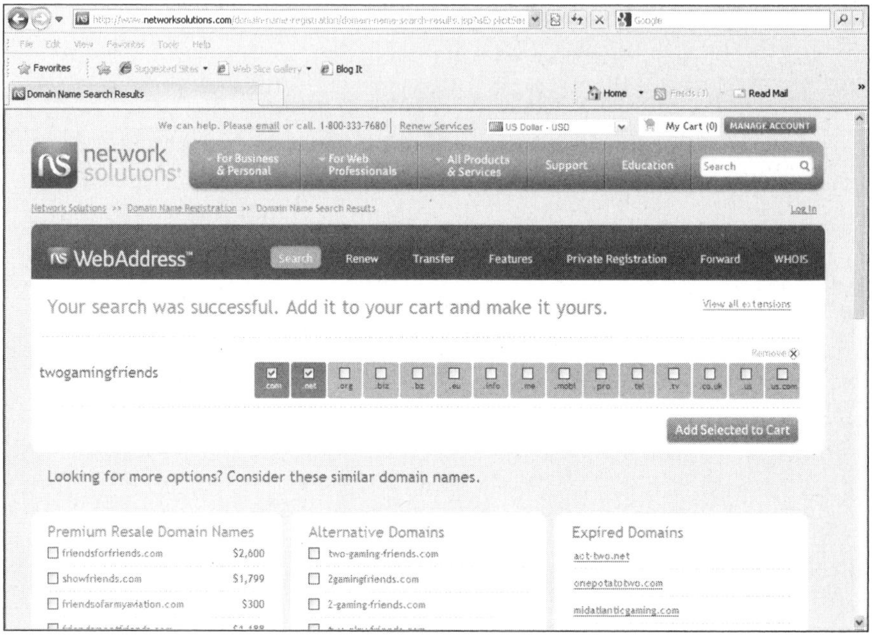

Figure A-4:
A sample
Network
Solutions
search
results
page.

4. Click to select any items you want to buy.

5. Click to deselect any items you don't want to buy.

6. Click the Add Selected to Cart button.

7. Choose whether you'd like to register your domain name publicly or privately.

8. Complete the transaction as instructed online.

Yahoo! Small Business

Just like the other registrars we've listed, Yahoo! Small Business allows you to search for your domain name and then purchase the name if it's available. Figure A-5 shows where you can find the search function on the Yahoo! Small Business home page.

Search box

Figure A-5:
Yahoo!
Small
Business
domain
name
search
function.

Visit Yahoo! Small Business (smallbusiness.yahoo.com) and then follow these instructions to search for domain name availability:

1. **Click inside the search box, and type the domain name you're looking for,** *including* **the extension you'd like (such as** .com**).**

2. **Click the Search button.**

   You see a page (similar to Figure A-6) that tells you the domain name is available and invites you to purchase it or tells you the domain name is unavailable. If the domain name is unavailable, the page lists similar domain names that are available and gives you the option to search for another name.

3. **If the original domain name is available, click Continue, and complete the steps for purchasing the name.**

4. **If the original domain name isn't available, but you'd like to buy one of the other domain names, follow these instructions:**

   a. **Click to select the name you want to buy.**

   b. **Click Continue.**

   c. **Follow the online instructions to complete the transaction.**

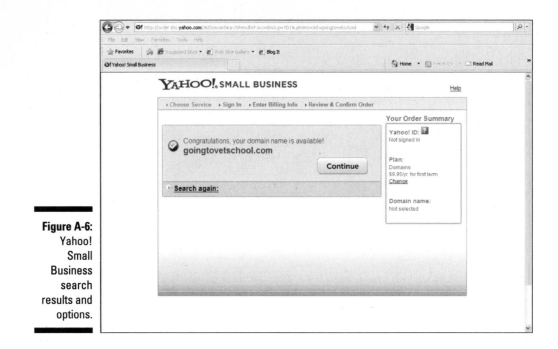

Figure A-6:
Yahoo!
Small
Business
search
results and
options.

PairNIC

PairNIC is the final registrar we discuss. Figure A-7 shows the PairNIC home page, where you can start your search for your domain name.

To search for domain name availability at PairNIC, visit its site (`www.pairnic.com`) and then follow these instructions:

1. **Click inside the search bar, and type the name of the domain you want to purchase.**

   Do not type the extension (such as `.com`).

2. **From the pull-down menu, choose the extension (for example, `.com` or `.net`) that you'd like to search for.**

3. **Click to select the Register This Domain Name Now option.**

4. **Click the blue Continue button.**

   A page appears that tells you whether your domain is available, as shown in Figure A-8. If the domain is not available, PairNIC provides a list of similar domain names that you may be happy with.

Search box

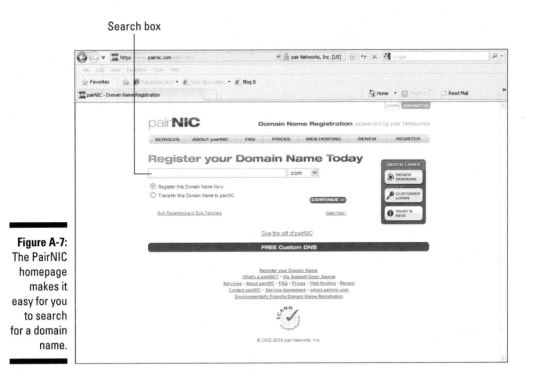

Figure A-7:
The PairNIC
homepage
makes it
easy for you
to search
for a domain
name.

Figure A-8:
PairNIC lists
results of
your domain
name
search
and offers
options.

5. **Select the domain name(s) you'd like to buy.**

   If the original name wasn't available, you might want to select an alternative.

6. **Click Continue.**

7. **Use the pull-down menu to choose which plan you'd like to purchase.**

8. **Use PairNIC's instructions for completing the transaction.**

If you don't see a name that suits your needs, do another search until you find something that works for you.

Mapping Your Domain Name to Your TypePad Account

After you register (that is, buy) your domain, you need to map it to your existing TypePad blog. *Domain mapping* is simply pointing a domain name (that is, URL) to your current blog. To do that, you have to change a few items at your domain's registrar site. This section explains how to map your domain by using any of the four registrars we've discussed.

Begin the domain-mapping process

Regardless of your registrar, before you begin, you need to go to the Domain Mapping page in your TypePad account by choosing Account⇨Domain Mapping. Then follow these initial instructions before you look at the instructions for your particular registrar. These instructions tell TypePad how you want to use your domain name in relation to your TypePad blog(s); later in this chapter, the instructions for a particular registrar explain how to map your domain to TypePad.

1. **Click the gray Begin Here: Map a Domain Name button.**

   A page appears, asking for some basic information about how you'd like to use your domain name with your TypePad blog(s). You may want to refer to Figure A-9, which shows the Domain Mapping page.

2. **Type your domain name in the first text box (be sure to include www).**

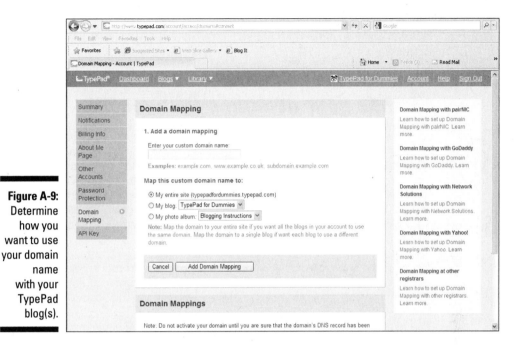

Figure A-9:
Determine
how you
want to use
your domain
name
with your
TypePad
blog(s).

3. **Click to select the blog(s) or parts of your site that you want to associate with this domain name.**

    Your options are

    - **My Entire Site:** If you map the domain to the entire site, all blogs associated with your TypePad account are included.

    - **My Blog:** You can choose a specific blog to map your domain to. If you have multiple blogs and want a different domain associated with each one, this is the option to choose.

    - **My Photo Album:** You can opt to have a photo album, instead of your blog, associated with your domain.

4. **Click Add Domain Mapping.**

    A page appears, asking you to configure your domain's DNS record. At this point, you need to go to your registrar (the Web site where you bought your domain) and change the necessary information (such as the CNAME record; we provide instructions in the next section, "Change your domain's DNS record"); then return to this page to complete your domain mapping.

We strongly suggest that you open a new browser tab or window when visiting your registrar's site to change your DNS. Having both tabs or both windows open (one with your TypePad account and one with your registrar) makes it easier to move from one site to the other and check setting information if necessary.

Change your domain's DNS record

As you've probably noticed as you've become more familiar with your TypePad account, Six Apart (and, therefore, TypePad) has a close relationship with certain companies, including GoDaddy. You can search for, buy, and access your GoDaddy account right from the TypePad Knowledge Base. Because Six Apart and TypePad have integrated GoDaddy, and GoDaddy appears to be the easiest way to map a domain with TypePad, we provide specific instructions for using GoDaddy and more generic instructions for the other registrar sites.

At this point, we suggest that you find your registrar in this section and follow the instructions for changing your DNS so that you can complete the domain-mapping task for your TypePad account.

You must change your DNS settings (specifically, CNAME) to map your domain to your TypePad blog. If you aren't comfortable doing this yourself, we suggest opening a help ticket with your registrar to request assistance.

GoDaddy

Visit the GoDaddy site (godaddy.com) and then follow these instructions to change your DNS settings:

1. **Sign in to your GoDaddy account.**

2. **Use the mouse to point to, but not click, the word *Domains* on the green toolbar.**

   A menu appears.

3. **Click My Domains.**

   A page appears with a list of the domains you've registered with GoDaddy.

4. **Click the domain name you want to map to your TypePad account.**

   A page appears that lists the information related to the domain name you chose. See Figure A-10.

5. **Make sure that your nameservers are set to the default.**

6. **Ensure that all Forwarding is off.**

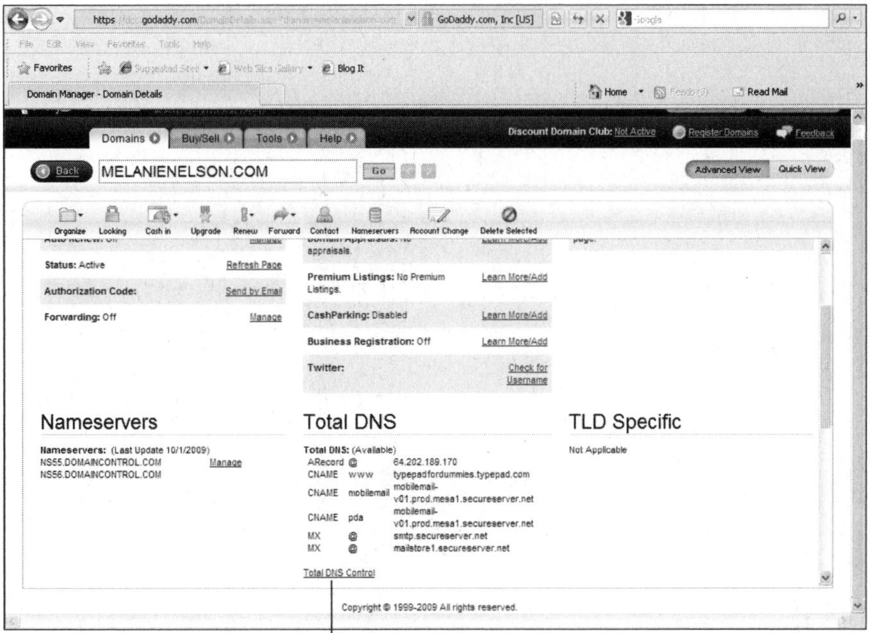

Copyright © 1999–2009 All rights reserved.

Figure A-10:
The GoDaddy Domain Manager page.

Click to change CNAME record

7. **Click the Total DNS Control link.**

   A page appears that looks a bit like a spreadsheet (see Figure A-11). You are about to edit your CNAME record.

8. **Click the pencil-and-paper icon on the line that says www (refer to Figure A-11).**

   A pop-up window appears, asking if you're sure you want to edit the CNAME for this domain.

9. **Click OK.**

   A screen appears that allows you to edit the CNAME information.

10. **Click inside the Points to HostName text box.**

11. **Replace the @ symbol with your TypePad URL.**

    Type only the domain name (for example, **blogname.typepad.com**). Do not type the `http://` prefix.

12. **Click OK.**

13. **Complete the domain-mapping process as instructed in "Finish the domain-mapping process."**

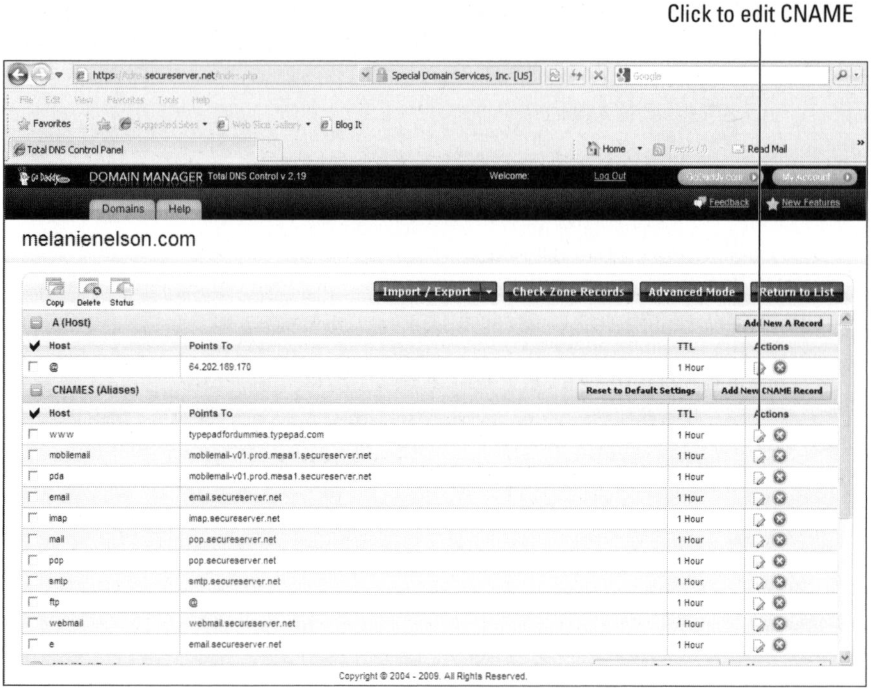

Click to edit CNAME

Figure A-11:
GoDaddy
Total DNS
Control
page.

Network Solutions

To change the DNS settings for your Network Solutions account, visit its Web site (www.networksolutions.com) and then follow these instructions:

1. **Sign in to your Network Solutions account.**

2. **Click the Account Manager link.**

   Your account page appears.

3. **Click the domain name you want to map to your TypePad account.**

4. **Click the Manage Advanced DNS Records link.**

   The Manage Advanced DNS Records link appears.

5. **Click Add/Edit under Host Alias (CNAME Records).**

6. **Make the following changes:**

   a. Alias: Type **www** (don't type a period).

   b. Refers to Host Name: Deselect so that the option is blank.

    c. Other Host: Click to select this option and type **blogname.typepad.com**. Note that *blogname.typepad.com* should reflect your TypePad blog's URL.

7. **Click Continue.**

8. **Complete the domain-mapping process as instructed in "Finish the domain-mapping process."**

Yahoo! Small Business

Visit Yahoo! Small Business (`smallbusiness.yahoo.com`) and then follow these instructions to change your DNS settings:

1. **Sign in to your Yahoo! Small Business account.**

2. **Navigate to the My Services page.**

3. **Click the Domain Control Panel link.**

   The Domain Control Panel appears.

4. **Click the Managed Advanced DNS Settings link.**

5. **Click the Add Record link.**

6. **Make the following changes:**

   a. Source: Click inside the text box and type **www** (don't type a period).

   b. Destination: Click inside the text box and type **blogname.typepad.com**. Note that *blogname.typepad.com* should reflect your TypePad blog's URL.

7. **Click Submit.**

   A pop-up window asks if you'd like to confirm the creation of a CNAME record.

8. **Click Submit.**

9. **Complete the domain-mapping process as instructed in "Finish the domain-mapping process."**

PairNIC

PairNIC specifically suggests using Domain Name Parking if you'd like to map your domain to your TypePad blog. To do this, follow these instructions:

1. **Sign in to your PairNIC account.**

   Your account page appears.

2. **Click the Manage Domain Names link.**

   A page is returned with a list of your domain names.

3. **Click the domain name you want to use with your TypePad blog.**

4. **Click the E-Mail Forwarding and Web Site Forwarding and Parking link.**

5. **Click the Domain Name Parking option.**

   A warning appears, alerting you that you are choosing Domain Name Parking.

6. **Click Continue.**

7. **Click inside the box marked Destination Domain Name, and type** blogname.typepad.com.

   Note that *blogname.typepad.com* should reflect your TypePad blog's URL.

8. **Click the Add Domain Parking button.**

9. **Complete the domain-mapping process as instructed "Finish the domain-mapping process."**

Using Domain Name Parking with PairNIC changes your nameservers. After the nameservers are changed, it can take up to two days for the changes to resolve.

Finish the domain-mapping process

Now that you've initiated the domain-mapping process in your TypePad account and have changed the CNAME at your domain name registrar, you're ready to finish the process:

1. **Return to the Domain Mapping section on the TypePad Dashboard.**

2. **Click the Activate link in the Domain Mappings box at the bottom of the page, as pictured in Figure A-12.**

   The Domain Mapping page appears with a note highlighted in yellow at the top of the screen: You have successfully activated the selected domain.

It can take up to 48 hours for the CNAME changes to resolve, so you may not see your changes immediately when you type your domain name in a browser.

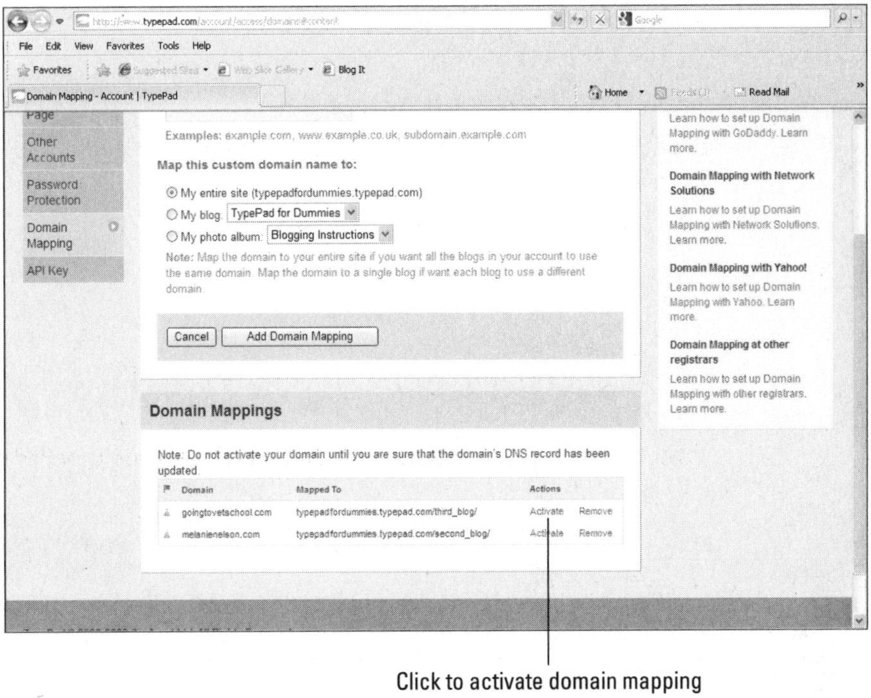

Figure A-12:
Domain
Mapping
page.

Click to activate domain mapping

Deactivating Domain Mapping

If you no longer want to map a specific domain to your TypePad blog, you can deactivate it. To do that, go to your Account page, and choose the Domain Mapping tab. Scroll down to the Domain Mappings box at the bottom of the page. Click the Deactivate or Remove link. The Deactivate link simply deactivates domain mapping from your blog; if you ever want to reactivate domain mapping, simply click the Activate link. The Remove link removes the mapping completely — if you ever wanted to reactivate domain mapping, you'd have to go through the entire process again.

If you deactivate domain mapping, any images you uploaded while the domain map was active will no longer appear. When you deactivate domain mapping, the links that call the images are broken. You have to fix those links by hand.

Appendix B

Third-Party Stat Counters

*B*eing aware of your statistics is a significant part of the blogging gig. Particularly for bloggers who seek to blog professionally or want to establish credibility as experts in their field, it's impressive to colleagues and marketers when you can show measurable results of your blog's performance. When you deal with advertisers, they have every right to ask you about your blog's traffic — you'll need to be able to show your blog's reach and audience.

TypePad tracks your statistics for you; in Chapter 5, we explain how you can see your most recent page views and referrals on the front page of the blue blog-level navigation bar. These numbers may be helpful as a quick reference, but TypePad's Dashboard statistics don't provide the in-depth information most professional bloggers may require from their statistics-tracking software. As a result, we recommend that you install a third-party statistics tracker (also referred to as a *stat counter)* on your site.

In this appendix, we give you an overview of the subject of blog traffic, defining the terminology and helping you understand more advanced tools such as FeedBurner and Google Analytics. Entire books have been written on how you can use sites like these to track and interpret your blog's data, but if you're a beginner to blog traffic, this appendix gives you a nudge in the right direction.

If you want to really understand how to leverage your statistics, we suggest checking out *Web Analytics For Dummies,* by Pedro Sostre.

Keeping it all in perspective

If you're blogging to build your business, tracking and understanding your blog statistics are important because you'll use these numbers to stay aware of what's working and what's not.

Remember, however, that keeping a close eye on your stats is optional, especially if you blog as a hobby. It's tempting to let the concrete measurements of page views, referrals, subscribers, and so on entirely define your blog's success. Instead, make your measure of success your own personal sense of satisfaction from producing good content and the valuable relationships that will likely spring up from your blogging. To keep a healthy perspective, many hobbyist bloggers check their statistics at only designated times (for example, on the same day each week or month). Still others don't check them at all!

Watch your stats if you need to, for the sake of your business, or if it's the kind of thing that suits your competitive or curious personality. If you blog just for the love of it, though, don't let your stats become a source of stress. They should inform you, not define you.

Understanding Basic Traffic Terminology

If you're new to the subject of blog traffic, it's helpful to have a firm understanding of some basic concepts. Not every traffic counter uses exactly the same technology and algorithms to assess your numbers, but you need to know and understand fundamental information to use your data effectively:

- ✔ **Pageviews:** Each time someone visits your site, it counts as a pageview (different traffic counters may call it by a different name, such as *total visits*). If, for example, readers click around in your archives, visiting four different posts or pages, your statistics counter most likely records four different pageviews. Pageviews are based on how many times a page is loaded into a browser, not on how many different users are loading the page. In other words, the same person may come to your site five times in a day, and each visit is included in your pageview count.

- ✔ **Unique users:** The number of unique users reflects the individual people who have visited your site. The data collected here is based on a computer's IP address (which is basically the computer's identifying information that all Web sites collect). Whereas pageviews include how many times a page as has been loaded (regardless of whether it was the same user visiting over and over), unique users (or *uniques,* as they're often referred to) is a record of individual IP addresses — no computer is counted twice. Advertisers in particular are interested in your number of monthly unique visitors because it's considered the most accurate measure of your blog's actual traffic.

✔ **Keyword analysis:** You'll want to know what search terms people are using to locate your blog, and keyword analysis does just that. Most statistics sites tell you which search engine results are directing people to your blog, which helps you solidify your search engine optimization (SEO) strategies (see Chapter 1). If you find that a post of yours is a popular entry point for Google searchers, you know that this is a popular topic, and you might want to tackle it further, and maybe you should include the post in a "Best Of" TypeList in your sidebar (see Chapter 8).

Even if SEO isn't your cup of tea, understanding your search engine traffic is interesting and sometimes highly amusing. For example, Figure B-1 shows an afternoon of keyword analysis at one of our personal blogs (using www.statcounter.com).

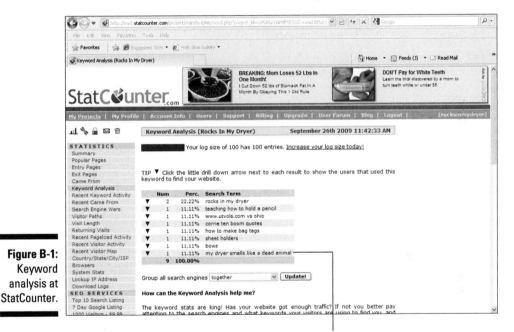

Figure B-1: Keyword analysis at StatCounter.

A very bad day!

✔ **Referrals:** Your referrals let you know which blogs or other Web sites are sending traffic your way by linking to you. If a blogger with a significant amount of traffic links to you, you can usually expect to see a pleasant spike in your traffic. Any time you notice someone sending traffic your way, it's a nice, professional gesture to send them a comment or e-mail of thanks!

Plenty of additional, more advanced metrics are available to bloggers, and we discuss those further along in this appendix.

Choosing a Stat Counter

No shortage of sites track and interpret your traffic, and many even do it for free. When you sign up for the service, the site gives you a snippet of code you can place in your sidebar by using a Notes TypeList or the Embed Your Own HTML widget (see Chapter 8 for instructions on how to use both options). Then you sign in to your account on the statistics site to gain access to your traffic reports.

If you install multiple statistics trackers, you may be surprised to see that each one produces a different number. This is because sites may not use identical methods to estimate traffic. If you notice discrepancies, don't sweat it — unless the discrepancies are large. If this happens, check your stat counter's help page for assistance or contact the site directly with your questions.

Following are a few tried-and-true statistics counters that are popular with many bloggers. All offer free versions of their service, and the first three offer access to upgraded, more advanced metrics for a fee. Most hobby bloggers (and many professional ones) find that the free version of these services is usually sufficient:

- ✔ Site Meter (`sitemeter.com`)
- ✔ StatCounter (`statcounter.com`)
- ✔ ShinyStat (`www.shinystat.com`)
- ✔ BlogTracker (`tracker.icerocket.com`)
- ✔ My BlogLog (`www.mybloglog.com`)

This list is a good start, but if you're looking for other options, type **blog statistics tracker** in a search engine, and browse the numerous results until you find the stat counter that best suits your needs.

Implementing FeedBurner

In both Chapters 5 and 15, we tell you a little more about FeedBurner (`feedburner.com`), a site for managing your RSS feed. You can easily burn your RSS feed through FeedBurner (Chapter 5 shows you how), and we highly recommend that you do so. Having a feed tracked via FeedBurner gives you access to some powerful subscription-tracking software — you'll likely find it most helpful as a benchmark for your blog's performance. We could fill an entire book with pointers on maximizing your FeedBurner account, but in this section, we hit on just a few of the most important elements. For more expansive instructions, click the Help link in the top-right corner of your FeedBurner page.

FeedBurner is owned by Google. Because it sits under the Google umbrella with Google Analytics (see the next section), FeedBurner concentrates more heavily on interpreting your *subscriber* data (how many people subscribe to your blog's feed) than on your *traffic* data (how many people visit your blog). Some information on page views and clicks is available via FeedBurner, but not in the same depth that you'll find in its Google partner, Google Analytics.

Getting started

If you haven't already burned your feed through FeedBurner, that's your important first step. Follow the steps in Chapter 5, or visit feedburner.com and sign in with your Google account. On FeedBurner's front page, click the Claim Your Feeds Now button, and FeedBurner walks you through the steps of getting your feed up and running.

After your FeedBurner RSS feed is established, you'll see, after signing in, a page titled My Feeds. It looks similar to the one in Figure B-2 — we're using one of our own FeedBurner accounts to demonstrate.

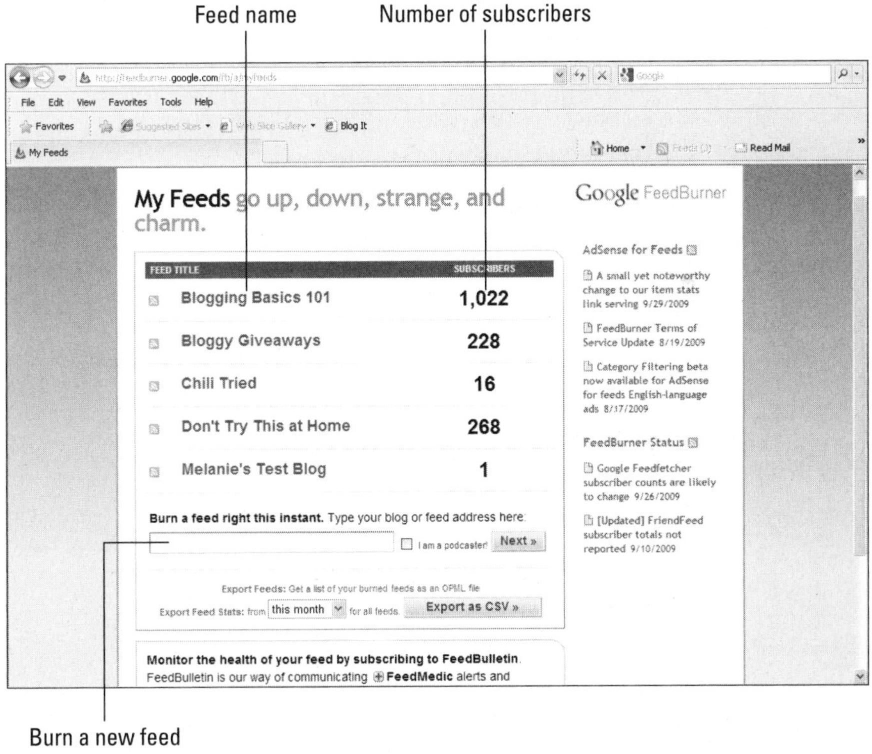

Feed name   Number of subscribers

My Feeds go up, down, strange, and charm.

Google FeedBurner

FEED TITLE	SUBSCRIBERS
Blogging Basics 101	1,022
Bloggy Giveaways	228
Chili Tried	16
Don't Try This at Home	268
Melanie's Test Blog	1

Burn a feed right this instant. Type your blog or feed address here.

☐ I am a podcaster   Next »

Export Feeds: Get a list of your burned feeds as an OPML file

Export Feed Stats: from this month ▾ for all feeds. Export as CSV »

Monitor the health of your feed by subscribing to FeedBulletin. FeedBulletin is our way of communicating ⊕ **FeedMedic** alerts and

AdSense for Feeds

A small yet noteworthy change to our item stats link serving 9/29/2009

FeedBurner Terms of Service Update 8/19/2009

Category Filtering beta now available for AdSense for feeds English-language ads 8/17/2009

FeedBurner Status

Google Feedfetcher subscriber counts are likely to change 9/26/2009

[Updated] FriendFeed subscriber totals not reported 9/10/2009

Figure B-2: My Feeds page at FeedBurner.

Burn a new feed

In the example in Figure B-2, five feeds are burned under one account. To burn another feed under this same account (a good idea if you're managing multiple blogs), simply enter the URL in the text box below Burn a Feed Right This Instant, and click Next. FeedBurner walks you through the steps of burning additional feeds.

No additional feeds to burn? Now you're ready to look at your blog's FeedBurner stats.

Understanding your FeedBurner stats

From your My Feeds page (refer to Figure B-2), click the name of the feed you want to work with. Your Feed Stats Dashboard appears, as shown in Figure B-3.

Across the top of the screen, note the navigation tabs titled Analyze, Optimize, Publicize, Monetize, and (so cleverly) Troubleshootize. You can find a ton of information under each of those tabs, but here's a general rundown of what each one offers you:

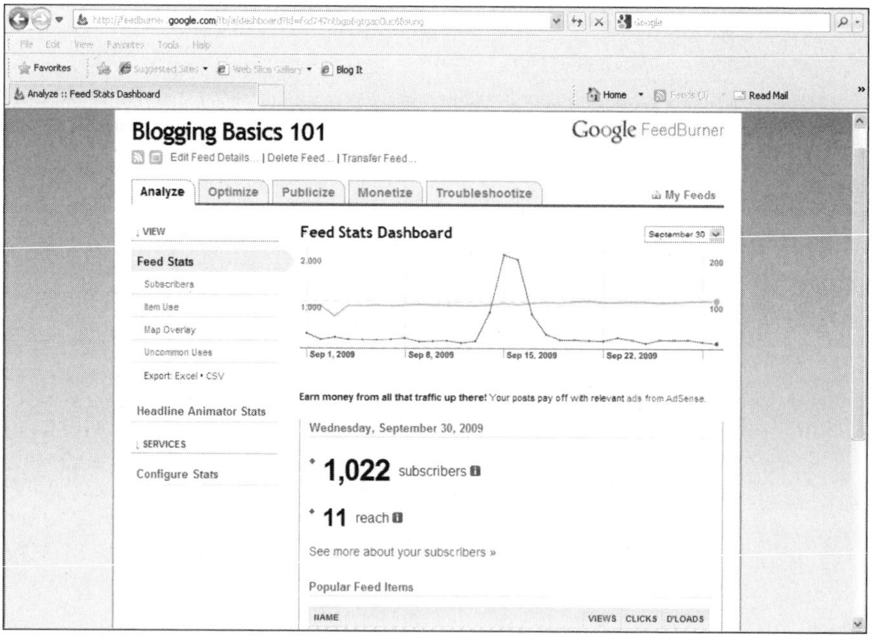

Figure B-3:
Feed Stats
Dashboard
page on
FeedBurner.

✔ **Analyze:** This tab gives you a snapshot of information about your blog's subscribers. In the bar graph, the green line tracks your number of subscribers (hover the mouse over the line for more information). The blue line tracks your *reach,* FeedBurner's word to describe the number of times readers have interacted with the content on your site (such as a click). Clicking the Subscribers link under Feed Stats (on the left) shows you which feed readers are being used to follow your blog. Don't be afraid to click around and explore the Analyze tab — you'll find several helpful tools to help you interpret your traffic.

✔ **Optimize:** Want to add a podcast feed to your blog? Or maybe share your Bloglines or Delicious links with readers? The Optimize tab allows you to make the most of your RSS feed with just a few clicks.

✔ **Publicize:** Use this tab to generate a *chicklet,* or graphic, showing readers how to subscribe to your site easily. You can also generate a button displaying how many subscribers you have. As we explain in Chapter 15, you can also use this tab to offer your readers the e-mail subscription option. Click around this tab for more tools to promote your feed.

✔ **Monetize:** This tab allows you to use your Google AdSense account to insert ads directly into your feed. Your readers see these ads without ever having to click over to your site. This tool assumes that you already have some working familiarity with Google AdSense — for more information, see *Google AdSense For Dummies,* by Jerri L. Ledford.

✔ **Troubleshootize:** Use this tab for a quick-and-easy list of solutions to common FeedBurner problems, such as a feed that won't update. At the bottom of the page, don't miss the link to Open the FeedBurner Help Group in a New Window. This takes you to a forum where FeedBurner troubleshooters can share tricks of the trade.

Incorporating Google Analytics

Google Analytics is the blogging-industry standard for tracking your site's statistics. This powerful, comprehensive tool allows you to see who is visiting your site, where they came from, how long they stayed, and which pages they visited. In addition, you can track how many times a specific link was clicked, which keywords are performing well for your blog, what your most popular content is, and much more. The best part? Google Analytics is free. With the high performance of Google Analytics, however, comes a higher degree of complexity.

You need to have a Gmail account (www.google.com/accounts/New Account) to set up your Google Analytics account. If you already have a Gmail account, you can go directly to Google Analytics (www.google.com/analytics) to set up your account.

TypePad allows you to integrate your Google Analytics account with your blog by sharing your UA number (this is your User Account number, and is assigned when you establish an account with Google Analytics). To link your Google Analytics account with your TypePad blog, click your blog's Settings tab and then click the Stats link. Type your UA number and then click Save Changes.

Using Google Analytics tools

As we've stated, Google Analytics is the industry standard and the most robust option for tracking your blog's statistics. If you have a third party relying on you for accurate information (for example, an advertiser who wants to know how many people clicked his or her link), that third party is more likely to trust the Google Analytics information than a less well-known or trusted statistics program.

In addition, Google Analytics allows you to track many elements of your blog. This section explains some of the main tools of Google Analytics and how you can use them with your TypePad blog.

Keep in mind that you use your Google Analytics UA number to link your Google Analytics account with your TypePad account, but you will continue to view all your statistic information at the Google Analytics site, not on your TypePad blog's Overview page.

The first thing you see when you sign in to your Google Analytics account is your My Analytics Accounts page, which looks similar to Figure B-4. This page lists the Web site Profiles you've established. (If you have several blogs, you can establish a Profile for each and manage them all from this page — you can have up to 50 Profiles.)

Navigating your Google Analytics Dashboard

When you click the name of the Profile you want to work with, the first thing you see is the Dashboard for that Profile. Your Dashboard, as seen in Figure B-5, is the hub of your blog's statistical data.

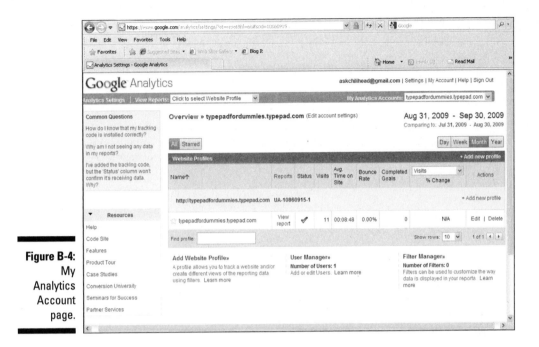

Figure B-4:
My
Analytics
Account
page.

Menu of links   Graph

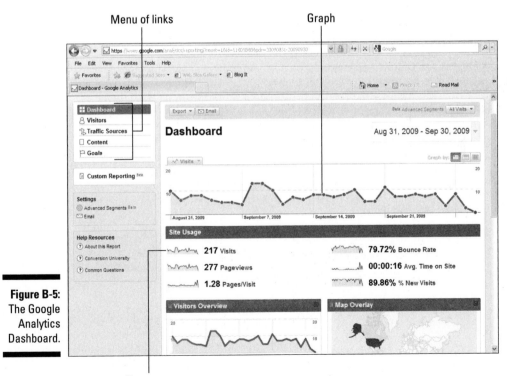

Figure B-5:
The Google
Analytics
Dashboard.

Site usage

The Dashboard gives you an overview of the activity on your site for a specific period of time. Refer to Figure B-5 as we explain each module:

- **Graph:** This graph is a visual representation of your basic site statistics. You can choose to view visits, pageviews, pages/visits, average time on the site, bounce rate, or percentage of new visits. You can also choose whether you want the graph to show daily, weekly, or monthly trends. A bonus is the ability to compare two metrics. For instance, if you choose to compare visits and pageviews, you'll have an idea of how many visitors surfed through your site and saw different pages or posts and how many just clicked away after reading what they came for.

  The *bounce rate* is how long visitors stayed at your site; the higher the bounce rate, the shorter they stayed — aim for a bounce rate of about 50 percent.

- **Site Usage:** This section of the Dashboard gives you information at a glance. You can easily see how many visits and pageviews your site has enjoyed, the average pages readers browsed per visit, the bounce rate, the average time a visitor spent at your site (this correlates to your bounce rate), and the percentage of your visitors that were new.

- **Menu of Links:** This menu lets you discover specific information about your statistical data. For instance, if you click Visitor, you can see information on visitor trending, benchmarks, loyalty, which browsers visitors use, and network properties. You can add any of these links to your Dashboard as a module by clicking the link in the menu and then clicking the Add to Dashboard link.

- **Modules:** Below the Graph and Site Usage information are several modules. These modules can be deleted or moved around to suit your interests and needs. The default modules are as follows:

  - **Visitor Overview:** This module shows pretty much the same information that the default graph shows. You can see the number of visitors to your site over the last month.

  - **Map Overlay:** This module shows a map of the world and highlights the areas where your visitors are coming from. Dark green indicates the highest concentration of visitors; light green indicates fewer visitors.

  - **Traffic Sources Overview:** This module shows you how your traffic found you. The pie chart is segmented according to those who found you via search engines, referring sites (other sites that have linked to you), direct traffic (those who typed your URL directly), and other.

  - **Content Overview:** This module is extremely useful because it shows you at a glance which pages of your blog are most popular. You can quickly see the top five pages your readers are interested in and how many pageviews each had over the past month.

Each module has a View Report link so you can see even more detailed information about the data.

You can change the order of the modules by clicking and dragging a module to a new place on the Dashboard. If you'd like to delete a module, just click the X in the top-right corner of the module. If you'd like to add a module to the Dashboard, click the link from the menu of links for the topic you want to include and click the Add to Dashboard link at the top of the module.

Doing more with Google Analytics

As you can see, Google Analytics offers the same options other stat counters provide. However, Google Analytics offers many options beyond just basic visitor statistics. Your Google Analytics account allows you to track your readers' specific behavior and report on how your site is helping or hindering your goals. For instance, if you'd like to track how many people are signing up for your newsletter, you can do that. Or if you'd like to track how many people are clicking a specific link or advertisement on your site, you can do that. The best part? The features are free and included in your Google Analytics account. If you want that sort of functionality from another program, you'd likely pay for it.

Google Analytics is so robust, we could write an entire book on it. Unfortunately, we don't have that kind of room, so we're going to show you how to do the two most-asked-for tasks: setting and tracking goals, and tracking click-throughs.

Setting and tracking goals

A Google Analytics *goal* refers to a specific task that measures how well your site fulfills a business need. When you think of a goal as it relates to your Web site, you most likely consider the goal as an idea — something to achieve. Obviously, Google Analytics can't track ideas, but it can track Web pages. When you're working with Google Analytics, your goal is a Web page. If your "idea" goal is to have readers sign up for a newsletter or make a purchase, your Google Analytics goal is related to a Web page that confirms that behavior is completed.

Here's an example. Let's say your goal is to increase newsletter subscribers. To encourage your readers to sign up for your newsletter (and thus increase your subscriber number), you provide a link inviting readers to subscribe to your newsletter. That link takes readers to a subscription page with a sign-up form (though you don't have to have a form to set a goal). After readers have completed the form and clicked the button to submit that information, they are taken to a Thank You page. This Thank You page is your Google Analytics goal, because if readers have made it to this page, you are sure they have subscribed to your newsletter. Tracking how many times readers make it to the Thank You page allows you to see how your readers are using your site and whether you're successful with your goal of increasing newsletter subscriptions.

To set up a goal, follow these instructions:

1. **Sign in to your Google Analytics account.**

2. **Click the View Report link next to the Profile you want to work with.**

3. **Click Goals on the menu of links in the left sidebar.**

   The Goals Overview page appears.

4. **Click Set Up Goals and Funnels.**

   A new browser window opens, with your Profile Setting page. This page also allows you to set up your goal(s). Scroll down until you see the table named Conversion Goals and Funnel. Let's set up your first goal.

5. **Click Edit in the first row of the Conversion Goals and Funnel table.**

   The Goal Settings page appears.

6. **Complete the Goals Settings page as follows:**

   - **Active Goal:** Click to select On so you can activate your goal. If you ever decide to deactivate this goal, simply return to this page and click to select Off.

   - **Match Type:** Choose Exact Match if you want the URL you enter as your goal URL to match the URL shown in the report. Choose Head Match if your site has dynamically generated content (for example, users have dynamically generated IDs, and those are part of the URL). Choose Regular Expression Match if you are using regular expressions.

   If you're just starting out with Goals, choose Exact Match if you're unfamiliar with dynamically generated content or regular expressions.

   - **Goal URL:** Type the URL of your goal page (for example, the Thank You for Subscribing page we used in the earlier example).

   - **Goal Name:** Type the name you want this goal to have (for example, newsletter subscriptions).

   - **Case Sensitive:** Click to select this box if capitalization is important within the URL you entered in the Goal URL box.

   - **Goal Value:** Assign a numeric value to your goal.

Tracking click-throughs

Being able to track which links your readers are clicking is an extremely useful tool. In particular, tracking whether your readers are clicking an advertiser's link allows you to see which advertisements and products are of interest to your readers and which are not (or, if you're not selling anything, which links to further information are working). In turn, if you're selling your own ads (and aren't part of an advertising network), you'll know which advertisements to accept and which to decline based on your user's interest and behavior. Or you'll be able to tell what information your readers are most interested in finding based on which articles they're clicking to. To track links, you need to insert specific Google Analytics code into your link HTML. The following instructions explain how.

Tracking click-throughs for a link requires that you insert HTML code. If the code is not inserted correctly, Google Analytics will not track click-throughs for the link. You won't break your blog, but you won't be tracking your link, either.

1. **Create your link in the TypePad Compose editor.**

   (See Chapter 5 for instructions on making a link.. The original link looks something like this, but with your information:

   ```
   <a href="http://www.blogname.com">your link text</a>
   ```

2. **Change your link to look like this:**

   ```
   <a href="http://www.blogname.com/" onclick="pageTracker._
           trackEvent('category', 'action', 'label', 'value');">your link
           text</a>
   ```

   - **Category:** This field is required. Type a simple name for the category you are tracking. For instance, if you're tracking click-throughs for links, you might name the category `links`. If you're tracking video downloads, you might name your category `video`. You can reuse the category name for items that are the same (that is, use `links` for all links being tracked).

   - **Action:** This field is required. Type the action you are tracking. If you're tracking click-throughs for a link, you might name your action `click`. If you're tracking how many people play a video at your site, you might name the action `play`. Again, you can reuse the action name as necessary.

   - **Label:** This field is optional. Use this item to determine which link is being tracked, and name it something that reflects the link. For instance, if you're tracking how many people click the link for

Blogging Basics 101, you can name the label bb101. When you view your Google Analytics stats for your events (instructions follow), you can clearly see which links are being clicked more than others.

 • **Value:** This field is optional. You can assign a numeric value, if you like.

Here, we've made a link that sends the reader to *Blogging Basics 101.* We've assigned the category as links, the action as click, and the label as bb101:

```
<a href="http://www.bloggingbasics101.com" onclick="pageTracker._
          trackEvent('links', 'click', 'bb101');">Blogging Basics 101</a>
```

If you choose a name with more than one word for your category, action, label, or value, use hyphens between the words. For example, if you want to name your category test links, type **test-links** as your category.

3. **Save and publish your post.**

   You can track your click-throughs via Google Analytics.

   Google Analytics won't show your statistics until 24 hours later.

4. **Sign in to your Google Analytics account.**

5. **Click the View Report link next to the Profile you want to work with.**

6. **On the menu of links in the left sidebar, click Content and then click Event Tracking.**

7. **Click the metric you want to view.**

Finding out more about Google Analytics

Are you interested in learning to use Google Analytics to its full potential? Google has a blog at analytics.blogspot.com and a YouTube channel that contains many video tutorials for using Google Analytics with your blog. To find out more, follow these steps:

1. **Type** www.youtube.com/user/Google **in your browser's address bar and press Enter.**

2. **Click the Playlist link.**

   A new page appears with a list of Google's video playlists.

3. **Scroll down the page until you find Google Conversion University, and click that title.**

   A new page appears that lists the video tutorials for Google Analytics.

4. **Click the title of the video you want to view.**

Index

• *B* •

Business/Accounting & Bookkeeping

Bookkeeping For Dummies
978-0-7645-9848-7

eBay Business
All-in-One For Dummies,
2nd Edition
978-0-470-38536-4

Job Interviews
For Dummies,
3rd Edition
978-0-470-17748-8

Resumes For Dummies,
5th Edition
978-0-470-08037-5

Stock Investing
For Dummies,
3rd Edition
978-0-470-40114-9

Successful Time
Management
For Dummies
978-0-470-29034-7

Computer Hardware

BlackBerry For Dummies,
3rd Edition
978-0-470-45762-7

Computers For Seniors
For Dummies
978-0-470-24055-7

iPhone For Dummies,
2nd Edition
978-0-470-42342-4

Laptops For Dummies,
3rd Edition
978-0-470-27759-1

Macs For Dummies,
10th Edition
978-0-470-27817-8

Cooking & Entertaining

Cooking Basics
For Dummies,
3rd Edition
978-0-7645-7206-7

Wine For Dummies,
4th Edition
978-0-470-04579-4

Diet & Nutrition

Dieting For Dummies,
2nd Edition
978-0-7645-4149-0

Nutrition For Dummies,
4th Edition
978-0-471-79868-2

Weight Training
For Dummies,
3rd Edition
978-0-471-76845-6

Digital Photography

Digital Photography
For Dummies,
6th Edition
978-0-470-25074-7

Photoshop Elements 7
For Dummies
978-0-470-39700-8

Gardening

Gardening Basics
For Dummies
978-0-470-03749-2

Organic Gardening
For Dummies,
2nd Edition
978-0-470-43067-5

Green/Sustainable

Green Building
& Remodeling
For Dummies
978-0-470-17559-0

Green Cleaning
For Dummies
978-0-470-39106-8

Green IT For Dummies
978-0-470-38688-0

Health

Diabetes For Dummies,
3rd Edition
978-0-470-27086-8

Food Allergies
For Dummies
978-0-470-09584-3

Living Gluten-Free
For Dummies
978-0-471-77383-2

Hobbies/General

Chess For Dummies,
2nd Edition
978-0-7645-8404-6

Drawing For Dummies
978-0-7645-5476-6

Knitting For Dummies,
2nd Edition
978-0-470-28747-7

Organizing For Dummies
978-0-7645-5300-4

SuDoku For Dummies
978-0-470-01892-7

Home Improvement

Energy Efficient Homes
For Dummies
978-0-470-37602-7

Home Theater
For Dummies,
3rd Edition
978-0-470-41189-6

Living the Country Lifestyle
All-in-One For Dummies
978-0-470-43061-3

Solar Power Your Home
For Dummies
978-0-470-17569-9

Available wherever books are sold. For more information or to order direct: U.S. customers visit www.dummies.com or call 1-877-762-2974.
U.K. customers visit www.wileyeurope.com or call (0) 1243 843291. Canadian customers visit www.wiley.ca or call 1-800-567-4797.

Internet

Blogging For Dummies,
2nd Edition
978-0-470-23017-6

eBay For Dummies,
6th Edition
978-0-470-49741-8

Facebook For Dummies
978-0-470-26273-3

Google Blogger
For Dummies
978-0-470-40742-4

Web Marketing
For Dummies,
2nd Edition
978-0-470-37181-7

WordPress For Dummies,
2nd Edition
978-0-470-40296-2

Language & Foreign Language

French For Dummies
978-0-7645-5193-2

Italian Phrases
For Dummies
978-0-7645-7203-6

Spanish For Dummies
978-0-7645-5194-9

Spanish For Dummies,
Audio Set
978-0-470-09585-0

Macintosh

Mac OS X Snow Leopard
For Dummies
978-0-470-43543-4

Math & Science

Algebra I For Dummies
978-0-7645-5325-7

Biology For Dummies
978-0-7645-5326-4

Calculus For Dummies
978-0-7645-2498-1

Chemistry For Dummies
978-0-7645-5430-8

Microsoft Office

Excel 2007 For Dummies
978-0-470-03737-9

Office 2007 All-in-One
Desk Reference
For Dummies
978-0-471-78279-7

Music

Guitar For Dummies,
2nd Edition
978-0-7645-9904-0

iPod & iTunes
For Dummies,
6th Edition
978-0-470-39062-7

Piano Exercises
For Dummies
978-0-470-38765-8

Parenting & Education

Parenting For Dummies,
2nd Edition
978-0-7645-5418-6

Type 1 Diabetes
For Dummies
978-0-470-17811-9

Pets

Cats For Dummies,
2nd Edition
978-0-7645-5275-5

Dog Training For Dummies,
2nd Edition
978-0-7645-8418-3

Puppies For Dummies,
2nd Edition
978-0-470-03717-1

Religion & Inspiration

The Bible For Dummies
978-0-7645-5296-0

Catholicism For Dummies
978-0-7645-5391-2

Women in the Bible
For Dummies
978-0-7645-8475-6

Self-Help & Relationship

Anger Management
For Dummies
978-0-470-03715-7

Overcoming Anxiety
For Dummies
978-0-7645-5447-6

Sports

Baseball For Dummies,
3rd Edition
978-0-7645-7537-2

Basketball For Dummies,
2nd Edition
978-0-7645-5248-9

Golf For Dummies,
3rd Edition
978-0-471-76871-5

Web Development

Web Design All-in-One
For Dummies
978-0-470-41796-6

Windows Vista

Windows Vista
For Dummies
978-0-471-75421-3

Available wherever books are sold. For more information or to order direct: U.S. customers visit www.dummies.com or call 1-877-762-2974.
U.K. customers visit www.wileyeurope.com or call (0) 1243 843291. Canadian customers visit www.wiley.ca or call 1-800-567-4797.

How-to?
How Easy.

Go to www.Dummies.com

From hooking up a modem to cooking up a casserole, knitting a scarf to navigating an iPod, you can trust Dummies.com to show you how to get things done the easy way.

Visit us at Dummies.com

Dummies products make life easier!

DVDs • Music • Games •
DIY • Consumer Electronics •
Software • Crafts • Hobbies •
Cookware • and more!

For more information, go to
Dummies.com® and search
the store by category.

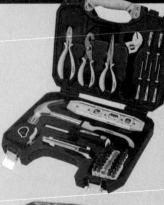

BIBLIO RPL Ltée

G - JUN 2010

Making everything easier!™